The Psychology of Saving

The Psychology of Saving

A Study on Economic Psychology

Karl-Erik Wärneryd

Professor Emeritus of Economic Psychology, Stockholm School of Economics, Sweden

Edward Elgar
Cheltenham, UK • Northampton, MA, USA

Published by
Edward Elgar Publishing Limited
Glensanda House
Montpellier Parade
Cheltenham
Glos GL50 1UA
UK

Edward Elgar Publishing, Inc.
6 Market Street
Northampton
Massachusetts 01060
USA

A catalogue record for this book
is available from the British Library

Library of Congress Cataloguing in Publication Data

Wärneryd, Karl-Erik, 1927–
    The psychology of saving: a study on economic psychology / Karl-Erik Wärneryd.
    Includes bibliographical references and index.
    1. Saving and investment—Psychological aspects. 2. Economics—Psychological aspects. I. Title.
    HB822.W37 1999
    332'.0415'019—dc21   98–31080
                                                                    CIP

ISBN 1 84064 016 2

Printed and bound in Great Britain by Bookcraft (Bath) Ltd.

List of Figures

Contents

List of Tables

Preface

The work on this book started long ago. The idea of writing a book on the psychology of saving first came to me in 1985 when I listened to Franco Modigliani's lecture after he received the Economics Prize in Memory of Alfred Nobel. The lecture dealt with many problems that could be clothed in psychological terms. The emphasis was on the consequences of the fact that man was forward-looking. Modigliani indicated that the concept of thrift which earlier economists had often used to explain savings was not necessary in his saving theory. While I was intrigued with the idea of the dominant influence of the forward-looking property of man which had been mostly neglected by psychologists, I began wondering what modern psychology could do with 'thrift' to explain why forward-looking did not always result in provision for the future. The whole book is an attempt to reconcile views of thrift which I use as a very comprehensive concept to summarize a number of psychological variables, and views of the forward-looking property which in economics is often seen as just mathematical expectation.

What had the psychologists done towards the clarification of saving? In 1970, Ölander and Seipel who were members of my research team at The Stockholm School of Economics published a review of psychological approaches to saving. They found that there was little contribution to theory, but that there were empirical studies of saving behavior and that those were interesting and promising. The work of George Katona was outstanding in this context.

When I retired from The Stockholm School of Economics at the end of 1992, I was invited to the CentER for Economic Research at Tilburg University. A research program was started there as a collaboration between econometricians, economists, and economic psychologists. It was financed by the VSB bank and was called the VSB Panel Project. In all, I came to spend around three years working within the project. While the main idea was to create a database on household saving in the Netherlands by means of repeated interviews, the Program also comprised contacts with researchers on saving from many other countries. Frequent interactions with econometricians and economists as well as with economic psychologists who all had a deep interest in studying saving further strengthened my idea that a book on the psychology of saving would be timely. I started, therefore, making notes and writing papers. The main writing was done after my return to Sweden.

I want to express my sincere thanks to CentER and especially to its Director, Professor Arie Kapteyn, for letting me stay in an environment ideally suited for research and encouraging my psychological thinking although it is pedestrian and deviates considerably from the elegance of present-day economics. In my work on the book, I have received valuable comments from Rob Alessie, Hermann Brandstätter, Herman Camphuis, Werner Güth, Erich Kirchler, Ellen Nyhus, and Paul Webley. I want to thank them and especially Ellen who devoted much time to reading and commenting on the whole manuscript. In some cases, the comments of the others referred to papers that were drafts of some of the contents of the book. All are of course innocent of the weaknesses of the book. I use some data collected under the VSB-CentER Savings Project. The data are commonly referred to as the VSB Panel.

Finally, I should frankly admit that I am in favor of saving money and may thus be biased in my description of the psychology of saving. There are at least three good reasons for my positive attitude towards saving:

1. It is good for an individual to be capable and willing to save. It adds to the well being of the household
2. The macroeconomic consequences of saving are, with few exceptions, favorable to a country
3. Serving the need for economies in the use of nonrenewable resources presupposes control of expenditure and saving of money.

Stockholm, August, 1998

Karl-Erik Wärneryd
Professor Emeritus of Economic Psychology

Introduction

Man hört nur die Fragen, auf welche man im Stande ist eine Antwort zu finden.
[One hears only the questions to which one is able to find an answer].
German proverb

The present volume is intended to furnish ideas to stimulate research on saving behavior. Most ideas in the discussion of the psychology of saving originated in economics. Saving has simply been of little concern to psychologists, with the exception of economic psychologists, too few in number. A review of ideas may hopefully arouse a revived interest in the subject matter among economists and a novel interest among psychologists. It may also supplement the Life-Cycle Hypothesis, using the psychological thinking of early economists and utilizing the concepts and methods of modern cognitive and social psychology to elaborate the concept of 'thrift'.

The principal focus is on the *psychology* of saving. The book is in no way meant to be a complete coverage of economic saving theories. I concentrate on saving behavior rather than on savings and rely on psychological discussions and findings rather than on economic theory. The latter is, however, in my view a good source for finding variables that can explain saving, especially if one goes back to the classical economists. They used psychological insights rather than the academic psychology of their time. Besides, in early times psychology and economics were rather close partners in the endeavor to explicate human behavior.

The main reason for economist (and politician) interest in the psychology of saving is the issue of what are considered inadequate savings in national economies. 'If we are to understand why people are saving so little and are to make helpful recommendations as to how to get people to save more, we have to incorporate more of the psychology of saving into our economic theories . . . In the standard life-cycle framework the only policy variable is the after-tax rate of return to saving' (Thaler, 1994, p.186). Stimulating consumption is an easier task than stimulating saving. Still, in a depression when more consumption could invigorate the economy it may be a hard job to make people save less and spend more.

In some countries and in some time periods, people seem to be saving too much and consuming too little. Keynes (1936) maintained that saving should be discouraged and consumption animated in periods of recessions or de-

1

pressions. Katona (1960) who was a leader in the empirical research on saving stressed the role of the consumer in economic growth. Increased consumer spending could revive an economy that was down and he proved his point using expectations that were elicited from businessmen and consumers.

The message of the book is that in the study of saving, there is a place for more psychological research, pursuing the economic-psychological approach *and* basic psychological research on what 'forward looking' implies for behavior. The economic-psychological approach, in my view, involves two major things. It means (1) a focus on breakdowns of the macroeconomic level into segments of the population, usually described in psychological terms based on their tendencies to react differently to economic stimuli; (2) purveying richer descriptions and explanations than economics alone can provide for use in public policy making and financial marketing contexts, such as policy discussions and programs to stimulate saving. In this study, economic-psychological research could well use more of modern cognitive and social psychology. Saving behavior is a function of perception of the future *and* the act of providing for the future, paying respect to social influences. So far, little research along these lines has been conducted in the discipline of psychology.

Psychological explanations are necessary at different levels in the economy: from the micro to the macro level. It is in economic psychology common to deal with segments of the population and to base the segmentation on differences in some psychological variable. Segmentation has for a long time been a frequently used concept in the area of marketing. The basis for segmentation was originally a psychological variable called 'benefit'. A benefit is the perception of the utility that is expected from a product or service. This way of construing economic psychology leads to the inclusion of ideas from other disciplines, not only from economics which is, of course, close to economic psychology, but also from sociology, political science, and consumer behavior.

The relationships between economics and psychology, or perhaps it should be formulated between a growing number of economists and psychology, are developing in an interesting, and to a psychologist maybe fearsome way. Schumpeter (1954) asserted that economists had always done what they found convenient to do with psychology, with little respect for what the psychologists thought appropriate. What is happening now is somewhat different. Economists are creating a psychology of their own. They are often well read in the psychological literature, make choices of concepts that they find potentially useful, fitting them into economic theory; in essence using them to expand utility theory and to make the psychological concepts congruous with the rationality postulate.

Economic analysis starts with an ideal model, based on rationality and perfect information on the part of decision-makers. Rationality means that a decision maker has a utility function embodying her/his preferences and maximizes utility. Since the ideal model without exception deviates from reality, the model is supplemented with constraints of different sorts and with attempts to incorporate new aspects in the utility function. Psychology, notably economic psychology, starts with rather simple hypotheses about relationships between empirical phenomena. These hypotheses are tried out on empirical data, in the tradition of psychology through (laboratory) experiments, but in economic psychology predominantly with survey data. There is the danger that the research ends up with a multitude of empirical relationships without integration and context. This may be interpreted as a need for a little more abstraction in economic-psychological theory and more clearly specified models.

Questions arise as I go through theories and empirical research on saving behavior. In some cases, it is possible to find preliminary answers by looking at the VSB Panel database of CentER for Economic Research, Tilburg University. When the VSB Panel was initiated, the wise decision was made to include a number of psychological variables whose selection was guided by advice from economists, econometricians, and psychologists and by perusal of the literature. By coincidence, the same literature (and some more) has been used for the present book and there is now a chance to get some more answers from data.

The plan of the book is a mixture of several principles. It does not observe the categories or sequences usually employed in psychological texts although many areas of psychology are drawn into the discussion. Those are only touched upon since the purpose is to relate everything to saving behavior. Chapter 1 introduces economic psychology and elucidates the historical and current relationships between economics and psychology. It goes a little beyond the title of the book since it deals with relations in general between economics and psychological science and not only with respect to saving. The purpose is to provide a better understanding of the roots of the differences. The scope and role of economic psychology is discussed and the field of macroeconomic psychology is defined. This serves as a background to the later presentation of psychological research related to the topic of saving.

In Chapter 2, the concept of saving is introduced and some of the problems of defining and measuring saving and savings are discussed. Some statistical data on saving rates in different countries are given. Using data from the Dutch VSB Panel Study, the question of what people mean by saving is approached. Finally, the psychology of saving is defined and commented on.

Chapter 3 is devoted to a historical perspective on the psychology of saving. It traces the use of psychological concepts in the discussion of accumulation of money over the centuries up to the early neoclassical economists Marshall, Pigou, and Fisher. It is an attempt to enrich the present discussion of saving by an overview of how psychological insights have been used in earlier economics. 'Industriousness' and 'thrift' keep popping up throughout this review which also reveals factors behind these concepts.

Chapter 4 covers the main economic theories of savings. First, a background based on Fisher's concept of 'time preference' is given. Via Keynes's absolute income hypothesis and 'psychological law', the focus is shifted to later theories like Duesenberry's relative income hypothesis, and to the now dominant theories of saving – the Permanent Income Hypothesis and the Life-Cycle Hypothesis. The chapter ends with some recent psychological additions to saving theories. The Behavioral Life-Cycle Hypothesis that was introduced as an alternative to the pure economic Life-Cycle Hypothesis is presented. A closer examination of the psychological underpinnings of the Life-Cycle Hypothesis is saved until Chapter 8. Some developments in the study of time preference are reviewed in the final part of the chapter.

Chapter 5 deals first with psychological or, if the reader prefers another concept, behavioral research on saving. Such research has often been carried out in cooperation between psychologists and economists. Brief reviews of empirical studies are given. This includes descriptions of some models used in the empirical study of saving behavior. While many studies have tried to explain saving by means of sets of economic, sociodemographic and psychological variables, only a few studies have devoted attention to the question whether different types (segments or groups) of savers can be distinguished and meaningfully interpreted. Some ongoing laboratory research on saving behavior is also reviewed and, finally, qualitative research on saving is briefly discussed.

Chapter 6 is devoted to some psychological concepts that have been used in the study of saving. The focus lies on cognitive concepts. Expectation is a concept used both in economics and psychology – with different meanings and implications. Expectation theories are reviewed and the role of expectations in saving is dealt with. It is noted that the forward-looking aspect of human behavior implies an important role for expectations and that this role has not been investigated. Uncertainty and risk attitudes constitute an area of common interest to psychologists and economists. Uncertainty and the cognate concept of risk play a role in the theories of saving and both concepts are elucidated in the chapter. In behavioral theories of saving, the concept of mental account is becoming important. The concept is first introduced as belonging to the Behavioral Life-Cycle Hypothesis in Chapter 4 and is further discussed in Chapter 6.

Chapter 7 treats another set of psychological variables and assesses the roles of those in the psychology of saving. Attitudes towards saving are according to many studies quite favorable among people in general. The question is to what extent they have explanatory and predictive power if they are commonly shared. Psychologically phrased motives for saving were suggested and used by many classical and neoclassical economists and they have been investigated in surveys of saving behavior. A personality characteristic, called 'thrift', appeared as a main factor in many economist explanations of saving. An important personality factor that was assumed to explain differences in thrift was self-control or as it was often called 'willpower'. There are now survey data indicating that there is potential use for personality variables in the study of saving. Finally, the chapter takes up the broad issue of social influence on saving.

Chapter 8 is an attempt to provide an integrative approach to the psychology of saving. The Life-Cycle Hypothesis has deficiencies and economists are busy trying to improve its explanatory and predictive power. Among other things, they are trying out concepts that are close to psychology. The psychological underpinnings of the theory are examined and related to psychological theory. When used by economists, isolated psychological concepts and simple hypotheses about relationships have been frequent in the study of saving behavior. A psychological schema is presented. It is aimed at integrating a number of concepts that have been used earlier and putting them into a meaningful context. The schema conveys the idea that saving is a function of perceived future needs and 'a prompt to action' and that 'control of expenditure' is important in this context. The purpose of the schema is to stimulate coherent psychological research on saving and to suggest ideas for supplementing the dominant economic theories of savings.

The final chapter is preoccupied with implications of what we already know about the psychology of saving or can make educated guesses about. A major reason for interest in the psychology of saving is the fact that, as Thaler (1994) pointed out, the dominating economic theory of saving can primarily suggest manipulation of the interest rate (and taxes) to influence saving. While the psychology of saving may not yet be highly advanced, it is rich in ideas about what could be done to influence saving. This is essential not only to public policy makers, but also to banks, insurance companies and many types of educators who want to promote saving.

1. A Closer Look at Psychology and Economics and at Economic Psychology

Actually, however, economists have never allowed their analysis to be influenced by the professional psychologists of their times, but have always framed for themselves such assumptions about psychical processes as they thought it desirable to make. On the one hand, we shall note this fact occasionally with surprise because there exist problems in economic analysis that might be attacked with advantage by methods worked out by psychologists.

Schumpeter (1954, pp.27-8)

The historical perspective in Chapter 3 will make it evident that psychological science contributed very little to the psychological thinking in economics. In this chapter, the first part will be devoted to some explication of why psychology did so little. The rest of the chapter confronts the question of the possible role for economic psychology in an era when many economists are picking up psychological concepts and theories and dressing them into the appropriate economic garb.

In order to facilitate the presentation of economic ideas the distinction between macro- and microeconomics is given here. Macroeconomics is

primarily concerned with the study of relationships between broad economic aggregates, the most important of which are NATIONAL INCOME, aggregate SAVING and consumers' expenditure, INVESTMENT, aggregate employment, the quantity of money [. . .], the average price level [. . .] and the BALANCE OF PAYMENTS. (Bannock et al., 1985, p.277)

Microeconomics focuses on the behavior of single decision units such as

consumers and business firms and the way in which their decisions interrelate to determine relative PRICES of goods and FACTORS OF PRODUCTION and the quantities of these which will be bought and sold. Its ultimate aim is to understand the mechanism by which the total amount of RESOURCES possessed by society is allocated among alternative uses. (Bannock et al., 1984, p.296)

Since the 1930s a special meaning has been attached to the concept of macroeconomics. Keynes (1936) developed a way of reasoning about aggre-

6

gate phenomena that seemed appropriate as a basis for economic policy under different stages in the business cycle. It gave a new role to economists and provided them with new tools (Scitovsky, 1986). The meaning of macroeconomics is not always clear and there are approaches that differ widely with the Keynesian notion (see e.g. Klamer, 1984, for a review of the so-called 'new classical' or 'rational expectations' macroeconomics). Although the focus lies on aggregate phenomena, macroeconomics is in principle based on assumptions about the behavior of individual households and business firms. The assumption is made that individual behaviors can be aggregated with little bias. Attempts are constantly made to explicate macroeconomic phenomena in terms of microeconomic behavior, usually by means of the rationality postulate (see e.g. Lucas, 1986). There are, however, established macroeconomic theories with little founding in microeconomic theory.

A BRIEF HISTORY OF PSYCHOLOGICAL SCIENCE

Like economics, psychology can be said to have started with the philosophers in ancient Greece. Aristotle (384–322 BC) discovered many interesting things about the human mind, the human senses and personality traits. In his view, mind was located in the heart, an idea that was much later rejected by the medical scientist Galen (ca. 129–199 AD). In *De Anima* (known by its Latin title) Aristotle provided a framework on human senses, human learning and memory that dominated psychological thinking through the ages (see for example, Murphy, 1951). His ideas about mind and body relations, that is, between sensation and perception, laid an early foundation for associationism that was later to enable psychology to become an experimental science.

> Most influential of all his specific teachings is to the effect that we remember things by virtue of 'contiguity, similarity, and contrast' (reference to contiguity and similarity had been made by Plato). We think of Paul because he was with Peter, or because he is like Peter, or because he contrasts with Peter . . . This doctrine of association later became the doctrine that all the operations of the mind depend upon associations laid down in experience. (Murphy, 1951, p.9)

In *Ethics*, Aristotle discussed the appropriateness and advantages of being 'temperate' (in the English translation). Temperance means moderation in action, thought, or feeling and is close to self-control. Moderation and self-control are still considered to be important factors in explaining saving. The role of these concepts was for many years played down in psychology, but they are gaining some new acceptance albeit under new labels such as self-regulation of behavior. Aristotle's psychological theories were in the Middle Ages mixed with theological thinking and less interest in natural observation was displayed. With the Renaissance, his ideas were again combined with naturalism. Philosophers like Descartes made physiological discoveries that influenced the discussion of psychological phenomena, in the first place, mind-body problems. The development of the natural sciences on the basis of observation and experiment had an influence also on psychology, which came to depend on physiology to an important extent.

While psychological theory after Aristotle was part of philosophy, the practical use of psychology belonged in other disciplines. Psychology was for many centuries a fundamental part of many other sciences and was taught within and as part of those (Schönpflug, 1993). There thus existed applied psychology that was quite independent of philosophy and the parent discipline was busy with more theoretical thinking about psychological problems, mostly consciousness and mind-body problems.

> However, before the end of the 19th century, there was no attempt at a concept of an applied discipline of psychology. There was rather a body of psychological expertise that spread and expanded when the initial pragmatic disciplines of politics and economics dissolved into several practical disciplines. These were typically disciplines that dealt with human action and with the impact of the human factor in general. Thus, issues of applied psychology such as training, communication, evaluation, selection, and placement were often implicitly or explicitly treated in medicine, law, education, and cameralistics . . . applied psychology was cultivated in other disciplines that were ahead of psychology in the race for independence. (Schönpflug, 1993, p.13-14)

Kant (Boring, 1950; Danziger, 1990, p.19) declared that psychology could never become a science because psychology could neither use mathematics nor experiments. Kant's successor Herbart who wrote a widely used textbook on psychology showed that psychology could use mathematics so one step towards making psychology a science was taken. When psychologists started becoming oriented towards physiology, the experimental method and mathematics turned out not to be a problem. An important step was the new thinking about associations. Associationism started with the assumption of supposedly irreducible mental elements and assumed that learning and the development of higher processes consisted mainly in the combination of those elements.

Boring (1950) stressed the role of the father, James Mill, and the son, John Stuart Mill, for making it possible for psychology to become a science

> The nineteenth century saw the culmination of associationism in James Mill and its modification from mental mechanics to a mental chemistry by John Stuart Mill. It saw associationism made over by Bain into the system that was to become the substructure for the new physiological psychology, and it saw the new theory of evolution first to bear upon psychology by another associationist, Herbert Spencer . . .

The two Mills and Bain brought philosophical psychology to the point where scientific psychology could take it over. (Boring, 1950, p.219)

The birth of scientific psychology is often dated to 1879 when Wilhelm Wundt founded his laboratory in Leipzig. His work in the laboratory was essentially a combination of physiological psychology which had received an important push forward through James and John Stuart Mill's work on associationism and Fechner's work on psychophysics which was published in 1860. Mind-body relationships and consciousness were the main preoccupations of the new psychological science. The approach meant that stimulus-response associations were seen as purely mechanical. There was no room for expectations. This view was further enhanced in Watson's behaviorism and reached its apogee in Skinner's operant conditioning theory (Skinner, 1974).

Philosophy was for many centuries the parent science of all other sciences. It embraced both psychology and economics. At some point in time separate disciplines started diverging from the main source. As sciences closely related to philosophy, psychology and economics had many common interests and the same thinker could give significant contributions to both sciences. David Hume, Adam Smith, Jeremy Bentham, James and John Stuart Mill all gave important contributions to both sciences, but the contributions were mainly held in different compartments. Economics was sometimes seen as a subdivision of psychology and at any rate psychological knowledge was held to be fundamental to economic theory.

Towards the end of the 19th century, psychology was rapidly developing as an experimental science. The new science was in the tradition of philosophy and of physiology busy with problems of sensation and perception. This was a classical problem area in philosophy and thanks to the new experimental physiology it became possible to explore lawful relationships between physical stimulation and individual experience. The experimental psychologists took their problems from philosophy rather than from everyday life or the work place. This is one explanation of why they seemed of little help to economists, who needed psychological findings on actions, that is, much broader categories than the narrowly defined relationships in the experimental psychology. William James's (1890) work meant a change. It was a huge effort to summarize and systematize psychological knowledge in such a way that different dimensions of human life were covered with the best knowledge of the day. It was suggested that economists had better observe the progress in psychological science, a notion that was emphatically rejected by most economists.

Psychology has developed many branches and unlike in economics there is little common basis for the branches. Earlier, most of those who received academic training in psychology received a solid background in experimental psychology and test theory. This is no longer the case. Psychological researchers may have very different educational backgrounds depending on the field of interest. In later chapters, I shall rely primarily on cognitive psychology and social psychology for ideas. Cognitive psychology, which in the early 1960s became legitimate again after an interval where behaviorism prevailed, has gained wide acceptance for many of its findings. Research on cognitive phenomena is carried out in many disciplines, including economics. Herbert Simon has been a leader in this research and gave the field early respectability by combining cognitive psychology and computers (Simon, 1979).

WHO IS AN ECONOMIST AND WHO IS A PSYCHOLOGIST?

On Christmas Day, 1923, Mary Paley [Marshall's wife] recorded that after long reflective silence for the whole of their dinner, Marshall had said, 'If I had time to live my life over again, I should have devoted it to Psychology. Economics has too little to do with ideals; if I said much about them, I should not be read by businessmen.

Groenewegen (1995, p.729)

An economist is according to the dictionary someone who is a specialist in economics or someone who is economical (*Webster's New Collegiate Dictionary*, 1977). What type of training does it take to become an economist? The obvious answer is training in economics. I shall give a pertinent long quotation from a British economist, G. Shackle, who is very well known among economists for his creative thinking (see Frowen, 1990). In 1955, he wrote: 'to be a complete economist a man need only be a mathematician.'

That was, however, not the whole truth, so he added a few things: 'a philosopher.' Even this was not the end of the requirements, in the third place there follows: 'a psychologist' which I note with great pleasure. After that he added a number of specialities: 'an anthropologist, a historian, a geographer, and student of politics, a master of prose exposition, a man of the world with experience of practical business and finance, an understanding of the problems of administration, and a good knowledge of four or five foreign languages. All this in addition, of course, to familiarity with the economic literature itself.'

Shackle concluded

This list should, I think, dispose at once of the idea that there are, or ever have been, any complete economists and we can proceed to the practical question of what arrangements are likely to provide us with men who will feel not wholly confounded when an important economic decision confronts them. (Shackle, 1955, p.241)

The gist of this thinking and an important implication is that if you are an economist, you can only deal with certain aspects of economic behavior. It illustrates the idea that one has to use interdisciplinary approaches in the study of economic problems. Shackle himself had a research team with representatives from different disciplines, among them psychology.

A psychologist is defined as a person who is trained to perform psychological analysis, therapy, or research (*Webster's*, 1977). This definition hardly corresponds to the popular notion that everybody is able to practice psychology and that some people are good while others are poor in their exercise of psychology. It was mentioned above that while, for many centuries, psychology as part of philosophy was preoccupied with mind-body and consciousness problems, many other disciplines developed psychological knowledge of their own. In everyday thinking a psychologist is not necessarily thought of as good at using psychology. Psychological knowledge from research often competes with psychological knowledge based on everyday experience, intuition, and speculation. Common-sense psychology and scientific psychology do not always agree. More will be said about this later in this chapter.

Psychology is associated with the study of single individuals and social psychology with the study of individuals in groups. Economic problems at the aggregate level often have psychological dimensions, but are usually not conceived of as the business of psychologists. Everyday psychology is often seen as more congenial than scientific psychology for handling psychological dimensions in societal problems. Judging from the mass media focus of interest and knowledge, clinical psychology is practically the only psychological area of real interest to the general public. People who have some knowledge about psychology as a field of study tend to think of psychology as being split between schools and approaches. To some extent this may be true, but scientific psychology can still contribute to a better understanding of many problems in society. Cognitive psychology, which to the general public is relatively unknown, is one of the most important developing areas in scientific psychology and has attracted the interest of researchers in many other sciences where human behavior is concerned.

ECONOMICS AND PSYCHOLOGY

Economics as the Study of Self-Interest, Pleasure and Pain

The economic science was by Aristotle in his *Nicomachean Ethics* said to have wealth as its end. The science dealt with household and property management. Economics, which was early on called a science, like psychology also comprised practical knowledge and was practiced outside of the supremacy of philosophy. There thus existed applied economics and applied psychology that were quite independent of philosophy and the more theoretical thinking in the parent discipline.

Some of the best discussions of psychological problems relating to economic behavior can be found in the publications of the classical and early neoclassical economists. Before Adam Smith economics was a science without human actors. There were two dominating schools. The *mercantilists* studied foreign trade and stressed its importance for a national economy. The role of the government was confined to controlling trade and, in a way, to serving the merchants. The *physiocrats* who were mainly French saw agriculture and mining as the only real sources of wealth generation and all other activities were parasitic. The only role for government was to make sure that property was secure.

Adam Smith ([1776] 1982) introduced psychology into political economy by stressing the good consequences if men pursued their self-interest (self-love) and heeded some natural instincts. The forces of the market would then take care of creating a balanced economy – the work of the invisible hand. After Smith and later Bentham, economics, mostly called political economy, became the science that dealt with human pleasure and pain. Jevons (1871) and Böhm-Bawerk (1888) although using somewhat different words both saw economics as the study of pleasure and pain, which included the study of human emotions. In a passage on economics and ethics Jevons ([1871] 1911, p.23) described economics as follows: 'The theory which follows is entirely based on a calculus of pleasure and pain; and the object of Economics is to maximize happiness by purchasing pleasure, as it were, at the lowest cost of pain.' Böhm-Bawerk (1888) described the subject matter of his field in terms of happiness that are clearly related to feelings of pain and pleasure, at the same time as he said that he rejected hedonism and utilitarianism. Many contemporary psychologists were also interested in pleasure and pain, but mostly in the more physiological aspects.

Later, the experimental psychologists working on learning adopted the label of *reinforcement* to designate the effects of pleasurable or painful events. Boring (1950) referred to this as 'a hedonism of the past' meaning that these psychologists were not interested in intentions ('hedonism of the future'), but rather in consequences following rewards and punishments. More focus on intentions rather than reinforcements would probably have made psychology appear more useful to economists. Reinforcement is still an important concept in the psychology of learning, especially in Skinner's (1974) theory which has had some acceptance among economists who want to enrich economic theory (see Lea, 1978; Alhadeff (1982).

In his introduction to *Principles of Economics*, Marshall ([1890] 1990, p.1) said that economics is both a study of wealth and a branch of the study of man: 'POLITICAL ECONOMY or ECONOMICS is a study of mankind in the ordinary business of life; it examines that part of individual and social action which is most closely connected with the attainment and with the use of the material requisites of wellbeing.' This is still a highly psychological phrasing of the subject. It is noteworthy that Marshall used the words 'A study of mankind in the ordinary business of life', presumably to distinguish the subject matter from that of psychology. The science of psychology was at that time still closely related to problems experienced in philosophy rather than in everyday life.

Edgeworth ([1881] 1967), an economist who is sometimes mentioned also in the history of psychology took up a critical scrutiny of Jevons's idea of economics as the science of pleasure and pain. He asked for numerical measurements for the mathematical reasoning to be meaningful

> Professor Bain has shown [. . .] how one may correct one's estimate of one's pleasures upon much the same principle as the observations made with one's senses; how one may correctly estimate the pleasures of others upon the principle 'Accept identical objective marks as showing identical subjective states', notwithstanding personal differences, as of activity or demonstrativeness. This 'moral arithmetic' is perhaps to be supplemented by a moral differential calculus, the Fechnerian method applied to pleasures in general. For Wundt has shown that sensuous pleasures may thereby be measured, and, as utilitarians hold, all pleasures are commensurable. The first principle of this method might be: Just perceivable increments of pleasure, of all pleasures for all persons, are equatable. (Edgeworth ([1881] 1967, p.60)

As a support for his contention that utility could be measured, Edgeworth thus cited Fechner, Bain and Wundt, all three of whom are classified as psychologists in the history of psychology, although Fechner was a physiologist, Bain like Jevons a logician, and Wundt a medical doctor and philosopher. Edgeworth treated the Utilitarian Calculus of pleasure which was the basis for ethics as something separate from the Economical Calculus of Pleasure, which was the basis for economics. Earlier the two were treated as belonging together, but Edgeworth saw them as distinct. Attempts are nowadays being made to bring ethics and economics closer together again (Sen, 1979; 1987; Etzioni, 1988).

It is interesting to compare the economists' notions of feelings of pleasure and pain as needing no definition and the psychologists' efforts at about the same time to establish the true nature of feelings and emotions. The psychologists were influenced by the physiologists in their dealing with such matters. William James who became widely known for his *The Principles of Psychology* which was published in 1890, is also known for his theory of feelings and emotions which was based on physiological theory and his own work in the laboratory (the James-Lange theory of emotions).

Towards the end of the 19th century, economics became more and more dependent on mathematics. Alfred Marshall (1890) presented a highly coherent economic theory, which was based on mathematics and became a standard textbook in university courses. Far from all economists adopted the abstract, mathematical approach to economics. The reliance on history did not give up that easily. There was a 'Methodenstreit' in Germany involving Carl Menger who was in favor of abstract reasoning and Friedrich Schmoller who represented the historical approach (Caldwell, 1986). To some extent the History School has returned into focus with institutional and evolutionary economics (Hausman, 1988, p.37).

Controversies between Economists and Psychologists in the Early 1900s

Economics is certainly a peculiar science. Many of its premises are platitudes such as: Individuals can rank options; or individuals prefer more goods to fewer; or individuals choose that option that they most prefer. Other premises are simplifications such as: Commodities are infinitely divisible or individuals have perfect information. Upon such platitudes and simplifications, such as 'premises assumed without evidence, or in spite of it,' economists have erected a large theoretical edifice. This edifice possesses immense mathematical sophistication, but its conclusions, although not 'necessarily erroneous,' are often inapplicable.

Hausman (1988, p.1)

The progress in scientific psychology led to criticism of the psychological underpinnings of economics. Gabriel Tarde (1902) accused Smith of having forgotten the psychology that he espoused in his *The Theory of Moral Sentiments*, when he wrote *The Wealth of Nations*. Smith was blamed for missing the fact that humans were social beings, interacting with others, and not exclusively pursuing their self-interest. For many years both before and after Tarde it has been held that Adam Smith changed his concept of man from *The Theory of Moral Sentiment* to *The Wealth of Nations*. Whereas Smith in the former book stressed consideration of other men's happiness in the pursuit of one's own, he apparently spoke in favor of self-interest as the guiding principle in the latter.

While Smith (1759) talked about three components of virtue: prudence, benevolence and justice, and self-command, the same Smith ([1776] 1981, p. 119) asserted 'It is not from the benevolence of the butcher, the brewer, or the baker, that we expect our dinner, but from their regard to their own interest. We address ourselves, not to their humanity but to their self-love, and never talk to them of our own necessities but of their advantages.' Smith praised the effects of division of labor and according to more recent thinking this involved no disregard for benevolence. There is no incongruity between the first book and what is said in the later book according to the editors of Smith ([1759] 1982, pp.20-5). They noted that Smith himself did not see any difference. Hayek ([1978] 1985) said

> It is an error that Adam Smith preached egotism: his central thesis said nothing about how the individual should use his increased product; and his sympathies were all with the benevolent use of the increased income. He was concerned with how to make it possible for people to make their contribution to the social product as large as possible and this he thought required that they were paid what their services were worth to those to whom they rendered them. Hayek ([1978] 1985, p.268)

The controversies between economics and psychology often concerned the hedonistic assumption of a single motive for economic behavior and the construction of utility theory. These questions also caused considerable argument among economists before ultimately a broad consensus was achieved. Economic theory has been the object of attacks from such different approaches as behaviorism, psychology of Verstehen and psychoanalysis (if the latter is subsumed under psychology). Lewin (1996) gives an interesting account of the controversies around the turn of the century.

In the Anglo-Saxon countries there was a fight between psychology and economics in which some economists grabbed arguments from the well-known psychological works of William James, William McDougall and John Watson (see Coats, 1976). Mainstream economists vehemently rejected the psychological arguments. Florence (1927), a British economist, who was on the whole favorable towards using psychological theories in economics, rejected McDougall's (1908) theory of instincts as a foundation for economics. He did this on the ground that instincts left no room for considering costs or sacrifices. Some deliberation of utility versus costs and other sacrifices was according to him a necessary feature of consumer choice.

Psychological attitude theories have later repeatedly been criticized for disregarding the cost or sacrifice aspects of behavior and for too much concentration on benefits and attractiveness (see Meyer, 1982). To a large extent the criticism has been valid, but it should be noted that the attributes measured according to leading attitude theories comprise both costs and benefits. Models like the new 'Theory of Planned Behavior' combine attitudes with such variables as 'social norms' and 'perceived control' to predict behavior (see Ajzen, 1991).

The development towards abstract theory involved that economics became depsychologized (Coats, 1976; 1988). John Neville Keynes, the father of John Maynard Keynes, in very clear terms, stated the independence of economics from psychology

The bare facts that other things being equal men prefer a greater to a smaller gain, that under certain conditions they will forego present for the sake of future gratifications, and the like, are psychological facts of great economic importance. But they are assumed by the economist, not established by him. He does not seek to explain or analyse them; nor does he investigate all the consequences to which they lead. Economic laws in the strict sense are different from the above. They are not simple laws of human nature, but laws of complex social facts resulting from simple laws of human nature. (Keynes [1917] 1988, p.84)

A decisive blow to the role of psychology was dealt by Lionel Robbins ([1935] 1979). He discussed the nature of economics and formulated a much-quoted definition of economics: 'Economics is the science which studies human behaviour as a relationship between ends and scarce means which have alternative uses.' The definition did not mention need satisfaction, which had often earlier been part and parcel of definitions of economics. This underscores the fact that Robbins was hostile towards the science of psychology. He was particularly emphatic in his rejection of behaviorism, which in his view had misled some economists into rejecting the economic theory of subjective value as non-scientific since value could not be observed.

The borderlands of Economics are the happy hunting-ground of minds averse to the effort of exact thought, and, in these ambiguous regions, in recent years, endless time has been devoted to attacks on the alleged psychological assumptions of Economic Science. Psychology, it is said, advances very rapidly. If, therefore, Economics rests upon particular psychological doctrines, there is no task more ready to hand than every five years or so to write sharp polemics showing that, since psychology has changed its fashion, Economics needs 'rewriting from the foundations upwards'. As might be expected, the opportunity has not been neglected. Professional economists absorbed in the exciting task of discovering new truth, have usually disdained to reply; and the lay public, ever anxious to escape the necessity of recognizing the implications of choice in a world of scarcity, has allowed itself to be bamboozled into believing that matters, which are in fact as little dependent on the truth of fashionable psychology as the multiplication table, are still open questions on which the enlightened man, who, of course, is nothing if not a psychologist, must be willing to suspend judgement. (Robbins [1935]1979, p.40)

Economists as enlightened men are themselves psychologists who are independent of psychological fashions. Like many other economists, Robbins referred to common-sense psychology as a support for the rationality postulate. 'All that we need to assume as economists is the obvious fact that different possibilities offer different incentives, and that these incentives can be arranged in order of their intensity.' (Robbins [1935] 1979, p.40). Robbins translated the rationality concept into something that was a pure logic of choice, with the main emphasis on consistency. It just involved knowing one's preferences and acting in accordance with them. Contrary to what is often assumed, Robbins made some room for apparently inconsistent behavior: 'The marginal utility of not bothering about marginal utility is a factor of which account has been taken by the chief writers on the subjective theory of value from Böhm-Bawerk onwards.' (Robbins [1935] 1979, p.42)

Robbins's arguments are interesting and are still worth considering. Let us look at them more closely.

1. Robbins asserted that the psychological foundations of economics had nothing to do with psychological science. Similar to John Stuart Mill (see Chapter 3), he viewed economics as based on a simple psychological law which could be observed in everyday life: people prefer more to less of something that gives pleasure and less of what gives pain. Little can be objected to this law in the abstract although it is easy to find exceptions to this law in reality.
2. Even if economics needed psychological science, the latter would not be able to furnish any truths that could last for some time. Robbins apparently referred to the intense debates between representatives of different schools in psychology such as those between holistic Gestalt psychology and atomistic behaviorism. There is still no long-lasting, coherent theory of behavior, which could replace the simple psychological law that Mill talked about. There is, however, in psychology a possibility of making cafeteria choices of ideas and methods for economists. The new cognitive psychology has found use in many disciplines besides economics.
3. Psychologists make use of the fact that people seem to forget that they live in a world of scarcity and have to make choices, that is, to make priorities and preference scales, however primitive. Psychologists have with some right been accused also by other economists of having a one-valued rather than a two-valued logic: psychologists tend to measure attractiveness of objects (attitudes) and neglect the cost or sacrifice aspects (Florence, 1927; Meyer, 1982). Recently augmented attitude models like Ajzen's Theory of Planned Behavior are an answer to this criticism (see Chapter 7).

More Recent Developments

While over the last century the two disciplines diverged more and more as the problems in focus and the methodological approaches were developing, there are now signs of a growing use of knowledge from the other discipline and some cooperation. Maybe both disciplines had to become established sciences first. It has been said that when economists started to develop abstract theory, economics took an important step away from history and it became a science that could make predictions (Manicas, 1987). While psychology is mostly centered on description and explanation, economics is preoccupied with prediction. Friedman's so-called F-twist (1953) asserted that the true measure of the value of economics was the accuracy of the predictions it made. The assumptions made could be false, but they remained valid as long as the predictions were better than those made with any other assumptions. This closed the door for the psychologists' criticism of the psychological underpinnings of economic theory. The F-twist has been widely accepted by economists, but there is rejection by some (see Cyert and Grunberg, 1963; Thaler, 1980) and by philosophers of science (Nagel, 1963; Musgrave, 1981). The psychologists only approve realistic assumptions.

Mainstream economics has developed a rather strict paradigm for research. Caldwell (1986) gave the following description of the typical procedure in economic research.

> If one were to reflect on what comprises scientific procedure in economics, the following set of instructions might emerge: Find a problem, model it as a maximization problem, derive some testable hypotheses (the predictions of the model), find empirical proxies for the theoretical constructs, do the econometrics, get your results. (It might well be added: If the results agree with the model, publish them; if not, find out why, and then publish them). (Caldwell, 1986, p.10)

Caldwell noted that in the 1950s and 1960s, many macroeconomists did not follow this paradigm since their models did not yield any testable propositions.

Mainstream economists still see little room for scientific psychology in the realm of economics. Recent developments under the label of 'behavioral economics', however, involve a more accepting attitude towards psychology. In fact, researchers from both fields have found that they may again have something to learn from each other. Psychologists have become involved in the study of economic behavior, especially as it is related to decision making, and economists accept survey data, have adopted psychological research methods like the laboratory experiment and utilize concepts and hypotheses from social and cognitive psychology.

These new crossings of the disciplinary borderlines are more than mere fishing expeditions into unexplored areas. With some oversimplification it can be said that (some) economists have found it useful to enrich microeconomic theory with psychological concepts and theories in their attempts to explain and predict macroeconomic phenomena. Psychology is focused on individual experience and behavior and often has little to offer at the aggregate level. This leaves ample room for the use of common-sense psychology and introspection at this level. There is also use of sociology, but surprisingly little. Economic sociology is again making progress after a slow start with Schumpeter long ago (Granovetter and Swedberg, 1992; Swedberg, 1993).

Some concepts that are used at the aggregate level do not have any correspondence at the micro level. Laws of behavior can sometimes differ depending on whether the macro or the micro level is studied. Neglecting the differences between micro and macro is in economic texts referred to as 'the fallacy of composition' (see Samuelson and Nordhaus, 1992, p.6). In other social science texts it is called 'the ecological fallacy' (Langbein and Lichtman, 1978). The fallacy concepts are signs of the awareness that micro relationships and macro relationships may differ. Still, when a relationship is discovered at the macroeconomic level, there typically begins a quest for a micro model that is compatible with the macro findings. The consumer choice theory and the utility function will perhaps over time be broadened so as to cover earlier unexplained macroeconomic phenomena (see Leibenstein, 1979; see also Chapter 8).

Despite the common charge (see Radnitzky and Bernholz, 1987) that economics is an imperialistic science, economic models have not penetrated into psychology to any noteworthy extent, except in the study of decision making and in economic psychology where they suggest problems for study (see Lea et al., 1987). I have a feeling that there is often a confounding of economists' influence on society and their (much smaller) influence on other social sciences. Nonetheless, in this field of endeavor, the contributions of psychologists have often concentrated on proving deviations from rationality (Kahneman and Tversky, 1979). Psychologists working in Skinner's tradition have found economic analysis of demand very useful (see Hursh and Bauman, 1987). Psychological research in general has received little influence from economics and stayed away from studying economic problems. The pervasive use of psychology in marketing and personnel administration does not count in this context. There was some influence from the early Austrian economists on contemporary psychologists. Menger's (1871) ideas informed some study of religious behavior according to Schumpeter (1954). Böhm-Bawerk is said to have contributed ideas to Act psychology, which later became Gestalt psychology.

Arrow has suggested that Freud was influenced by the Austrian economists of his time when he formulated his theory of libido and what was called 'the economic principle' of balance between the ego and the id.

> Freud's use of the term 'economic' in his discussions of metapsychology is remarkably precise. He is referring to the allocation of the scarce resources of the libido among competing uses, just as the individual allocates his scarce income among competing commodities. It might be interesting for the historian of thought to see what, if any, influence the thought of economists had in Freud's development. Vienna in the 1870s and 1880s was the center of a great school of economists who were very much interested in the utility theory – indeed, this group was one of its originators. (Arrow, 1963, p.726)

In recent years, the communication between the fields of psychology and economics has increased within certain research areas. Research on decision making under uncertainty and risk is nowadays a truly interdisciplinary area in the sense that several disciplines are involved in the research, but real co-operative efforts are still rare. Edwards (1954) made the first presentation of economic and statistical research on decision making under uncertainty and risk to psychologists. His article aroused a lot of interest among psychologists for experimental work in the area. Herbert Simon has had considerable influence on cognitive psychology, but not as an economist, rather as a computer scientist and psychological researcher.

Hursh and Bauman (1987) represented a new field within psychology, which they said was heavily influenced by economics: *behavioral analysis*. These authors have found economic theory an inspiring source of concepts and ideas for their psychological research, which belongs to Skinner's tradition. An early account of this common ground was given by Lea (1978). Ainslie (1975) relied to some extent on classical and neoclassical economists in his discussion of specious rewards and how to overcome addiction. In a recent book, he has launched the concept of picoeconomics to designate economics within an individual, a sort of serial decision making (Ainslie, 1992).

One reason for the psychologists' lack of interest in economic theory may primarily lie in the fact that most of them have a critical attitude towards the rationality concept. This may have kept psychologists from studying economic behavior that in principle should be at least as interesting as other behavior. The laws governing behavior are presumably also valid for economic behavior. The question then becomes one of the researcher's inclination to confirm findings within an area about which s/he knows little and which is the guarded specialty of another discipline. Those psychologists who have been interested in economic behavior have seen it as an area of application rather than basic research and many of them have been attracted by business as consultants and employees. This started at the beginning of this century when Hugo Münsterberg (1913) gave advice on psychology and industrial efficiency and John Watson, the father of behaviorism, joined the advertising world.

Psychology is not a well-integrated science with a dominating research paradigm such as in economics. There are conflicting paradigms, sometimes still called 'schools', and there is a focus on developing theory for limited behavioral areas rather than for behavior in general. This trend is reflected in the training of psychologists. Nowadays the basic training seems to vary much more than earlier on and there is more of an early specialization. Economic psychology is still a rare option among specializations offered to psychology students. For economists who are looking for complementary training in psychological research there are also very few opportunities. The In-

ternational Association for Research in Economic Psychology (IAREP) ar-
ranges annual meetings, workshops, and with some intervals summer schools
to encourage psychologists and economists to undertake interdisciplinary
research on economic behavior.

The economic model of human behavior is sophisticated, but with respect
to the individual behavior highly simplified and abstract. The abstract nature
makes it possible to use the same basic micro model for deriving a variety of
conclusions at the macro level. Despite the presumable oversimplification of
the behavioral assumptions in the postulate of rationality, there is still the
possibility that psychologists who are less abstract in their approaches can
learn something from its uses. Some of the work in cognitive psychology
may be critical of the rationality postulate, but important research is inspired
by attempts to improve (or disprove) the theory (see Kahneman and Tversky,
1979; Hogarth, 1987).

Some innovative uses of psychology in economics involve converting a
psychological theory into something that is compatible with the rationality
postulate. The use of cognitive dissonance theory in economic contexts is a
well-known example (Hirschman, 1965; Akerlof and Dickens, 1982). Thaler
and Shefrin's theory of self-control (1981) is another example. More will be
said about this in Chapter 8.

In empirical studies, economists tend to be mainly interested in results of
analyses at the macro level, not in individual data. This is illustrated in
Keynes's (1936) formulation in his psychological law: 'as a rule and on the
average' (see Chapter 4). Epstein (1980) and Schachter et al. (1986) pleaded
for more and better use of aggregate measures in psychology. Economists
refrain from directly measuring certain concepts which are either through
deductive analysis proven to be dispensable or are replaced through 'proxies'
that can be estimated. 'Proxies' are used to replace actual measurements of
phenomena that are considered elusive and hard to measure directly. Economists seem to do better at creating interesting 'proxies' than psychologists
who tend to stick to 'indicators' that are close to observations. Psychologists
are often hesitant about what Gergen (1982) called 'generative' use of theory,
i.e., innovative generalizations of findings (see Wärneryd, 1986b).

The Use of Scientific Psychology and Common-Sense Psychology

*Economic theory has been steadily purged of psychological content, to the point
where even the minimal interdisciplinary contact afforded by mutual mockery has
largely ceased.*

Lea (1981, p.246)

J.N. Keynes ([1917] 1988) and Robbins ([1935] 1979) and many other
economists emphatically rejected the possibility and desirability of relying on

scientific psychology; reliance on everyday experience sufficed for making the simple psychological assumptions in economic theory plausible. Also according to Arrow (1963, p.738), economic theory is fundamentally based on observations that are non-scientific in most psychologists' eyes: 'The whole axiomatic approach can be thought of as crystallizing everyday or introspective observations.' When the early economists out of concern for societal issues discussed psychological problems they took examples from everyday life and they freely used introspection. The contemporary psychologists were preoccupied with research problems inspired by philosophy, but typically rejected introspection as inferior to the experimental method.

To what extent did the early economists use the results of scientific psychology? This is perhaps not a relevant question judging from what Schumpeter (1954, pp.27-8) said in his *History of Economic Analysis*. He attacked the view that psychology was the basis from which economics like every other social science must start and from which all fundamental explanation must be taken (see the vignette introducing this chapter). He declared that using a psychic fact did not mean borrowing anything from professional psychology: 'I am simply formulating what rightly or wrongly I believe to be a fact of common experience. If we place ourselves on this standpoint, we shall find that there is much less of psychology about economic propositions than one might think at first sight.'

While Schumpeter devoted some attention to scientific psychology in his history of economics, his view was in the end quite similar to that of Robbins. Schumpeter was more concerned about the neglect of what he, following Max Weber, called 'economic sociology'. He distinguished between three component parts in economics: *economic theory* in which he included statistics, *economic history*, and *economic sociology*. He voiced the opinion that the use of psychoanalytic theory could be very useful in economic history.

Schumpeter was probably right in his assertion that the economists used professional psychology when they found it useful, and that, mostly, they did not find any use for it. Did they then mainly depend on common-sense psychology? First, a few words should be said about what scientific psychologists think about common-sense psychology. Fletcher (1984, p.204) defined common sense in the following manner: 'a cultural group's body of shared beliefs about the world'. Common-sense psychology is then psychological beliefs that are shared by some cultural group. According to this view it can be studied through everyday language (ordinary language). Psychological knowledge has always been an ingredient in everyday life and more or less taken for granted. Psychological science has had difficulties finding its way with common-sense psychology. The latter is partly more advanced, partly lagging far behind scientific psychology according to Kelley (1992).

Psychologists have a tendency to be somewhat doubtful about common-sense psychology. This is mainly because it is too easy to be unaware of the influence of common-sense psychology on psychological findings and especially of its influence on interpretations of research results. There is always a temptation to evaluate findings against common sense, which may be good, but may also lead to false rejection or acceptance of hypotheses. Fletcher (1984, p.203) concluded that '. . . common sense is a valuable but inherently dangerous resource available to psychologists.' This may also hold true for economists using common-sense psychology. Skinner (1974), like most other behaviorists, was very hostile towards common-sense psychology

> The disastrous results of common sense in the management of human behavior are evident in every walk of life, from international affairs to the care of a baby, and we shall continue to be inept in all these fields until a scientific analysis clarifies the advantages of a more effective technology. It will then be obvious that the results are due to more than common sense. (Skinner, 1974, p.234)

If common-sense psychology is defined as above, it is probable that the classical and neoclassical economists did not entirely depend on common-sense psychology. Psychology did not exist as a scientific discipline that could give answers to questions concerning those problems that were of greatest concern to economists. Every social science and natural sciences like medicine had their own psychology (Schönpflug, 1993). While observations of psychological phenomena were made by other scholars, those philosophers who were interested in psychology were devoted to exploring more abstract thinking. Scholars who needed psychological knowledge often made rather astute observations of human behavior and were more discerning than the philosopher-psychologists. In certain periods, there were apparent similarities in the thinking of economists and scientific psychologists. Schumpeter (1954, p.796) attributed these similarities to 'phraseological' influences and the effects of Zeitgeist rather than to actual influence from psychology.

There are also some differences in how the early economists related to what was contemporary scientific psychology. Was Adam Smith depending on common-sense psychology or on more systematic observation when he wrote the following passage which is essentially the contents of prospect theory and lies emphasis on loss aversion ('losses loom larger than gains')? (Kahneman and Tversky, 1979)

> We suffer more, it has already been observed, [. . .] when we fall from a better to a worse situation, than we ever enjoy when we rise from a worse to a better. Security, therefore, is the first and the principal object of prudence. It is averse to expose our health, our fortune, our rank, or reputation, to any sort of hazard. (Smith [1759] 1982, p.213)

One way for economists to deal with psychology was to cite, as support for their reasoning about human behavior, ideas and results from the works of psychologists. Jevons (1871), for example, cited his colleague Alexander Bain who is considered to be the first British psychologist. He did so in many contexts and in particular when discussing feelings and emotions as part of developing marginal utility theory. As indicated above, Edgeworth (1881) who contributed to economic theory by using 'mathematical psychics', referred to psychological research results from Fechner, Bain and Wundt, sometimes criticizing them.

Böhm-Bawerk (1888) took a different approach to psychological science. He noted that he based his psychological thinking on his own observations. This is typical of the Austrian school and the members of the School can no doubt be accused of armchair psychologizing rather than heeding the findings of scientific psychology. Böhm-Bawerk gave an excuse for daring to deal with psychological issues. He complained that professional psychologists were as yet devoting little attention to the psychological problems that were of interest to the economist. His colleague Menger (1871) did not cite any psychological research, but developed some psychological theory of his own, a need hierarchy which is similar to the one of Maslow (1954). Pareto (1909) more or less developed his own psychology and said that the attempts to refer to Fechner's law as a support for the idea of diminishing utility were unnecessary. Except for that, he seems to have given few references to psychological science in his economic texts. According to Albou (1984) there is still a lot to learn from Pareto's reasoning for researchers in economic psychology.

It would seem that some economists like Jevons, Edgeworth and Marshall who first developed the mathematical approach to economics were more inclined to cite the results of the science of psychology. They somehow took the substance of their theory from psychology and used it as an argument and support for the chosen mathematical form. Fisher (1930) used psychological concepts in his development of economic theory. In his discussion of what factors determined interest rates, he talked about subjective or psychic income and he suggested that 'impatience' could be used instead of 'time preference' when spending versus saving was discussed. Coats (1976) mentioned that Fisher in his doctoral dissertation treated the potential role of psychology in economics and found that the developments in scientific psychology were of little use. Fisher did not make any explicit references to scientific psychology. According to him, a major source of psychological ideas was a book by John Rae *The Sociological Theory of Capital* (Rae, 1834). This book was written by an educator with some background studies in medicine and political science. It contains a discussion of the desire to accumulate wealth that had influence on such economists as J. S. Mill, Böhm-Bawerk, Marshall, and Fisher (see Chapter 3).

In some contexts, Keynes (1936) used the concept of *animal spirits* to designate what many other authors call 'psychological factors'. He defined it as a kind of spontaneous optimism that made entrepreneurs optimistically invest money in their own ideas. Interestingly, Keynes may have been influenced by psychoanalysis when he formulated some of the ideas in his *General Theory* (Winslow, 1986). Keynes was close to the so-called Bloomsbury group, which also included advocates of psychoanalysis. Winslow found indirect evidence for psychoanalytic influences in Keynes's discussion of liquidity preference (anal fixation) and of animal spirits. In his earlier work *A Treatise on Money*, Keynes discussed some of Freud's ideas in footnotes, but in *General Theory* he did not refer at all to psychoanalysis. Hayek ([1978] 1985, p.284) who like Schumpeter was not much of an admirer of Keynes said: 'Widely read as Keynes was in many fields, his education in economics was somewhat narrow.' Keynes may have known more about psychoanalysis than about psychology, except for the psychology based on his own observations. Much of his psychological reasoning was related to the uncertainty of the future and expectations that replaced certain knowledge, an area unexplored by psychologists in those days (Schmölders et al., 1956).

The increasing focus on utility maximization, equilibrium theory, indifference curves and revealed preferences saved economists from having to pay attention to individual idiosyncrasies of human beings. Still, psychological problems that have been suppressed under the elegant theory of economics keep cropping up and can no longer be handled by pure economics. The interesting fact to note now is that economics has finally reached the stage where serious use is found for results and methods from scientific psychology. The degree of acceptance, to be sure, differs among economists and there is a tendency to make psychological concepts compatible with the rationality concept. Survey data on business and consumer expectations, approaches like the controlled laboratory experiment, and some selected concepts, especially if they can be made compatible with the rationality postulate, are nowadays rather widely appreciated. There are economists and others who have wanted to reject the rationality postulate and completely rewrite economic theory. Scitovsky (1976, 1986) is a notable example and so are Alhadeff (1982) and Maital (1982). Their economist colleagues have not met their efforts with much enthusiasm.

There are differences in approaches and interpretations with respect to the interdisciplinary problems. Economists are, for example, used to working with specified models in mathematical form whereas psychologists tend more towards employing cruder, often verbal models or what economists call 'box-and-arrow' models (which for them are harder to read than mathematical texts). The design and interpretation of laboratory experiments differ somewhat between the disciplines (Hey, 1992)). Concepts like expectation, attitude, risk perception and risk aversion are denotatively and connotatively different in the two disciplines (Arrow, 1982; Selten, 1991; Smith, 1991).

Table 1.1 Some Characteristics of Economics and Psychology

Economics	Psychology
Founded on a few fundamental assumptions, by Becker (1976) called 'The Economic Approach to Human Behavior'	Mostly inductive, with low-level empirical theory Concentration on explanation of individual behavior
utility maximizing behavior stable preferences market equilibria	Often strivings for descriptive details of processes Learning is a central concept
Deductions based on these assumptions	Hypotheses close to observations
Mathematical language and specified models; econometrics	Experimental and statistical methods, scaling methods
Objective data, use of proxies based on objective data	Observational and subjective data, also on emotions and feelings
Interest in aggregate phenomena (macro), outcomes rather than processes	Interest in general behavioral laws and individual differences
Assumptions about individual behavior serve 'as if' and do not have to be true	Assumptions about individual behavior must be realistic (agree with psychological knowledge)
Psychological concepts are reinterpreted in economic terms so as to be compatible with the rationality concept	Typically ignores context, structural, and system variables

(Based on Wärneryd, 1994, p.45)

Table 1.1 summarizes the previous discussion of characteristics of economics and psychology. More will be said about economic and psychological approaches to saving research in later chapters. Chapter 3 gives a historical perspective on the psychology of saving and this gives another chance to review some psychological issues in economics.

THE THREE MEANINGS OF ECONOMIC PSYCHOLOGY

Many uses of psychology in economics may be seen as fishing for new explanatory concepts. There are also systematic attempts to utilize the interdisciplinary possibilities. These attempts can be classified under the umbrella labels of *economic psychology* or *behavioral economics*. These are sometimes seen as synonymous. While the concept of economic psychology is often used when psychologists deal with economic problems, behavioral economics usually refers to the attempts by economists to include psychological thinking and research methods in the sphere of economics. With the psychological perspective that dominates this book, the focus here will naturally be on economic psychology, but first a definition of behavioral economics should be given

> Behavioral economics is concerned with studying human behavior in economic matters. It deals with modeling 'real man' rather than simply 'economic man', by considering the behavioral, especially socio-psychological, mechanisms underlying economic behavior. It is aimed at enriching analytical economics by giving economic models a more realistic point of departure and thus improving their relevance. Such an approach is necessarily interdisciplinary, borrowing insights from behavioral and social sciences and applying them to economics. (Maital, 1986, cover text)

Economic psychology actually represents a broad spectrum of attempts to combine knowledge from the two fields. I would like to submit that the concept of economic psychology is used in at least three senses:

1. The psychological foundations of economics
2. A field of applied psychology
3. A separate field of study.

I shall first make a brief presentation of the three uses, then advance some ideas about the possible future of economic psychology. My own preference is the third use.

The Psychological Assumptions behind Economics

Occasionally, authors dealing with the psychological underpinnings of economics have used *economic psychology* to designate the psychological assumptions underlying economic theory. The concept is occasionally found in writings by leading economists and historians of economic thought, e.g. Schumpeter (1954), Hayek (1978), and Coats (1976). It is employed when the meaning of the utility maximization or rationality postulate is discussed, that is, the psychological underpinnings of economics.

Gabriel Tarde (1902) wrote that he launched the concept of economic psychology in 1881 when he published a critique of economic theory. He conceded that some members of the Austrian School in economics also used economic psychology in the sense of the psychological foundations of economics. The Austrians seem to have used 'Wirtschaftspsychologie'. In the 1902 text, Tarde seriously criticized Adam Smith (1776) for being a poor psychologist, disregarding human interaction, when he formulated his economic theory. In Tarde's view, Adam Smith was dealing with economic psychology when he proposed that human actors had an important role in the development of markets. According to Smith, the pursuit of self-interest, the division of labor, and the exchange of goods were the basic elements of human action. Exchange was the main characteristic that distinguished humans from animals. Tarde found that these notions insufficiently considered how humans influence one another. He proposed that social interaction, what he called 'l'interpsychologie', should be a basis for economics rather than the rational pursuit of the self-interest. Similar views can be found in Caporael et al. (1989) who thoroughly reviewed the psychology of selfishness.

Few economists question the rationality postulate. Many economists today seem to think in accordance with Lakatos' (1978) research program

> The basic unit of appraisal must be not an isolated theory or conjunction of theories but rather a *'research programme'*, with a conventionally accepted (and thus by provisional decision 'irrefutable') *'hard core'* and with a *'positive heuristic'* which defines problems, outlines the construction of a belt of auxiliary hypotheses, foresees anomalies and turns them victoriously into examples, all according to a preconceived plan. (Lakatos, 1978, p.110)

In general, Lakatos' thinking about research programs seems to be gaining wide acceptance in economics (cf. Latsis, 1976; de Marchi and Blaug, 1991). The basic postulate of rationality is kept as the hard core of economic theory. Models derived from this postulate can be rejected without any effect on the hard core. Attempts are made to foresee anomalies and turn them into examples. This implies that findings in scientific psychology can never affect the rationality postulate. They can very well inspire and enter into models in the belt of auxiliary hypotheses. Behavioral economists are actually exploring such possibilities.

Economic psychology in the sense of the psychological underpinnings of economic theory does not imply that the rationality concept is being opposed.

Despite many objections that can be raised against the rationality postulate, this paradigm is hard to replace for its elaborate structure and elegance, its proven usefulness and for lack of something better. Despite the fact that economic reasoning often proceeds from a model of individual behavior, the main aim is to explain the behavior of large aggregates of individuals over time, not the behavior of single individuals. The analysis of individual behavior is carried out 'as if' the individual acts rationally.

It is possible to use psychology without reflecting on the rationality assumption, both for descriptive and explanatory purposes. Lea et al. (1992) proposed a focus on the consequences rather than on the axioms of rationality, which means that psychologists should leave the rationality concept alone and concentrate on other issues of relevance to economic behavior. Researchers can use psychology to elaborate descriptions of behavior or to gather data that provide measures of economic concepts that are otherwise hard to appreciate. Unfortunately, psychology is sometimes used as a cafeteria in which choices of theory fragments can be made to fit almost any preconceived notion about human behavior and humans.

Economic theory has major advantages as a normative theory, but is deficient as a descriptive theory of individual behavior according to the psychologist Herrnstein (1990). He said

> We start with a paradox, which is that the economic theory of rational choice (also called optimal choice theory) accounts only poorly for actual behavior, yet it comes close to serving as the fundamental principle of the behavioral sciences. No other well articulated theory of behavior commands so large a following in so wide a range of disciplines . . . The theory of rational choice, I conclude, is normatively useful but is fundamentally deficient as an account of behavior. (Herrnstein, 1990, p. 356)

Herrnstein proposed an alternative, descriptive theory that he called 'melioration' (Herrnstein and Prelec, 1992).

Thaler (1992) focused attention on a number of *anomalies* in economic behavior, which could not be explained by economic theory and showed how they could be understood by using results from cognitive psychology and experimental economics. He cited two reasons for the avoidance of economic models with assumptions of less than fully rational behavior

> First, it is not generally possible to build good descriptive models without collecting data, and many theorists claim to have a strong allergic reaction to data. Second, rational models tend to be simple and elegant with precise predictions, while behavioral models tend to be complicated, and messy, with much vaguer predictions. But, look at it this way. Would you rather be elegant and precisely wrong, or messy and vaguely right? (Thaler, 1992, p.198)

Although, overall, I opt for the second alternative, I have to concede that with messy models and vague predictions it is often difficult to know whether one is right or wrong. Besides, Thaler speaks of understanding and economists request predictions.

Research in economic psychology in the first sense may attempt to work with some of the difficulties of present economic theory, essentially by providing more and better descriptive details about human behavior. Psychologists can conceivably add to the discussion by contributing data on circumstances under which rationality does or does not occur and thus help explain anomalies. Their results can to some extent make irrational behavior predictable (cf. Akerlof and Dickens, 1982). They can also look at what constitutes utility, what the relations are between revealed preferences and subjective utility (cf. Sen, 1979). Economists like Gary Becker (1976) tend to see anomalies as minor deviations from rationality which can be explained in terms of rationality or which are random and thus insignificant. Some economists explore whether economic theory can handle the found anomalies pushing economic reasoning a little further (see Machina, 1990).

Psychological experiments that indicated frequent and large deviations from economic rationality, notably research inspired by prospect theory (Kahneman and Tversky, 1979), have met considerable interest among economists, but also met criticism, based on experimental work carried out by economists. The results from the psychological studies have been questioned, among other things, for lack of mundane realism, for non-use of monetary incentives in the experiments, and for disregarding learning effects (see Machina, 1990; Smith, 1991; Hey, 1992).

Hausman (1991) accused economists of dogmatism and reluctance against new evidence. He reviewed the *preference reversal phenomenon*, found it well established experimentally, and criticized economists for playing it down because it clashed with some fundamental economic theory. The preference reversal phenomenon involves stable findings that choices among pairs of gambles are primarily influenced by probabilities of winning and losing, whereas buying and selling prices of choice options are primarily determined by the dollar amounts that can be won or lost. This means that preferences may not be stable and that different ways of measuring preferences will give different results. The preference reversal is predictable, but not very well explained (see Tversky et al., 1990).

Economists, in the first place behavioral economists, are increasingly accepting psychological research that enriches economic models or gives access to new types of data. Typically, these economists try to comply with or cope with the rationality concept by reinterpreting psychological concepts so that the latter become compatible with the rationality postulate. Akerlof and Dickens (1982) who developed dissonance theory in rationality terms and applied it in the study of safety behavior provided a well-known example. This theory had earlier been used by Hirschman (1965), an economist who has frequently relied on psychology and especially on dissonance theory in his discussion of how to make attitudes change in economic development. Thaler and Shefrin (1981) gave another example with their theory of self-control and saving. These economists seem to feel free to adopt psychological thinking and use it in their models as long as they can make it compatible with the rationality postulate.

Economic Psychology as a Field of Applied Psychology

A second way of defining economic psychology starts with psychological theories as a basis for the study of economic behavior. Economic behavior is seen as an area of application where scientific psychological knowledge can be put to the test and used for solving new kinds of practical problems. In a textbook on applied psychology, Anastasi (1964) described economic psychology as follows

> A branch of consumer psychology that has been taking shape since World War II is economic psychology. Cutting across the fields of economics and psychology, this area of research employs some of the data-gathering procedures developed in consumer opinion surveys and in the (previously discussed) food acceptance methodology. In its analysis of consumer data, economic psychology combines concepts taken from psychology, mathematics, and economics. (Anastasi, 1964, p. 277)

Anastasi cited some examples of pertinent research. Her first examples concerned product development problems. Given that the price of a product cannot exceed a certain amount, which quality grade is optimal? She correctly referred to this research as belonging to operations research. Another example was taken from a study of meal preferences assessed through mail questionnaires distributed to the members of a faculty club. Every day there was a choice between three differently priced dishes in the restaurant. Combining meal preferences and price preferences, Jones (1959) was able to make rather accurate predictions of actual choice in the faculty restaurant. As a research assistant in the Psychometric Laboratory at the University of Chicago I was involved in the early stages of this study (without knowing that it was economic psychology). The other examples cited by Anastasi were taken from George Katona's work. They dealt with economic expectations, attitudes and buying behavior.

In the USA, economic psychology is still primarily seen as the empirical study of economic expectations and, in particular, the regular surveys of consumer confidence which, by the way, usually include a few questions on

saving. In the Preface of the *Handbook of Consumer Behavior*, Robertson
and Kassarjian (1991) declared

> Few areas in consumer behavior can claim the persistence and longevity of eco-
> nomic psychology. Based on the work of Katona and the Michigan Survey Re-
> search group, this view suggests that consumer spending patterns are heavily influ-
> enced by consumer expectations of their economic well-being and by consumer
> sentiments (pessimism, optimism, or confidence). (Robertson and Kassarjian,
> 1991, p. ix)

They added: 'Economic psychology was not destined to enjoy rapid expan-
sion in the United States. In Europe, however, interest has been steadily
growing.'

In addition to the study of consumer and business expectations and attitudes, economic psychology in Europe comprises many other aspects of consumer and business economic behavior. Commonly, the label of consumer
behavior or in some case consumer psychology is employed to cover a broad
field, usually with close ties to marketing theory. While consumer behavior
study has had a strong managerial orientation, the economic-psychological
study of consumer psychology has more of a theoretical orientation, attempting to construct more general theory which can serve more purposes than just
managerial uses (see Lea et al., 1987, pp.541-3; Wärneryd, 1988; Ölander,
1990). Consumer behavior researchers may not always like the idea that their
well-established field could be classified as part of economic psychology as
the tendency is in Europe. They may prefer the view that economic psychology is restricted to expectations, saving behavior, and well being.

Economic psychology in the applied sense has meant a constant influx of
methods and hypotheses from basic psychological research into reality-
oriented application. At the turn of the century, there were already prominent
psychologists who worked at least part-time with problems in economic behavior, mostly with personnel selection or advertising problems. Schönpflug
(1993) maintained that applied psychology in general had been independent
of basic research and that there had rather been an inflow from practice to
basic research. As far as consumer behavior is concerned, there is no doubt
that applied research has borrowed heavily from basic research. Some developments in the applied field of economic psychology have been important for
progress in basic psychology. Much theory-oriented research on judgments,
human information processing and decision making is carried out in the consumer behavior area. Attitude research has received important inputs from
consumer behavior studies.

Researchers who are interested in developing basic psychological theory
should find economic behavior a fascinating behavioral field to study. People
are generally concerned with economic problems and it is comparatively easy

to motivate potential subjects and not only college students to serve as subjects or respondents. Private economic problems can apparently be essential contributory factors to minor and sometimes even major emotional disturbances in everyday life and to the developing of neuroses. Very little research attention in psychology has been devoted to this area. Somehow, psychologists have hesitated to deal with the role of economic affairs in everyday life.

When psychologists study economic problems, the focus lies on the use of psychological thinking with little regard for economic variables. Economic psychology in the true sense of the study of what influences economic behavior should be genuinely interdisciplinary using both economic and psychological variables and models based on theory from both fields. More psychologists working on economic behavior problems with a view towards developing psychology would, however, give helpful contributions to economic psychology as an applied field. The applied field can be better served with new theories, models, and methods if basic psychological research devotes more interest to economic behavior.

Economic Psychology as a Special Field of Study

Effectual demand consists of two elements, the power and will to purchase. The power to purchase may perhaps be represented correctly by the produce of the country whether small or great; but the will to purchase will always be the greatest, the smaller the produce compared with the population, and the more scantily the wants of society are supplied . . . In short, I by no means think that the power to purchase necessarily involves a proportionate will to purchase.
Malthus, Works, VI (pp.131-2; quoted from Ekelund and Hébert, 1990, pp.156-7)

A third way of viewing economic psychology is to treat it as an emerging science of its own, combining psychology and economics and formulating theories that tie the two disciplines together. The focus is on the study of economic behavior and includes the study of the individual/the household as well as decision-makers in business and in the public sector. George Katona who was by his first training a psychologist and later studied economics instituted the first research program in economic psychology. After a career as an economic journalist and investment advisor, he fell ill and had to change to a quieter occupation so he again started to do psychological research. His specialty was to utilize Gestalt theory in the study of learning and problem solving. His *Organizing and Memorizing* is a classic in its field and still widely cited. When World War II broke out, Katona used some of his psychological knowledge to warn against uncontrolled inflation, which he had experienced in Germany after the First World War. His book *War without Inflation* aroused interest among some leading economists. He was offered a job with the Cowles Commission, which had the task of conducting research that could help solve the problems of a war and after-war economy.

In the middle 1940s, Katona started a research program that involved asking consumers and businessmen about their expectations of their own financial status and the national economy. Katona first used economic psychology to designate the new field, but later changed the name to psychological economics and even later to behavioral economics. Economic psychology then became identified with the empirical study of expectations and attitudes regarding economic problems. The use of such studies quickly spread to other countries and became the concern of economists and to some extent statisticians. Katona's research, however, comprised much more than the study of expectations. It included consumer spending habits, saving, saving motives, attitudes towards inflation, and consumer motivation in general.

Katona was highly critical of abstract economic theory. He was mainly concerned with macroeconomic issues like the sales of durable goods, saving, and reactions to inflation. He complained that economic theory made completely wrong assumptions about behavior at the micro level so that aggregate predictions were mostly wrong. Economists tended to overlook the fact that most consumer behavior was based on routines and that the factors influencing genuine decision-making were important to study empirically. He seems to have become more and more convinced that it was necessary to build up a special field of study (see Katona, 1975, 1979, 1980). He advocated an economic-psychological theory that was descriptive and low-level, i.e. close to empirical observations. This theory was meant to be a valuable complement or even replacement of the abstract economic theory and the empirical research based on it.

Similar ideas about the role of psychology as a provider of data on actual economic behavior are found in Simon (1986)

> At the level of the business firms and the consumer, classical theory gives few hints as to how real human beings make real decisions in a world that rarely provides them with the data and computational resources that would be required to apply, literally, the theory of the textbooks. We need empirically valid theories of how business organizations operate, of how investment decisions are actually made, of how the levels of salaries and wages are determined, and of the growth and sizes of business firms. (Simon, 1986, pp.xv-xvi)

This involves constructing empirical theory in the spirit of George Katona rather than to try to improve economic theory by attacking or trying to supplement the rationality postulate. It does not preclude further explorations of the limits of rationality in real life, for example, looking at how compatible with individual goal hierarchies behavioral acts are.

In Europe, economic psychology is now usually defined as the psychological study of economic behavior at different levels of aggregation, from the individual/household to the decision-makers at the macroeconomic level, and of factors influencing such behavior. It is mostly associated with the study of consumer behavior in a much broader sense than in Katona's work and it is thus in this respect similar to consumer psychology. The field also covers a number of other areas such as the psychology of saving, fiscal psychology, entrepreneurship, and unemployment.

Reviewers of recent publications in economic psychology have pointed out that there is no coherent framework. In fact, Katona had a simple micro model, which was useful also at the macro level: saving/consumption is dependent on *ability* to save/consume and *willingness* to save/consume (cf. Malthus in the vignette above). Consumer ability to save/consume is defined as disposable income and willingness is assessed through interview data on financial expectations and attitudes. Later attempts at providing a more integrated framework for the field have been made, the most advanced being the work by Lea et al. (1987) who tried to combine psychological and economic reasoning. Baxter (1988, 1993), an economist, has in two volumes developed a framework for the use of psychological knowledge in economic analysis. Lane (1991) provided a critique of the rationality postulate standing alone, and added human satisfaction as another magnitude to maximize. His volume is an excellent review of much research related to economic psychology.

When economic psychology is interpreted in this way it is neither completely within the bounds of economics nor completely within those of psychology. It is notable that some of the professorial chairs in economic psychology are in psychology departments whereas the rest are in schools of business or in economics departments.

Psychological research is in principle aimed at establishing behavioral laws and at the same time it is focused on individual differences. Individual differences are the substance of much applied psychology. Much research is devoted to finding the contingencies that cause the individual differences. Many of the research questions are of the following type: under what circumstances does Y follow from the occurrence of X and under what circumstances does Z follow? This means that in economic psychology the idea is to look for *intervening variables* between economic stimuli and business or consumer reactions. The intervening variables can in the case of consumers be used to distinguish *segments* of the population, characterized by psychological variables, for example consumers who have different attitudes towards a product or service. Whereas there are significant differences between segments, each segment is homogeneous for a psychological characteristic.

A fundamental idea in economic psychology is that there are clusters of consumers (citizens). They share certain characteristics within each cluster while the clusters are distinct from one another. Wahlund and Wärneryd (1987) studied clusters based on saving motives. In their study of taxpayers, Wärneryd and Walerud (1982) distinguished between three clusters of tax-payers differing in their attitude towards tax evasion and in self-reported tax evasion. Knowing some important characteristics of each cluster (segment) gives a better understanding of potential reactions to tax evasion policies. Katona (1975) distinguished between degrees of optimism-pessimism in society. This dimension can easily be interpreted at a given time in terms of segments – one segment composed of optimists and the other of pessimists. Reactions to economic and financial policy measures can be expected to vary between segments with different psychological characteristics. Katona noted differences between optimists and pessimists in reactions to a tax cut.

Macroeconomic predictions have often failed during the last decades and there is some disagreement about theories; somehow, in the public eye the theories do not live up to their promise. Some economists suggest that descriptions and explanations at less aggregated levels than the macroeconomic level are necessary for arriving at better macroeconomic explanations and predictions. There is then a quest for something like the market segment concept used in marketing theory and marketing practice and familiar in economic psychology.

Even when skillfully used by behavioral economists, psychology is usually given a minor role. It is given a service role and is not seen as a major means of making progress in economics. Subjective data are at best treated as supplementary and are on the whole, in the mainstream economist's opinion, better avoided as unreliable. When psychologists deal with economic problems their focus is normally on what psychology rather than economics can get out of the study. Researchers are in the first place interested in developing the field in which they have their basic training. Expeditions into other disciplines are undertaken on the main proviso that the basic discipline profits. Psychologists tend to avoid economic variables that are important to economists and do not relate their findings to the rationality concept. Economists do not use psychology to its full potential, but select single concepts that often do not work out very well. So there is room for a separate field of study in which economic and psychological thinking can be combined: economic psychology. Lea et al. (1992) and Winnett and Lewis (1995) have put forth similar ideas.

Rather than being a source of critique leveled against economics, economic psychology is in this sense a challenge to economics to the extent that the research can provide descriptions and explanations of economic behavior that at least for some purposes are better than those advanced by economic theory. For psychology, economic psychology as a separate field of study involves the study of a specific category of behavior, namely economic behavior, also using non-psychological variables and models that are derived from economics. It needs to be separated out from psychology since the study presupposes consideration not only of economic and psychological factors, but also some understanding of the economic research paradigm, which takes some special training.

The relationship between economics and psychology, according to Lunt (1996a) now runs the risk of being dominated by the economists' newly aroused interest in cognitive psychology and neurophysiology. 'It is then proposed that economic psychologists stop adopting economists' agendas and start to examine economic theory to open new lines of collaboration that will allow them to apply their own conception of psychology to economics.' (Lunt, 1996a, p.275) Lunt especially deplored that economists had little interest in the social aspects of economic behavior. He may, in my opinion, have somewhat underestimated the wide range of psychological loans in today's behavioral economics and among the economist advocates of socioeconomics.

Research in economic psychology is carried out by economists and psychologists and by many researchers trained in management and business administration. In earlier centuries, thinkers could contribute to the development of both economics and psychology. Bernard Mandeville, David Hume, Adam Smith, Jeremy Bentham, and above all, James and John Stuart Mill, all gave important, but strictly compartmentalized insights to both disciplines. For the major part of the 20th century, there has been little understanding and communication between the two sciences. The last few decades have again witnessed contributions to both sciences from researchers like George Katona, Herbert Simon, Daniel Kahneman, and Amos Tversky, to cite a few outstanding contributors. This is a sign of increasing convergence after, say, 100 years of clear divergence between the disciplines. The news is that the contributions are no longer strictly compartmentalized.

The meaning attached to economic psychology does have consequences for the type of studies made in the field of saving. If economic psychology is interpreted as the psychological underpinnings of economics, the research on saving concentrates on providing psychological variables and hypotheses that relate to economic theory and can help economists in their dealing with saving. If it is applied psychology, the interest lies on research to study applied economic behavior problems and to give feedback, if any, to psychology rather than to economics. If the focus lies on economic psychology as a special field of study the research is aimed at providing models explaining and predicting economic behavior. In this endeavor, the field engages both psychological and economic thinking and to some extent also sociology. Applied in the study of saving, this approach involves the study of differences in saving between segments of the population and attempts to explain such differences with psychological and economic concepts. Improving the prospects for economic psychology as a separate field of study will require building an economic-psychological theoretical framework that to some extent at least can integrate ideas and results.

MACRO(ECONOMIC) PSYCHOLOGY

The Use of Aggregate Measures

Aggregation means summing objects and can be done at different levels, that of the national economy being only one possibility. While some forms of aggregation, e.g. over members of a group, are common in psychology, aggregate measures at the level of the national economy are rare. Schachter et al. (1986) argued for more use of aggregate measures in psychological research

> The single number that summarizes the daily sales of department stores may seem of primary interest to merchants, but it is also the kind of number that can be of compelling interest to social scientists. It is an aggregate number – the resultant of the buying behavior and decisions of an entire population. Though aggregate numbers and variables are virtually the substance of much of economics, they are not the kind of variables that have been of particular interest to psychologists – essentially still absorbed in a search for laws and regularities of individual behavior, with no systematic attempt to extrapolate research findings and relationships on the individual level to aggregate or collective behavior. (Schachter et al., 1986, p. 237)

In everyday parlance, nations are described in terms that are similar to the personality traits of individuals. Psychological concepts and behavioral laws that are supposed to regulate individual behavior are applied to the actions of nations with little hesitation. Nations are said to be 'thrifty' or 'wasteful', 'reliable' or 'irresponsible', 'bellicose' or 'peaceful', even (more or less) 'stubborn'. If 'people' is used instead of 'nation', it is even more obvious that personal attributes which derive from individual, common-sense psychology are employed to characterize aggregates of people.

Psychological concepts are used to characterize nations, apparently on the basis of assumptions that a majority (or almost all) of a population possess the characteristic in question. Behind such concepts there are usually no attempts at measurement. In principle, it is feasible to construct such measures through assessing the prevalence of the characteristic in the population and reporting frequencies or through some kind of indicators, e.g. the number of savers as an indicator of thrift. In his study of achievement motivation, McClelland (1961) used content analysis of children's books to assess the degree of achievement motivation in different nations.

Aggregation gives rise to problems concerning the relationships between individual and aggregate behavior (see Borgatta and Jackson, 1980). One problem is whether relationships between phenomena found at the aggregate level can be applied to individual behavior. The converse problem is whether relationships found at the individual level can be generalized to the aggregate. In psychological research there has been comparatively little interest devoted to the problem of aggregation (cf. Epstein, 1980; van Raaij, 1984).

Relationships between macro and micro are in the social sciences often treated under the label of 'ecological inference'. The initial question is usually whether aggregate data and relationships found at the aggregate level can be applied to individuals. Aggregated data may reveal relationships that cannot be found in individual data (Langbein and Lichtman, 1978; Adams, 1965; Bouwen, 1977; Katona, 1979). There are also occasions when relationships that are significant and interesting at the individual level disappear at the aggregate level. The outcome is that the efforts bestowed on psychological details at the individual level may be lost at the aggregate level and that it may be necessary to look for new psychological variables at the macro level.

Bernard Mandeville (1729) asserted in *The Fable of the Bees* that individual saving was a disaster to society. If the citizens of a nation could afford to waste money they should do so, otherwise the economic machinery would stop. Mandeville who may not have been the first to note that individual behavior and corresponding aggregate behavior could have different consequences, aroused a lot of dispute when he asserted that 'private vice' was 'public benefit'. Keynes (1936) observed that economic behavior, assessed at the aggregate level, could have implications and consequences different from individual behavior. As briefly noted before, in economics, a problem of ecological inference is known as 'The Fallacy of Composition'. According to Samuelson and Nordhaus (1992, p. 6) the fallacy is the misconception that what is true for a part is therefore true for the whole. One of the examples they gave had to do with savings and is similar to what Mandeville asserted: attempts of individuals to save more in a depression may reduce a community's total savings. There is a contradiction in pointing out the composition fallacy and at the same time claim that the macroeconomic assumptions should rest on a solid foundation of microeconomics.

Is There a Need for Macro(economic) Psychology?

Can psychological concepts and theories that are essentially based on individual behavior be reconciled with macroeconomics? If measurements can be meaningfully aggregated over individuals, the answer is yes. If there is aggregation bias (composition fallacy), there will be room for psychological concepts that refer to aggregates. One implication of the macro concept is that behavior assessed at the aggregate level can have different consequences than individual behavior. Consequently, behavioral laws may have to be different at the aggregate level, and there may be a need for psychological measures that have no counterpart at the individual level. There is, in my view, a good argument for a *macroeconomic psychology* with ties to macroeconomics.

Katona (1979) said that economists were earlier unwilling to accept the idea of differences in models at the individual and the aggregate level

> It would surely be very difficult to construct a plausible model of human behavior, even allowing for much purely random and idiosyncratic differences among individuals, on which attitudes could influence subsequent behavior of large groups without influencing the behavior of those who were observed to hold them. (Consultant Committee on Consumer Survey Statistics, 1955, p.61; quoted from Katona, 1979, p.120)

The quotation reflects the opposition to the idea that a psychological concept at the macroeconomic level can exist independently of the micro level. Theory in macroeconomics is in principle based on micro level theory. Microeconomic theory may be wrong in its assumptions about individuals, but right at the macroeconomic level. The possibly wrong microeconomic theory of consumer choice and rationality may serve macroeconomics better than any alternative! When Friedman (1953) talked about good predictions, he certainly meant predictions that could be tested at the aggregate level.

The economist's explanations and predictions are not intended to be adequate and valid for single individuals. It is sometimes debated whether there is a real need for a theory of individual behavior to build and construe macroeconomics. The received view is that there must be a microeconomic theory based on the behavior of individual decision-makers that are assumed to act rationally. Psychological problems are hidden and not made explicit in macroeconomic theories which becomes apparent when shortcomings of economic policy measures are discussed post hoc. Psychological assumptions are often introduced after the fact to explain unexpected developments.

There is a close relationship between macroeconomics and national economic policy making. Keynes pointed out the danger of overproduction, a high saving ratio and underinvestment and he proposed ways of keeping both inflation and unemployment under control and stimulating total demand. His macroeconomic theory has been an inspiration for government advisors to suggest policy measures to control the effects of business cycles, the 'fine-tuning' of economies by appropriate government interventions. The actual effects of such fine-tuning attempts have been questioned and criticized. Although many politicians and economist advisors to government may be fond of the idea of fine-tuning economies, actual developments have argued against it. The emergence of 'stagflation' – high inflation and high unemployment – refuted the prevalent theory.

New thinking in economics has favored policies that stimulate supply rather than demand. The failures of macroeconomics have led to a search for ways of improving the theory and for better descriptions of economic reality. In the thinking of at least some macroeconomists this opens up for inputs from psychological research, e.g. research on expectations (Lindbeck, 1989), buying and saving motives, work incentives, and well-being (Scitovsky, 1986). Lea et al. (1987) reviewed many of the psychological questions behind macroeconomics.

Macroeconomic Psychology Defined

Macropsychology is little debated and most psychologists probably think that the concept is an oxymoron since psychology is based on the study of individuals. Lea et al. (1987, p.59) said that macropsychology was actually tantamount to sociology. Van Raaij (1984) proposed a four-field table crossing individual/collective and time-series/cross-section dimensions. He described the types of studies that were carried out in each field and the possible cross-overs between macro and micro. He concluded that no separate macro-psychology should be developed. Macroeconomic psychology is usually not strictly defined. Rather the main problem areas are enumerated. Apparently, macroeconomic psychology has been used in three senses:

1. Macroeconomic psychology is the study of macroeconomic problems using psychological theories and methods. Taxation, saving, and unemployment are typical areas
2. In a more restricted sense, macroeconomic psychology means the use of *macropsychological* concepts that may or may not correspond to a concept at the individual level. The use of some consumer confidence measures is a case in point (Chapter 5).
3. In a wider sense, it also includes aggregate economic phenomena that are *not* actually covered in macroeconomics, e.g. entrepreneurship and innovation and issues of well-being and quality-of-life.

To the extent that there are valid general laws of behavior that can be applied to aggregate phenomena and behaviors that can be summed over individuals to give a meaningful aggregate measure, there is little need for special macro-psychological concepts or theory. Some purely macropsychological concepts and measures without equivalents at the individual level may, however, be wanted and ineluctable to handle certain psychological problems at the level of society. It is sometimes desirable to assess, for example, the mood of a population or its degree of entrepreneurship.

To me, it seems appropriate to use the term on all concepts and theories that are applied to aggregates, also when there is no corresponding concept or theor, at the individual level. An example of a concept in the latter category is the measure of consumer confidence known as 'Index of Consumer Sentiment' (Katona, 1979). Macroeconomic psychology can be described as economic psychology related to the study of macroeconomic problems such as *financial expectations, saving, taxation, unemployment, inflation* and it also includes problems that are not usually treated under macroeconomics, notably *level of innovation and entrepreneurship* and *consumer satisfaction* in a society. Research has focused mostly on these areas while such macroeconomic areas as balance of payments and quantity of money have received little psychological attention. The problems studied typically originate from problems in economic reality. The research is not primarily theory-driven, neither by economic nor by psychological theories. Since the problems pertain to economic behavior, the range of problems studied naturally shows more similarity to economics than to psychology. The latter serves as a provider of ideas and methods for reformulating the problems in such terms that they become amenable to psychological measurement.

In economic psychology, aggregation is often done at sublevels of the economy. In marketing, for example, segments of buyers are often distinguished based on psychological characteristics that are common to groups of the consumer population. The focus is on markets or market segments rather than on individual consumers. The data underlying segmentation are mostly collected from individuals. Measures that pertain exclusively to the total market are frequently used in research on consumers. Sales figures and data on market shares, collected from business firms, are, for example, used as dependent variables in multivariate analyses of consumer behavior in which socioeconomic and psychological variables are jointly used. As noted above, Schachter et al. (1986) recommended increased use of such measures in psychology.

THE FUTURE OF ECONOMIC PSYCHOLOGY

The future of economic psychology will depend on whether there is a demand for its services. Macroeconomic psychology, in particular, has to prove itself. The crucial question is to what extent the results are seen as interesting and useful not only by researchers but also by practitioners in various positions. Keynes (1936) noted the importance to practical men of what economists say

Practical men, who believe themselves to be quite exempt from any intellectual influences, are usually the slaves of some defunct economist . . . for in the field of economic and political philosophy there are not many who are influenced by new theories after they are twenty-five or thirty years of age, so that the ideas which civil servants and politicians and even agitators apply to current events are not likely to be the newest. (Keynes, 1936, pp.383-4)

The usefulness of psychological research in matters pertaining to the micro level, especially the consumer choice of products, is well established. There is a demand for such research from practitioners and from academic disciplines related to marketing and management. There is less demand for macro-psychological research on economic behavior, sometimes even resistance to the whole idea. The ideas of some defunct economists may be an encumbrance not only to practitioners, but also to theoreticians.

Who listens to a psychologist when s/he is talking about such economic affairs as the saving ratio, tax incentives for stimulating saving and developments at the stock exchange? The answer is now that there is some listening and even requests for research results, opinions and information are directed to economic psychologists. There is some realization in the mass media and in business that psychological factors affecting economic behavior can be fruitfully studied and commented on not only by economists, but also by (some) psychologists. It is essential that there is a demand for more complex and thus interdisciplinary answers to many economic questions and that there is insight that segments of the population, differing with respect to psychological properties, often must be closely examined to properly answer apparently macro level questions.

2.   What Saving Is and Is Not

Thus a store of savings is to the working man as a barricade against want; it secures him a footing, and enables him to wait, it may be in cheerfulness and hope, until better days come around . . . Economy, at bottom, is but the spirit of order applied in the administration of domestic affairs: it means management, regularity, prudence, and the avoidance of waste . . . Economy also means the power of resisting present gratification for the purpose of securing a future good, and in this light it represents the ascendency of reason over the animal instincts. It is altogether different from penuriousness: for it is economy that can always best afford to be generous. It does not make money an idol, but regards it as a useful agent.

Smiles ([1859] 1969, pp.285-6)

The most laborious population, inhabiting the most fertile territory, if they devoted all their labour to the production of immediate results, and consumed its produce as it arose, would soon find their utmost exertions insufficient to produce even the mere necessaries of existence.

Senior ([1836] 1908, p.58)

PROVISION FOR THE FUTURE: A PREREQUISITE FOR SURVIVAL WITH SCARCE RESOURCES

The Origins and Major Functions of Savings

Saving is as old as human culture. Alfred Marshall (1890) asserted that as soon as man devoted time to doing things that did not involve immediate consumption but provided for future consumption, there were savings in the shape of weapons, tools, and housing. The first savings were *consumer capital goods*. For the person or family to survive during periods when weapons and tools were made and during seasons when supplies were scarce, saving in the form of *storage* of provisions was necessary. Agriculture presupposed that seeds could be put aside from immediate consumption. Saving meant as a rule that some consumption was postponed to safeguard future living. Later, commerce led to investments in goods and means of transportation which often required funds from credits and savings. Saving *money* became important and could mean gains.

44

Economics is often defined as the science that deals with the optimal utilization of scarce resources to satisfy human needs. Scarcity is a fundamental concept in economics and in a sense, it is fundamental in everyday life. Most people have limited liquid assets, deriving from earnings and wealth, and have to be careful in their spending of money to be able to satisfy the most urgent needs. People differ in how well they develop their skills to deal with scarcity now and in the future. Savings or wealth that ensure the satisfaction of future needs vary among people; wealth may exist without any saving. The word wealth has assumed a meaning that goes far beyond the immediate or future capacity of assets to satisfy needs. In modern welfare societies, there is besides directly owned assets also wealth in the form of entitlements created by sickness insurance and private and public old-age pension systems.

Wealth in the dictionary (*Webster's New Collegiate Dictionary*, 1977) is defined as follows: a: all property that has a money value or an exchangeable value b: all material objects that have economic utility; *esp*: the stock of useful goods having economic value in existence at any one time. In the same dictionary, *Capital* is defined: (1) a stock of accumulated goods esp. at a specified time and in contrast to income received during a specified period; *also*: the value of these accumulated goods; (2) accumulated goods devoted to the production of other goods; (3) net worth.

In the 19th century discussions of capital and saving, definition (2) was usually employed. Jevons (1871) said, for example

> We are told with perfect truth, that capital consists of wealth employed to facilitate production; but when economists proceed to enumerate the articles of wealth constituting capital, they obscure the subject . . . Capital, as I regard it, consists merely in the *aggregate of commodities which are required for sustaining labourers of any kind or class engaged in work*. A stock of food is the main element of capital; but supplies of clothes, furniture, and all the other articles in common daily use are also necessary parts of capital . . . The single and all-important function of capital is to enable the labourer to await the result of any long-lasting work, – to put an interval between the beginning and the end of an enterprise. (Jevons [1871] 1911, pp.223-4)

The simple rule is accordingly that if it takes a year before you can get a new harvest it is necessary to have a year's supply to take you over. This touches one of the fundamental reasons for saving, that is, refraining from consumption now to make provision for the future. A surplus of assets can arise if nature provides abundant gifts or the resources are skillfully managed. This is true both at an aggregate level and at the individual household level. The nonrenewable resources in the world will last longer than was feared some years ago, but, clearly, slow depletion of resources as well as environmental protection are furthered by reduction in current consumption.

Restraint of Consumption

Restraint of consumption is not only desirable, but also necessary at both the aggregate level and the household level since resources are scarce. At the individual household level there is nowadays in many countries a social security net that protects the individual to a large extent even if he or she makes little provision for the future. These social security nets have advantages for the individual at the same time as they may have disadvantages for society, such as encouraging consumption now and waste of resources at the expense of one's own future needs and the needs of future generations.

Many factors affect consumption and saving which often makes it difficult to explain and predict savings. Klein (1954) noted

> Expenditures on durables and many components of savings are not determined by habitual decisions. They fluctuate and thereby influence general economic activity, but their predictability is enhanced by a study of their relation to income, past income change, past liquid assets, and consumer attitudes or expectations . . . Some components of saving, which can be specifically measured and identified in survey data, are determined by contract or by routine and do not play the same instigating role in economic fluctuation. (Klein, 1954, pp.7-8)

The question of what saving is worth to the individual and to the national economy is multifaceted. While restraint of consumption is generally held to be laudable both for the individual and the nation, some individual saving resembles avarice and there are stages in the business cycle where there may be too much restraint, at least according to certain economic theories. Saving and investment belong together. If there is too much saving and too little investment, there will be no economic growth. According to the prevalent economic theory, more of what is saved should then be spent on consumption and increased consumption will lead to more optimism among investors. An objection is that such increases in demand will lead to increases in prices and higher inflation and may not increase the entrepreneurs' willingness to invest in new plants and machinery and create new employment opportunities.

The welfare systems vary to a considerable extent among countries and over time. What the public sector finances in one country, may in other countries be a matter of taking private insurance such as health or sickness insurance or joining pension plans. Whereas in the first case, all citizens (and some visitors) are covered, in other countries people remain who are outside the public safety net and have to provide for themselves as best they can. Some otherwise important reasons for saving are missing in countries with well-developed welfare systems. Can the determinants of saving then be the same in all countries? Can saving theory be so general that the same theory can explain savings and saving behavior at all times and in all countries? Obviously, there are differences in the structure of savings and the behaviors of savers in countries such as the USA, Japan, Italy, Germany and the Scandinavian countries, to take those countries where most studies of saving and savings have been carried out.

The Life-Cycle Hypothesis (LCH), is based on the assumption that people restrain their consumption in certain periods to be able to afford approximately the same consumption in other periods when income is lower (see Figure 2.1). People are assumed to want to spend approximately the same amounts at each stage in the life cycle ('permanent income'). Young people may borrow money to be able to afford the consumption they want, middle-aged people save money for old age consumption and old-age pensioners dissave to maintain a desired level of consumption. These assumptions appear plausible, but there is a need for many qualifications as will be seen in the following.

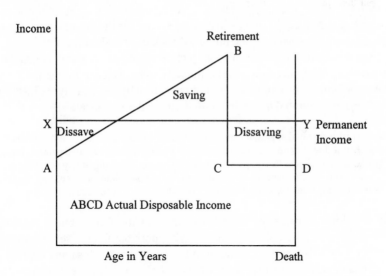

Figure 2.1 The Basic Life-Cycle Hypothesis

A Look at Saving Definitions

In economic contexts, whether in theory or empirical study, saving is mostly defined as 'excess of income over consumption expenditure in a period' or as 'the difference in net worth at the end of a period and the net worth at the beginning of the period'. Both definitions treat savings as residuals and not as primary activities. Classical economists described and treated saving or the accumulation of capital as an active process that required self-command. Adam Smith (1776) envisaged a conflict between present enjoyment and future profit. Saving meant giving up the former in favor of the latter. Like Rae (1834), Jevons (1871) and many later economists, Smith saw saving as an accumulation of capital which would give more in return in the future. The accumulation of wealth was seen as an act of sacrificing something now for being better off in the future.

These economists thus focused on the use of money, now or in the future. Fisher (1930, p.5) said: 'Money is of no use to us until it is spent.' He made a distinction between spending and investing. 'To spend is to pay money for enjoyments which come very soon. To invest is to pay money for enjoyments which are deferred to a later time.' There was little recognition of the fact that people may want to own rather than use money. Fisher's main purpose was to explain how interest rates arose and changed. People tended to be impatient and their impatience could be measured through their subjective discount rate, also called time preference. Not being able to postpone consumption and spending all the money instead of saving for the future was a sign of high discount rates which made future values look less significant now.

The essence of the definitions that picture saving as an action is that saving involves refraining from consumption of some resource in one period to give a possibility for consumption in a later, usually not exactly defined period. Keynes illustrated this in his somewhat jocular statement

> An act of individual saving means – so to speak – a decision not to have dinner today. But it does *not* necessitate a decision to have dinner or to buy a pair of shoes a week hence or a year hence or to consume any specified thing at any specified date. Thus it depresses the business of preparing to-day's dinner without stimulating the business of making ready for some future act of consumption. (Keynes, 1936, p.210)

The definition contains the act of providing for the future, but it excludes reasons for saving as well as goals involving possible future uses. There is a negative tone to the second sentence in the quote: an act of saving depresses some business. In an earlier work, Keynes (1930, p.172) gave a slightly different definition of saving: 'Saving consists in the negative act of refraining from spending the whole current income.' Katona (1960) noted that this definition did not reflect the manner in which people tended to view saving.

> For most people saving is something positive. Subjectively it is not merely a consequence of not spending but rather the result of substantial pressures directed toward achieving highly valued goals of life. Saving is considered most important and its absence is greatly regretted. In all these respects the acquisition of money and wealth resembles the acquisition of goods of permanent value, such as homes and durables. (Katona, 1960, p.101)

A similar view can be found in Pareto (1909) who noted how deeply rooted the motive for saving money and other resources was. Pareto ([1909] 1971, p.323) said: 'Saving is only partially determined by the income one receives from it; it results in part also from man's desire to have in reserve goods which can be consumed from time to time; it is also the result of an instinctive act of man, who behaves in this respect like many animals.' Saving money to get more or something better in the future was thus not the only or even primary goal of saving. Pareto indicated that there was a precautionary motive and that savings had some utility in themselves.

What is not consumed during one period involves saving for later periods. Consumer durables present special problems. Household appliances and automobiles are bought to serve for many years.

> Consumption thus would include the value of all goods and services actually consumed during the period. That is, consumption should refer literally to consuming – the eating of food, wearing of clothing, and so forth. If a consumer purchased a suit of clothes out of income for $100, wore it for two years, and then threw it away, in the first year he would be regarded as having saved $50 and consumed $50, and in the second year as having engaged in negative saving of $50 and consumption of $50. (Lansing, 1954, p.26)

A distinction should be made between *saving, saving behavior* and *savings*. Saving refers to the activity or process of saving. Saving behavior is synonymous to saving, but puts an emphasis on the behavioral aspects. Savings, finally, represent the outcome of saving activities and saving processes (cf. Katona, 1975). Mainstream economists seem to have a tendency to prefer 'savings' rather than 'saving' and also use 'savings behavior' rather than 'saving' or 'saving behavior'. In ordinary language, savings behavior means the behavior of savings, whatever that may be, and not the behavior of savers.

Waste is often seen as the alternative to saving, implying that refraining from some consumption is always possible. The absence of savings can be caused by poverty without any waste of money. Economists and other social thinkers and educators have elaborated on the causes of waste and searched for the answers in sociodemographic and personality characteristics.

HOARDING, SAVING, AND INVESTING

Capital Accumulation

The making of a fortune may no doubt enable some people to 'enter society', as it is called; but to be esteemed there, they must possess qualities of mind, manners, or heart, else they are merely rich people, nothing more.

Smiles ([1859] 1969, p.301)

Thinkers discussed capital accumulation as a human activity in ancient times. While it was generally seen as a legitimate activity, there was also a discussion of what it was legitimate to do in order to accumulate capital. Aristotle and Cicero had very definite views on what were inappropriate ways of making money (see next chapter). Through the centuries, there has remained a conflict between the desirability of being industrious, frugal and saving money, on one hand, and the possession of capital, on the other. Religious influences have enhanced this conflict. Political ideologies like socialism and Marxism have rejected the idea of capital accumulated at the individual level. The fact that private ownership of means of production was considered inappropriate did not preclude small-scale saving and ownership of consumer durables. In the earlier communist countries, there was plenty of individual saving. The purpose was mostly to save up for buying attractive capital goods like automobiles. It has been said that particularly in Soviet Russia individual households used to have money over because there was not much to spend the money on.

When the concept of capital accumulation is used rather than saving, an association to profit seeking and gain is provoked. Capital accumulation and capitalism are so closely associated that the general sense of capital accumulation is obfuscated. Hirschman (1977) noted that the prevalent critique of capitalism accused capitalism of doing what it was meant to do: quenching the influence of the passions.

> In one of the most attractive and influential of these critiques, the stress is on the repressive and alienating feature of capitalism, on the way it inhibits the development of the 'full human personality.' From the vantage point of the present essay, this accusation seems a bit unfair, for capitalism was precisely expected and supposed to repress certain human drives and proclivities and to fashion a less multifaceted, less unpredictable, and more 'one-dimensional' human personality. (Hirschman, 1977, p.132)

In the public eye and in many mass media contexts in Western Europe, the word 'capital' often seems to connote vested interests and financial power.

Hoarding and Saving

From a behavioral standpoint, capital accumulation can be divided into three activities with rather floating boundaries between them: (1) hoarding, (2) saving and (3) investing. Hoarding means keeping goods for future use. Animals such as hamsters and squirrels are known for their hoarding habits. They store food for future use and often more than they can consume. Lea et al. (1987, p.227) citing among others Lea and Tarpy (1986) called hamsters 'spectacular food hoarders'. The latter authors found that hamsters that had been deprived of food for a day hoarded increased quantities of food when it again was available. Lea et al. (1987, p.227) suggested that hoarding and similarly some saving could be seen as the result of a primary biological drive.

Hoarding is also used to designate that cash money is stowed away or held on to so that there can be no investment. Hoarding is

> The withdrawal of money from active circulation by accumulating it rather than spending it on consumption or buying assets. It can be thought of as a withdrawal of money from the market for borrowing and lending in order to hold it in idle balances. It represents, therefore, the net change in stocks of idle balances. (Bannock et al, 1984, p.202)

Putting money in a piggy bank and keeping it there is thus hoarding. When the money in the piggy bank is placed in a bank account the money is saved according to this distinction. While the distinction may be useful in some contexts, it will not be observed in the following and saving will be used to cover also hoarding in piggy banks.

Stock measures of savings are based on estimates of total savings, which are usually tantamount to total wealth. *Flow* measures are derived from changes in savings. The saving during one period, say, a year, can be measured in many ways as will be discussed below under 'Measurement of Saving'. All the measures are essentially measures of flow whether they are differences between the stock at the year's end and the year's beginning or subjective reports on whether anything was saved and on how much was saved during the year.

The economists' notions of capital accumulation were in the early history of economics associated with agriculture. When somebody did not consume all his/her goods in one period and thus had an excess over the need in that period, the surplus could be used in different manners, to some extent depending on the nature of the goods. If the goods were used later, it was just a question of hoarding implying that the supply was hidden or stored for later use. A surplus of grain, potatoes etc. could be used as seed which leads to new crops, it could be stored for future consumption, it could be given to laborers who worked on the farm for the owner or it could be sold. If sold, the money received could be used in different ways, e.g., for hiring workers to work in the fields and increase production or it could be lent to somebody who used it in a business.

Saving and capital accumulation have often been seen as the same thing. J.S. Mill said: 'The essence or attribute of wealth was the power to be accumulated – essentially a concept of physical production.' (Corry, 1962, p.24) Connotatively, there may be big differences. At the individual level, the conflict between spending now and saving for the future has been described as the conflict between the passions and the interests (Hirschman, 1977). While saving is commonly held to be a virtuous activity, capital accumulation may be seen as doubtful, in particular if it is done on a large scale. The focus in discussions of saving and capital accumulation can be on the act itself, its outcome, or its purpose or motive. The purpose of a saving act is provision for the future. An act of capital accumulation may be associated with a focus on making profit and, in the mind of some, with greediness and profit hunger.

While the distinction between saving and hoarding is now mostly neglected, the early economists stressed the use aspect of saving. In his *Political Economy*, J.S. Mill said about capital:

> If merely laid by for future use, it is said to be hoarded; and while hoarded it is not consumed at all. But if employed as capital, it is all consumed . . . Saving, in short, enriches, and spending impoverishes, the community along with the individual; which is but saying in other words, that society at large is richer by what it expends in maintaining and aiding productive labor, but poorer by what it consumes in its enjoyments. (Corry, 1962, p.25)

Saving and Investing

Whereas saving has to do with refraining from spending, investing refers to putting money into something in order to gain. This is clear from the dictionary definition of *invest* (*Webster's New Collegiate Dictionary*, 1977): 1 to commit (money) in order to earn a financial return 2 to make use of for future benefits or advantages. In these definitions, there is a profit motive connected with investing. It is implied that the investor has the expectation of getting more back than s/he invested or in times where the risk of losses in value is high, at least keep the real value of the investment. This view of the relationship between saving and investment differs from that of classical and neo-classical economics in which saving and investment are only two sides of the same coin: in the absence of hoarding, what is saved is invested (Corry, 1962).

A dictionary of economics has the following to say

> Strictly defined, investment is expenditure on real capital goods. However, in everyday language, it is also taken to mean purchase of any asset, or indeed the undertaking of any commitment, which involves an initial sacrifice followed by subsequent benefits. For example, one may speak of the purchase of an ordinary share or the decision to go to university as an investment. However, in the theory of income determination, investment means strictly expenditures on capital goods. In this sense, investment is the amount by which the stock of a firm or economy changes, once we have allowed for replacement of capital which is scrapped. (Bannock et al., 1984, p.241)

Investing can be interpreted in different ways. Total investment in a country refers to money spent on assets that last more than one budget period. In early economics, the economics of agriculture dominated the thinking. At the macro level, the relationships between saving and investing could then be divided into three categories:

1. Saving and investing were the same. Saving, in this sense, meant postponing consumption to a later date implying either that the goods could be used as seed for new crops or used to pay labor. The goods that were not immediately consumed could be said to be an investment. If the goods were just hoarded, they were not an investment even if they were later consumed.
2. The goods that were not consumed could be exchanged against other goods or money. In the first type of exchange, individual saving and investment completely coincided. In the second case, the money could be kept as cash, which is usually not held to be an investment unless it is lent to somebody.
3. If the money saved was loaned to other people or was put into shares, bonds, or real estate it was considered to be an investment.

If consumers bought durables, the purchases were not treated as an investment by the classical economists, despite the fact that there was multiperiod use of the durables. Jevons (1871) noted this and criticized Adam Smith for introducing the idea. He expressed his astonishment at the fact that when households acquired capital goods, those were no longer counted as capital. They kept their value as capital as long as they stayed with producers

> It leads to the absurd conclusion that the very same thing fulfilling the very same purposes will be capital or not according to its accidental ownership. To procure good port wine it is necessary to keep it for a number of years, and Adam Smith would not deny that a stock of wine kept in the wine merchant's possession for this purpose is capital, because it yields him revenue. If a consumer buys it when new, and keeps it to improve, it will not be capital, although it is evident that he gains the same profit as the merchant by buying it at a lower price. If a coal merchant buys in a stock of coal when cheap, to sell when dear, it is capital; but if a consumer lays in a stock, it is not. (Jevons [1871] 1911, pp.260-1)

In present-day studies of consumer wealth, some possessions of durables like automobiles and large pleasure boats, but probably not well-stocked wine cellars, are sometimes counted as investments. The possession of consumer durables may be important when savings are calculated, but they are often left out when budget (cross-sectional) data are used. To what extent do consumers include acquisition and possession of consumer durables when they answer questions about saving? This will be dealt with below on the basis of data from the VSB panel at the CentER for Economic Research.

Financial Saving and Real (Estate) Saving; Time Horizon and Savings

At the macro level, a distinction is made between financial saving and saving in real terms, that is, in real estate. The former consists of savings available for business and government investment purposes and the latter is direct investment on the part of households. 'Real saving' is investment in real estate and mostly involves that households acquire houses for their own living. Household savings are the sum of net accumulation of financial assets and tangible (real) assets. 'Financial savings' comprise savings and other bank accounts, investments in shares, bonds, insurance savings, and surpluses from other operations in financial markets. Real or tangible savings are (net) investments in owner-occupied homes and second homes like summer cottages.

In agricultural contexts, which dominated economic thinking in the early 19th century, it was natural to think in periods of one year. What was saved one year was spent for next year's crop. Wealth was accumulated by annual growth in the productive capital involved. How many years did people take into consideration? Many factors probably affected the time horizon people had. Poor people with a short life expectancy and living in insecure environments certainly had very short time horizons – they had no prospectiveness as Marshall (1890) put it. At the same time there were apparently people, even from humble and poor origins, who systematically accumulated money over long periods of time. As will be shown in the next chapter, classical economists devoted considerable attention to the factors that influenced thrift, which in its turn is related to time horizon.

A common definition of saving involves that current income is not all spent on consumption in the same period and that there is an excess of income. Keynes's above cited definition points out that saving does not involve any decision about how and when the money is to be spent in the future. The Permanent Income Hypothesis (PIH) and the Life-Cycle Hypothesis (LCH) include the idea of a future time horizon as an important element for determining savings. While the PIH presumes an infinite time horizon, in practice the time horizon is often assumed to be shorter, say, three to five years (cf. Friedman, 1957, p.227). The LCH calculates with the total life span when the individual makes saving decisions. Life expectancy turns out to be a very important component of the theory.

A debated question is whether the time horizon stops with the expected time of death. The consideration of future generations enters into considerations of how much wealth should be consumed and how much should be left for posterity. The fact that one does not expend one's wealth during one's lifetime may be a sign that there is a bequest motive. Rawls (1973) dealt with savings for bequests as a problem of justice between generations. Barlow et al. (1966) found that among wealthy people there was a feeling that one should bequeath at least as much as one had inherited.

With respect to retired people, a distinction is sometimes made between *annuity wealth*, which provides a fixed income stream during the life of the owner and *bequeathable wealth*, which may be consumed at a rate determined by the owner or which can be bequeathed (Hurd, 1990). It is, of course, possible that a strong bequest motive can make people save out of their annuity income in addition to not spending any of the bequeathable wealth.

Debts and Saving

It is also difficult for a man who is in debt to be truthful; hence it is said that lying rides on debt's back. The debtor has to frame excuses to his creditor for postponing payment of the money he owes him; and probably also to contrive falsehoods.
Smiles ([1859] 1969, p.288)

Debt, credit, and loan have some shared meaning: the fact of owing something to someone else. They are not synonyms and the differences are important from an economic-psychological point-of-view. A dictionary defines debt as a sum of money or other property owed by one person or organization to another. Debt comes into being through the granting of credit or through borrowing capital. Credit means: 'Granting the use or possession of goods and services without immediate payment' (Bannock et al., 1984). Lea et al. (1993) made the following, more psychological distinction

by 'credit' we usually imply an arrangement to borrow money over some more or less defined period, with an assumption that repayment is within the borrower's means at all times. House mortgages and hire-purchase or installment credit schemes fall in this category, at least at the point when they are arranged. In contrast, 'debt' implies an obligation that the borrower is either unable to discharge or is trying to avoid discharging, at least at the time when it should be discharged. Thus credit implies a willing lender (often, indeed, the loan is made on the lender's initiative) while debt implies an unwilling lender. (Lea et al., 1993, p.86)

Debts are not in the first place synonymous to mortgages and loans. They are associated with bills that have not been paid, buying on installment plans and short-term loans that have to be paid back in a near future (Lea et al., 1995). Katona (1960) pointed out that the availability of credit was an important factor that influenced consumer behavior and thus the US economy. He said about debts and savings

Finally, what of the effect of *installment buying* on American thrift? It has been said that the ease of such buying has removed any reason to save for the purpose of acquiring cars, large household goods, and many other things. We do indeed find that saving to buy durable goods does rank among the important reasons for saving. But the same was found to be true ten or fifteen years ago, and probably even much earlier. Most people have viewed, and still view, the acquisition of durable goods as expenditures which ought to be paid out of income, either in cash or in the form of time payments. (Katona, 1960, p. 100)

Earlier on, having debts usually meant that there were no savings in the household. Savings were used before the household was likely to incur debts. While there are still many households with debts and no savings, the situation today is that households have savings, loans and debts (cf. Livingstone and Lunt, 1992). From an economic point of view, it is rational and makes sense to have loans if the savings are invested in such a way that they yield more than what the debt costs. In a country with high inflation and tax deductible interest payments, it could pay to take loans and invest in real estate and shares. This was the case in Sweden before the changes in the tax system in the early 1980s and some profits could still be made up to 1991 when a comprehensive tax reform was enacted (see Wahlund, 1991).

Incurring debts and at the same time increasing savings are psychologically compatible. Taking a new mortgage may be held separate from saving for a reserve in terms of a buffer capital. Mortgage holders tend to accumulate money in bank accounts to pay interest and amortization on mortgages. Psychological reasons may dictate that the household maintains buffers for unforeseen events and simultaneously uses credit to cover expenditures, for example, for a new automobile or new kitchen appliances (Lunt and Livingstone, 1992, pp.36-7). Katona (1975, pp.276f) used the heading 'Borrowing as a Sign of Prosperity' for his discussion of a new household tendency to borrow money even though the household had savings. He compared household investment with business investment, which is often based on loans.

In a consumer survey (Katona, 1975, p.277) the following question was asked: 'Speaking of buying a car on time, Mr. Smith has done so, although he has enough money in the bank to pay cash; why do you think he bought the car on time?' The most frequent answer was that the money in the bank was earmarked for something else. 'Bank deposits should be kept for rainy days', many people said. Another reason given was that savings were hard to replace. When you buy a car it is easy to get credit. When you are struck by ill events, it may not be so easy. The installment plan is contractual saving; albeit at a cost, it may be an aid against human frailty. Lea et al. (1995) who studied a sample of people who were in debt to a water supplier found that serious indebtedness was a sign of poverty rather than prosperity.

A First Glance at Reasons for Saving

When saving is defined in a passive mode like the excess of income over expenditure no objective or goal is implied. The excess of income over expenditure can arise as a consequence of deliberate acts or by default, the latter implying that income is ample and that saving requires no extra effort. More active definitions of saving make goals or motives clear or those are at least implicit in the definition. Refraining from consumption now implies consumption later and suggests that the later consumption is a motive or goal for saving. Classical and neoclassical economists provided a number of saving goals, which they held to be prevalent. In the next chapter, some of these authors will be introduced since they have contributed not only to the development of economics, but also to the psychology of saving.

While saving in popular parlance may comprise both money and goods of different kinds, in economic theories the concept is usually restricted to the saving of money and tied to the possibility of using the money for investment purposes, through a bank or investments of different kinds. In the broader sense of saving, the following reasons can be distinguished:

1. Remainder or surplus arises without explicit intention to save ('by default'; 'abundance')
2. Hoarding for recurrent needs or greater needs in the future (example: hoarding by squirrels and hamsters)
3. The growth of assets is expected to give increased possibility of need satisfaction in the future (saving seeds or lending against interest)
4. Reserve for uncertainty and risk (precautionary motive)
5. Voluntary contractual commitment (amortization plan on mortgages, paying in to pension schemes or self-imposed, forced saving)
6. Widened time horizon ('thinking of future generations'; bequest motive, consideration of nonrenewable resources).

There are reasons for not saving and for dissaving. Some reasons are implied by the LCH while others are not. Waste is not necessarily the converse of saving. Thrift is compatible with not saving any money if the financial means are barely sufficient for mere subsistence. Here are some rather obvious reasons for not saving

1. Higher future income or other positive changes in the opportunity set are expected
2. The probability of less or no utility at all in the future may be deterring. Money saved can be lost or diminished through taxes, inflation, through robbery and dishonest management of deposits (financial advisors) and many other ways
3. Lessened ability to enjoy consumption in the future (with high age)
4. Short life expectancy and time horizon does not extend beyond death
5. The adopted life style presumes spending.

Everyday observation suggests that differences in life style influence saving behavior. While certain life styles seem to contain immediate spending of current earnings, other life styles are characterized by restraint of consumption, making saving of money possible (with the same income level as that of the non-savers). Research on life styles usually involves studies of activities, interests, and opinions, employing so-called AIO-scales. In market research, many attempts have been made to develop life-style scales and correlate the scales with consumption patterns and purchases of specific brands of goods. At best, very low correlations have been obtained (see Engel et al., 1986).

Discretionary Saving

Katona (1975) distinguished between three types of saving, based on motives for saving: (1) contractual, (2) discretionary, (3) residual saving.

Contractual saving is similar to the precommitment ideas brought forth by Strotz (1956). This type of saving may involve arranging with the employer or a bank to transfer money from wages/salary every month to a savings account. Buying on installment necessitates later regular saving since the debt must be paid off; buying life insurance or joining a pension scheme involves a contract to save regularly and usually for long periods of time.

Discretionary saving is Katona's original concept. It relates to the room for genuine decisions that many people have in affluent societies. They can choose between attractive alternatives since there is money left after the basic needs have been satisfied. This makes consumption in society harder to predict without special study of the decision processes. People may decide to save for many reasons such as wanting to purchase an expensive durable, to go on a long vacation or just desiring to have money available if opportunities for attractive spending arise. Katona (1975) declared that most of saving was 'for a rainy day' (cf. Fisher, 1930). As will be explained later, Katona's criticism of Keynes's psychological law was based on the idea of the prevalence of discretionary consumption and saving in modern Western societies.

Residual saving refers to money that has not yet been spent because revenues and expenditures are not perfectly synchronized and because revenues may at least temporarily happen to exceed expenses. The money is saved by default rather than planning and may involve a need for cash management, a temporary repository (Lindqvist, 1981b).

Functional Saving

E[xperimenter]: If you were saving up, how would you do it?
C[hild]: I'd try and save up and keep it in my money box and forget about it and once
mum gives me some more money, put it in my money box and forget about it again.
Sonuga-Barke and Webley (1993, p.56)

Sonuga-Barke and Webley (1993) introduced the concept of 'functional saving'. It is associated with income constraint. 'When the cost of a desired item of consumption exceeds levels of income, combining income over a period of time allows that item to be bought. This saving requires the integration of a series of choices between present and future spending.' (Sonuga-Barke and Webley, 1993, p.17). The authors explored functional saving in children in a series of laboratory simulations under realistic conditions.

Functional saving is related to what the authors call 'the socio-developmental approach' to children's economic behavior (see also Webley and Lea, 1993). The main thesis involves that children's economic actions are functional expressions of socially determined ideas of acceptable economic goals. The authors noted that their approach implied that children should be taught and learn the function of saving and not only be encouraged to save (Sonuga-Barke and Webley, 1993, p.85) Functional saving has some similarity with the type of saving that is usually called 'goal saving' in surveys of saving. Goal saving refers to the fact that a respondent states a definite goal for the saving, such as buying a house, a consumer durable or an automobile or saving up for a vacation.

EMPIRICAL MEASURES OF SAVING AND SAVINGS

Aggregate Saving

Saving is defined as the excess of income over expenditure in a period

$$S = Y - C$$

where S = saving, Y = disposable (after-tax) income, and C = consumption. Maital and Maital (1991) used what they called a simplified version of the 'sources and uses of resources' model. With slightly changed notation, it looks like this

$$Y_d + BS + T + IM = C + I_n + CC + G + EX$$
$$\text{(Sources)} = \text{(Uses)}$$

where Y_d = disposable income, BS = business saving (retained earnings), T = net taxes (taxes minus transfer payments), IM = imports, C = private consumption, I_n = net domestic investment, CC = capital consumption, G = public consumption, EX = exports.

If $EX–IM = I_f$ (investment abroad), then

$$I_f + I_n + CC= Y_d–C \text{ [personal saving]}$$
$$+ BS \text{ [business saving]}$$
$$+ (T–G) \text{ [government saving]}$$
$$\text{(Gross Capital Formation)} = \text{(Gross National Saving)}$$

Aggregate saving is usually measured as aggregate income minus aggregate consumption. The estimates are notoriously uncertain and erroneous, due both to difficulties of defining consumption and deficient data. In fact, estimates of total savings are often revised from time to time and the new values may be quite different from earlier estimates. Estimates of savings are, however, regularly produced and published. While such data suffer from many weaknesses, they are used for comparisons between years and countries and there is a constant search for explanations of variations. The following characteristics of savings statistics should be kept in mind when looking at Table 2.1:

1. Savings are usually defined as the difference between total income and total consumption in an economy. The consumption figures are subject to what is defined as consumption and what is defined as investment and depreciation in durables and in real estate
2. Data about households, small enterprises, and voluntary associations are usually mixed so that no separate figures for household savings can be obtained
3. Even if the aggregate data were perfect, they might conceal important facts about savings in segments of the population
4. Attempts at influencing saving behavior presuppose more detailed knowledge about savers, saving motives etc. which requires data from special surveys.

The data in Table 2.1 give an impression that there is some decrease over time in the saving rates for most of the countries and little change for the remainder. This seems to hold, independent of the saving rate. The table shows that household saving rates are very high in Japan and they seem stable over the ten years. According to the OECD publication, which is the source of the data, the rates were even higher at the end of the 1970s. Germany is also consistently high, but the rates were slightly higher in the late 1970s. The saving rates in France, Italy and the United Kingdom are based on gross savings and are thus not directly comparable to those of other countries. For the UK, the rates have varied considerably over the years. In contrast, they have been more stable at a quite high level for France and Italy.

Table 2.1 Household Saving Rates 1986–95 in Some OECD Countries. Percentage of Disposable Household Income

	1986	1987	1988	1989	1990	1991	1992	1993	1994	1995[1]
USA	6.2	4.5	4.5	4.1	4.3	5.1	5.2	4.6	4.2	4.5
Japan	16.1	14.7	14.3	14.6	14.1	15.1	15.0	14.7	15.2	16.3
Germany	12.3	12.6	12.8	12.4	13.8	12.6	12.9	12.3	11.7	11.3
France[2]	12.9	10.8	11.0	11.7	12.5	13.2	13.7	13.8	13.3	14.0
Italy[2]	18.2	17.8	16.9	16.7	18.2	18.2	17.7	15.8	14.8	13.6
UK[2]	8.7	7.1	5.7	7.1	8.1	10.1	12.2	11.4	9.4	9.6
Netherl.[3]	2.5	2.5	2.4	4.2	6.0	1.3	2.4	1.0	0.8	1.4
Sweden	1.3	−2.8	−4.8	−4.9	−0.6	3.1	7.7	7.9	8.3	6.5

Notes
(1) For 1995, estimated saving rates.
(2) For France, Italy, and United Kingdom: gross saving.
(3) For the Netherlands: excluding mandatory saving through occupational pension schemes.
Source: OECD Economic Outlook 58 (1995), Annex Table 26.

The data for the Netherlands are a little unexpected. The Dutch have over the centuries had a reputation of being thrifty (see Mandeville, 1729; Smith, 1776; Rae, 1834). Weber ([1930] 1952, pp.172-3) said: 'But also in Holland which was really only dominated by strict Calvinism for seven years, the greater simplicity of life in the more seriously religious circles, in combination with great wealth, led to an excessive propensity to accumulation.' In Poor Richard's Almanack, Benjamin Franklin rhymed: 'The thrifty maxim of the wary Dutch, is to save all the money they can touch.' Now their saving rates are among the lowest in the OECD countries. The exclusion of the mandatory saving through occupational pension schemes is an important part of the explanation. Many employees contribute from their salaries/wages to pension schemes where the employers pay the remainder of the cost.

The gloomy picture for the Netherlands is changed if gross national saving is expressed as a percentage of nominal GDP. Figure 2.2 shows the gross national saving as a percentage of nominal GDP for 1986-93 in four selected OECD countries. Japan is at the top and is followed by The Netherlands, which soars above the USA and Sweden. The figures for the Netherlands may be partly due to large collective and business savings and mean rather small household savings, except savings for retirement purposes.

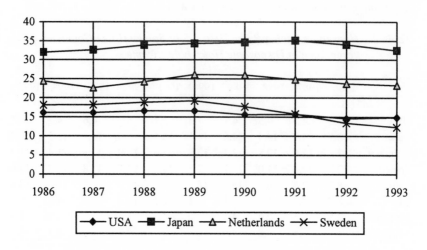

Source: OECD Economic Outlook 58 (1995), Annex Table 27.

Figure 2.2 Gross National Saving in Four OECD Countries as Percentage of Nominal GDP

Why do countries differ and why do the same countries show variation in willingness to save over a period of time? Obviously, economic and socio-demographic factors are important, but there is still some unexplained variance when such factors have been taken into account. A recent study of 17 OECD countries over a period of 20 years showed that cross-country variance explained 83 percent of the total variance in per capita savings and time-series variance explained only three percent (Kessler et al., 1993).

Kessler et al. (1993) found that while differences in economic and demographic factors explained much of the cross-country variance, there was also a significant contribution of what they called 'sociological factors'. Those included values, attitudes, religion and culture. The LCH was not sufficient to explain the differences. The 'sociological factors' are similar to what early economists called 'thrift'. They used differences in 'thrift' to explain differences in savings that were not explained by the socioeconomic variables. Thrift which is a psychological characteristic has in economic discussions been assumed to vary between population segments and countries and over time. Self-control and willpower were assumed to determine thrift and different population groups had different amounts of these characteristics.

Survey Studies of Saving

The first representative sample surveys of savings and saving behavior seem to have been carried out in the 1940s at the University of Michigan (Klein, 1954; Morgan, 1967; Katona, 1975). Surveys have since then become increasingly important as a supplement to aggregate statistical data on household savings. In survey studies of saving, the researcher has to make many decisions (cf. Lansing, 1954).

1. Define the sample
2. Define the decision unit; it usually means defining a household
3. Decide on who should be interviewed in a household; interviewing one person may not be enough
4. Define the time period to be covered
5. Decide when during the year to make the interviews
6. Define income, wealth, and savings
7. Find a way of adding income and savings of household members.

Interview surveys of savings and saving behavior are usually based on representative samples of individuals or households. Due to non-response, that is, failure of some sample units to participate whether for lack of willingness or other reasons like illness, the actually interviewed sample can deviate considerably from the intended one. It is common to try to compensate for non-response by weighting the observations so as to ensure that categories like age and perhaps income agree with those of the sampled population.

There is a tendency in economic and consumer behavior literature to talk about households as decision-making units and treat individuals as representative of households and pay little attention to relations between individuals in the household. The ideal household to study is, of course, the one-person household. While one-person households may be ideal respondents, they are hardly representative of the population. They may be studied for certain specific purposes (cf. Dahlbäck, 1991). When there are two or more members in a household, the question arises how the different members should be treated.

Is there such a thing as a genuine household decision? Studies of family decision making indicate that family decisions can often be a complex affair and that family members may pursue different strategies. There are many studies of how husbands and wives divide decisions and somewhat fewer of the influence of children on joint purchase decisions (see Kirchler, 1988, 1995). An assumption of division of labor in the family is often made in such studies and to some extent the validity of this idea is borne out by empirical data on purchases (Davies, 1976). While simple questions about financial decisions have been included in many studies (for overviews, see, Davis,

1976; Kirchler 1988), few studies have specifically dealt with saving behavior. In a study of around 300 newly married young couples' asset accumulation, Ferber and Nicosia (1972, p.185) found that in many cases husbands and wives did not agree about asset decisions. They concluded: 'Hence, an explanation of these decisions may lie not in treating the family as a unit but in considering each of its major component parts and [of] how they interact with each other.'

There are some indications that the wife has somewhat more responsibility for saving in bank accounts and the husband has more responsibility for saving that can be characterized as investing. Dual career couples with double incomes may have separate saving accounts and invest money independently of one another at the same time as they have joint savings.

In surveys of saving, the assumption is often made that one household member, usually the husband, is competent to answer questions about the household saving behavior. This assumption presupposes that someone is the *financial manager* of the household. Studies of family decision making suggest that this can be a questionable assumption.

Detailed interviews on income, wealth, and savings are best carried out when income tax returns have just been filed. The respondents have a better chance to remember amounts and probably have more of the basic documents available. A disadvantage may be that those who have filled out income tax returns may not be favorably inclined towards new inquiries about their finances.

Survey studies of savings and saving behavior run into problems of defining saving in such a way that people can make reliable reports on their behavior. When saving is defined as excess of income over consumption expenditures or difference in net worth over a year, it is necessary to ask for detailed data on assets and revenues (see Lansing, 1954, for a full description). Psychological studies of saving too often focus on relationships between subjective reports from the same interview. Attitude scores are, for example, compared with subjective reports on savings during the last 12 months. This may be acceptable for lack of better measures, but the generality of the findings should be treated as being rather limited. At the aggregate level, simple subjective reports on saving have turned out to have predictive power for aggregate savings (van Raaij and Gianotten, 1990).

Psychological data typically refer to individuals while savings to a large part or altogether belong to the family. This makes it difficult to use data on individual characteristics in studies of saving if actual savings are estimated rather than subjective reports on the activity of saving. If a presumed financial manager is interviewed, it may seem natural to use her/his psychological characteristics. Data on the characteristics of different family members make it possible to improve the analyses. Gunnarsson (1996) found considerable differences in risk attitudes between husbands and wives. It is perfectly conceivable that the partners in a household have quite distinct habits of handling money. Short-run survival of a family may, for example, be possible because the thrift of one spouse is compensating for the impatience to spend of the other (in the long run the conflict may be solved by divorce).

When the first surveys of savings were carried out in the 1950s, much care was put into defining the assets that would be included in the estimates of savings (see Lansing, 1954). By the saving of an income unit was usually meant the sum of the changes during the year of the assets and debts of the income unit, excluding changes due to changed evaluations of the household's financial and real capital. Increases in assets and decreases in debts were counted as positive saving.

Changes in the market value of houses, shares, and bonds give rise to some questions whether such changes should be counted as saving. Higher market values of homes can be used to increase mortgages and the increase can thus be used for consumption. In this limited sense, it seems appropriate to treat the value increase as saving. Subjective reports on saving in many cases do not seem to claim that such changes are saving or dissaving (see below). Buying a new car is certainly an investment leading to consumption during a hopefully longer period than one year, but it is usually counted as consumption by people in general (Katona, 1975, p.231).

Lansing (1954) pointed out that the definitions of savings and saving should vary depending on the purpose of the study. If the purpose was to find out how much money consumers made available for business investments, there was little reason to include expenditures on consumer durables like automobiles and pleasure boats. If the purpose was to look at consumer welfare such assets should be included.

Survey Questions

Saving and savings are operationally defined through the phrasing of interview questions and their meaning can vary considerably. In the following, a number of questions that have been used in the VSB Panel Project at CentER for Economic Research are presented as illustrations. Savings during a year can be estimated through changes in different wealth components, assessed either by means of direct questions: 'How much has the balance of your saving accounts changed over the last twelve months?' Or indirectly: 'How much money did you have in your saving accounts a year ago? How much do you have now?'

A variety of questions have been used to ascertain household saving, besides asking for more or less detailed data on assets and revenues. Some questionnaire makers ask about saving while others try to avoid mentioning saving. A typical question in the first category is: 'Did your household save money during the last twelve months?' It is sometimes followed by: 'How much did you save?

The second type of question asks about the finances of the household

How is the financial situation of your household at the moment?
    (1) We are incurring debts
    (2) We are drawing on our savings
    (3) We can just about manage
    (4) We have some money over
    (5) We have a lot of money over.

This question has for many years been used in regularly conducted surveys in the EU countries. The question requests a description of the financial situation right now and the answers report whether there is money left over. It is not known how people will respond when they have just increased their debts through taking out a new mortgage and at the same time are regularly saving money in bank accounts. Presumably only very few respondents fall into this category. The answers may not coincide with the answers to the following question that covers the financial situation over a whole year

Over the past year, would you say that (your/your family's) spending
    exceeded (your/your family's) income,
    that it was about the same as your income,
    or that you spent less than your income?
(Spending should not include any investments you have made.)

A follow-up question runs as follows

Did any of that spending include purchases of a home or automobile or spending for any investments?
If yes Including only monthly payments on your house or car and leaving aside any spending on investments, over the past year, would you say that (your/your family's) spending exceeded (your, your family's income), that it was about the same as your income, or that you spent less than your income?
If spending exceeded income To make up the difference, did you borrow additional money, did you spend out of savings or investments, or did you do something else?

Another way of asking the crucial question combines two approaches

Which of the following statements on this page comes closest to describing your (and your husband's/wife's/partner's) saving habits?
    Don't save – usually spend more than income
    Don't save – usually spend about as much as income
    Save whatever is left over at the end of the month – no regular plan
    Save income of one family member, spend the other

Spend regular income, save other income
Save regularly by putting money aside each month.

What Do People Mean by Saving?

The VSB Panel respondents were asked: 'To what extent do you consider the following acts as ways of saving? (1 = has nothing to do with saving; 7 = a pure form of saving).' The answers are shown in Table 2.2.

Table 2.2 Acts Considered as Saving

	1	2	3	4	5	6	7	d.k.
Put money in sav. account	1.4	1.3	2.2	6.2	9.9	22.2	53.7	3.2
Put money in check account	33.0	21.7	12.1	14.1	9.0	4.3	2.5	3.4
Buy securities	9.7	5.3	8.8	20.9	20.6	15.0	6.7	13.0
Open time deposit	7.4	4.0	5.5	13.4	12.8	17.8	18.0	21.0
Put money in savings box	18.4	9.7	9.1	13.2	15.2	11.4	19.5	3.4
Buy shares	10.2	6.4	9.8	20.8	22.3	13.7	5.5	11.4
Buy bonds	7.9	4.8	7.4	16.1	20.0	19.7	9.6	14.5
Participate in mutual funds	7.1	4.6	7.6	16.8	20.5	20.8	6.9	15.8
Speculate with money	35.7	17.2	13.4	13.8	5.1	1.9	0.7	12.2
Pay off mortgage	18.1	9.2	8.3	15.2	16.7	16.4	7.9	8.3
Consume less than income	13.9	7.6	8.1	16.5	20.1	16.4	12.5	4.9

N = 3675

Source: Data from the 3rd Interview Wave, VSB Panel.

It may seem strange that, for example, 'put money in savings box' does not receive higher values. The explanation is probably that people tend to think of 'saving' as a major activity like putting money in a savings account. Why, then, is there so much dispersion in the latter category? While putting money in a savings box is actually a form of hoarding (see above) until the money is moved back into circulation when put in a bank account, money in a savings account seems by definition to be saving. There may be a time dimension to saving, suggesting that money should be kept a certain minimum time to be counted as saving. Cash management, whether the liquid resources are in a bank account or in a box at home is apparently not always seen as saving. Many respondents do not see 'Buying securities' as saving. There may be more than one reason for this. Buying securities may be seen as investing rather than saving. There is uncertainty associated with securities while bank savings accounts are usually perceived as riskless. Finally, if money is taken from a savings account to pay for the securities, there is no new saving.

A principal components analysis of the above data yielded four factors (with eigenvalues > 1) that together explained 69 percent of the variance. The first factor was characterized by high loadings for the categories 'buy shares' (0.89), 'buy bonds' (0.88), 'invest in mutual investment funds' (0.88), 'buy securities' (0.86), and 'open time deposit' (0.64). This factor suggests that saving is equal to investing. The second factor shows high loadings for the categories 'put money in savings account' and 'put money in savings box'. 'Put money in checking account' (0.79) and 'speculate' (0.61) had high loadings on the third factor and 'pay off mortgage' was the only high-loading item on the fourth factor. Saving is clearly a multi-faceted phenomenon.

In another interview wave, the respondents were asked in a different manner about what they meant by saving. The question specifically referred to which changes in assets the respondent had included when answering the question about saved amounts.

> We would like to know what you mean by 'saving' or 'putting money aside'. On the following screens a number of alternatives will be mentioned. When you have to calculate how much you have saved over the last twelve months, which of these alternatives do you then include in your calculation? You can put 1, 2, or 3 after each alternative, where 1 = 'included in my estimate of saved amount,' 2 = 'not included in my estimate of saved amount,' 3 = 'not applicable'.

The answers are summarized in Table 2.3. A large majority included increase in savings accounts in their estimates. No other category showed the same clear pattern. A slight majority of those who had shares and bonds included changes in the value of those in savings. It is possible that they thought of new acquisitions rather than changes in value. Despite the fact that increased house value can be consumed through new mortgages, a sizable majority excluded such value changes from their calculation of savings. Very few considered changed values for automobiles, boats, antiques etc. as savings during the year. Paying back loans was excluded from savings reports in a slight majority of cases.

Unfortunately, no response alternative for 'payments to pension schemes' was included. In a study on the prototypicality of the saving concept, Groenland et al. (1996) found that pension scheme saving was rated as highly typical saving.

Table 2.3 What VSB Panel Respondents Included in Estimates of Savings

	Included	Excluded	Not applic.
	Percent	Percent	Percent
Increase in savings account	68.4	8.4	23.2
Increase in checking account	26.7	39.2	34.1
Increased value of shares, bonds	16.1	13.0	70.9
Increase in value of own housing	12.4	40.1	47.4
Increase in value of car, boat, motorcycle	6.7	38.2	55.1
Paying back loans	17.9	19.8	62.4
Money lent to others	3.5	9.8	86.6
Increased value of antiques, art, jewelry	3.1	21.2	75.7
Increased value of life insurance	8.3	28.0	63.7
Other things	5.0	95.0	0
N = 3 052			

Source: Data from the 2nd Wave, the VSB Panel, CentER for Economic Research

The VSB panel also makes it possible to compare the results of several defi-nitions of saving. Here the interest is restricted to subjective reports on sav-ing. Table 2.4 shows the relationships between the reports on saving given by a simple question on saving over the last 12 months (yes-no) and the question whether income exceeded or was less than expenditures. Most of those who said that they had not saved over the last 12 months either had expenses higher than income or expenses about equal to income. Those who answered that their expenses had exceeded their income were asked whether they had included the purchase of a house, an automobile or any other large invest-ment in the expenses. Most of those who reported a deficit said that they had broken even or had a surplus if they did not include the purchases. The an-swers to the two questions seem to agree well.

Table 2.4 Comparisons between Answers to Questions about Saving

	Did not save in last 12 months	Saved in last 12 months	Total
Expenses higher than income	18.0	8.1	10.8
Expenses and income equal	65.0	38.9	46.0
Expenses lower than income	17.1	53.0	43.2
N (=100)	1003	2672	3675

Source: Data from the 3rd Wave, the VSB Panel, CentER for Economic Research.

Another comparison can be made with the answers to six statements about saving. The results are reported in Table 2.5. The first two columns report on

The Psychology of Saving

the answers to the question about saving during the last 12 months. The last three columns are based on the question reported in Table 2.4. It may be a surprise that so many of those whose expenses exceeded their incomes saved regularly by putting aside money every month. This is more understandable if one considers that many of those had made a large purchase.

Table 2.5   Answers to Differently Phrased Questions about Saving

	Did not save	Saved	Expense larger than in-come	Expense equals income	Expense less than income
	Percent	Percent	Percent	Percent	Percent
Usually spend more than income	8.6	0.4	15.3	1.5	0.4
Don't save, usually spend about as much as income	35.5	0.7	13.4	17.2	0.9
Do not really save, but usually have some money over at the end of the year	23.3	5.8	5.4	12.5	9.2
Save whatever is left over at the end of the month – no clear plan	16.7	23.9	9.3	17.5	29.8
Spend regular income and save other incomes	6.2	6.4	5.7	8.7	4.0
Save regularly by putting aside money each month	9.7	62.8	50.8	42.6	55.7
N (=100)	893	2593	366	1591	1529

Source: Data from the 3rd Wave, the VSB Panel, CentER for Economic Research.

The purchase was often a house. People who have mortgages or who have bought automobiles on installment plans may have to save regularly at least for some time, to accumulate money for paying interest and amortization.

Empirical Measures of Household Wealth and Saving

Survey estimates of saving during a period are usually based on differences between the net wealth (net worth) at the end of the period and the net wealth at the beginning of the period. This measure does not correspond exactly to the definition 'excess of income over consumption in a budget period'. The measure is a flow measure and should be distinguished from the household's total savings. The latter is a measure of the stock and is equivalent to net wealth. Calculation of net wealth is usually based on detailed questions about assets and liabilities.

Table 2.6 reports on estimates from Dutch data, collected from the Socio-Economic Panel of the Central Bureau of Statistics in the Netherlands. The Panel consists of around 5 000 households that are interviewed every year. The table shows that almost all households had at least one checking account. The majority had savings accounts. For many households, the residence where they lived was an important asset. Relatively few owned bonds and shares.

Table 2.6 Assets, Debts, and Savings in Dutch Households 1987–88

	Percent owner- ship 1987	Means for own- ers Dfl	Percent owner- ship 1988	Means for own- ers Dfl	Savings 1987-88 Dfl
Assets					
Checking accounts	99.3	4 19	99.5	3 354	−475
Savings, deposit accounts	65.8	13 45	68.6	14 023	948
Saving certificates	4.7	13 26	4.9	12 901	70
Bonds and mortgage bonds	2.9	49 02	3.6	45 101	191
Shares, options, other securities	6.3	46 70	6.9	42 480	−50
Antiques, jewels, coins	23.7	9 44	28.6	9 133	335
Value of own residence	45.5	149 04	45.9	153 990	4331
Other real estate	6.0	127 09	5.5	138 349	−256
Own automobile	68.2	10 49	69.3	11 827	1182
Net worth of own business	5.7	123 99	5.3	126 840	72
Claims against private persons	5.1	9 85	5.6	12 609	34
Assets not mentioned. above	5.8	14 07	5.3	17 462	130
Cash value of life insurance mortgage	-	20 46	-	22 260	81
Debts					
Personal loan or revolving credit	21.8	12 18	21.0	11 125	131
Hire-purchase	3.2	3 31	2.5	3 460	28
Balance of mortgage	38.6	88 10	38.8	92 933	−2112
Other loans	7.5	16 37	7.4	22 654	99
Net wealth (▲net wealth 88-87)	100	73 72	100	75 994	4739

Source: Tables 6, 7 and 10 in Camphuis (1993).

SO WHAT IS THE PSYCHOLOGY OF SAVING?

Reading the classical economists, one finds two sets of factors that are psychological and that influence saving. One set has to do with perception of future needs and the other with provision for the future, that is, undertaking some act that will provide for the future. The perceptions, the actions and the links between them are the subject matter of the psychology of saving. The fact that people see a future need does not in all cases lead to acts of provision. In the first place, inadequate financial means may be a sufficient explanation. In other cases, something more is needed to explain saving and differences in saving. The psychological links between perception and action, 'the prompt to action', and the factors influencing those turn out to be important. Many concepts have been attempted as explanatory links. Here are some: willpower, self-control, values, attitudes, and saving motives.

Psychology is defined as *the science of experience and behavior*. This definition indicates that psychology deals with subjective matters and with how subjective perceptions, judgments, values and attitudes relate to actions and other units of behavior. A prominent feature of the psychology of saving is that it tries to answer the question 'why'. 'Why do people save, why don't people save?' The answer to the question will differ depending on how saving is defined. Baxter (1993, p.231) pointed out that the definition of saving determined which age groups saved. With a wide enough definition also younger people saved.

When saving is the excess of income over consumption in a period, the question is: 'Why do people have an excess of income over consumption expenditures?' It is patently clear that an adequate answer to this question first requires the use of variables relating to financial conditions and perhaps sociodemographics before any psychological variables come to mind. This, of course, does not preclude that psychological variables may also be interesting. If saving is defined as 'refraining from consumption now', the question is clearly different: 'Why do people refrain from consumption now in favor of future consumption?' This question obviously implies the primary use of psychological variables, with financial and sociodemographic variables as supplementary.

Microeconomic theory is based on subjective perceptions and preferences, but there is a strong tendency not to rely on subjective data and to replace them with objective data such as 'revealed behavior' that can be observed in the market place. While psychologists do rely on subjective data, they may also use objective data as 'proxies' of subjective data. In the view of some psychologists, this should occur more often (Epstein, 1980; Wärneryd, 1986b). The psychology of saving deals with subjective data on factors relating to saving and savings and with reports on savings and saving behavior that may be subjective.

Research in the economic psychology of saving often combines objective data on finances and sociodemographics with subjective data in the analysis. This means, in my view, that the future psychology of saving is not necessarily identical to the present economic psychology of saving. The psychology of saving can profitably be studied as a more pure psychological phenomenon than has hitherto been achieved. This study involves the important question of how humans relate to the future. If the psychology of saving is seen as the same as the economic psychology of saving, there is more of a focus on what psychological and economic variables together can explain of saving behavior. It focuses on subjective reports on saving and their relationships to more objective measures. It also incorporates an interest in the interactions between psychological and economic variables that can explain saving.

Through many centuries, saving was explained by reference to a kind of personality characteristic or trait, called 'thrift'. Thrift was a summary concept for all sorts of psychological factors that were assumed to affect savings. Thrift was used both to designate individual behavior in economic matters and the behavior of nations; some nations were notably thriftier than others and better economic stability and growth was expected for those countries.

More elaborate psychological variables were introduced into the discussion of saving in the later part of the 19th century. Saving motives became a focus of discussion and this continued up to 1936 when Keynes formulated his psychological law, which focused the economists' attention on the role of income for saving. At the same time, he discussed a number of individual motives for saving before he announced that they, being stable, had little macroeconomic significance.

The psychology of saving focuses on the *process* in which money is not spent in one period and which makes it possible to consume in a later period if needed. The process comprises perception of future needs and provision for the future and can in principle be studied by frequently repeated observations, preferably by means of diaries. In practice, at best, a few observations at different points in time in the form of panel studies are possible. The process is often investigated through retrospective interviews, which leave the door open for memory errors in addition to other biases like unwillingness or inability to report all the facts. For lack of better alternatives, these methods have to be accepted, but the results should be interpreted with some caution. At any rate, in the psychology of saving, the *how?* and the *why?* of this process are of primary interest rather than the outcome.

For many purposes, it seems sufficient to use subjective reports on saving and savings. It should be noted that the subjective reports may include detailed descriptions of household finances, based on the respondents consulting documents. Interview data may hardly be less reliable than data from income tax returns as is sometimes implied by hard-core economists who do not trust interview data. In fact, income statements in properly conducted interviews may even be more accurate than the figures in income tax returns. Whereas estimates of saving based on detailed data from households never seem to yield more than modest correlations with presumed explanatory variables (except earlier saving), subjectively reported saving often shows high correlations with explanatory factors (also subjectively reported).

It is obvious that even a simple and clear definition of saving like 'the excess of income over consumption expenditure' involves considerable problems when it is more closely examined. Income and consumption expenditure must be clarified. Should, for example, windfall gains like lottery wins and inheritances be counted as income? Economists who study the consumption function attribute in their analysis a special role to what they call 'permanent income' that they do not consider equivalent to current income. Some behavioral economists – who are in many ways similar to economic psychologists – speak about different 'mental accounts' and tend to think that temporary income by the earner is treated differently than regular income. The role of the acquisition and possession of consumer durables must be specified to clarify savings. Browning and Lusardi (1996, p.1812) pointed out that the acquisition and use of consumer durables could be a way of smoothing consumption over the life cycle.

It is little wonder that saving at the aggregate level is defined as a residual or the difference between total income and total consumption and not defined by cumbersome collection of survey data. As said earlier, the aggregate data suffer from the fact that the calculation of total income and total consumption are rather inexact, due to reporting errors, definitional problems and periods used. Surveys are not only a complement to aggregated data, but they are necessary to assess the importance of psychological variables. Collecting the necessary data at the household level means asking detailed, for many respondents, boring questions about household finances which may lead to difficulties with response rates. Such data are nowadays available in many countries and they are certainly a desirable addition to aggregate estimates of savings even if they are far from perfect.

3. A Historical Perspective on the Psychology of Saving

We find here a good illustration of the fact that however careless a savage race may be for the future, it cannot avoid making some provision for it. A bow, a fishing-net, which will do its work well in getting food for to-day, must be of service for many days to come: a horse or a canoe that will carry one well to-day, must be a stored-up source of many future enjoyments. The least provident of barbaric despots may raise a massive pile of buildings, because it is the most palpable proof of his present wealth and power.

Marshall ([1890] 1990, p.183, footnote 2)

The Purpose of the Chapter

The purpose of the chapter is to trace psychological thinking in the historical discussions of saving and savings. The main focus lies on the use of psychological factors to explain saving. In a way, the chapter also deals with how much thrift, profit seeking, and accumulation of capital have been appreciated over the centuries. While with few exceptions – some of which will be commented on below – saving has been held in high esteem, capital accumulation and, in particular, profit seeking have been exposed to questions whether they have been good for society and for the individual.

The brief history of the psychology of saving is not meant to be a complete history of how the ideas about saving and savings have developed over the centuries. Some prominent thinkers more clearly than others employed concepts and sketched processes that were psychological and they sometimes used the best scientific psychological knowledge of their time. Mostly, they appear to have relied on their own, often astute observations of family and business life, and on introspection.

I want to look primarily at discussions that still can teach us something and help us understand the psychology of saving. While modern economic texts on saving are mostly devoid of psychological concepts, classical and neoclassical economists often cited support in common-sense psychology and sometimes in contemporary academic psychology. What there is of a psychology of saving owes more to classical and neoclassical economists than to psychologists, except for the work of George Katona (1975). Economic psychologists have carried out empirical research on saving, but have not developed much theory about the psychological factors influencing saving behavior. In general, psychologists have devoted little interest to the psychology of saving and have largely neglected expectations and reactions to the future.

Rambling through history, I may make many errors of omission and leave out important ideas that can be said to belong to the psychology of saving. My main purpose is to sort out some interesting concepts for further use rather than to do justice to history. Doing this, I may be prone to make mistakes of a well-known type

> We then proceed to read much of our more sophisticated present-day understanding back into the work of earlier writers whose analysis was inevitably more fragmentary and incomplete than the later achievement. It was this retrospective view which doubtless inspired Whitehead to say somewhere that everything of importance has been said before – but by someone who did not discover it. (Rosenberg, 1976, p.79, cited from Barro, 1989, p.39)

ARISTOTLE AND OTHER ANCIENT THINKERS ON CAPITAL ACCUMULATION

Xenophon, a soldier and philosopher who died in 355 BC is held to be one of the earliest economists if administration of resources is included in the practice of economics (Ekelund and Hébert, 1990, pp.15-16). Sen (1987) noted that there were traces of even earlier economic books in Indian culture. In his writings, Xenophon stressed leadership with good administrative skills and efficiency. 'Although the leader is motivated by self-interest, acquisitive behavior as such is not considered 'natural'. Rather, the economic process consists of intelligent man using perception and reason to extract from nature what is necessary to fulfill human needs and to avoid discomfort.' (Ekelund and Hébert, 1990, p.16) Xenophon accepted self-interest, but the acquisition of resources should stop at what was necessary for a good life. Property could be wealth or not wealth, depending on how it was handled

> The same things are wealth and not wealth, according as one understands or does not understand how to use them. A flute for example, is wealth to one who is competent to play it, but to an incompetent person it is no better than useless stones . . . unless he sells it,' in which case 'it becomes wealth' . (Ekelund and Hébert, 1990, pp.16-17)

Wealth was what could be used more than once or could be sold for a profit and it thus implied utility.

Aristotle (384–322 BC) discussed the accumulation of wealth and distinguished between two kinds, one of which was laudable and the other objectionable. It was laudable to accumulate wealth with the purpose of living well. It was objectionable to accumulate property for its own sake and without limit

> in both, the instrument is the same, although the use is different, and so they pass into one another; for each is a use of the same property, but with a difference; accumulation is the end in the one case, but there is a further end in the other. Hence some persons are led to believe that getting wealth is the object of household management, and the whole idea of their lives is that they ought either to increase their money without limit, or at any rate not to lose it. (Aristotle, *The Politics*, p.14)

The honorable way to get wealth was through household management.

> There are two sorts of wealth-getting, as I have said; one is a part of household management, the other is retail trade: the former is necessary and honourable, while that which consists in exchange is justly censured; for it is unnatural, and a mode by which men gain from one another. The most hated sort, and with the greatest reason, is usury, which makes a gain out of money itself, and not from the natural object of it. For money was intended to be used in exchange, but not to increase at interest. And this term interest, which means the birth of money from money, is applied to the breeding of money because the offspring resembles the parent. That is why of all modes of getting wealth this is the most unnatural. (Aristotle, *The Politics*, p. 15)

Aristotle clearly recognized the usefulness of possessing money: 'What money does for us is to act as a guarantee of exchange in the future: that if it is not needed now, it will take place if the need arises; because the bearer of money must be able to obtain what he wants.' (Aristotle, *Ethics*, p.185). Money was there to be spent and hoarding or accumulation were unnatural and thus condemned by him. (Ekelund and Hébert, 1990, p.23). Receiving interest on money was also unnatural and similar to usury.

Cicero (106–43 BC) wrote to his son on duties and distinguished between three categories of men. Men who ruled the republic were greatest and showed the greatest spirit

> Many men of great spirit, however, have lived and still live lives of leisure. Some limiting themselves to their own business, investigate and examine great matters of some kind. Others have taken a middle course between philosophy and the administration of the republic: enjoying their own personal wealth, they neither increase this by every possible method nor prevent those close to them from making use of it, sharing it rather with friends and the republic too if the need arise. (Cicero, *On Duties*, p.36)

Cicero summarized

Their wealth should in the first place be well won, and not dishonourably or in-
vidiously acquired. Secondly, it should be increased by reason, industriousness,
and thrift. Thirdly, it should be available for the benefit of as many as possible,
provided they are worthy of it, and be at the command not of lust and luxury but of
liberality and beneficence. (Cicero, pp.36-7)

Both Aristotle and Cicero granted the gentleman the right to acquire and hold
wealth on the condition that the acquisition was honorable and the wealth
was moderate. Good management of resources, industry and thrift were pre-
requisites and the wealth should be there with a view to spending it wisely for
real enjoyment. Real enjoyment included sharing the pleasure with others and
some responsibility towards the republic. Accumulation of wealth as an end
in itself was disgraceful.

SAVING IN THE MIDDLE AGES

Aristotle's works dominated the thinking of scholars long after his death and
traces of his ideas can still be discovered in modern thinking about science
and ethics. In early Christian thought, wealth was looked upon as a gift of
God and was furnished to promote human welfare. Those who did not have
wealth should not seek after it and those who had wealth should administer it
wisely so as to serve this purpose (Ekelund and Hébert, 1990, p.25). This
appears to be a slightly more passive view of capital accumulation than that
held by, for example, Aristotle in ancient Greece. In the Middle Ages feudalism was the dominant form of economic organization. Serfs, servants and
poor farmers who had little property rights and some artisans constituted the
majority of the population. For many centuries, thrift was a necessity in
Europe for mere survival. Many succumbed at an early age to epidemics,
starvation and other ills, despite being thrifty. In modern terms, the opportunity sets in the environment were not opulent enough. With increasing trade,
a new merchant class with some prosperity emerged. They were often in conflict with the land-owning nobility.

The Scholastic economists were religious men who tried to interpret and
elaborate on Aristotle's ideas at the same time as they scrutinized what the
Christian Bible said. The Scholastics took some important steps in clarifying
human wants, discussing aggregation of wants and scarcity of resources, and
in sketching demand functions (Ekelund and Hébert, 1990, p.34).

Wealth accumulation was seen as a matter for kings. The latter needed to
create treasuries to be able to be successful in the wars that sooner or later
became necessary for their own survival (Machiavelli [1513] 1995; cf. Heckscher [1935] 1994, pp.208-10) In the 14th century, saving was considered a
virtue when practiced by commoners. The reasons behind this were not quite

unselfish and pure on the part of the mentors. Those tried to enact and enforce the so-called sumptuary laws to curb consumption and implant the desired virtuous behavior, apparently with little success. The sumptuary laws prescribed in detail how people of low rank in society could dress and what property like horses and carts they were allowed to possess

> Expenditure of money by commoners pained the nobles not least because they saw it benefiting the merchant class rather than themselves. The clergy considered that this expenditure drained money from the Church, and so condemned it on the moral ground that extravagance and luxury were in themselves wicked and harmful to virtue. In general the sumptuary laws were favored as a means of curbing extravagance and promoting thrift, in the belief that if people could be made to save money, the King could obtain it when necessary. Economic thinking did not embrace the idea of spending as a stimulus to the economy. (Tuchman, 1979, p.20)

THE RENAISSANCE AND THE RISE OF CAPITALISM

The First Steps towards Capitalism

Ever since Aristotle's time, economics had two branches, which were not always kept separate. One branch was part of philosophy and was close to ethics. It dealt with questions of what was good for society. The other branch was closer to mundane matters. It dealt with household management and in particular how agriculture should be successfully pursued. Later, in the Middle Ages, especially towards the end, this branch merged with mechanics, which divorced from philosophy as a kind of technology to take advantage of the developing natural sciences. The joint efforts were known as 'cameralistics' which consisted of practical arts and administrative knowledge and skills (Sen, 1987). Bookkeeping, which attained perfection in 15th century Italy, was an important feature of these skills. Reality became more complex and special skills were rewarded by success, which led to professionalization.

With the Renaissance, work became more recognized as a legitimate, even honorable activity for the middle classes. The Protestant ethic was one factor in this development. With the exception of the nobility, people who were able to work should work and not be idle. Thrift and saving became desirable characteristics of the emerging middle class.

In the 16th and 17th centuries, many countries and population segments in Europe converted to new religions. In many ways, this instigated and encouraged new economic conduct. While the roots of capitalism may be found in the Middle Ages' thinking of some Scholastics, the Protestant ethic is credited as an important contributor to economic development. In his work *The*

Protestant Ethic and the Spirit of Capitalism, Max Weber expounded the hypothesis that religion influenced and shaped economic behavior. He suggested that Protestant asceticism made capital accumulation not only acceptable, but also highly commendable.

Weber ([1930] 1952, pp.175-6) quoted the founder of the Methodist Church, John Wesley: 'We ought not to prevent people from being diligent and frugal; we must exhort all Christians to gain all they can, and to save all they can; that is, in effect, to grow rich.' He added: 'There follows the advice that those who gain all they can and save all they can should also give all they can, so that they will grow in grace and lay up a treasure in heaven.' Weber remarked that Wesley's view was very close to his own interpretation of capital accumulation.

It may look as though capital accumulation was permissible only when the savings were used for the good of other people. There were some doubts about selfish spending for one's own exclusive good, especially if the spending involved luxuries. Nevertheless, the fact that money was bestowed on others meant that the donor was rewarded in heaven (which could be a selfish purpose).

Weber's hypothesis about the role of Calvinism for the development of capitalism has been severely criticized as being too simple and as exaggerating the role of a single factor that may have had some influence. Tendencies towards capitalism appeared at about the same time also in other religious contexts, for example, in certain catholic groups. This development included that, in the 16th century, the views on work started to change in certain population segments. In ancient Greece, a gentleman did not really work. Certain things could be done, but it was understood that a gentleman should have plenty of time for diversions such as conversations with other gentlemen. Slaves and servants were there to fulfill the needs of the nobility and they carried out the work. This upper-class view on work continued through the centuries. While work became recognized as a legitimate, even honorable activity in the middle classes, the nobility still maintained their rejecting attitude, except for certain honorable duties. The emerging merchant class was held in low esteem.

People who were able to work should work and not be idle. Azuelos (1996) noted with respect to England

> The passing of the 1576 Act for the Setting of the Poor to Work and for the Avoiding of Idleness, which placed parishes under the obligation of building workhouses and providing raw materials whereby the idle poor might be set to work – both to be financed through the levying of poor rates – marks an important step in this growing awareness of the economic dimension of this phenomenon. Azuelos (1996, pp.876-8)

For the poor people, thrift was a necessity and did not lead to a much better life. 'Only the upper tier of city society, which comprised successful traders, craftsmen, lawyers, doctors and the like, tried to join the ranks of the rising merchant class by adopting a work ethic and developing a sense of thrift. Not surprisingly, it was among those circles that Puritan influence was most strongly felt.' (Azuelos, 1996, p.879) Thrift and saving became characteristics of the new middle class.

Adam Smith remarked on the spreading rejection of idleness

> It would be necessary that almost every man should be a man of business, or engage in some sort of trade. The province of Holland seems to be approaching near to this state. It is there unfashionable not to be a man of business. Necessity makes it usual for almost every man to be so, and custom every where regulates fashion. As it is ridiculous not to dress, so is it, in some measure, not to be employed, like other people. As a man of a civil profession seems awkward in a camp or a garrison, and is even in some danger of being despised there, so does an idle man among men of business. (Smith [1776] 1981, p.113)

In the framework of mercantilism, somewhat different ideas developed. While Mirabeau created the label 'Mercantilism' in 1763, the first signs of the creed date back to the early 16th century. The mercantilists had some fundamental notions about the way in which an economy should work to promote economic growth. They abandoned the idea of personal salvation and devoted themselves to the real world. Many of them came from the new merchant class. 'And although their overall social goal of "state power" was subjective, their opinions on the workings of the economic system were a clear reflection of real-world habits of thought' (Ekelund and Hébert, 1990, p.44). Mercantilism was a set of economic creeds that characterized a period between feudalism and liberalism and was more or less a consequence of the emergence of the nation-states and the birth of capitalism (Ekelund and Hébert, 1990).

According to Eli Heckscher ([1935] 1994), the mercantilists had the belief that whenever money changed hands, it created new income. This led to a belief in the utility of luxury and the evil of thrift. It appears that they saw disadvantages to the economy of the country when people were hoarding money. Money should be spent or made available for investment.

> Thrift, in fact, was regarded as the cause of unemployment, and for two reasons: in the first place, because real income was believed to diminish by the amount of money which did not enter into exchange, and secondly, because saving was believed to withdraw money from circulation . . . In 1695 the same argument was put forward by Cary with even more clarity, if that were possible. He stated that if everybody spent more, all would obtain larger incomes 'and might then live more plentifully'. There then arose, in his opinion, a 'flux of wealth', causing variety of Fashions, which add Wings to Men's Inventions. (Heckscher [1935] 1994, pp.208-9).

Mandeville, Malthus and, much later, Keynes concurred with the idea that thrift could be disastrous for society. Schumpeter (1954, p.287) remarked that the physiocrat Quesnay had a view on saving that was strikingly similar to that of Keynes: 'in itself, saving is sterile and a disturber; it must be "offset," and this offsetting is a distinct act that may or may not succeed. A fairly strong anti-saving tradition thus acquired additional support shortly before it almost vanished into thin air.' Schumpeter only briefly mentioned the views of Mandeville who was quoted by Keynes (1936) in support of non-saving.

The Conflict between the Passions and the Interests: The Growth of Capitalism

Capital accumulation presupposed industriousness and thrift. Those who favored capital accumulation emphasized that the money saved should ultimately be used and that there should be moderation and consideration of other people's needs. Capitalism, which was at first based on commerce and later on industrialization, meant something additional. It embodied the idea that money could be used to make money, something that Aristotle had not accepted as legitimate. It should be noted that in the Middle Ages interest on loans was not permitted (Tuchman, 1979). Industrial capitalism meant that the ownership of machines and factories gave opportunities for making profit without work, which Karl Marx later repudiated.

The Enlightenment of the 18th century favored the use of reason and rejected old doctrines. Man was admonished to become rational and less inclined to follow passions. The pursuit of passions meant pursuing short-run goals. Adam Smith pointed to 'present enjoyment' at the cost of future consumption. Humans should pursue their interests, which involved calculation of the future. Interests corresponded to self-interest in the long run and they were in conflict with the passions (Hirschman, 1977).

Vico (1668–1744) who was an Italian philosopher recognized the significance of identifying and controlling passions by turning them into virtues. He argued

> Out of ferocity, avarice, and ambition, the three vices which lead all mankind astray, [society] makes national defense, commerce, and politics, and thereby causes the strength, the wealth, and the wisdom of the republics; out of these three great vices which would certainly destroy man on earth, society thus causes the civil happiness to emerge. This principle proves the existence of divine providence: through its intelligent laws the passions of men who are entirely occupied by the pursuit of their private utility are transformed into a civil order which permits men to live in human society. (Quoted from Hirschman, 1977, p.17)

Hirschman (1977) proposed that commerce that was necessary for capitalism to develop meant a quest for tranquillity and peace. By pursuing his material interests man would become inured against the passions. He further made the observation that the poor actually had little opportunity to yield to their passions and that the richer people got, the more they could disregard their interests (Hirschman, 1977, p.125).

The room for rational pursuit of interests had its limits.

> But the idea that men pursuing their interests would be forever harmless was decisively given up only when the reality of capitalist development was in full view. As economic growth in the nineteenth and twentieth centuries uprooted millions of people, impoverished numerous groups while enriching some, caused large-scale unemployment during cyclical depressions, and produced modern mass society, it became clear to a number of observers that those caught in' these violent transformations would on occasion become passionate – passionately angry, fearful, resentful. (Hirschman, 1977, p.126)

Capitalism, which was the pursuit of a new type of elite and was in conflict with feudal concerns, had effects on society by creating a new balance between the passions and the interests. The new elite was the intellectual, managerial, and administrative leaders. While the money-making activities were not approved in themselves by the thinkers, they were thought to have a most beneficial side effect. They put pressure on societal leaders to keep calm and peace in the nation.

> Weber claims that capitalistic behavior and activities were the indirect (and originally unintended) result of a desperate *search for individual salvation*. My claim is that the diffusion of capitalist forms owed much to an equally desperate search for a way of *avoiding society's ruin*, permanently threatening at the time because of precarious arrangements for internal and external order. Clearly both claims could be valid at the same time: one relates to the motivations of the aspiring, new elites, the other to those of various gatekeepers. (Hirschman, 1977, p. 130)

Capital accumulation had turned into capitalism, which had some ideology behind it, but was on the whole apparently based on pragmatic thinking. More and more of what Aristotle had considered as less honorable ways of accumulating money were accepted and even seen as natural ways of controlling the passions in favor of the interests. In a recent article, the philosopher Norman Bowie (1994) discussed the Enlightenment view that markets were 'civilizing' rather than destructive or feeble. He expressed some hope of increased international understanding and of decreased degradation of the environment as a consequence of the civilizing effect of markets.

It may be noted that the ideas about the conflict between the passions and the interests at the individual level live on in psychoanalysis (the Ego and the Id). They have recently re-emerged in terms of the conflict between the Planner and the Doer in Shefrin and Thaler's (1988) Behavioral Life-Cycle Hypothesis, which will be presented in the next chapter.

Mandeville's Views on Private Vice as Public Benefit

The Dutch physician Bernard Mandeville (1670–1733) proclaimed the danger of saving money. In his famous poem 'The Fable of the Bees or Private Vices, Publick Benefits' and two volumes of comments, Mandeville presented the provocative view that saving was not a virtue. The mercantilists had earlier had similar views. This was what happened when people saved rather than spent their money freely (Mandeville [1729] 1924, p.32)

> For 'twas not only that They went,
> By whom vast Sums were Yearly spent;
> But Multitudes that liv'd on them,
> Were daily forced to do the same.
> In vain to other Trades they'd fly;
> All were o'erstocked accordingly.
> The Price of Land and Houses falls;
> Mirac'lous Palaces, whose Walls,
> Like those of *Thebes*, were rais'd by Play,
> Are to be let.

Mandeville was an immigrant from the Netherlands and lived in London where he had an apparently profitable practice as a physician. It is sometimes assumed that he wrote the poem to show his command and love of the new language. The poem caused an outcry from people who considered thrift and saving as a virtue and he faced accusations of attempting to corrupt society. His position as a physician with a good clientele was threatened. To defend himself and elaborate on his views, he published a series of comments, which were published between 1714 and 1729.

In a society that was not forced to frugality, there should be no frugality. No country had ever shown frugality without a national necessity. If people who could afford it stopped wasting money, the effects on society would be disastrous. All those who were gainfully employed through the spending of the wasters would lose their jobs. There would be overproduction, falling prices on property, and underconsumption. Mandeville assumed and tried to prove that while waste was private vice it could be public benefit. It was not desirable not to use luxuries in a society that could afford to be lavish. Lavishness stimulated creativity: 'Prodigality has a thousand Inventions to keep People from sitting still, that Frugality would never think of; and as this must consume a prodigious Wealth, so Avarice again knows innumerable Tricks to rake it together, which Frugality would scorn to make use of' (Mandeville, 1729, p.105). While the idea was not completely new and the mercantilists were rather close to similar thinking, the latter primarily hated hoarding.

People followed their self-interest, their passions according to Mandeville who in his comments considered cognitive, motivational-emotional and personality factors and emphasized individual differences.

> Experience teaches us first, that as People differ in their Views and Perceptions of Things, so they vary in their Inclinations; one Man is given to Covetousness, another to Prodigality, and a third is only <u>Saving</u>. Secondly, that Men are never, or at least very seldom, reclaimed from their darling Passions, either by Reason or Precept, and that if anything ever draws 'em from what they are naturally propense to, it must be a Change in their Circumstances or their Fortunes. . . . If any body would refute what I have said, let him only prove from History, that there ever was in any Country a National Frugality without a National Necessity. (Mandeville [1729] 1924, pp.182-3)

Mandeville apparently believed in stable personality traits and stable preferences. Changes could then be ascribed to changes in environmental circumstances or in wealth. This is similar to how economists reason today. He made a clear distinction between individual behavior and aggregate behavior, which was hardly common in his days. The distinction is evident already from the subtitle of his poem: 'Private vice, publick benefit'.

Keynes (1936) cited Mandeville when he described the possible ill effects of saving at the aggregate level. Economists sometimes talk about 'the Paradox of Thrift' to indicate that what is good at the individual level is not necessarily good for the national economy. An alternative name for the phenomenon is 'the Composite Error' or 'Composition fallacy', the error made when the aggregate is assumed to be simply the sum of the individual parts (Samuelson and Nordhaus, 1993).

The idea that good micro-level behavior could be bad at the macro level was bravely presented to the public. Mandeville's further reasoning around The Fable involved a creative use of some earlier thinking. He was a forerunner both to economics and to psychology (Hayek [1978] 1985). In his comments on the two volumes of text, the editor Kaye noted that Mandeville was a precursor both to some psychoanalytical thinking and to some economic thinking. In a footnote, he wrote

> The fundamental position of the *Fable* – that so-called good arises from a conversion of so-called evil – is really a form of one of the chief tenets of psycho-analysis – that virtues arise through the individual's attempt to compensate for original weaknesses and vices. Mandeville also forestalled another Freudian position when he argued [. . .] that the naturalness of a desire could be inferred from the fact of a general prohibition aimed at it, and the strength of the desire, from the stringency of the prohibition. (Mandeville [1729] 1924, p. LXIV)

The last point is known in social psychology as 'reactance theory'. Reactance theory says that a person will react against attempts to control her/his freedom of choice by valuing more highly that from which the person is blocked and by adopting attitudes contrary to those imposed upon her/him (Sutherland, 1995; Cialdini, 1988, p.232ff). Reactance theory may help explain why people resist or do not comply with attempts to influence their saving or spending behavior.

Through focusing on the individual, Mandeville made economics more psychological, a work that was later continued by Adam Smith. The latter elaborated in a creative way the idea of division of labor that Mandeville had proposed and also used some of his views on self-interest. Mandeville's notion about the importance of luxuries was foreign to many economists and social thinkers who tended to have a rather Spartan inclination. Finally, Mandeville maintained the idea that the economy should be left alone without interference by Government. This was the beginning of later laissez-faire theory in political economy. (Mandeville [1729] 1924, pp. CXXXIV)

SOME CLASSICAL ECONOMISTS AND THEIR VIEWS OF CAPITAL ACCUMULATION

Adam Smith on Frugality and Public Waste

Adam Smith (1723–90) is considered to be the founding father of classical economics and he was the first real system builder in economics. Classical economics dominated economic thinking for centuries and was represented by thinkers like Ricardo and John Stuart Mill. It is still influential and serves as a foundation of economic theory. Smith is worth mentioning also in the history of psychology since 17 years before he published his *Wealth of Nations*, he wrote a book on (moral) psychology with the title *The Theory of Moral Sentiments*.

Earlier economic thinking had focused on property and exchange of property, but with Smith it switched to an interest in human behavior. Human agents were now introduced in a systematic manner into political economy. Like Mandeville, Smith maintained that people should act in accordance with their preferences and pursue their self-interest. With a large number of independent decision makers equilibrium would be obtained and the economy seem governed by an invisible hand.

Smith had a theory of man, which accepted reality as he saw it. The principle of self-interest or self-love as Smith preferred to call it was explored in *The Wealth of Nations* and has been a dominant thought in economics ever since. A characteristic of all men was that they were in the first place interested in what was nearest to them. Smith said

Every man is, no doubt, by nature, first and principally recommended to his own care; and as he is fitter to take care of himself than of any other person, it is fit and right that it should be so. Every man, therefore, is much more deeply interested in whatever immediately concerns himself, than in what concerns any other man: and to hear, perhaps, of the death of another person, with whom we have no particular connexion, will give us less concern, will spoil our stomach, or break our rest much less than a very insignificant disaster which has befallen ourselves. (Smith, 1759, pp.82-3)

Many later economists like Jevons, Böhm-Bawerk, and Marshall have treated the implications of the preference for nearness in time and space. The economist Fisher (1930) much later applied the concept of time preference to the time dimension that Smith hinted at and gave the economists a way of measuring distance in time. Modern psychologists have developed scaling methods to measure what increasing distance in time and space means for human reactions. The Swedish psychologist Ekman (1970) reported some early results. Those confirm Smith's ideas. Smith's insight seems to be practiced every day in the selection of news in the mass media. He recognized that it would be hard for many to accept this principle: 'Though it may be true, therefore, that every individual, in his own breast, naturally prefers himself to all mankind, yet he dares not look mankind in the face, and avow that he acts according to the principle' (Smith [1759] 1982, p.83).

It should be added that Smith did not think that it was in anybody's self-interest to hurt or damage other people. This was made clear in *The Theory of Moral Sentiments*

There can be no proper motive for hurting our neighbour, there can be no incitement to do evil to another, which mankind will go along with, except just indignation for evil which that other has done to us. To disturb his happiness merely because it stands in the way of our own, to take from him what is of real use to him merely because it may be of equal or of more use to us, or to indulge, in this manner, at the expence of other people, the natural preference which every man has for his own happiness above that of other people, is what no impartial spectator can go along with. (Smith [1759] 1982, p.82)

Another human characteristic was the will to better oneself. Smith (1776) wrote

With regard to profusion, the principle which prompts to expense is the passion for present enjoyment; which, though sometimes violent and very difficult to be restrained, is in general only momentary and occasional. But the principle which prompts to save is the desire of bettering our condition, a desire which, though generally calm and dispassionate, comes with us from the womb, and never leaves us till we go into the grave . . . An augmentation of fortune is the means by which the greater part of men propose and wish to better their condition . . . Though the principle of expence, therefore, prevails in almost all men upon some occasions, and in some men upon almost all occasions, yet in the greater part of men, taking the whole course of their life at an average, the principle of frugality seems not only to predominate, but to predominate very greatly. (Smith [1776] 1981, pp.341-2)

Smith was confident that man was endowed with such defenses against waste of money that they were ordinarily enough. His views on saving constituted *the* theory of saving up to the works of Böhm-Bawerk who introduced a number of new ideas (Schumpeter, 1954). With Adam Smith, capital accumulation for self-interest purposes became established in theory as legitimate. Capital accumulation was good for industriousness. Smith also thought that there were strict limits as to how far the pursuit of money out of self-interest could go. This is especially clear in the volume on moral sentiments. Like many earlier and later writers, Smith attributed saving to thrift which he labeled parsimony and played down industriousness to some extent. Industry provides the resources that may be saved while parsimony leads to the real accumulation.

Capitals are increased by parsimony, and diminished by prodigality and misconduct. – Whatever a person saves from his revenue he adds to his capital, and either employs it himself in maintaining an additional number of productive hands, or enables some other person to do so, by lending it to him for an interest, that is, for a share of the profits. As the capital of an individual can be increased only by what he saves from his annual revenue or his annual gains, so the capital of a society, which is the same with that of all the individuals who compose it, can be increased only in the same manner. – Parsimony, and not industry, is the immediate cause of the increase of capital. Industry, indeed, provides the subject which parsimony accumulates. But whatever industry might acquire, if parsimony did not save and store up, the capital would never be greater. (Smith [1776] 1981, p.337)

As distinguished from Mandeville who found frugality unnatural and lauded prodigality, Smith (1776) believed that frugality was a characteristic feature of all humans. There were some exceptions due to individual differences and differences over time in a person's economic behavior. He was influenced by Mandeville's idea that it was important that the individual served his/her self-interest, but he praised individual thrift as part of self-love. At the same time he forcefully attacked the sumptuary laws that had been introduced so as to curb common people's consumption and asserted that the decision whether to spend or save could and should be left to the individuals themselves. Pursuing self-interest meant that individuals were independent and their preferences could be added up. They were complementary in the sense that there was productive division of labor. The invisible hand governed nations so that equilibria became possible.

Smith firmly believed in the balancing effect of the invisible hand and consequently saw serious economic problems in a nation as being caused by government intervention rather than by individual wasters of money.

> It is the impertinence and presumption, therefore, in kings and ministers, to pretend to watch over the economy of private people, and to restrain their expense, either by sumptuary laws or by prohibiting the importation of foreign luxuries. They are themselves always, and without any exception, the greatest spendthrifts in the society. Let them look well after their own expense, and they may safely trust private people with theirs. If their own extravagance does not ruin the state, that of their subjects never will. (Smith [1776] 1981, p.346).

The pursuit of self-interest as a characteristic of all humans remained in economic theory. To Bentham self-interest was the same as utility and utility was governed by two sovereign masters, pain and pleasure (Ekelund and Hébert, 1990, p.127ff). Bentham and utilitarianism focused the interest of political economy on the problems for a government to create maximum happiness for its population. Unlike Adam Smith, Bentham did not expect maximum happiness to occur without government intervention.

Self-interest was held to be the only motivation of human action and hedonism, which the Greek philosophers had pleaded for, became the main psychological tenet of economics. Bentham and utilitarianism proclaimed the greatest good of the greatest number of people and saw this as a fulfillment of the self-interest. Each individual was assumed to be driven by the search for pleasure and the avoidance of pain, but also respecting the greatest good of the greatest number. In this manner, utilitarianism could be the foundation both for economic theory and for ethics. Later authors have found it more difficult to reconcile self-interest and hedonism with utilitarianism (see e.g. Sen, 1979).

John Rae, the Effective Desire of Accumulation, and the Prompt to Action

John Rae (1796–1872) who, late in his life, wrote a biography of Adam Smith, started writing a book which was meant to be a critique of *The Wealth of Nations*. In 1834, he published a book which was republished in 1905 under the new title *The Sociological Theory of Capital* because of high demand from economists. Rae expounded a theory of accumulation of capital and drew attention to time preference. Economists like John Stuart Mill (1848), Böhm-Bawerk (1888), Marshall (1890), and Fisher (1930) later elaborated on many of his ideas. Rae captured important aspects of saving in the following two sentences: 'The determination to sacrifice a certain amount of present good, to obtain another greater amount of good, at some future period, may be termed *the effective desire of accumulation*. All men may be said to have a desire of this sort, for all men prefer a greater to a less; but to be effective it must prompt to action. (Rae [1834] 1905, p.53) 'All men prefer a greater to a less' is the foundation of the rationality postulate that was later formulated in similar terms and further explored by John Stuart Mill and Jevons.

The effective desire of accumulation did not lead to accumulation unless it prompted to action. What can be a possible link between a desire and actual action? Rae had some ideas as to when the desire could prompt to action. The circumstances that seemed to contribute most to strengthening the desire to accumulate were the following three:

1. The prevalence throughout the society of the social and benevolent affections, or, of that principle, which, under whatever name it may be known, leads us to derive happiness from the (future) good we communicate to others
2. The extent of the intellectual powers, and the consequent prevalence of habits of reflection, and prudence, in the minds of the members of the society
3. The stability of the condition of the affairs of the society, and the reign of law and order throughout it. (Rae [1834] 1905, p.58)

The desire of accumulation is weakened, and strength given to the desire of immediate enjoyment, by three opposing circumstances:

1. The deficiency of strength in the social and benevolent affections, and the prevalence of the opposite principle, a desire of mere selfish gratification
2. A deficiency in the intellectual powers, and the consequent want of habits of reflection and forethought
3. The instability of the affairs of the society, and the imperfect diffusion of law and order throughout it. (Rae [1834] 1905, pp.58-9)

In modern terms, the first condition is similar to the bequest motive for saving which is also named 'altruism' and which by Keynes (1936) was called 'pride'. The second resembles what Hirschman (1977) called 'the interests', some economists called 'foresight' and is now often handled under the precautionary motive for saving. The third 'prompt' to accumulate capital may be equivalent to consumer confidence for which there is nowadays a measuring instrument in the shape of 'The Index of Consumer Sentiment'. This prompt may also be subsumed under 'uncertainty' In fact, Rae repeatedly stressed the uncertainties of life. Despite these ideas which have later been elaborated by economist thinkers, the links between desire of accumulation and saving behavior are, to this day, still puzzling researchers.

As Loewenstein (1992, pp.5-7) noted in his review of time preference, Rae pointed to two strong factors that worked against the proclivity to accumulate capital. The first factor was the brevity and uncertainty of life. This made people value present consumption higher than future consumption. When people felt safe, they had a tendency to be more frugal than when they lived under hazardous conditions. The second factor was the psychological discomfort of delaying gratification, of refraining from something now. Rae said

> The prospects of future good, which future years may hold out to us, seem at such a moment dull and dubious, and are apt to be slighted, for objects on which the daylight is falling strongly, and showing us in all their freshness just within our grasp. There is no man perhaps, to whom a good to be enjoyed today, would not seem of very different importance, from one exactly similar to be enjoyed twelve years hence, even though the arrival of both were equally certain . . . Everywhere we see that to spend is easy, to spare, hard. (Rae [1834] 1905, p.54)

The vivid visibility of present goods in comparison with future goods was an important factor deciding the choice in favor of the former. It was the task of the philosophers to interpret the facts of wealth accumulation and the causes behind it. When asked, people could describe the components of their wealth, but not explain the origins of wealth. They did not understand why wealth accrued.

> However complicated the social system of which any person engaged in the acquisition of wealth makes a part, he has no difficulty in tracing the manner in which that portion of it which he possesses has been acquired, nor in explaining how it forms to him a certain amount of what he calls capital . . . Though, therefore, he can easily tell how he got that which constitutes his wealth, and how to him it comes to be wealth, he will yet probably confess that he is unable to say what constitutes wealth in general, from whence it is derived, or what are the exact laws regulating its increase or diminution. (Rae [1834] 1905, p.3)

The Ricardian Equivalence Principle

David Ricardo (1772–1823) systematized political economy. Like other classical economists, he had a tendency to think in terms of agricultural production when he searched for solutions to economic problems. This inspired the economists to use a single commodity and annual production periods in their analysis (Corry, 1962). Saving and investing amounted to the same thing; what was saved was invested and in Adam Smith's terms was used for consumption, but by 'a different set of people' (Smith [1776] 1981, pp.337-8). The interest rate ensured that all savings were used for investment.

Barro (1989) revived the interest in one of Ricardo's ideas, which he called 'The Ricardian equivalence principle'. The influence of public debt on saving ratios has recently been debated as a consequence of increasing public debt in many Western countries, including the USA. Increased public debt is usually assumed to stimulate consumption and thus reduce the room for savings at the same time as higher real interest rates crowd out investment. Ricardo's ideas about public debt were similar to his ideas about individual debt. If the individual foresees a deficit in the future, s/he will save now.

Do people then react in the same way to increases in public debt as to increases in their own debts? The equivalence principle means

> A decrease in the government's saving (that is, a current budget deficit) leads to an offsetting increase in desired private saving, and hence to no change in desired national saving . . . Since desired national saving does not change, the real interest rate does not have to rise in a closed economy to maintain balance between desired national saving and investment demand. Hence, there is no effect on investment, and no burden of the public debt or social security . . . In a setting of an open economy there would also be no effect on the current account balance because desired private saving rises by enough to avoid having to borrow from abroad. (Barro, 1989, p.39)

In simple terms, the principle involves that people foresee that public debts will have to be paid back and this can only be done through increases in taxes. Therefore, people increase their savings as a preparation for higher taxes. Public debts are financed through treasury bills, bonds etc., which are bought and stored by the public. Psychologically, people may be concerned that the future prospects for the nation will affect themselves and save money for pure precautionary motives.

An objection against the Ricardian equivalence hypothesis is that people do not live forever and that they do not care about taxes levied after their death. Public debt may mean an intergenerational burden that leads to a smaller stock of capital for future generations. Future generations will have to pay back the debts and will need the savings. To what extent do people really care about the after-tax expenditures of future generations and how is saving affected by such considerations? In consonance with Adam Smith's thinking, primary consideration of the needs of one's own offspring and little consideration of the country's future needs seem most likely. Consideration of the country's future finances, except in so far as the future of oneself and one's offspring is concerned, seems rather unlikely. Bequeathing government bonds would be one way of ensuring that the offspring had money for paying raised taxes.

The Ricardian equivalence principle assured that government debt-making spun off household saving due to the expectation that future taxes would be levied to pay off the debt. In this assumption, there is probably hidden a sense of responsibility towards future generations. How much national debt is justified to finance present consumption at the expense of future generations? Investments with long-term beneficial effects can certainly be financed with long-term debts, but what about other government expenditures? There is some debate in economics about Ricardo's equivalence principle, but little attention is paid to its social and behavioral implications. The philosopher Rawls (1973) dealt with some aspects of the problem (see Chapter 7).

Senior's Psychological Wealth Concept

We propose in the following Treatise to give an outline of the Science which treats of the Nature, the Production, and the Distribution of Wealth. To that Science we give the name of Political Economy. Our readers must be aware that that term has often been used in a much wider sense.

Senior ([1836] 1938, p.1)

Nassau Senior (1790–1864) published a volume on political economy which was for some time a highly influential textbook. His main preoccupation was the production of wealth and he used a mentalistic approach to this issue. He distinguished three constituents of wealth or value of an article of wealth: *utility*, *limitation in supply*, and *transferableness*. All three constituents were necessary to make something an article of wealth.

'Utility' was the power of the article, direct or indirect, 'of producing pleasure, including under that term gratification of every kind, or of preventing pain, including under that term every species of discomfort' (Senior [1836] 1938, p.6). Senior carefully explained that utility was no intrinsic quality in the things called useful. It was an expression of their relations to the pains and pleasures of mankind.

And, as the susceptibility of pain and pleasure from particular objects is created and modified by causes innumerable, and constantly varying, we find an endless diversity in the relative utility of different objects to different persons, a diversity which is the motive of all exchanges. (Senior, 1836, p.7)

The next constituent of wealth, 'limitation in supply', is similar to the fundamental economic concept of scarcity.

Whenever, therefore, we apply the words *limited in supply*, as a comparative expression, to those commodities of which the quantity can be increased, we refer to the comparative force of the obstacles which limit the respective supplies of the objects compared. (Senior, 1836, p.8)

Senior admitted that 'transferableness' was an awkward term. He meant that all or some portion of the power of giving pleasure or preventing pain were capable of being transferred either definitively or for a period. Two classes of things were imperfectly transferable. The first class seems to correspond to affective value and the second class comprised most of our personal qualities. By including affective value and human capital in the discussion of wealth and maintaining that they were partly transferable, Senior deviated from what other economists thought of as capital or wealth.

The limitation in supply was the most important factor for value. 'The chief sources of its influence on value are two of the most powerful principles of human nature, the love of variety, and the love of distinction. The mere necessaries of life are few and simple' (Senior [1836] 1938, p.11; cf. Scitovsky, 1976). Senior ranked a number of needs for which variety and distinction were desired. First, variety in food came, then variety of dress, last the desire to build, ornament, and to furnish. Senior added something that resembles diminishing marginal utility.

> It is, however, that our desires do not aim so much at quantity as at diversity. Not only are there limits to the pleasure which commodities of any given class can afford, but the pleasure diminishes in a rapidly increasing ratio long before those limits are reached. Two articles of the same kind will seldom afford twice the pleasure of one, and still less will ten give five times the pleasure of two. (Senior [1836] 1938, pp.11-12)

Senior formulated four principles on which the science of political economy rested. The first one is the only one of interest here: 'That every man desires to obtain additional Wealth with as little sacrifice as possible.' This was accompanied by his idea about the importance of abstinence. He discussed three instruments of the production of wealth or capital: *human labor*, *the agency of Nature* (land and raw materials in the first place), and *abstinence*. Abstinence, which involved postponing consumption and the saving of goods or money, was crucial. 'The most laborious population, inhabiting the most fertile territory, if they devoted all their labour to the production of immediate results, and consumed its produce as it arose, would soon find their utmost exertions insufficient to produce even the mere necessaries of existence.'

Senior wanted to stress somewhat different dimensions than those the economists usually associated with 'capital'. While he used abstinence, which means refraining from expenditure, rather than 'frugality' since the latter was associated with labor, he stressed that abstinence often involved some degree of labor and actually could be painful. He argued

> To abstain from the enjoyment which is in our power, or to seek distant rather than immediate results, are among the most painful exertions of the human will . . . but of all the means by which man can be raised in the scale of being, abstinence, as it is perhaps the most effective, is the slowest in its increase, and the least generally diffused. Among nations, those that are the least civilized, and among the different classes of the same nation those which are the worst educated, are always the most improvident, and consequently the least abstinent. (Senior [1836] 1938, p.60)

The assertion in the last statement can be tested against Table 2.1 (or can't it?). Senior also had the idea that interest paid on loans was a compensation for abstinence. He used the psychological concept of abstinence as a factor in the production of capital and not as a factor making lendable funds available.

This idea had some acceptance, but Böhm-Bawerk and Fisher (see Loewenstein, 1992, pp.8-9), later emphatically rejected it.

The Mills: Contributors to Both Economics and Psychology

Names like Jeremy Bentham, James Mill (1773–1836), and the son of the latter, John Stuart Mill (1806–73) appear in the history of both psychology and economics (see for example, Boring, 1950; Murphy, 1951; Blaug, 1985; Danziger, 1990; Ekelund and Hébert, 1990). James Mill made significant contributions both to economics and psychology. His system of political economy was closely allied to that of Bentham who was a close friend of his. He fully accepted the pleasure-pain philosophy and the doctrine of hedonism, that human actions were motivated solely through self-interest.

> In seeking to outline a comprehensive political economy, he thus included a treatment of ethical and psychological questions. In general, Mill and the utilitarians favored the principle of free exchange without government interference; they believed that individual self-interest would bring about social welfare if economic (that is, from Mill's viewpoint, psychological) laws were left to themselves. (Murphy, 1951, p. 103)

In Mill's work *Analysis of the Phenomena of the Human Mind* which, after many years of work in his spare time, he published in 1829, he analyzed concepts like consciousness and treated the distinction between sensation and perception, a classical psychological question for philosophers to deal with.

Associationism began with Aristotle's three relations between elements: similarity, contrast, and contiguity. The principle of association starts with supposedly irreducible mental elements and assumes that learning and the development of higher processes consist mainly in the combination of those elements. James Mill formulated associations as mechanical laws that tied together sensations and more complex mental entities. Schumpeter (1954, p.447) noted that like Hume James Mill treated economic theory independently of psychological associationism. 'Its propositions are completely independent of associationist psychology and are just as compatible with any other.'

John Stuart Mill further developed psychological associationism, which prepared the way for psychological laboratory experiments. In this way the old problem of mind-body relationships could be experimentally studied in the laboratory. Many of John Stuart Mills important ideas were published as comments added to his father's *Analysis of the Phenomena of the Human Mind*. The work was republished in the 1860s. He modified his father's strict mechanical associationism and admitted that the mind was an active, not a passive, thing that could create new syntheses. It was a significant step from mental mechanics to mental chemistry.

In his economic works, James Mill explored hedonism, but he also relied upon observations of reality as an employee in the East India Company. Among the economists in the early 19th century, capital accumulation and its relation to economic growth was a dominant topic (Corry, 1962). The national economy was essentially seen as one big farm. The general view was 'Saving is spending'. Behind this view, the idea was that what was saved was immediately spent on labor or on the production of producer goods, such as were used in farming. James Mill declared

> Whatever is saved from the annual produce, in order to be converted into capital, is necessarily consumed; because to make it answer the purpose of capital, it must be employed in the payment of wages, in the purchase of raw material to be worked into a finished commodity; or lastly, in the making of machines. (Corry, 1962 p.23)

John Stuart Mill's major contribution to political economy was *Principles of Political Economy* which was first published in 1848 and for many years was the leading textbook in England and highly influential on economic thinking. In it, Mill made an important and clear distinction between *normative* and *descriptive* economics. He signaled very carefully when he made any policy recommendation.

Already in 1836, John Stuart Mill had formulated the basic tenets of political economy in a succinct way and created the much-debated 'economic man'.

> All these operations, though many of them are really the result of a plurality of motives, are considered by Political Economy as flowing solely from the desire of wealth. The science then proceeds to investigate the laws which govern these several operations, under the supposition that man is a being who is determined, by the necessity of his nature, to prefer a greater portion of wealth to a smaller in all cases, without any other exception than that constituted by the two countermotives already specified [aversion to labour and desire of present enjoyment of costly indulgences]. Not that any political economist was ever so absurd as to suppose that mankind are really thus constituted, but because this is the mode in which science must necessarily proceed. (Mill [1836] 1988, p.53)

Three things are outstanding in this quotation. (1) Although there may be a plurality of motives behind economic behavior, economic theory considers them all as depending on the desire of wealth. (2) Man prefers greater to less unless s/he is averse to work or intent on present enjoyment rather than on something in the future (preferring the minor good today to the larger in the future). (3) No economist is foolish enough to believe that this is the whole truth, but 'this is the mode in which science must necessarily proceed'. The science of economics began to sort out a few psychological laws and left the rest, even though the economists knew they did not cover the whole story.

It is clear from the long quotation above that Mill saw the desire of effective accumulation as a characteristic of all humans. He recognized the role of saving: 'The essence or attribute of wealth was the power to be accumulated – essentially a concept of physical production' (Corry, p.24). He also said: 'To consume less than is produced, is saving; and that is the process by which capital is increased' (Corry, p.25).

Mill was in favor of applying economics in the attempts to solve problems in society and saw the work on social reforms as an integral part of economics. He put his ideas into practice as an active Member of Parliament. He did not trust the laissez-faire principles that Adam Smith's invisible hand invoked, and like Bentham he favored some government intervention to improve the situation of the poor and affect the income distribution to some extent

> we may suppose this better distribution of property attained, by the joint effect of the prudence and frugality of individuals, and of a system of legislation favouring equality of fortunes, so far as is consistent with the just claim of the individual to the fruits, whether great or small, of his or her own industry. (Mill [1848] 1985, p.115)

Mill devoted considerable attention to taxation. One of the purposes of his suggestions was to create incentives for work and another to make sure that wealth created through work was not too heavily taxed. Saving was too important to be hampered by government intervention. Taxes could be imposed on inheritance since wealth through inheritance was not achieved by work. He opposed, in particular, the tax on land transactions that was the same independent of the size of the transaction. This was a clear disadvantage to small farmers and constituted a disincentive to save. If those managed to save, there were no reasonable investments at hand because of the constraints of the legal system. (Ekelund and Hébert, 1990, p.214)

Karl Marx – 'A Minor Post-Ricardian' (Paul Samuelson)

Paul Samuelson called Karl Marx (1818–83) 'a minor Post-Ricardian' because Marx was concerned with questions of what constituted product value and his ideas were similar to those of Ricardo. Both had the view that the amount of labor was decisive for the value. Accepting Ricardo's labor theory of value, Marx held that human labor was the source of economic value. The capitalist paid his workers less than the value that their labor added to the goods. The pay was usually only enough to maintain the worker at a subsistence level. This created a 'surplus value'. Marx argued that the capitalist appropriated this surplus value and made a profit, thereby exploiting the laborer.

Marx was highly critical of capitalism whose rise he described in the following terms

> The starting point of the development that gave rise to the wage laborer as well as to the capitalist was the servitude of the laborer. The advance consisted in a change of form of this servitude, in the transformation of feudal exploitation into capitalist exploitation. To understand its march we need not go back very far. Although we come across the first beginnings of capitalist production as early as the 14th or 15th century, sporadically, in certain towns of the Mediterranean, the capitalistic era dates from the 16th century. (Marx [1859] 1990, p.136)

Marx did not pay any attention to individual industry, thrift and saving. The important thing was to him the rise of classes in society and how they developed. In the end there would only be the capitalists and the proletariat.

> In proportion as the bourgeoisie, i.e., capital, is developed, in the same proportion is the proletariat, the modern working class, developed – a class of laborers, who live only so long as they find work, and who work only so long as their labor increases capital . . . The lower strata of the middle class – the small tradespeople, shopkeepers, and retired tradesmen generally, the handicraftsmen and peasants – all these sink gradually into the proletariat, partly because their diminutive capital does not suffice for the scale on which Modern Industry is carried on, and is swamped in the competition with the large capitalists, partly because their specialized skill is rendered worthless by new methods of production. Thus the proletariat is recruited from all classes of the population. (Marx [1859] 1990, p.120)

Thrift apparently did not save anybody from sinking into the proletariat due to strong structural forces.

> Under capitalism, all business people try to acquire more surplus value in order to increase their profit. Surplus value is, by definition, derived from labor. Thus we might expect capitalists to seek out labor-intensive production methods in order to maximize their profits. In fact, however, they continually strive to substitute capital for labor . . . In addition, capitalists generally seek to offset a falling rate of profit by lowering wages, imposing longer workdays, introducing child and female labor, and so forth. All this contributes to the absolute misery of the working class. (Ekelund and Hébert, pp.276-7)

Marx criticized political economy, which he saw as promoting capitalism. 'When, for example, it defines the relationship of wages to profit, it takes the interest of the capitalists to be the ultimate cause, i.e., it takes for granted what it is supposed to explain . . . The only wheels which political economy sets in motion are *greed* and the *war amongst the greedy – competition*.' (Manuscripts, pp.106-7; quoted from Ekelund and Hébert, 1990, pp.268-9)

Jevons on Anticipation and Uncertainty

A big step towards establishing economics as a science that was independent of philosophy and psychology was taken in the early 1870s when three treatises that developed marginal utility analysis were published (Jevons, 1871; Menger, 1871; Walras, 1874). The three authors had independently of each other elaborated the idea that product value was constituted by utility, not by amount or cost of work put into the product. Jevons (1835–82) presented a theory of utility that he expressed in mathematical terms. While Menger produced a theory that is interesting from a psychological point of view and will be treated under a separate heading, Walras does not appear to have contributed to the psychology of economic behavior or saving theory. Suffice it to say that he saw mathematics as the natural language of economics analogous to how it was used in mechanics, that he launched the important concept of equilibrium, and presented a highly elaborate definition of capital.

Whereas Smith and the Mills had contributed to the development of both psychology and economics, although in different contexts, Jevons's work was exclusively aimed at developing political economy as a science of its own. In the preface to his work he noted that some people had been thinking that economics had already acquired a nearly perfect form.

> I believe it is generally supposed that Adam Smith laid the foundations of this science; that Malthus, Anderson, and Senior added important doctrines; that Ricardo systematized the whole, and, finally, that Mr. J.S. Mill filled in the details and completely expounded this branch of knowledge. Mr. Mill appears to have had a similar notion . . . Yet, in the other sciences this weight of authority has not been allowed to restrict the free examination of new opinions and theorems; and it has often been ultimately proved that authority was on the wrong side. (Jevons [1871] 1911, Preface to The First Edition, p. V).

Jevons said he ventured to think that he could add something to political economy by introducing mathematics and ideas from physics. 'It is clear that Economics, if it is to be a science at all, must be a mathematical science' (Jevons [1871] 1911, p.3). True to the tradition from Bentham, Jevons treated political economy as a 'Calculus of Pleasure and Pain'. He suggested that the science should emulate physics and start with some fundamental principle. 'The nature of Wealth and Value is explained by the consideration of indefinitely small amounts of pleasure and pain, just as the theory of statics is made to rest upon the equality of indefinitely small amounts of energy (Jevons [1871] 1911, Preface). He cited Mill's assertion that 'an obvious psychological law' should be the foundation for economics. A suitable starting point was the fact that 'a greater gain is preferred to a smaller one'. From that Jevons continued 'we may then reason downwards, and predict the phenomena which will be produced in society by such a law'. (Jevons [1871] 1911, pp.16-17)

Jevons's approach involved the deductive use of mathematics to explore the consequences of a few fundamental assumptions and the use of statistical data to test hypotheses. This approach still characterizes economics albeit many economists have added much sophistication since then. It involved

> That every person will choose the greater apparent good; that human wants are more or less quickly satiated; that prolonged labour becomes more and more painful, are a few of the simple inductions on which we can proceed to reason deductively with great confidence. From these axioms we can deduce the laws of supply and demand, the laws of that difficult conception value, and all the intricate results of commerce, so far as data are available. The final agreement of our inferences with *a posteriori* observations ratifies our method. But unfortunately this verification is often the least satisfactory part of the process, because, as J.S. Mill has fully explained, the circumstances of a nation are infinitely complicated, and we seldom get two or more instances which are comparable. (Jevons [1871] 1911, p.18)

Jevons was not sure whether it was right to call the reasoning deductive since it usually started with some observation of reality. As he was very much in favor of using statistical data, he carefully pointed out that the results of the deductive reasoning should be compared with reality as represented by statistical data.

Using the idea that pleasure and pain could be represented by infinitesimal units, Jevons arrived at an important distinction between total utility and degree of utility (marginal utility). He used differential calculus to express the idea. He even dealt with the problem of measuring such mental phenomena.

> A unit of pleasure or of pain is difficult even to conceive; but it is the amount of these feelings which is continually prompting us to buying and selling, borrowing and lending, labouring and resting, producing and consuming; and *it is from the quantitative effects of the feelings that we must estimate their comparative amounts*. We can no more know nor measure gravity in its own nature than we can measure a feeling; but, just as we measure gravity by its effects in the motion of a pendulum, so we may estimate the equality or inequality of feelings by the decisions of the human mind. (Jevons, [1871] 1911, p.11)

Jevons came close to revealed preference theory, apparently inspired by the contemporary British psychologist Alexander Bain. 'As Mr. Bain says, "It is only an identical proposition to affirm that the greatest of two pleasures, or what appears such, sways the resulting action; for it is this resulting action that alone determines which is the greater".'

The emerging psychological science asserted that subjective experience could be measured. It was not necessary to rely on only revealed behavior as Jevons suggested. Edgeworth ([1881] 1967), an economist who is sometimes mentioned also in the history of psychology took up a critical scrutiny of Jevons's idea of economics as the science of pleasure and pain. He asked for numerical measurements for the mathematical reasoning to be meaningful and he contested Jevons's view that the utility of one person could not be compared with that of another. As a support for his contention that utility can be measured, Edgeworth cited Fechner, Bain and Wundt, all three of whom are classified as psychologists in the history of psychology. Edgeworth treated the Utilitarian Calculus of pleasure which was the basis for ethics as something separate from the Economical Calculus of Pleasure, which was the basis for economics. Earlier the two were treated as belonging together. Attempts are nowadays being made of bringing ethics and economics closer together again (e.g. Sen, 1987; Etzioni, 1988).

While Jevons in his theory of capital did not bestow any special attention on the problem of saving, his theory of utility contained some innovative ideas about intertemporal choice

> This power of anticipation must have a large influence in Economics; for upon it is based all accumulation of stocks of commodity to be consumed at a future time . . . We may safely call that man happy who, however lowly his position and limited his possessions, can always hope for more than he has, and can feel that every moment of exertion tends to realise his aspirations. He, on the contrary, who seizes the enjoyment of the passing moment without regard to coming times, must discover sooner or later that his stock of pleasure is on the wane, and that even hope begins to fail . . . In admitting the force of anticipated feeling, we are compelled to take account of the uncertainty of all future events. We ought never to estimate the value of that which may or may not happen as if it would certainly happen . . . If the probability is only one in ten that I shall have a certain day of pleasure, I ought to anticipate the pleasure with one-tenth of the force which would belong to it if certain. (Jevons [1871] 1911, pp.35-6)

Jevons had important things to say about utility over time. When a stock of commodities was to be expended over a certain period of time, the science of economics must point out the mode of consuming it to the greatest advantage, that is, with a maximum result of utility.

> To secure a maximum of benefit in life, all future events, all future pleasures or pains, should act upon us with the same force as if they were present, allowance being made for their uncertainty. The factor expressing the effect of remoteness should, in short, always be unity, so that time should have no influence. But no human being is constituted in this perfect way: a future feeling is always less influential than a present one. (Jevons [1871] 1911, p.72)

There were two reasons for counting with lower values for future goods; one was uncertainty (see above) and the second the human weakness to prefer present goods to future goods. Despite the uncertainty, anticipation could give pleasure. While Senior stressed the pains of considering the future, Jevons saw the present utility of anticipated pleasure.

> It is certain that a very large part of what we experience in life depends not on the actual circumstances of the moment so much as on the anticipation of future events. As Mr. Bain says, 'The foretaste of pleasure is pleasure begun: every actual delight casts before it a corresponding ideal'. (Jevons [1871] 1911, pp.33-4)

The economists used the notions of pleasure and pain without defining them. At about the same time, the psychologists went to great efforts to establish the true nature of feelings and emotions. Bain's theories influenced Jevons, but the work of the later experimental psychologists seemed to have little influence on economists, maybe because of a focus on physiological aspects. William James (1890) who became widely known for his comprehensive *The Principles of Psychology* is also known for his theory of feelings and emotions which was based on physiological assumptions and his own laboratory work (the James-Lange theory of emotions).

In this context, it is interesting to note what the psychologist Francis Galton wrote in an appreciative letter to Edgeworth in 1881 after having read a review of the latter's *Mathematical Psychics*, published by Jevons in the journal *Mind*: 'As regards a few details: – mixed modes of utilitarianism – I should have thought your view was the one to be formulated, so as to serve the entire range of cases, the value of a neighbour's happiness as compared to one's own being represented by a variable, = 0 in pure economics, = 1 in pure altruism.' (Quoted from back cover of *The Journal of Political Economy*, 1977, 85, No. 1). The psychologist Galton thus thought that economics had already at that time been completely divorced from ethics (cf. Sen, 1979).

Menger and the Hierarchy of Needs

The Austrian Carl Menger (1840–1921) used no mathematics. Like Jevons, he employed the subjective value of a commodity as the starting point for the discussion of price formation. Utility was not in the commodity, but in the relationship between the individual and the commodity. 'Emphasizing all-important *subjective* factors, Menger defended self-interest, utility maximization, and complete knowledge as the grounds upon which economics must be built. Aggregative, collective ideas could not have adequate foundation unless they rested upon individual components' (Ekelund and Hébert, 1990, p.323). Menger was heavily opposed by the Historical School, which rejected the emphasis on individual behavior and stressed the importance of dynamic institutions in society. .

Menger did not explicitly cite any psychologists, but was rather anxious to clarify which type of psychology was proper to the psychologists and which type to the economists. He declared that those economists, who were grappling with the causal contexts of goods and causal laws connected therewith, were mistaken about the task of economics. He meant that such tasks that related to the nature of objects were a matter for the natural sciences including psychology and that economists should deal with the meaning of goods to humans. 'We [the economists], on the contrary, have to deal with goods as means for human purposes, explore their context in the goal consciousness of the trading men (their teleological context) and establish their laws' (Menger [1871] 1923, p.21; my translation from the German original. I have not been able to find this footnote in the English translation of the book).

The basis for Menger's concept of marginal utility was the *need hierarchy*, which is pictured in Figure 3.1. The basic idea was that need groups could be ordered in terms of how demanding they were and that there were levels of satisfaction. The most demanding need group was the need for nourishment (I). When some satisfaction was given, the urgency of this need group diminished and another need group was attended to. Menger suggested that need group V could be the need for tobacco, which was attended to when the four higher need groups each had received a certain degree of satisfaction.

NEEDS ORDERED AFTER URGENCY

I	II	III	IV	V	VI	VII	VIII	IX	X
10	9	8	7	6	5	4	3	2	1
9	8	7	6	5	4	3	2	1	0
8	7	6	5	4	3	2	1	0	
7	6	5	4	3	2	1	0		
6	5	4	3	2	1	0			
5	4	3	2	1	0				
4	3	2	1	0					
3	2	1	0						
2	1	0							
1	0								

Figure 3.1 Menger's Hierarchy of Needs

Suppose that a person spends one DEM on the highest-ranking need (I) and gets 10 units of satisfaction. Spending another DEM in this category would give nine additional units and a third DEM would give eight units, altogether 27 units. If the person spent two DEM on the satisfactions of the first need group and one DEM on the second need group, s/he would get 28 units of satisfaction. This implies the principle of marginal thinking. The person is assumed to make comparisons at the margin to obtain maximum utility for scarce means.

Although Menger's marginal utility theory was not the only one, it made an important contribution to developing utility theory by focusing on new aspects. One implication of Menger's utility theory was opportunity cost, the value you forego by not choosing another alternative. If you spend your money now and do not save, the opportunity cost is what you could have acquired for the money in the future (discounted to its present value, to make the comparison fair).

Maslow (1954) much later conceived a need theory that is similar to that of Menger. While Maslow's need hierarchy has received a lot, according to some critics undeserved, attention, especially in social psychology, it has not inspired the same type of quantitative precision as the theory of marginally diminishing utility. It is said that some Austrian psychologists were inspired by Menger's marginal utility theory to use the ideas in their study of religious behavior (Schumpeter, 1954).

Böhm-Bawerk on the Psychology of Saving

Another non-mathematical approach to economics was presented by the Austrian economist Böhm-Bawerk (1851–1914) who was critical of Jevons's use of psychology and his attempts at quantification of subjective concepts. Böhm-Bawerk dealt thoroughly with the motives for capital accumulation and for the rate of interest. He was particularly engrossed in the question why there was interest on capital and what determined a certain interest rate. He formulated a kind of psychological theory which came to be known as the *impatience theory of saving* (Fisher, 1930).

The basic assumption was that people preferred a good here and now to goods in the future and that they demanded a compensation for abstaining from the good now. 'Present goods are as a rule more highly valued than future goods of the same kind and number' (Böhm-Bawerk [1888] 1912, p.426). From this fact, the phenomenon of interest rate in all its shapes was explained. To compensate for the difference in value between now and later, the individual asked for interest, by Böhm-Bawerk neutrally called 'agio'. The explanation of the interest on capital was simply the influence of time on human evaluation of goods. While Adam Smith and later classical econo-mists had also noted this phenomenon, Böhm-Bawerk dealt in detail with the demographic and psychological factors that affected this behavior.

Böhm-Bawerk propounded that there were three circumstances behind the constant undervaluation of future goods:

1.   Erroneous beliefs due to lacking imagination and ability to understand

2. Weakness in will, making people choose a smaller utility now before a larger utility later
3. Uncertainty about the future.

Böhm-Bawerk brought something new and original to the discussion of what was earlier described as present indulgence or enjoyment and now is often called 'myopic' behavior. The first factor was imperfect information which he expressed in terms similar to what is now called 'limited cognitive capacity'. The second factor involved problems of will, which now would be called motivation or self-control. Böhm-Bawerk hinted that professional psychologists might not make that distinction and treat the two reasons as one. The lacking willpower could possibly be explained by the fact that the future good was less vividly imagined than the present good and therefore had less influence than it deserved (Böhm-Bawerk [1888] 1912, pp.447-8; cf. Rae above). Overall, Böhm-Bawerk seems to have been cognitive rather than motivational in his approach to human behavior, albeit he often talked about 'weakness of will' (Willensfehler). Loewenstein (1992, p.14) suggested that Böhm-Bawerk's cognitive theory was close to what Tversky and Kahneman (1982) called 'availability'.

The third factor was the degree of uncertainty about the future and the brevity of life. Böhm-Bawerk gave an example

> A utility of 100 with a probability of 50 percent that we do not experience it, we certainly estimate differently than a present utility of 100, but rather like one of 50, and I am convinced that every one of us who is promised a birthday present of 100,000 florins for the 100th birthday, would be willing to exchange this large, but somewhat uncertain gift for a much smaller fraction of it in present goods. (Böhm-Bawerk [1888] 1912, p.448; my translation)

Like many other economists of his time Böhm-Bawerk saw economics as based on psychological underpinnings. He thought those had to be understood by economists to enable them to develop economic theory. Here is an example of his fundamental ideas about economic behavior

> Humans strive for happiness. This is the most common, although also vaguest expression for a multitude of strivings, all of which have the aim of promoting such events and circumstances that are as pleasant as possible to our feelings and emotions and avert those that are unpleasant. If one wants to change the words, one can say instead of 'Striving for Happiness' also 'Striving for Self-Composure and Self-Development', or 'Striving for as much Life Enhancement as Possible', or just as well, also, 'Striving for as complete Need Satisfaction as Possible'. (Böhm-Bawerk [1888] 1912, p.6; my translation)

Böhm-Bawerk was actually apologetic because he so much depended on psychological thinking in developing his theory of capital and interest. He made the observation that psychologists were looking for more general behavioral goals and that the finer details of economic behavior might escape the psychologists while the economists had become more aware of such things and thus could rely on their own observations.

In the third edition of his book on capital theory, Böhm-Bawerk wrote a long, psychological afterword to the theory of value where he discussed the role of psychology in economics. He said that psychological thinking was necessary to develop the theory of value of goods. Mostly, he had to rely on everyday observation since professional psychologists had not devoted any attention to the problems. He discussed the problems connected with crossing borders between sciences and stated his reasons for doing so, among them the fact that some economists had introduced dilettantish psychology into economics. One of those thus referred to was Jevons. The main argument against the latter was apparently that he had said that subjective feelings could not be directly measured, but must be replaced by objective measures (similar to revealed preferences) that could be treated with statistics and mathematics. Böhm-Bawerk consequently attempted to show that the amount of feeling ('Fühlungsgrösse') could be subjectively estimated.

It is said that Böhm-Bawerk's work influenced the Austrian act psychologists who later reached fame as Gestalt psychologists (Endres, 1987). Their opposition against the elementism and atomism that characterized experimental psychology had some similarities with what Böhm-Bawerk asserted about the contemporary psychologists in his book on capital.

NEOCLASSICAL ECONOMISTS

Alfred Marshall – Who Wished He Had Been a Psychologist

Thus it [Economics] is on the one side a study of wealth; and on the other, and more important side, a part of the study of man. For man's character has been moulded by his every-day work, and the material resources which he thereby procures, more than by any other influence unless it be that of his religious ideals; and the two great forming agencies of the world's history have been the religious and the economic.
Marshall ([1890] 1990, p.1)

The founding father of neoclassical economics, Alfred Marshall (1842–1924), devoted great interest to psychological problems although he rarely used the word psychology. He entitled Book III (there were six) in his *Principles of Economics* 'On Wants and Their Satisfaction.' He wrote

Reckoning is made for the greater force measured by a shilling in the case of a poor man than a rich: but economics seeks generally for broad results that are little affected by individual peculiarities . . . Habit itself is largely based on deliberate choice . . . Economic motives are not exclusively selfish. The desire for money does not exclude other influences; and may itself arise from noble motives. ([1890] 1990, pp.XVII in Contents)

Although Marshall made economic theory more mathematical, he carefully avoided mathematics in his main text and relegated diagrams and formulas to footnotes and appendixes. This makes his book *Principles of Economics* readable to a wider audience.

Marshall dealt with what he called 'deferred pleasure'. Like Jevons and Böhm-Bawerk, he noted that there was uncertainty involved in deferring utility, but he was more explicit about a second factor affecting postponement of consumption, the subjective treatment of remoteness.

> A prudent person will endeavour to distribute his means between all their several uses, present and future, in such a way that they will have in each the same marginal utility. But in estimating the present marginal utility of a distant source of pleasure a twofold allowance must be made; firstly, for its uncertainty (this is an *objective* property which all well-informed persons would estimate in the same way); and secondly, for the difference in the value to them of a distant as compared with a present pleasure (this is a *subjective* property which different people would estimate in different ways according to their individual characters, and their circumstances at the time). (Marshall [1890] 1990, p.100)

A discount was therefore made even when the future good was certain

> in fact human nature is so constructed that in estimating 'the present value' of a future benefit most people generally make a second deduction from its future value, in the form of what we may call a 'discount', that increases with the period for which the benefit is deferred. (Marshall [1890] 1990, p.100)

The discount rate varied over people and circumstances and it was important for how much was consumed or saved.

> The rates at which different people discount the future affect not only their tendency to save, as the term is ordinarily understood, but also their tendency to buy things which will be a lasting source of pleasure rather than those which give a stronger but more transient enjoyment; to buy a new coat rather than to indulge in a drinking bout, or to choose simple furniture that will wear well, rather than showy furniture that will soon fall to pieces. (Marshall [1890] 1990, pp.100-1)

The preference for present goods could be very strong

> Cases are not rare of men who alternate between earning two or three pounds a week and being reduced to the verge of starvation: the utility of a shilling to them when they are in employment is less than that of a penny when they are out of it, and yet they never attempt to make provision for the time of need.

In a footnote he added: 'They "discount" the future benefits . . . at the rate of many thousands per cent per annum' (Marshall [1890] 1990, p.187).

Marshall emphasized the cognitive aspects of the motivational forces. Talking about the definition of interest (as a reward for waiting), he said that the accumulation of wealth was dependent on man's *prospectiveness*, that is, her/his faculty of realizing the future. This quality in a person made it possible to resist the vivid exposure to present goods which Rae and Böhm-Bawerk mentioned. The growth of wealth 'involves in general a deliberate waiting for a pleasure which a person has (rightly or wrongly) the power of commanding in the immediate present, and that his willingness so to wait depends on his habit of vividly realizing the future and providing for it' (Marshall [1890] 1990, p.233).

Marshall presented a number of reasons for saving. He asserted that most saving arose out of family affection. This involved saving money for the well being of the family both before and after one's death.

> That men labour and save chiefly for the sake of their families and not for themselves, is shown by the fact that they seldom spend, after they have retired from work, more than the income that comes in from their savings, preferring to leave their stored-up wealth intact for their families; while in this country alone twenty millions a year are saved in the form of insurance policies and are available only after the death of those who save them. (Marshall [1890] 1990, pp.189-90)

Mandeville had seen frugality in a nation as something arising out of necessity and not as a virtue at all. Smith had seen frugality as a characteristic that was more or less part of human nature and effective under most circumstances. Marshall's views were similar to those of Mandeville. Frugality arose out of necessity, but could continue as a commendable individual habit when it was no longer necessary to save to the same extent.

> The greatest savings are made by those who have been brought up on narrow means to stern hard work, who have retained their simple habits, in spite of success in business, and who nourish a contempt for showy expenditure and desire to be found at their death richer than they had been thought to be. (Marshall [1890]1990, p.190)

According to Marshall, many people found it important to provide for the future when they could no longer earn enough income. They reasoned that the extra gratification they could get from spending the money now was smaller than the comfort they could get from the same amount when they had retired from active life. They could even be willing to pay something for the certainty of having such means in their old age. This meant that a negative interest rate could be possible. (Marshall [1890] 1990, pp.192f)

Marshall also pointed out a factor that inhibited saving, namely, the possible insecurity of money saved

> The thriftlessness of early times was in a great measure due to the want of security that those who made provision for the future would enjoy it: only those who were already wealthy were strong enough to hold what they had saved; the laborious and self-denying peasant who had heaped up a little store of wealth only to see it taken from him by a stronger hand, was a constant warning to his neighbours to enjoy their pleasure and their rest when they could. (Marshall [1890] 1990, p.187-8)

Some people took special pleasure in amassing wealth. They did not save for the future enjoyment they could get out of their wealth. To some, the following may sound like a description of certain types of investors who have been active in recent years and especially in the late 1980s.

> They are prompted partly by the instincts of the chase, by the desire to outstrip their rivals, by the ambition to have shown ability in getting the wealth, and to acquire power and social position by its possession. And sometimes the force of habit, started when they were really in need of money, has given them, by a sort of reflex action, an artificial and unreasoning pleasure in amassing wealth for its own sake. (Marshall [1890] 1990, p.189)

Fisher's Impatience to Spend Income vs. Opportunity to Invest

> *He proceeded from dependence on his wife's wealth to maintain his household to a millionaire on his own whose optimism about the future knew no limits. Despite his financial success, by at the end of the 1920's he faced, along with the rest of the country, economic ruin.*
>
> Allen (1993, p.178)

Böhm-Bawerk was for some time minister of finance in Austria, something that probably contributed to his perception of the world. Fisher (1867–1947) was an American economist who for some time was a multi-millionaire, but who died with a large debt after unlucky investments. Fisher had great influence on the theory of saving through his work on interest rates and time preferences. The latter will be treated in the next chapter. Fisher's (1930) book had the full title of: 'The Theory of Interest. As Determined by IMPATIENCE to Spend Income and OPPORTUNITY to Invest It.' It was a thoroughly revised edition of a volume first published in 1907.

The book was introduced with a chapter that explained Fisher's view on income and capital. Income was in his view a series of events. 'For each individual only those events which come within the purview of his experience are of direct concern. It is these events – the psychic experiences of the individual mind – which constitute ultimate income for that individual' (Fisher, 1930, p.4). He proceeded to label such income 'enjoyment or psychic income'. 'Money is of no use to us until it is spent. The ultimate wages are not paid in terms of money but in the enjoyment it buys. The dividend check becomes income in the ultimate sense only when we eat the food, wear the clothes, or ride in the automobile which are bought with the check' (Fisher, 1930, p.5).

Enjoyment income is a psychological entity and cannot be measured, but can indirectly be approximated through the *real income*. The latter 'consists of those physical events in the outer world which give us our *inner* enjoyments' (p.6). A variety of events are included in the real income, for example, the shelter of a house, the use of clothes, the earning of food, and the reading of a newspaper. The only way real income can be measured is to measure the money the individual paid to get them. Fisher thus arrived at the cost of living as a measure of real income and as an indirect assessment of enjoyment income.

A third income was then added, *money income*, 'consisting of the money received by a man for meeting his costs of living' (Fisher, 1930, p.11). Money income was usually meant when the concept of income was used, but the enjoyment income was the most fundamental.

The distinction between enjoyment income and money income means that a difference is made between a hedonic income concept that is close to the one used by utilitarians and a pure economic concept with objective indicators. Studying the former is apparently the task of the psychologist who at least today can rely on subjective scales that have been developed after Fisher wrote his book. The link to hedonism is reflected in recent discussions of the psychology of utility. Kahneman (Kahneman and Varey, 1991; Kahneman, 1994) has in various contexts discussed the idea of two fundamentally different concepts of utility. One type of utility is close to the hedonic utility that Bentham and the two Mills talked about. Kahneman calls it *experience or hedonic utility*. It is related to Fisher's enjoyment income. The second type of utility is the utility revealed in actual choices among objects, i.e., revealed preferences, and is labeled *preference utility*. Kahneman pointed out important consequences of the differences between the two types of utility.

Fisher (1930, p.12) also defined capital: 'Capital, in the sense of capital *value*, is simply future income discounted or, in other words, capitalized. The value of any property, or rights to wealth, is its value *as a source of income* and is found by discounting that expected income.' He noted that savings increased capital value, the income being decreased by the same amount as the capital was increased. 'These savings thus diverted from income and turned back into capital will, except for mischance, be the basis for real income later' (Fisher, 1930, pp.28-9).

Fisher accepted Böhm-Bawerk's arguments about impatience. The degree of impatience affected the utility of future goods and was thus important for the rate of interest that the individual was supposed to calculate with. An individual's impatience to spend or time preference depended on four characteristics of his income stream (Fisher, 1930, p.65).

1. The size of an individual's expected real income stream
2. Its expected distribution in time; whether it was constant, increasing, or decreasing
3. Its composition – to what extent it consists of nourishment, of shelter, of amusement, of education, and so on (cf. mental accounts with different consumption propensities)
4. Its probability, or degree of risk or uncertainty.

The effects of these characteristics were not the same for every person. A number of personal factors operated in addition to the income factors. Like Senior, Jevons and Böhm-Bawerk, Fisher had the opinion that certain population groups were more impatient to spend than others. Low age, low income and low social class were characteristics of such groups. He believed that the degree of impatience varied between people and that it varied over time for one and the same individual. There was a typical development in the degree of impatience from childhood to old age, but there could also be abrupt conversions from spendthrift to thrift and vice versa. Six personal characteristics made the impatience to spend greater: (1) short-sightedness, (2) a weak will (the lack of self-control), (3) the habit of spending freely, (4) emphasis upon the shortness and uncertainty of life, (5) selfishness or the absence of any desire to provide for survivors, (6) slavish following of the whims of fashion.

The factors that decreased impatience to spend were the reverse of the above-mentioned: (1) a high degree of foresight, 'which enables him to give to the future such attention as it deserves'; (2) a high degree of self-control, 'which enables him to abstain from present real income in order to increase future real income'; (3) the habit of thrift; (4) emphasis upon the expectation of a long life; (5) the possession of a family and a high regard for its welfare after one's death; (6) the independence 'to maintain a proper balance between outgo and income, regardless of Mrs. Grundy and the high-powered salesmen of devices that are useless or harmful, or which commit the purchaser beyond his income prospects' (Fisher, 1930, p.89).

Fisher made a distinction between foresight and self-control similar to that of Böhm-Bawerk. 'Foresight has to do with *thinking*; self-control, with *willing*. Though a weak will usually goes with a weak intellect, this is not necessarily so, nor always. The effect of a weak will is similar to the effect of inferior foresight' (Fisher, p.83).

According to Fisher (1930, pp.504-5), the causes leading to high impatience could be influenced through training that gave insight into the need for providing 'for the proverbial rainy day' and for self-control. It meant building up habits of thriftiness, providing incentives for taking better care of children and future generations, and, finally, but not least, modification of fashion in favor of less ostentatious and harmful expenditures for lavish living. Caring for the family was to Fisher one of the important reasons for saving money, but he did not emphasize it as strongly as Marshall did.

Fisher generalized his observations of individual characteristics to whole nations, aggregating individual to national characteristics

> Where, as in Scotland, there are educational tendencies which instill the habit of thrift from childhood, the rate of interest tends to be low. Where, as in ancient Rome, at the time of its decline, there is a tendency toward reckless luxury, competition in ostentation, and degeneration in the bonds of family life, there is a consequent absence of any desire to prolong income beyond one's own term of life, and the rate of interest tends to be high. (Fisher, 1930, p.504)

The dominating theories of saving are developments of ideas that derive from Fisher's theory of intertemporal choice. Fisher noted that time preference was similar to what Rae called 'the effective desire for accumulation' and Böhm-Bawerk thought of as the tendency towards undervaluation of the future. 'All preference, therefore, for present over future goods resolves itself, in the last analysis, into a preference for early enjoyment income over deferred enjoyment income' (Fisher, 1930, p.65). Fisher devised ways of estimating time preferences through discount functions and 'impatience schedules' that were similar to the methods nowadays used in surveys to assess time preferences.

Pigou and Welfare Economics

Pigou who is known for his contributions to welfare economics, broadly defined economic welfare as that group of satisfactions and dissatisfactions that can be brought into relation with a money measure. This relation was not a direct one, but was mediated through desires and aversions. He recognized the importance of factors intervening between economic stimuli and reactions. 'In other words, the effects of economic causes are certain to be partially dependent on non-economic circumstances, in such wise that the same cause will produce somewhat different economic effects according to the general character of, say, the political or religious conditions that prevail' (Pigou [1920] 1952, p.21). This situation forced economists always to add 'other things being equal' (ceteris paribus).

Pigou made an interesting, somewhat puzzling psychological distinction, 'the money which a person is prepared to offer for a thing measures directly, not the satisfaction he will get from the thing, but the intensity of his desire for it' (Pigou [1920] 1952, p.23) He complained that the use of the term utility which naturally carried an association with satisfaction was also used to represent intensity of desire. The idea sounds similar to subjective expected utility, but the exact role of intensity of desire is not quite clear. Pigou said that his distinction was especially important when attitudes towards the future were involved. He had some doubts about people's willingness to abstain from consuming now because of the higher intensity of present desires.

> Generally speaking, everybody prefers present pleasures or satisfactions of given magnitude to future pleasures or satisfactions of equal magnitude, even when the latter are perfectly certain to occur. But this preference for present pleasures does not – the idea is self-contradictory – imply that a present pleasure of given magnitude is any *greater* than a future pleasure of the same magnitude. It implies only that our telescopic faculty is defective, and that we, therefore, see future pleasures, as it were, on a diminished scale. (Pigou [1920] 1952, pp.24-5)

The notion of a defective telescopic faculty is a metaphor that has been much cited. Pigou elaborated

> Hence there is nothing to set against the fact that, if we set out a series of exactly equal satisfactions – *satisfactions*, not objects that yield satisfactions – all of them absolutely certain to occur over a series of years beginning now, the desires which a man will entertain for these several satisfactions will not be equal, but will be represented by a scale of magnitudes continually diminishing as the years to which the satisfactions are allocated become more remote . . . When they [people] have a choice between two satisfactions, they will not necessarily choose the larger of the two, but will often devote themselves to producing or obtaining a small one now in preference to a much larger one some years hence. The inevitable result is that efforts directed towards the remote future are starved relatively to those directed to the near future, while these in turn are starved relatively to efforts directed towards the present. (Pigou [1920] 1952, p.25)

The defective telescopic faculty could cause large errors. 'It follows that the aggregate amount of economic satisfaction which people in fact enjoy is much less than it would be if their telescopic faculty were not perverted, but equal (certain) satisfactions were desired with equal intensity whatever the period at which they are destined to emerge' (Pigou [1920] 1952, p.26). Another reason for the low valuation of future consumption was the fact that life expectancy was limited. The person to whose efforts the utility was due did not always enjoy such fruits of work or saving as accrued after a considerable interval.

> It follows that, even though our desires for equal satisfactions *of our own* occurring at different times were equal, our desire for future satisfaction would often be less intense than for present satisfaction, because it is very likely that the future satisfaction will not be our own. This discrepancy will be more important the more distant is the time at which the source of future satisfaction is likely to come into being; for every addition to the interval increases the chance of death, not merely

> to oneself, but also to children and near relatives and friends in whom one's inter-
> est is likely to be most keen. (Pigou [1920] 1952, p.26)

Pigou did not necessarily mean that there was no bequest motive for trying to keep one's wealth, rather that the value of future goods decreased very rapidly for long time intervals. In a footnote, he argued that the future value of one pound to oneself or to one's heirs could be equally persuasive for investment.

Like J.S. Mill, Pigou was concerned that taxes could affect saving.

> all taxes which differentiate against saving, as compared with spending, must
> diminish welfare. Even without differentiation there will be too little saving. Prop-
> erty taxes, where they exist, and death duties, obviously differentiate against sav-
> ing. The English income tax, though it appears to be neutral, in fact, as is shown
> elsewhere, also does this. (Pigou [1920] 1952, pp.28-9)

Too much accumulation of wealth on the part of some people may, however, make it desirable to accept from the government some differentiation against savings. Pigou already in his preface noted that one of the objectives of economics was to make it possible to reduce unfair distribution.

Pigou pointed out an obvious, but rarely recognized possible causal link between savings and the protection of environment and natural resources. He emphasized the link between nature's exhaustible resources and provision for the future. People tended, because of intense desires, to use up exhaustible stores more quickly than was consistent with the general interest. Governments had the responsibility to protect the interests of future generations. (Pigou [1920] 1952, pp.28-30)

A NEGLECTED DIMENSION – WHAT DOES SAVING MEAN TO THE INDIVIDUAL?

Industriousness and thrift were virtues. This implied that the appropriate be-havior was more or less of a duty and the reward for the individual was in the first place a good conscience. Classical economists considered what was good for society even though their analysis often started with the individual. Saving was important because it was good for economic growth and conse-quently for society. What was good for a nation was also good for the citizen. To a psychologist, an obvious additional question concerns what good saving does to the individual and the household and what ill no saving means to in-dividual welfare. Kahneman's (1994) appeal that more interest should be devoted to the difference between experience utility and preference utility is highly relevant in this context. What is the experience utility of saving for different individuals?

Many economists struck a moral note when they discussed individual savings. Beside economists, many other writers extolled the duty of saving and for many years paid little attention to the hedonic consequences of saving or of non-saving. Two educators are worthy of notice because they focused on the individual's wellbeing: Benjamin Franklin and Samuel Smiles.

Benjamin Franklin (1706–90) wrote *Advice to a Young Tradesman* which by Max Weber was considered as a manifesto of modern capitalism and included almost in its entirety in his book *The Protestant Ethic and the Spirit of Capitalism*. Franklin published a number of newspaper columns in which he tried to enlighten and educate the public, using the pseudonym Poor Richard. Those were later published as *Poor Richard's Almanack* and as the collection *The Way to Wealth*. In many ways they were a collection of proverbs and maxims: 'If you know how to spend less than you get, you have the philosopher's stone.' 'If you would be wealthy, think of Saving as well as of Getting.' 'Rather go to Bed supperless than rise in Debt.' (Baida, 1990, pp.24-5) In his columns, Franklin sometimes provided tables to prove how much saved money grew and the saver gained over time with compounded interest.

Saving had earlier been promoted with arguments that saving was good for societal reasons and for religious reasons. With Franklin the notion that saving was good for the individual started to spread. This was consonant with the ideas of the Enlightenment, which cherished the idea of man's intrinsic power of self-development. Industriousness meant never to do something useless and thrift was never to spend money on anything that was of no good to oneself or anybody else.

Smiles (1812–1904) who was born in Scotland wrote a book about thrift (Smiles, 1875) in which he praised saving. In the earlier book *Self-Help* he emphasized the importance of exerting willpower in one's life. He also devoted much space to thrift and saving (Smiles [1859] 1969). 'It is *will* – force of purpose – that enables a man to do or be whatever he sets his mind on being or doing' (Smiles, 1859, p.230). 'Hence the lesson of self-denial – the sacrificing of a present gratification for a future good – is one of the last that is learnt.' (p.282)

> Economy, at bottom, is but the spirit of order applied in the administration of domestic affairs: it means management, regularity, prudence, and the avoidance of waste . . . Economy also means the power of resisting present gratification for the purpose of securing a future good, and in this light it represents the ascendancy of reason over the animal instincts. It is altogether different from penuriousness: for it is economy that can always best afford to be generous. It does not make money an idol, but regards it as a useful agent. (Smiles [1859] 1969, p.286)

Savings banks were first established towards the end of the 18th century. The stated purpose was to encourage small savers who were left out by the commercial banks to save small amounts regularly and have security for their savings. An important argument was that the small savers could gain from the interest paid on their savings accounts. The purpose of providing loans to small farmers who wanted to improve their farms was later added. There were upper limits to how much could be saved in a savings account. In the early 19th century, the problem of taking care of the poor elderly factory workers arose. This became an important motive for encouraging saving among low-income earners and was another argument for opening savings banks where even small sums of money could be deposited or borrowed.

Early advertising for savings banks tended to dramatize reasons why savings were important and good for people who saved. Drinking habits were frequently pictured as a major obstacle to saving money. There was often an admonition in the advertising appeals: if you do not save money, ill consequences will strike you. The happy destinies of people who saved money were compared with the misfortunes of people who did not save. In modern welfare societies in which there is a desire to stimulate saving through information or advertising campaigns, it is hardly possible any more to use such themes. It is not seen as legitimate to scare people for such purposes.

WHAT CAN WE LEARN FROM THE EARLY ECONO-MISTS ABOUT THE PSYCHOLOGY OF SAVING?

The following are typical measures of rational economic action:
(1) The systematic allocation as between present and future of utilities, on the control of which the actor for whatever reason feels able to count. (These are the essential features of saving.)
(2) The systematic allocation of available utilities to various potential uses in the order of their estimated relative urgency, ranked according to the principle of marginal utility.(3) . . . (4)

Weber (1968, p.71)

The fact that, in economics, saving is seen as rational behavior has not kept economists from launching additional psychological explanations, some of which seem difficult to combine with the maximization of economic utility. What there is of a psychology of saving is in fact mostly found in texts authored by classical and neoclassical economists. While classical and neo-classical economists from Malthus up to Keynes put much emphasis on the willingness to spend, with Keynes the main and sole focus became ability to spend, at first current income, later past income, and now, predominantly, future income. The psychological insights of earlier economists were converted into mathematics or disappeared altogether.

In the 1950s, willingness to spend was brought back into focus through survey research, carried out by George Katona. His economic-psychological model of saving assumed that savings depended on both ability and willingness to consume/save and that both could be measured. Malthus said that effectual demand consisted of two elements, the power to purchase which was tantamount to total income and the will to purchase. He concluded: 'I by no means think that the power to purchase necessarily involves a proportionate will to purchase' (Malthus, Works, VI, pp.131-2; quoted from Ekelund and Hébert, 1990, pp.156-7). Katona showed that the will to purchase could be assessed through interview surveys. Survey research on saving owes much to his work. In today's economic-psychological research, the willingness to consume/save comprises an increasing number of psychological variables as will be demonstrated in Chapter 5.

Here I shall briefly summarize major ideas or concepts that appeared in the discussions of saving and briefly comment on them. In Chapter 8, I shall put a number of the psychological concepts into a framework, which is aimed at integrating the concepts, and suggesting models for psychological research on the psychology of saving.

The most important psychological insights to take back from the brief historical review are:

1. The prevalent desire for effective accumulation and improvement
2. The assumed importance of thrift and thrifty habits
3. Self-control and willpower as determinants of thrift
4. Uncertainty of (about) the future and the role of expectations
5. Selective perception and limited cognitive capacity
6. Time horizon or attitude towards the future.

The desire for *effective accumulation* (Rae's expression) and *improvement* was accepted as a general characteristic of all humans. The essence of rationality is that people prefer more to less of something attractive (unless there are special circumstances). Mostly, it was assumed that there was a limit to the fulfillment of this desire. Men were either by nature generous to others when they had enough resources or they should feel an ethical and moral obligation to be so. Maximization of the desire of accumulation was no longer permissible when a person had resources enough for her/his own enjoyment (cf. Aristotle and Cicero). Even Marshall condemned those who saved money for the sake of accumulating wealth and did not think of their enjoyment.

Given that everybody had the desire for accumulation and betterment, differences among people were explained as due to differences in *thrift*, which was often, for example, by Adam Smith and Senior, combined with industriousness. Thrift had to do with willingness and industriousness with creating ability to save. The most common assumption was that 'thrift' was the main psychological factor. The roots of thrift were sought in characteristics such as age, income, wealth and education, but also in deep-rooted personality factors. The latter could be changed by situational factors (Fisher, 1930). Thrift was inculcated early in life. Such inculcation was more common in certain countries and in certain socioeconomic groups.

Although, unwittingly, people could always have some savings in the form of tools and other property, most savings depended on conscious attempts to make provision for the future. Even with a pervasive desire of accumulation some people did not save. *Insufficient willpower and lack of self-control* were held to be important explanations of deficiencies in individual thrift. These concepts lived on in economic discussions, but not in psychology. After William James's (1890) thorough treatment of the concept of will, new trends in psychology dispensed completely with the concept of will and it was banished for many years in the dominating schools of thought.

The future was uncertain and the more distant the future, the more uncertain it was. In making provisions for the future the individual had to take *uncertainty* into account. The relationship between uncertainty and saving was not simple. Some uncertainty made it seem meaningless to save. Other uncertainty made it imperative to save. Apparently, the degree of uncertainty could play a role for saving. Expectations which were also called anticipations always contained uncertainty.

Some economists pointed out the importance of imagining the future, the value of what now could be called perceiving the needs of the future and formation of expectations. Without *perception of the future needs* there would be little provision for the future. Böhm-Bawerk who spent extra time on dealing with perception and cognition suggested that perceptual and cognitive limitations were important explanatory factors for the prevalent tendency to undervalue the future. Marshall called attention to the importance of prospectiveness, which he defined as the ability to visualize the future in a vivid manner.

Time horizon may not have been used as a concept, but many discussions of intertemporal choice stressed the importance of the idea. It was often connected to life expectancy. People who did not expect to live long had little reason to be thrifty and save money. Money was in the first place saved by the already wealthy since they had a longer life expectancy. Besides, their time horizon did not stop with their own death, but encompassed their survivors. Already Adam Smith recognized that concern about the future decreased with increasing distance in time. Fisher suggested rate of *time preference* as a way of measuring time horizon by means of discount rates. To him, time preference was equivalent to the more psychological concept of impatience.

Today's economists who want to penetrate the field of saving in a deeper way have to go back to classical and early neoclassical economists to find the psychology that was lost. In the meantime psychologists have elaborated and sharpened their thinking on the psychological phenomena that occupied these economists and have, furthermore, developed methods for measuring the concepts in economic reality. Cognitive psychology has meant a major breakthrough and developments in social psychology also contribute to making psychology useful in the study of economic problems like saving. Even the banished concept of will is on its way back into acceptability, often under the cover name of volition or self-regulation (see Sjöberg et al., 1998).

4. The Psychology of Saving in Modern Economic Theories of Saving

THE DISCOUNTED UTILITY MODEL

The utility theory and its derivatives are supposed to take into account the important factors in consumer behavior. Anyone who insists on bringing in other elements can easily be regarded as a naïve realist in the same class with those people who argue from particular instances which contradict statistical results.

Duesenberry (1949, p.15)

In economics, the consumer is postulated to make choices between consuming and saving. Consumption is primary in the sense that savings are defined as what is left after consumption. Consumer choice is by assumption based on a utility function that has certain specified characteristics such as concavity upwards, which involves risk aversion. Rationality means that the consumer maximizes utility subject to the budget constraint, which sets a limit to how much can be spent. While everyday observation as well as behavioral research may throw some doubts on the realism of these assumptions, those are fundamental to economic analysis. The assumptions have their strength in being good for normative purposes. They are not a good description of how choices are made and are not intended to be descriptive of individuals.

Consumer choice that involves more than one period, 'intertemporal choice', is also based on utility functions. The utility function comprises current and future consumption. The latter is discounted to the present to be comparable to the present one. The 'discounted utility model' (DU) involves that what one gets in the future is less valued now than it will be later. It is assumed that the future value is divided by the market interest rate and that this discounted value is compared with the current value of the alternative.

All economic theories of saving are based on some form of the discounted utility model. Up to a point, it has served quite well since the theories have been able to explain saving and consumption in many contexts. The leading saving theories, the Life-Cycle Hypothesis (LCH) and the Permanent Income Hypothesis (PIH) have faced criticism for failure to explain important parts of modern savings. While suggestions for additions to the theories usually mean that the basic utility functions are provided with new components, the fundamental character of the functions has not changed. More will be said about this in Chapter 8.

Paul Samuelson formulated the definitive discounted utility model in 1937. Loewenstein (1992, pp.3-5) distinguished between four stages in its evolution. He presented a historical review of the economics of intertemporal choice which, at the same time, is the story of the stages that represent changing relationships between economics and psychology.

Senior (1836) and Jevons (1871) dominated the first stage. Both of them dealt with motivational factors and emphasized emotional and/or hedonic influences on behavior. Senior saw abstinence as highly painful and commented that abstinence was characteristic of the most civilized nations and the best-educated classes. Jevons based his discussion of utility on Bentham's principle of propinquity or remoteness and had a more elaborate view of the utility of future goods. He stressed that the value of a future good depended on its probability since the future was uncertain. He pointed out that anticipation of a future good gave pleasure. The present value of a future good should be affected by uncertainty, but in principle not by any other factors. He distinguished between what was normatively right and what was descriptive of reality. All future pleasures or pains should act with the same force as if they were present. 'But no human mind is constituted in this perfect way: a future feeling is always less influential than a present one' (Jevons [1871] 1911, p.72).

While Jevons did not suggest a discounting factor, he hinted that such a factor was necessary for a good description of actual behavior. Marshall (1890) explicitly mentioned two reasons for discounting the value of a future good or event. One had to do with uncertainty and was assumed to be objective and not differ among consumers. The other was subjective and depended on personal characteristics such as amount of self-control.

In the second stage, Böhm-Bawerk and later Fisher dominated. They represented a more cognitive approach to intertemporal choice, although both of them used personality concepts such as willpower and self-control. The former laid the foundation of modern time preference theory through his treatment of the relations between present value and future value of capital. His main principle stated that humans consistently undervalued the future wants and also the means, which served to satisfy them. Fisher translated Böhm-Bawerk's main idea into more precise, quantitative terms and devised methods of measuring time preferences (see below).

The third stage was characterized by attempts to eliminate psychology from the economics of intertemporal choice – and, in fact, from all of economics.

The psychological richness that characterized early discussions of intertemporal choice was supplanted by mathematical and graphical analyses that seemed to render psychology superfluous. Psychological concepts reflecting motivational and cognitive influences – *willpower* and *motivation* – gave way to nonevocative terms such as *time preference* that were deliberately agnostic about underlying causes. (Loewenstein, 1992, p.4)

The fourth stage comprises the last few decades and involves a new interest in psychology by economists. Loewenstein refers to the use of findings and methods in the new cognitive psychology and the field of decision-making studies that are nowadays a common interest among economic and psychological researchers. At the end of his interesting review, he compared the assumptions that the early economists made with present-day research and concluded that those were often surprisingly right.

TIME PREFERENCE ACCORDING TO FISHER

The dominating theories of saving are developments of ideas that derive from Fisher's theory of intertemporal choice. Fisher noted that impatience, which he used as a synonym to time preference, was related to what Rae called 'the effective desire for accumulation' and Böhm-Bawerk thought of as 'the perspective undervaluation of the future'. 'All preference, therefore, for present over future goods resolves itself, in the last analysis, into a preference for early enjoyment income over deferred enjoyment income' (Fisher, 1930, p.65). Fisher hinted at a way of estimating time preference in the following manner ' the degree of impatience is the percentage preference for *$1 certain* of immediate income, over *$1, also certain,* of income of one year hence, *even if all the income except that dollar be uncertain*' (Fisher, 1930, p. 77). The rate of time preference depended on socioeconomic and personality characteristics (see Chapter 3).

Impatience varied over the life cycle of a man (Fisher did not reveal anything about the impatience of women). Children who generally lacked foresight and self-control were highly impatient and so were young men, but for a different reason: they expected a large future income. Later, when the young men have families they may have a low degree of impatience because they think of the needs of the future. The breadwinner wants to provide for his wife and children in the future which means a high regard for the future and a lower regard for the present.

Then when he gets a little older, if his children are married and have gone out into the world and are well able to take care of themselves, he may again have a high degree of impatience for income, because he expects to die, and he thinks, 'Instead of piling up for the remote future, why shouldn't I enjoy myself during the few years that remain?' (Fisher, 1930, pp.90-1)

This description is strikingly similar to the ideas behind the Life-Cycle Hypothesis. Not finding it possible to represent such complex ideas with curves of the usual type in economics, Fisher used what he called 'impatience schedules' to further illustrate his notions of the relationships between income and time preference. As a first illustration, he constructed a table that crossed three income conditions and three types of persons and entered a percent figure in each field.

The income groups were (1) income small, increasing, precarious, (2) income of a medium type, (3) income large, decreasing, certain. The three groups of individuals were: (a) shortsighted, weakwilled, accustomed to spend, without heirs, (b) of a medium type, (c) farsighted, self-controlled, accustomed to save, desirous to provide for heirs. People in group 1a were characterized as having very high impatience and were given a time preference rate of 20 percent. People in group 3c had the lowest impatience and were assigned a time preference rate of 1 percent. The other groups were assigned values in between the two extremes, for example, 5 percent for group 1c. Fisher stressed that the groups were just meant to give a rough indication of what an impatience schedule would look like (Fisher, 1930, pp.95-6). From a certain point-of-view, the cross-tabulation is an attempt at segmentation of savers and it is an interesting attempt to combine economic and psychological variables.

Proceeding further along the same lines, Fisher suggested a demand schedule for loans and interest. He viewed it as analogous to the ordinary utility and demand schedule for commodities and prices. A prospective borrower was assumed able to tell for each successive bundle of 100 dollars added to present income how much he would give out of next year's income to have this amount added. This resulted in something like the following:

For the first $100, pay $120, which gives the impatience rate 20%
For the second $100, pay $115, which gives the impatience rate, 15%
For the third $100, pay $110, which gives the impatience rate 10%.
For the fourth $100, pay $106, which gives the impatience rate 6%
. . .

Attempts to measure time preference rates have often employed procedures similar to Fisher's impatience schedules. Like utility, impatience was marginally decreasing in this schedule. As noted earlier, Fisher indicated a number of factors that could produce differences among individuals and within individuals over time. He concluded that if incomes were not rigid and there was a loan market, individuals with high impatience would be willing to borrow and individuals with low impatience would be willing to lend. The effect of these operations will be that the high rates of time preference are reduced and the low ones are increased so that a common rate of interest, a market interest rate, is reached.

Fisher explained the interest rate as determined by time preferences that in their turn depended on income characteristics and personal factors. To some extent, the views on the interest rate reflected what the economist thought of saving. Nassau Senior and John Stuart Mill saw interest as the price paid for abstinence (Blaug, 1985). Böhm-Bawerk who like Marshall vehemently rejected the idea of saving as abstinence explained that the interest on capital was simply the influence of time on human evaluation of goods and capital. To compensate for the difference in value between now and later, the individual asked for interest, by Böhm-Bawerk neutrally called 'agio' which is Italian for the difference between the future and the present value.

Marshall (1890) defined interest on money as 'a reward for waiting'. He noted that relating interest to abstinence gave the wrong impression and had been ridiculed by some economists. Karl Marx had, for example, made fun of the abstinence of Baron Rothschild as compared to the non-abstinence of a poor worker. It was therefore better to define interest rate in terms of waiting for the enjoyment of material resources.

KEYNES AND THE ABSOLUTE INCOME HYPOTHESIS

Keynes's List of Saving Motives

With Keynes (1936) the role of the psychology of saving changed. To be sure, the increasing use of mathematics in economics had already de-psychologized economics, but thrift and some other psychological variables were still mentioned in the discourses on saving and there were attempts to find economic equivalents to these variables. In fact, Keynes provided a comprehensive list of saving motives, in many ways similar to those promulgated by Fisher (1930), but with some elaboration. He described eight main factors of a subjective character, which led individuals to refrain from spending out of their incomes: precaution, foresight, calculation, improvement, independence, enterprise, pride and avarice. A corresponding list of motives to consumption embraced enjoyment, shortsightedness, generosity, miscalculation, ostentation and extravagance (Keynes, 1936, pp.107-8).

'Precaution' meant building up a reserve against unforeseen contingencies. 'Foresight' included 'providing for an anticipated future relation between the income and the needs of the individual or his family different from that which exists in the present, as, for example, in relation to old age, family education, or the maintenance of dependents.' Browning and Lusardi (1996, p.1797) called this motive 'the life-cycle motive'. 'Calculation' referred to saving for a profit and indicated that a larger consumption at a later date was preferred to a smaller consumption now. 'Improvement' involved what Adam Smith called human betterment and is now labeled preference for a climax order: 'it gratifies a common instinct to look forward to a gradually improving standard of life rather than the contrary'. The 'independence' motive is the same as enjoying a sense of power to do things. 'Enterprise' leads to saving for going into business or speculating. 'Pride' is the same as the bequest motive. 'Avarice' is pure miserliness (Keynes, 1936, pp.107-8).

It is notable that Keynes in this way considered what saving could mean to the individual. Some of the motives were recognized as having different short-run and long-run effects. 'Several of the motives towards positive saving catalogued above as affecting individuals have their intended counterpart in negative saving at a later date, as, for example, with saving to provide for family needs or old age' (Keynes, 1936, p.109). The saving motives were assumed to change in a population only very slowly over time and their influence on the propensity to consume could thus be expected to be stable over long periods of time. Change in income was the really important influence on consumption and saving.

Keynes identified two decision dimensions in what he called psychological time preference. He called one 'the propensity to consume'. It operated under the influence of the motives listed above and determined how much of an individual's income was consumed and how much was saved. The second decision concerned the form in which the individual wanted to hold what had been reserved through the first decision. The second decision involved the individual's 'liquidity-preference', that is, how much s/he wished to retain in the form of cash.

The degree of liquidity-preference was defined as depending on (1) the transactions-motive, (2) the precautionary-motive, and (3) the speculative-motive. The first motive was the need of cash for current transactions in private and business exchanges. The second motive had to do with how much money was desired for future security. The speculative motive was 'the object of securing profit from knowing better than the market what the future will bring forth' (Keynes, 1936, pp.166-70). The interest rate was defined as 'the reward for parting with liquidity' and characterized as a measure of the unwillingness of those who had money to part with their liquid control over it. The motives for liquidity preference have often been interpreted as motives for saving rather than for the form of savings. This is a neglect of the distinctions made by Keynes. The concepts of propensity to consume and liquidity preference have found wide usage after Keynes.

The Psychological Law and The Absolute Income Hypothesis

In attempting to explain at an early stage the stock market crash of 1929, Keynes (1930) wrote

> The pessimism and the atmosphere of disappointment which the stock-market collapse engendered reduced enterprise and lowered the natural-rate of interest; whilst the 'psychological' poverty which the collapse of paper values brought with it probably increased saving. – The last point is important, and we may pause upon it for a moment. It may suggest a generalization of permanent value. A country is no richer when, for purposes of swopping titles to prospective gain between one of its citizens and another, people choose to value the prospects at twenty years' purchase, than when these are valued at ten years' purchase; but the citizens, beyond question, *feel* richer. Who can doubt that a man is more likely to buy a new motorcar if his investments have doubled in money-value during the past year than if they have been halved? He feels far less necessity or obligation to save out of his normal income, and his whole standard of expenditure is raised. For their paper profits and their savings out of current income are not kept by most men (as perhaps they should be) in entirely separate compartments of the mind. (Keynes, 1930, p.197)

Keynes drew the conclusion that owners of shares and bonds were more likely to 'save' when they were losing 'paper value' than when the paper values were rising, more likely to refrain from new extravagances and to pay off debts. This is an hypothesis of high current interest. As far as I know it has not yet been fully tested using behavioral data.

The 'consumption function' is the relationship between (aggregate) consumption expenditure and (aggregate) consumers' disposable income in an economy. In his discussion of the consumption function, Keynes (1936, p.96) formulated what he called 'a psychological law'.

> The fundamental psychological law, upon which we are entitled to depend with great confidence both *a priori* from our knowledge of human nature and from the detailed facts of experience, is that men are disposed, as a rule and on the average, to increase their consumption as their income increases, but not by as much as the increase in their income.

Keynes further explained

> For a man's habitual standard of life usually has the first claim on his income, and he is apt to save the difference which discovers itself between his actual income and the expense of his habitual standard; or, if he does adjust his expenditure to changes in his income, he will over short periods do so imperfectly. Thus a rising income will often be accompanied by increased saving, and a falling income by decreased saving, on a greater scale at first than subsequently. (Keynes, 1936, p.97)

In his *History of Economic Analysis*, Schumpeter (1954) was sarcastic about the psychological law

> I wish to advert to a type of pseudo-psychology which is nothing but an abuse. Keynes's well-known psychological law about the propensity to consume is an outstanding example . . . it is a statement of statistically observable fact which Keynes raised to the rank of an assumption. Nothing is gained, except a spurious dignity, by calling it a psychological law. (Schumpeter, 1954, pp.1059-60)

Katona (1975, pp.70-72) raised three serious objections to Keynes's law:

1. The law may have been true hundreds of years ago when people used all their income on bare necessities, but in affluent societies people have discretionary income, which they can use on durables. An increase in income, not used for habitual expenditures, would be used either for purchasing durable goods or for saving
2. Adjustments to income decreases cannot be considered as the reverse of adjustments to income increases. The habit lag is more likely to be valid for declines in income than for increases
3. Keynes forgot the role of expectations. Changes in consumer expectations tend to be uniform and to spread via the mass media and personal influences rather than to cancel out over a population.

After the psychological law was formulated, the interest in saving motives and other psychological concepts more or less disappeared from the economic discussion of the determinants of saving. Keynes made the strong assumption that saving motives were stable over time in a population. Earlier discussions of the determinants of saving had found room both for ability to save and willingness to save. With Keynes the research interest became solely focused on the role of income, on current income at first, then on past income, and, finally, on the role of future, expected income. The psychological law implies that the short-run marginal propensity to consume is lower than the long-run propensity to consume which is also is lower than the current propensity. With increasing national income savings are expected to increase since the marginal propensity to consume declines.

Keynes's theory became known as 'The Absolute Income Hypothesis' of saving since it focused on current income. It was subsequently submitted to many tests against empirical data on saving. On the whole, it did not test out well. Time-series analyses of long-run developments of savings in the USA indicated that the saving ratio was almost constant in spite of the fact that there had been substantial growth in real income. Cross-section analyses, on the other hand, tended to show that saving increased with income. While economists after Keynes focused on the role of income for saving, they made many attempts to improve the interpretation of income by looking at individual income over time. Past income and future, expected income became vitally interesting.

DUESENBERRY'S RELATIVE INCOME HYPOTHESIS

Duesenberry (1949) turned attention to past income rather than current income and launched the *relative income hypothesis*. Using cross-section data from 1935–6, he found that during the Depression a large number of families reported consumption expenditures in excess of income for the year. In the 1941 survey far fewer households showed those deficiencies. The absolute income hypothesis, which presumed that consumption followed income, could not explain this. Duesenberry noted that Keynes's absolute income hypothesis was inadequate for explaining saving variations over the business cycle. People apparently did not only pay attention to their present income, but to something else.

Duesenberry used, for an economist, unusually complicated psychological reasoning, borrowing ideas from social psychology and sociology. He assumed that people had a high standard of living as a social goal and that this goal via a drive for self-esteem and high social status led to a demand for high-quality goods. When the individual made comparisons with the living or consumption standards of other people, unfavorable outcomes inspired inferiority feelings.

> The strength of such feelings suffered by one individual varies with the frequency with which he has to make an unfavorable comparison between the quality of the goods he uses with those used by others. This frequency will depend . . . on the ratio of his expenditures to those of others with whom he comes into contact. – In view of these considerations it seems quite possible that after some minimum income is reached, the frequency and strength of impulses to increase expenditures for one individual depend entirely on the ratio of his expenditures to the expenditures of those with whom he associates. (Duesenberry, 1949, pp.31-32)

Duesenberry's theory involved that households made comparisons with other people's consumption level. This level was assumed to influence the expenditures and thus the saving of the individual household. While Duesenberry cited evidence for such effects from social psychological and sociological literature, he concluded his reasoning by suggesting a proxy that is far from these disciplines. He proposed to use the ratio between current income and the household's highest past income. The highest past income was thus assumed to represent the expenditures of those others with whom comparisons were made. If the past income had been higher, there was a pressure for the household to dissave and even make debts. Important factors in the pressure towards keeping the same standard of living were the social groups – reference groups – with whom the household compared its standard of living. Duesenberry referred to the effect as *demonstration effect* suggesting that people were influenced by what they saw in their social environment and by what characterized the standard of living of friends and acquaintances. Later versions of the theory employ the highest past consumption rather than the highest past income as a basis for comparison. This is more in line with Duesenberry's reasoning in the cited paragraph

The relative income hypothesis can be expressed like this

$$S / y_t = a + b(y_t / y_{max})$$

where S/y_t = household saving ratio
        y_t = disposable (net) income
       y_{max} = highest net income in earlier periods
          a and b are constants.

While the theory has not tested out very well as a general explanation of savings, there are many examples where it has turned out to have explanatory power. Berg (1982, p.45) who analyzed savings in Sweden using a life-cycle model, also ran a quick test of Duesenberry's theory on Swedish savings data 1951-1979. He arrived at the following estimate

$$S/Y = -50.6 + 54.7 \ Y/Y_{-1}$$
$$(17.4) \ (16.9)$$
$$R^2 = 0.2526 \quad D.W. = 0.5$$

Although the estimate was admittedly far from satisfactory, Berg calculated the long-run saving ratio on the basis of the equation and found to his surprise that there was good agreement between the actual and the calculated development. Per capita household disposable income increased by 2.3 percent per year during the period which together with the estimates of a and b yielded a long-run saving ratio of 5.3 percent: The latter was identical to the actual average ratio for the period in question.

A social psychologist may be a little disturbed by the fact that Duesenberry's comparison process is reduced to the ratio between current (Y) and last year's income (Y_{-1}) and that individual differences are assumed to cancel out so that they have no influence on the saving ratio. The ratio Y/Y_{-1} is an example of a proxy of the type often used by economists. The use of this proxy is legitimized by the fact that incomes, based on salaries and wages, had a tendency to increase every year and never to decrease (on average in those days).

Using British survey data on income satisfaction, Clark and Oswald (1993) found support for Duesenberry's hypothesis. They used a standard earnings regression model to calculate a comparison income (y^*) for each individual in the sample of employees (N = 5 195). As a check, external measures of comparison were also examined. According to the relative income hypothesis, the ratio y/y^* where y is (reported) income, should influence the level of consumption. The authors found that people who had an unfavorable ratio tended to save less.

Intuitively, many objections can be made. King (1985) had the following to say about the assumed comparison with the previously highest income level: 'Professional footballers who base their consumption plans on their highest income ever attained are seen in the bankruptcy courts from time to time, but most of their playing colleagues are evidently more careful' (King, 1985, p.230).

There is a disturbing question about the comparison income or comparison level of consumption in all studies. Do they really reflect social influence? In other words, is the social psychology of the reasoning really necessary? The basic assumption involves that a household in a social interaction process builds up a standard of living. The assumption of a demonstration effect is hardly utilized. With the proxy used, it can simply be assumed that the household resists changes in its standard of living, a kind of habit lag. This is exactly what Keynes (1936) maintained in his comment following the statement of the psychological law. When income rises there will be saving since the household will hesitate to change its standard of living. When income goes down there will also be slow adjustment to the new situation.

The idea of social influence could be exploited to assess the likelihood and speed of change. Households with little anchoring in social groups would be expected to make changes in consumption with less delay. In other households, the change process will at least take some time as a consequence of the fact that reference groups are not immediately changed. Psychological learning theories as well as sociological and some economic theory have hypotheses about 'habit lag' or 'habit persistence'.

It seems appropriate to look at what a social psychologist could have contributed to tests of Duesenberry's model. Typically, data from interviews would be required and questions asked about social influence. Such data have been collected and used in economic-psychological and econometric studies of economic behavior. The data are hardly of the type that, in principle, is desirable for testing the model. They rather purvey proxies that appear to be closer to social influence than the highest past income. A major drawback is that time series data can usually not be made available. In Chapter 7, the research on comparison or reference groups will be dealt with in more detail.

THE PERMANENT INCOME HYPOTHESIS

[I] generate multiple regressions these days at a rate that I never would have contemplated three or four decades ago – and many more than I would if I followed my own prescription for proper research procedures.

Milton Friedman (1992, p.36).

With Friedman's Permanent Income Hypothesis (PIH) research attention turned towards future income. Permanent income, which included present and future income, could be higher or lower than current income and this affected consumption. Friedman (1957) stated that under complete certainty there were only two reasons for spending less (or more) on consumption than what the household received in any time period.

The first is to 'straighten out' the stream of expenditures – by appropriate timing of borrowing and lending, the unit can keep its expenditures relatively stable even though its receipts vary widely from time period to time period. The second is to earn interest on loans, if the interest rate is positive, or to receive payment for borrowing, if the interest rate is negative. How it will behave under the influence of these motives depends, of course, on its tastes – the relative utility it attaches to consumption at different points of time. (Friedman, 1957, p.7)

The first model was based on strict demands on household knowledge. By complete certainty is meant that the household knows that it will receive a definite sum of money in each of a definite number of time periods. It also knows the prices and the rates of interest for each time period. If uncertainty is assumed, another reason for holding wealth is added: a reserve for emergencies, what Keynes called the 'precautionary motive'.

To introduce the idea of permanent income, Friedman used a graphic presentation that he borrowed from Fisher. The latter pictured intertemporal choice with a simple set of indifference curves, which he called 'willingness lines'. Along the x-axis he put income (consumption) year 1 and along the vertical axis income (consumption) year 2. Figure 4.1 depicts the temporal indifference curves of a single person. Each curve shows combinations of consumption year 1 and consumption year 2 between which the individual is indifferent. The dotted line comprises points that represent equal consumption in both years. Indifference curves at different heights show different combinations of consumptions during the two years. Higher curves mean more attractive combinations. At one end of a curve the consumption year 1 (C_1) dominates, at the other end the consumption in year 2 (C_2) dominates.

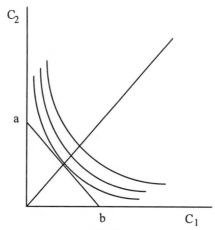

Figure 4.1 Indifference Curves for Intertemporal Choice

The budget line gives the height of the curve that the individual can choose. The budget line a-b represents different splits of the incomes between the two periods. In the Figure, the split is even and the consumption the same in both years. The slope of the tangent of the curve is the time preference or what Fisher as an alternative called 'human impatience'. He defined it as the marginal preference for present over future goods. Time preference is high when $C_1 > C_2$ and low when $C_1 < C_2$. If the household uses a high discount rate when calculating the present value of future consumption, present consumption prevails and the household is impatient.

Friedman proceeded with some simple equations. The maximum that the household could spend in year 1 was the income in year 1 (R_1) plus the income in year 2 (R_2) reduced by the cost of borrowing the second year income for use in year 1 (a). The maximum that could be spent in year 2 was the first year's income plus the interest (d = discount rate) that the household could receive when lending the first year income plus the second year income (b). These two points defined the budget line. In symbols, it looks like this

$$R_1 + \frac{R_2}{(1+d)} = a$$
$$R_2 + R_1(1+d) = b$$

The next step was to introduce the household's wealth in year 1 (W_1) as the sum of the incomes

$$W_1 = R_1 + \frac{R_2}{1+d}$$

Future income as a component of wealth may seem strange, but is in agreement with Fisher (1930, p.61). 'Capital wealth is merely the means to the end called income, while capital value (which is the sense in which the term capital is ordinarily used by interest theorists) is merely the capitalization of expected income.'

The consumption function is then written as

$$c_1 = f(W_1, i)$$

This consumption function makes it obvious that consumption in a period does not exclusively depend on income in this single period, but on expected income in the next period and interest rate (i). A change in R_1 does not affect consumption directly, but through its effect on W_1. If the change is accompanied by an opposite change in R_2 it may not affect consumption at all. Extended to an indefinite number of periods, this is the foundation of the *Permanent Income Hypothesis* (PIH) of consumption and saving. The permanent income is the income to which consumers adapt their behavior rather than to their recorded income. Permanent income cannot be observed directly. It must be inferred from the behavior of consumer units.

The empirical analyses reported in Friedman's book gave results that were consistent with

> a rather simple relation between permanent consumption and permanent income suggested by purely theoretical considerations, namely, a ratio between permanent consumption and permanent income that is the same for all levels of permanent income but depends on other variables, such as the interest rate, the ratio of wealth to income, and so on. (Friedman, 1957, p.221)

Friedman distinguished between permanent and transitory components of income. The permanent income represented what the consumer unit could count on with confidence. The transitory component was what the consumer unit saw as accidental or decided by chance. It did not affect long-term consumption plans and was assumed to cancel out over large groups of consumers. The length of the time period that the consumer took into consideration was called the consumer unit's 'horizon'. On the basis of different pieces of evidence, Friedman drew the tentative conclusion that the horizon was about three years.

The following equations summarize Friedman's theory

$$(\alpha)\, c_p = k(i, w, u) y_p,$$
$$(\beta)\, y = y_p + y_t,$$
$$(\gamma)\, c = c_p + c_t$$

Equation (α) shows that planned or 'permanent consumption' (c_p) is a fraction (k) of permanent income (y_p) that does not depend on the size of permanent income but does depend on other variables, in particular, the interest rate (i), the ratio of nonhuman wealth to income (w), and other factors affecting the consumer's tastes for current consumption versus accumulation of assets (u), 'such as the degree of uncertainty attached to the receipt of income, the consumer unit's age and its composition, and objective indexes of cultural factors like race or national origin' (Friedman, 1957, p.222).

The other two equations show that what Friedman called measured income (y) and measured consumption (c) each is the sum of two components: a permanent component and a transitory component. The latter reflects the influence on income regarded as chance or random by the consumer unit.

Is there any psychology in Friedman's permanent income hypothesis? The main thing to learn for a psychologist is how the future affects economic decisions (cf. Douglas and Isherwood, 1996, pp.29-35). The economists discovered the importance of future orientation and expectations long before the psychologists who are rarely preoccupied with studying reactions to the future. Psychological studies of uncertainty mostly lack a time dimension. The use of uncertainty may in principle be seen as a step toward psychology, but Friedman preferred objective indicators to subjective measurements. Although Friedman used subjective concepts when he talked about the consumer unit's characteristics and defined permanent and transitory income, he avoided all use of subjective measurements. He stated that permanent income could never be measured at the individual household level. It could only be inferred at the aggregate level. When Friedman discussed expected income he explicitly noted that he meant 'mean value'. Expectation is then tantamount to mathematical expected value and is not psychological.

Friedman's approach involves the assumption that consumption always can be separated from current income. It is a debatable, but interesting way of dealing with intertemporal choice. The psychologist can use the model and study it relying on subjective data. The question then arises whether it furthers psychological research on saving to assume that an individual acts in the way that Friedman suggests. To a psychologist with a slant towards cognitive experiments, it should be possible to test the question empirically in controlled experiments. It is feasible to construe experiments that can elucidate the role of transitory and permanent income for saving (see Chapter 5).

Since there are many similarities between the PIH and the Life-Cycle Hypothesis which will be examined next, further psychological comments are saved to the end of the next section and to Chapter 8.

THE LIFE-CYCLE HYPOTHESIS

A prudent person who thought that he would derive equal gratifications from equal means at all stages of his life, would perhaps endeavour to distribute his means equally over his whole life: and if he thought that there was a danger that his power of earning income at a future date would run short, he would certainly save some of his means for a future date. He would do this not only if he thought that his savings would increase in his hands, but even if he thought they would diminish.

Marshall ([1890] 1947, p.192)

The Basic Model

Modigliani and Brumberg (1954) gave an alternative to the Permanent Income Hypothesis. While the latter tested out well on cross-section data, it showed less success when tested on time-series data (Ando and Modigliani, 1963). The main difference between them is the time horizon and the role of age in the alternative model which was called the 'Life-Cycle Hypothesis' (LCH). It had the following characteristics. The model starts from the utility function of the individual consumer whose utility is assumed to be a function of her/his own total consumption in current and future periods. The individual is then assumed to maximize utility, subject to the resources available to her/him. The resources are the sum of current net worth and current and discounted future earnings over the individual's lifetime. The maximization assumption makes it possible to express the current consumption of the individual as a function of her/his resources and the rate of return on capital. The parameters are assumed to depend on age. The individual consumption functions thus obtained are then aggregated to arrive at the aggregate consumption function for the community. (Ando and Modigliani, 1963, p.56). A person's consumption in a period is assumed to be proportional to the present value of total resources accruing to her/him over the rest of the lifetime

$$c_t = g_t v_t$$

$$v_t = a_{t-1} + y_t + \sum_{t+1}^{N} \frac{y_t^{e\tau}}{(1 + r_t)^{N-1}}$$

where c_t is a household's total consumption in year t; a proportion of total lifetime resources

v_t is total lifetime resources at their present value

a_{t-1} is the sum of net worth carried over from the previous period
y_t is current income
$y_t^{e\tau}$ is what the household expects to earn in year t
N stands for the earning span, end of lifetime
r_t is the rate of return on assets, the discount rate

The second equation above is a slightly simplified version of the Ando-Modigliani model, but it should be sufficient to illustrate the main ideas of the basic LCH. Current consumption is seen as a proportion (g_t) of the life-time wealth, which consists of present assets, current income and expected income during the rest of the lifetime. There is no explicit role for past income. The household is assumed to know the amount of future income and the exact values of other variables that refer to the future. An alternative assumption is that a person acts *as if* s/he has perfect knowledge about the future. There is naturally uncertainty about future income, future interest rates, and remaining lifetime, but subjectively an individual may feel rather certain about the future on the basis of past experience. It should be noted that, in addition to the listed uncertainties, an individual could also be uncertain about the value of present net worth. There is no uncertainty in the basic model. Uncertainty is an important later addition and is often discussed as a precautionary motive for saving.

The life-cycle model is based on some assumptions about behavior:

1.   Individual behavior is forward looking
2.   Individuals optimize the use of their lifetime resources over their (expected) remaining lifetime
3.   Individuals tend to distribute their lifetime resources evenly over the lifecycle; saving is a consequence of consumption decisions
4.   When optimizing over their life span, households are sensitive to changes in interest rates, which influence their discount functions for future events
5.   Present income is mainly an indicator of what future income will be (generalization in psychological terms)
6.   The cost of acquiring information about the future is not so high or difficult that people use only information about the present when deciding on their current consumption.

An essential idea in the LCH is that individuals tend to distribute their lifetime resources evenly and to smooth consumption over the life cycle. They attempt to keep the marginal utility of expenditures constant over time (Browning and Lusardi, 1996, p.1799). In phases of life when the current income is lower than the proper share of the life resources, people borrow money, provided there is a functioning capital market. When the current income exceeds its proper share of the life income, money will be saved. On the basis of expectations that are rational the individual makes a budget for a period. This budget is independent of the size of current income, but serves as a criterion whether to save or dissave.

In a way, the household or the individual has to calculate annuities on the basis of current information in order to know how much to spend on consumption and to recalculate the annuities when there is new information about future income, future interest rates, or life expectancy. Thaler (1990) gave a succinct and slightly derogatory summary of the normative implications of LCH in the following words

> The essence of the life-cycle theory is this: in any year, compute the present value of your wealth, including current income, net assets, and future income; figure out the level annuity you could purchase with that money; then consume the amount you would receive if you in fact owned such an annuity. (Thaler, 1990, pp.193-4)

Hurd (1990) found that there was good agreement about the basic assumptions of the LCH

> A form of the LCH that most people could accept characterizes individuals and couples as forward looking in their consumption and savings decisions; as optimizing over their lifetimes (although, of course, distant events may be discounted so heavily that for practical purposes they do not matter); and as uncertain of their date of death . . . (Hurd, 1990, pp.606-7)

Changes in total savings are attributed to changes in economic growth, demographic changes, and changes in interest rates. Apart from random fluctuations, the saving ratio will be zero in a non-growth economy with a stagnant population. What the individuals/households save during one period of their life, they will consume at a later stage in life. When there is stagnation in the economy, saving will be exactly balanced by consumption. The major short-run influence on savings is change in the discount rate (Thaler, 1994).

The Critique of the Life-Cycle Hypothesis

> *Capital is accumulated not to smooth consumption over the life cycle (which im-plies that it is dissipated in due course), but because that is what you should do with capital.*
>
> Winnett and Lewis (1995, p.447)

What is said in the following is mostly also valid for the PIH and no distinction is made between the two models. In many respects, the LCH has tested out well and it is the leading theory of saving and as such has inspired an enormous amount of research. It has become clear that it has certain short-comings and lacks in explanatory value for some savings data. Many re-searchers have been working on improving the model and it is now claimed that the additions to the model make it possible to handle a number, but far from all of the problems (Browning and Lusardi, 1996).

The LCH predicts a positive relationship between economic growth and total savings. In many studies this relationship has not been substantiated and there is even a contradictory hypothesis that anticipated growth may actually discourage savings (Viard, 1993; Yoshikawa, 1995, p.201). In many studies, individuals or households at different stages in the life cycle have failed to show the expected saving behavior. (King, 1985; Courant et al., 1986; Juster, 1986; Thaler, 1990, 1992). The theory predicts definite differences in saving behavior over the life cycle (see Figure 2.1).

> under most plausible assumptions, savings will generally be low early in working life, will rise as earnings increase with age, and then will flatten out, becoming negative in retirement. This pattern implies a 'hump-shaped' profile for asset holdings over the life cycle. Although unsurprising, it suggests that failure to ob-serve a hump-shaped age profile for assets might constitute direct evidence against life-cycle savings behaviour. (King, 1985, p.236)

Young people save more than expected and old people do not dissave to the expected extent. There is, however, some disagreement about whether pen-sions paid to old people should be seen as using up wealth and thus tant-amount to dissaving or as income, part of which may be saved. Consumption over the life cycle seems to track current income too much and to be more in line with the absolute income hypothesis. Studies also show that consumers in general are not highly sensitive to changes in interest rates or changes in dividends (Juster, 1986).

Campbell and Mankiw (1989) suggested that there might be two types of consumers. One type lives up to the predictions of the PIH or LCH and takes into account life-cycle or permanent income, the other type simply spends what they earn and live up to the absolute income hypothesis. In a similar vein, Browning and Lusardi (1996, p.1797) said: 'It is unlikely that a single explanation will suffice for all members of a population at any given time or even for the same person over a long stretch of time.'

A common criticism of the basic LCH has been that it neglects the role of bequests for saving. While the LCH models people as optimizing over a very long period, usually their own lifetime, there is some conflict about the role of the next generation. The Ricardian equivalence principle implies that after public debt increases and tax cuts people start saving money because they recognize that higher taxes will follow. They may not live to pay the higher taxes, but their offspring will. There may be other reasons as well for a will to leave money to posterity. The will to bequeath money is often said to be a major instigator of saving behavior, especially among old-age people (Barlow et al., 1966; Kotlikoff, 1989; Hurd, 1990). The addition of a bequest motive is a major modification of the LCH. 'The leading alternative to the LCH is the LCH augmented by a bequest motive for saving' (Hurd, 1990, p.606).

The bequest motive also involves: 'A couple (or individual) gains utility from the knowledge that if both die, someone whose welfare they care about will receive their bequeathable wealth as a bequest' (Hurd, 1990, pp.606-7). Hurd gave an example of possible policy implications of the basic hypothesis and that of the alternative. Increases in Social Security will be saved if people have a strong bequest motive. In a footnote he noted that: 'According to this definition, saving by a couple to finance the consumption of a surviving spouse is not saving for a bequest.' Saving for precautionary motives presumably covers the welfare of a surviving spouse. Browning and Lusardi (1996, p.1846) suggested that 'the decumulation of couples can be lower than singles given that the expected "lifetime" of the household is greater for couples'.

The assumptions of the LCH have been defended by, for example, Modigliani (1986, 1988) who played down the potential role of the bequest motive. While King (1985, pp.285-6) admitted some shortcomings of the LCH in the light of empirical data, he suggested that the divergence between theory and reality could be a consequence of incorrectly specified questions. In the first place, there was a tendency to see the LCH as an all-or-none model. The reasonable assumption was that the LCH could explain the savings of the majority of savers and that the rest, which probably amounted to 20-25 percent of the consumers, was better explained through other theories. This implies types of savers as Campbell and Mankiw (1990; 1991) proposed.

It is also possible to differentiate between different types of savings. Three types of capital were distinguished in what was essentially a recapitulation of some of the saving motives of earlier economic thinkers, but couched in a more appropriate dress than subjective concepts (Kessler and Masson, 1987)

1. S-capital is mainly aimed at future consumption
2. K-capital consists of assets mainly held for their return. This can be seen as risk capital which is invested so as to maximize returns or at least secure high returns
3. H-capital is human capital; investment in education will for example give future returns.

The LCH corresponds to and covers only the first type of capital. Other motives characterize the other two types of capital such as power, influence, and self-actualization. The idea is to classify savings into these categories without having to ask people about their motives for saving. The distinction between

S-capital and *K*-capital is certainly interesting and implies that it is desirable to sort out investors from ordinary savers who have most of their wealth in bank accounts and home equity.

According to the LCH, wealth is not in itself a source of utility. The utility derives from the income or consumption that wealth permits. Samuelson and Nordhaus (1993) talked about 'the wealth effect', noting that a household with the same income but larger wealth than another household consumed more. There is also the observation that wealthy people save more of their income (Katona, 1975). Whether the wealth effect is positive or negligible, it refers to the income that wealth can yield, the utility of the capital income and not of the capital. Subjectively, savings and wealth may yield utility of the kind that Kahneman (1994) referred to as hedonic or experience utility, to be distinguished from preference utility.

Economists recognize that there can be considerable utility of wealth itself, only this insight is kept to side remarks and footnotes so as not to complicate the reasoning. A case in point is Fisher's footnote, referring to the income and wealth of Henry Ford: 'Except . . . he derives in addition to this obvious income other less tangible and more subtle income from the sense of possession, prestige, power, etc., which go with great wealth' (Fisher, 1930, p.27). Here Fisher contradicted his earlier statement that income was what was important with capital and that money was of no use until it was spent. Psychologically, the hedonic utility of wealth may have considerable weight.

In their critique of the LCH, Shefrin and Thaler (1988, p.609) observed that the failure of LCH to explain empirical data on savings had in many cases led to a number of ad hoc alteration attempts. Among those were the addition of a bequest motive, hypotheses about capital market imperfections, assumption that the utility function for consumption changed over time, and specifying a particular form of expectations regarding future income.

Browning and Lusardi (1996) who thoroughly examined microeconomic theories of saving distinguished between three major types of saving theory that were associated with the LCH. They preferred to employ other labels since there had been many developments after the original LCH. The first type of theory was like the first LCH based on certainty. The second type included a precautionary motive. A third type was based on the use of Euler equations and made it possible to include many other factors besides bequest and precautionary motives.

Carroll (1997) suggested a modification of PIH and LCH. He started with the observation that in surveys the most used response alternative to a question about motives for saving was 'being prepared for emergencies'. Next, he made the assumption that consumers were faced with important income uncertainty and were prudent, that is, they had a strong precautionary motive. They engaged in 'what I call 'buffer-stock' saving behavior . . . Buffer-stock savers have a target-wealth-to-permanent-income ratio such that, if wealth is below the target, the precautionary motive will dominate impatience, and the consumer will save' (Carroll, 1997, p.2). He conceded that the buffer-stock model was probably not valid for very wealthy people.

Changes in the demographic structure of a country can in some cases provide adequate explanations of a changing saving ratio. If, for example, as has been the case in many industrialized countries over the last decade, the number of old-age pensioners increases, the saving ratio is expected to go down. When demographic changes are considered in the analysis of, for example, US drops in the saving ratio, the explanatory power is improved but still far from perfect (Browning and Lusardi, 1996, p.1825).

The Saving of Old-Age Pensioners

Instead of piling up for the remote future, why shouldn't I enjoy myself during the few years that remain?

Fisher (1930, pp.90-1)

The fact that young people have been found to save more and older people have dissaved less than expected on the basis of LCH predictions has led to many discussions and attempts to supplement the theory. The LCH assumes that people try to maintain approximately the same consumption level over the life cycle. The household strives to smooth its consumption over time. Up to the retirement age people have higher incomes per person than they expect to receive after retirement and are thus expected to save. Retired people have less current income than their life-cycle income and use up their savings. This is quite similar to Fisher's description of the development of saving motives over the life cycle.

According to Kotlikoff (1989, p.239), the marginal propensity to consume is an increasing function of age. Individuals with only one more year to live will exhaust their remaining resources in their final year which means that they have a marginal propensity to consume that equals unity (calculated on an annual basis). The second oldest age group with two remaining years to live are assumed to allocate part of any additional resources to increasing next year's consumption and use the rest in the first year. Its propensity to consume is less than unity. In a simple version of LCH the marginal propensity to consume equals one divided by the number of remaining years to live.

Empirical studies of saving indicate that, on average, old-age pensioners save more or at least dissave less than expected. There is consumption lumping in certain life-cycle periods rather than consumption smoothing. There are now many studies showing that the LCH may fail to predict the saving of the elderly. Danziger et al. (1982) summarized the evidence showing that the elderly did not dissave and analyzed the 1972–73 Consumer Expenditure Survey data. Their results showed that the elderly spent less than the non-elderly at the same level of income and that the very oldest of the elderly had the lowest average propensities to consume (p.224). The propensity to consume decreased with age in each income bracket. Only if Duesenberry's relative income hypothesis was used, a difference in the expected direction was found. People with income above the median in their age cohort tended to have a decreased propensity to consume. The elderly dissaved only when their incomes were very low relative to the incomes of others in their cohort.

Using panel data, Hurd (1987) found that over a ten-year period the elderly in the data set dissaved at annual rates of 4.5 percent for singles and 1.6 percent for couples. These findings differed from most cross-section results. Hurd suggested that the LCH should be augmented to include a bequest motive, but his own test on the same data offered no support for a bequest motive. Burbridge and Robb (1985) found that in their Canadian sample, blue-collar households decumulated after retirement whereas white-collar households did not. The results suggested that it might be useful to think in terms of segments of the population, implying that some segments were closer to the overall rational model of the LCH. The Canadian results thus indicated that members of the working class complied more with the assumptions about old-age dissaving. Two factors seem to influence the consumption and to disturb the interpretation of the findings. One factor is presence or absence of retirement pensions and the other the wealth. Pensions can be seen as dissaving, at least when they arise out of pension plans that have involved individual payments. A considerable proportion of the USA population has surprisingly little wealth or assets and most of the wealth is home equity (Hubbard et al., 1994; Poterba et al., 1994).

> it is clear that many elderly reach retirement with very little. The most obvious explanation is that poverty after retirement is a reflection of a lifetime of poverty. Undoubtedly this is true in many cases, but other explanations should be explored. For example, in other data, differences in lifetime earnings seem to be much smaller than differences in wealth at retirement, indicating ex post differences in rates of saving. Yet, how much of the variation in saving rates is intentional and how much due to random events is not known. (Hurd, 1990, p.588)

The negative findings have not led to the rejection of the LCH in accordance with Popper's (1959) falsificationism, but rather to behavior similar to Lakatos' research program theory. The core of the theory is left intact and the interest is focused on auxiliary hypotheses that can preserve the core of the theory. Many more or less ad hoc explanations of the deviations have been advanced to supplement the theory. More than one of the suggested ad hoc explanations of the deviations from the LCH predictions may be valid and

different segments of the population may be characterized by different combinations of reasons for saving. This is in accordance with the general assumption in economic psychology that macroeconomic phenomena can be
better explained if the population is split up into segments, based on psychological characteristics. Here are the most common explanations of elderly
(non-dis)saving:

1. Old-age pensioners continue earlier saving habits which are facilitated
   through reduced consumption needs
2. Old-age pensioners save as a matter of precaution, so as always to
   have a buffer for unforeseen ill events and they do not know how long
   they or spouses will need the buffer
3. Old-age pensioners want to leave legacies to posterity, either for altruistic reasons or for buying favors now from prospective inheritors
   (the exchange-bequest motive)
4. Old-age pensioners do not dissave because of the illiquidity of assets
5. (Recently) retired people expect decreasing incomes and believe that
   their current income lies above the life-cycle income (permanent income).

On a common-sense level, all these explanations seem plausible enough.
Economists have tried to test the value of these explanations (for an overview, see e.g. Hurd, 1990). The bequest motive for saving is now integrated
in most LCH models. It is often studied through comparisons between families with and without children. The precautionary motive for saving has a
long tradition in economics. The empirical study of this motive is now
focused on the income uncertainty and life expectancy dimensions. Whereas
the prevailing tendency in economics is to infer psychological constructs
from economic behavior, these new attempts use interview data on incomes,
assets and to some extent also data on motives and attitudes.

From a behavioral point of view it seems likely that the explanations can
be valid for different segments of the population. The bequest motive can be
expected to have a close relationship to income and wealth. The precautionary motive may hold primarily for lower-income people who have earlier
experienced difficulties in making ends meet and have valued highly the
existence of a buffer capital (see Carroll, 1997). Continuing saving habits
may be a matter of controlling expenditures. Some people appear to have a
feeling that there is a limit to what they can indulge in. They set what they
think of as an appropriate level of consumption and may find that they have
money over after their consumption expenditures (Chapter 7).

The Saving Behavior of Young People

The rich are those whose families have had the 'luck' that all of their recent an-cestors died at the beginning of retirement, and so did not spend down their re-sources.

Weil (1991, p.163)

According to the LCH, young people have less income than their life-cycle income and they therefore tend to borrow money or dissave rather than save. Since young people generally expect rising income per household member, they are prone to borrow money. Studies of actual savings in Italy and Japan and also in some other countries indicate that there is considerable saving among the young (Ando et al., 1992). There is saving even though the current income is below the future income. Many attempts to explain this departure from the theory have been made:

1. Young people do not find it possible to borrow money against their future income (capital market deficiencies)
2. Young people are myopic and do not think in terms of future income against which they can borrow for current consumption
3. Young people do not wish to borrow heavily for consumption because they might be unlucky and not do well
4. The per capita income, for example, in a young couple with two wage earners, is higher than the expected income when the family grows.

The first three reasons try to explain the unexpected saving behavior by pointing to reasons for not borrowing money. They indicate that there may be a liquidity constraint that prevents dissaving. There may be a desire to borrow money against future income, but no functioning loan market. Another interpretation is that to achieve certain goals the young must first save to prove their ability to save and will then be able to borrow money. It may be a case of the 'downpayment motive' that Browning and Lusardi (1996) added to Keynes's list of motives. The second reason is strange in the sense that myopia is usually employed to explain the consumption of all income during the current period and lack of provision for the future. The main implication is that young people do not think that they can borrow money for their present consumption even when this is possible. The third explanation is a variant of the precautionary motive for saving. 'Utility gains from additional consumption now are more than offset by the value of having assets if bad luck strikes in the future' (Deaton, 1992, p.191).

The explanations thus give reasons for not making debts rather than explain the savings of young people. The Behavioral Life-Cycle Hypothesis (see below) assumes that there are different mental accounts and non-fungibility of money. Future income is according to this hypothesis referred to a mental account with a low propensity to consume. The willingness to make debts may be related to current rather than to future income. People in general, including young people, are much more myopic than what is presumed in LCH with its lifetime perspective. The planning horizons vary considerably for different consumption expenditures and usually do not comprise many years, except that there may be some concern about retirement pensions, starting early in life. The reasons may have some explanatory power, but little research has been carried out to decide how much they mean.

A slightly different explanation with clear psychological implications was suggested by Ando et al. (1992). They advanced a hypothesis that is the opposite of the myopic explanation

> We propose instead an explanation based on the hypothesis that, for very young households, due to the expectation of (future) consumption opportunities not available today, higher future income might be accompanied by larger needs. This creates a situation in which, at a later period, the marginal utility of income is higher even though expected income is higher than current income. (Ando et al., 1992, p.234) . . . We have outlined a theory in which current savings can be interpreted as a choice of flexibility, since the existence of future opportunities may be an incentive to postpone consumption until those periods in which it yields greater utility. (Ando et al., 1992, p.249)

The authors gave as an example young men who expected higher social status or promotion on the job. The higher social status would involve new opportunities for consumption and those would motivate current saving. The explanation involves that the marginal utility of the expected later income is higher although expected income exceeds current income. The discussant of the paper (Srinivasan, 1992, p.251) accepted that higher social status could have advance effects, but 'without a workable definition of social status and a data set in which the changes in income as well as in social status are documented, a direct empirical test of the theory is ruled out.'

A simple interpretation is that there is goal saving or what Browning and Lusardi (1996) called the 'downpayment motive', presumably for long-term goals. Young people may save to buy housing or consumer durables and they save money because they expect changes in family size that mean less income per capita in the foreseeable future. Some of the expected increases in needs may be a consequence of foreseen changes in social status and reference groups over time. This is particularly true for those young people who intend to make a career. Except for some form of goal saving, the hypothesis sounds a little far-fetched in my view.

It is possible that there are different segments of young people. Looking at the assumptions about the behavior of the young, one is tempted to say that the LCH assumptions have a distinct flavor of middle-class characteristics.

Middle-class youth tend to spend money on their education and are more likely to borrow money and dissave than to save. In Western European countries, it is common that young people borrow money against future income to pay for their studies and governments provide the necessary loans. After long training periods with little or no income and often borrowing they climb the career ladder and steadily increase their income. There are workers who after some short practice on the job have their highest income and purchasing power per capita when young. They may save because they expect decreasing per capita income for their households over time.

MODERN ECONOMIC SAVING THEORIES AND THE PSYCHOLOGY OF SAVING

Three questions are of particular interest for the present purposes:

1. Which are the psychological assumptions behind the LCH?
2. Are any relevant psychological concepts missing?
3. How can research on saving be improved by more psychology?

The LCH is based on a few assumptions that can easily qualify as psychological. Man is forward-looking and expectations dominate present behavior. The gist of the theory is, however, that there should be no subjective data. In theoretical contexts, subjective and objective data are assumed to be equivalent. In empirical contexts, every concept employed is economic (or possibly) demographic or is translated into such terms. Objective proxies that sometimes have very little similarity to the original concept replace subjective variables. The increased use of survey data has, however, changed the situation to some extent and subjective measures are increasingly being tried out.

The dominant saving theories, PIH and LCH, display few traces of the earlier detailed psychology of saving. Earlier economists paid a lot of attention to thrift, self-control and the saving motives behind thrift. The present focus is on ability to save. Willingness to save has almost dropped out of sight. The theories show signs of the mathematical transformation of psychological concepts that was initiated by Fisher and they start with the consumption function rather than with saving. As noted in Chapter 1, it is true that psychological concepts are coming back in new developments of economic theory. In theoretical contexts they are made compatible with the rationality postulate. This diminishes their similarity to the concepts used in psychological discourse.

Browning and Lusardi (1996) concluded their review of saving theory with the hope that behavioral, notably psychological factors might reduce some of the heterogeneity of the models.

> One immediate next step would be to explore how far we can reconcile behavioral models and standard optimizing predictions. More ambitiously, it may be that the heterogeneity that we allow for in standard models can be linked to psychological factors. This will allow parsimonious modeling of heterogeneity and may provide a link across many different life cycle decisions. (Browning and Lusardi, 1996, p.1850)

There are of course advantages to the economic approach. It simplifies grappling with macroeconomic problems and makes it possible to produce measurements that are otherwise not feasible. Simon (1990, p.6) expressed it like this: 'Accepting this assumption [of economic rationality] enables economists to predict a great deal of behavior (correctly or incorrectly) without ever making empirical studies of human actors (Simon, 1990, p.6).

While the explicit and hidden psychological assumptions in the LCH may not be wrong, they can be elaborated with the help of modern psychology. Psychological science may not be able to present relevant concepts and hypotheses in such a way that they can be integrated into economic savings theory, but application of some such thinking may lead to better descriptions and explanations of saving. Even if applications may not lead to better quantitative predictions of saving ratios, they contribute to a better understanding of processes in saving.

With respect to the psychology of saving, it should be noted that there is since a number of years economic research that includes many psychological variables. The Institute for Social Research at the University of Michigan is well known for such research. The US Federal Reserve Board carries out such studies. Right now there are ongoing projects on retirement and health that involve creative use of psychological variables (try AHEAD on the Internet!). In Europe, British, German and Italian survey studies can be mentioned. The VSB Panel project at CentER for Economic Research, Tilburg University, the Netherlands has furnished many of the ideas behind this book.

The psychological issues will be explored further in later chapters, especially in Chapters 6 and 7 where a number of psychological concepts will be treated more fully. Chapter 8 will deal in a more systematic way with the psychological issues connected with the saving models and present a schema that integrates some psychological concepts of potential use in saving studies.

THE BEHAVIORAL LIFE-CYCLE HYPOTHESIS

An Economic Theory of Self-Control

During the last decade, behavioral research on saving has been enriched with some new thinking, in the first place the Behavioral Life-Cycle Hypothesis and its predecessor 'An Economic Theory of Self-Control'. The economists Thaler and Shefrin (1981) developed the concept of self-control and applied it to saving behavior. They assumed that self-control was more or less by definition a question of conflict between opposing forces. Similar to agency theory in business economics, a long-term force, which the authors called *the planner* and a short-term force that they named *the doer* were postulated. In agency theory, these forces correspond to the forces acting in the presumed conflict between the owners of a firm and the hired managers. The former are long-run optimizers and the latter are short-run suboptimizers, intent on their own short-term interest. In a similar way, the planner is a long-run optimizer that tries to influence the way money is spent in each period by setting up rules for the doer. The doer would spend all the money in the current period without such rules.

While the theory may lack something as a theory of saving (cf. King, 1985), there are some implications of psychological interest. The theory is compatible with the postulate of rationality. Saving is defined as a conflict between two forces, both of which are assumed to operate rationally, but with different utility functions. In a manner of speaking, this means converting the Freudian theory of the ego, the superego and the id into the mathematical terms of the economic theory of rationality. The superego sets up rules to regulate the impulses of the id.

King (1985) raised the following objection against the model

> They formulate the problem as a principal-agent model. This does not seem appropriate. In their model it is possible for the higher self to ensure that the lower self always follows an optimal life-cycle savings plan. There is no asymmetry of information, and the essence of a principal-agent problem is lacking. More relevant would be a formulation in terms of a bargaining model in which the two opposing sets of values tussled for dominance in the individual's mind. (King, 1985, p.269)

Shefrin and Thaler (1988) called this a misplaced criticism and pointed out that their model implied a question of restricted control rather than asymmetric information; the planner (= the principal) had limited control over the doer (= the agent).

While self-control is a concept that is used in psychology, there is no real, accepted theory. Dictionary definitions call it the ability to inhibit impulsive or narrow goal-seeking behavior for the sake of a more inclusive goal. Self-control is often seen as the ability to delay gratification and there is a research tradition under this label, with Walter Mischel as the most prominent researcher (for overviews of this research, see Mischel, 1984; Mischel et al., 1992). In psychological personality theories, personality traits or factors related to the concept of self-control are common. The five-factor model (see Chapter 7) is the personality theory that has aroused most attention in recent years. It includes a factor called 'conscientiousness' which seems to be close to self-control.

Psychological Conflict

Thaler and Shefrin (1981) postulated that two forces were in conflict and they maintained that their thinking was close to ideas about conflict in psychology. There is some general resemblance to the psychoanalytic theory of conflict, but less to the most common psychological theories. There are several conflict theories in psychology. Some of those deal with interpersonal conflict rather than conflict within an individual and have little bearing here.

Lewin's vector theory, as interpreted by Bilkey (1951) described purchase decisions as a psychic conflict between the desire to acquire the object and the resistance against spending money and make other sacrifices to get the object. Katona (1951, 1975) used some of this thinking in his models of consumer behavior, but he pictured consumption or saving as routine behavior or occasional problem solving rather than conflict-ridden decision situations.

When psychological conflict is mentioned, reference is mostly made to Miller's theory. Miller (Dollard and Miller, 1950; Holzman, 1958) distinguished between three types of conflict: (1) approach – approach, (2) approach – avoidance, and (3) avoidance – avoidance.

'Approach – approach' conflict is the difficulty of choosing between two equally attractive goals that are at least partially not to be had at the same time (Buridan's Ass). Jevons's view that anticipated pleasure was an important source of utility may be interpreted as similar to this type of conflict. Immediate consumption is then assumed to give pleasure and saving gives anticipated pleasure. Except for the role of anticipated pleasure, Jevons's general thinking on the influence of pleasure and pain on utility seems more in line with the second type of conflict.

'Approach – avoidance' conflict develops when an individual has a desire for some goal (object), but has learned that s/he will be somehow punished if s/he tries to get it. The approach – avoidance conflict can be seen as a choice between status quo and an alternative which has both positive and negative consequences. This type of conflict is the conflict between pleasure and pain that classical economists used to talk about. Senior set 'abstinence' which involved saving as painful in contrast to consumption which was pleasure. He pictured saving as a matter of conflict. The balancing between pleasure and pain was also the foundation of Jevons's and others' theories of utility. Consumption gave pleasure, the pain meant sacrifice in terms of expenditure and of giving up alternatives (opportunity cost). To be able to afford the cost, the individual had to work which was painful and gave negative utility.

'Avoidance – avoidance' conflict is when the individual has to choose between two or more undesirable alternatives. The choice between going bankrupt or severely curtailing expenditure may involve such a conflict.

Most purchases for consumption are probably not seen as conflict since one gets a corresponding value in return. There is little uncertainty connected with ordinary product choice as Kahneman and Tversky (1984) pointed out. Psychologically, there is a clear difference between certain and risky choices. While a risky choice holds the possibility of a loss which people generally resent, a non-risky choice normally involves a cost. The notion of cost implies that something is gotten in return.

Resistance against spending money on a certain object can imply that another spending alternative is equally attractive which is similar to approach – approach conflict. The opportunity cost acts as a deterrence. It may involve that postponement of purchase (and presumably of consumption), thus saving money, is an attractive idea because of anticipated pleasure. This is also an approach – approach conflict. A third case is that the pain exceeds the pleasure, meaning that the sacrifice (cost) is too high – an approach – avoidance conflict.

Thaler and Shefrin (1981) visualized conflict in a way that most resembles an approach – approach conflict, that is, a choice between two attractive alternatives. If the focus is on future pain as a consequence of 'doer' dominance, the conflict is approach-avoidance. The economic theory of self-control was fashioned so as to explain some puzzling phenomena of intertemporal choice. The basic assumption was that saving presupposed an effort or an act of willpower. This assumption was elaborated in the more recent version of the theory (Shefrin and Thaler, 1988; Thaler, 1990; Shefrin and Thaler, 1992).

The Components of the Behavioral Life-Cycle Model

Shefrin and Thaler (1988, 1992) explicitly linked their model to the LCH and described it as an enrichment of LCH. It offers a way of grappling with some of the important issues in the critique of LCH. They call the new model the Behavioral Life-Cycle Hypothesis (BLCH). Three important behavioral features were incorporated in the model: (a) self-control, (b) mental accounting, and (c) framing.

The concept of self-control is one of the main aspects of the new model. In this respect, it is similar to many of the verbally formulated theories of classical and neoclassical economists. The authors included three elements in their discussion of self-control: (a) internal conflict, (b) temptation, and (c) willpower. The 'internal conflict' arises because of dual preference systems, one concerned with the long run and the other with the short run. Like in the earlier paper, the former is called 'the planner' and the latter is 'the doer'. The planner function in the model is essentially given the role of distributing income over the rest of the life cycle.

The authors of BLCH viewed 'temptation' as an absolutely necessary element and declared that models of saving without it were misspecified. The reason was simply that some situations or rather opportunity sets were more tempting than others and that this influenced saving. Experiments on delay of gratification clearly support the assumption of the importance of temptation. Children's willingness to wait for a more attractive reward decreases when the less attractive reward is physically present (Mischel et al., 1992). Early economists like Rae (1834), Böhm-Bawerk (1888) and Marshall (1890) also had the insight that present goods are more vividly represented than the future goods (see Chapter 3).

'Willpower' is said to represent the real psychic costs of resisting temptation. Exercising self-control is seen as a cost. It takes some effort, sometimes a lot of effort to postpone consumption. In this respect, the ideas are similar to those of Senior and his followers. The assumption makes it possible to express self-control as a behavioral cost, which can possibly be studied in the same way as other behavioral costs, experimentally through varying antecedent conditions, and through survey questions.

The authors also use 'mental accounting' and 'framing' to explain saving processes and savings. 'Framing' refers to how the individual describes an alternative to her/himself and chooses a reference point with which alternatives are compared. Wealth is framed into different 'mental accounts'. Money is assumed not to be fungible, which means that people distinguish between different kinds of money. The source of the money is assumed to have influence on the propensity to consume it. Three components are distinguished: (a) current spendable income, (b) current assets, and (c) future income. The temptation to spend a marginal dollar is assumed to vary for the three types of mental accounts. Current income is the most tempting to spend, that is, it is characterized by the highest propensity to consume. Current assets and then future wealth follow it. The propensity to spend wealth from dividends should then be lower than the propensity to spend current income.

The propensity to consume additions to wealth is assumed to depend on the form in which the wealth is received. If windfall money, say, a bonus, is paid in monthly payments, it is likely to be treated as current income and more of it will be consumed. If it is paid as a lump sum it is likely to be treated as belonging to the assets account and less of it is consumed. The authors cited support from a study in which subjects were asked how much they would spend out of wealth derived from different sources, which were assumed to represent different mental accounts. They also found support in Japanese studies that showed propensity of the Japanese to save out of lump-sum bonuses (cf. Yoshikawa, 1995). Winnett and Lewis (1995) hypothesized that the propensity to consume would be lower for a non-realized increase in share value than for an increase in dividend. Testing the idea on data from the VSB panel, they found that all income from capital tended to be seen as non-spendable, irrespective of the form in which it accrued. The relevant mental accounts seemed to be differently framed than the BLCH predicted (Winnett and Lewis, 1995, p.441).

Refraining from consumption requires willpower, willpower increases are painful and become more painful as additional willpower is applied. This agrees with Senior but not necessarily with Jevons who thought that there could be pleasure in anticipation. Willpower effort is said to become less costly as retirement draws near and saving is easier. Self-imposed constraints on the opportunity set can make it easier to resist temptation and spend less willpower. If the planner prevails and there is no cost for exercising willpower, the BLCH is identical to the LCH. The predictions of the two models diverge because this condition is not likely to be met (Shefrin and Thaler, 1988, p.613).

The BLCH will now be described in a slightly more formal way. The lifetime budget constraint is given by

$$LW = \sum_{t=1}^{T} y_t.$$

where LW = lifetime wealth

$y = (y_1, \ldots, y_T)$ is the lifetime income stream

T is the end of the lifetime

The life-time consumption stream $c = (c_1, \ldots, c_T)$ cannot exceed LW

$$\sum c_t = LW$$

While the BLCH is similar to the LCH, a major difference is that the individual frames wealth from different sources as belonging to different mental accounts, with different propensities to consume. The authors maintain that in reality there is always a conflict between short-run and long-run interest. The doer has a subutility function $U_t(c_t)$. The planner is concerned with maximizing a function of lifetime doer utilities.

At time t_i there is an opportunity set (X_i) of feasible choices for immediate consumption. If left free, the doer selects the maximum feasible value of consumption, that is, tries to maximize U_t on X_t. Nothing may be left for the future. The planner will try to avoid this, which requires the exercise of willpower (W_t). This is tantamount to a psychic cost that will decrease the utility U_t for the doer

$$Z_t = U_t + W_t$$

where Z_t is total doer utility, that is, the sum of the pleasure and the pain
(negative)
W_t is the necessary amount of willpower.

The willpower needed to make an individual choose c_t, given the opportunity set X_t, is expressed by the following function

$$\theta_t^*(c_t, X_t)$$

The required willpower is thus a function of how low the level of consumption will be and the temptation of the opportunity set. Three assumptions are made about willpower effort:

1. An increase in willpower effort is necessary to reduce consumption, that is, $\theta_t^*(.)$ is decreasing in c_t
2. Increased willpower effort is painful in the sense that reductions in consumption resulting from willpower are accompanied by reductions in Z_t
3. Increased willpower effort is not only painful, but becomes increasingly more painful as additional willpower is applied.

Willpower is costly, but the willingness to refrain from consumption is assumed to decrease with consumption level and income. In order to minimize the effort for each choice situation the planner works with internal and external rules. The internal rules are self-imposed and require more willpower than the external rules. An example of the former is a self-imposed defense to borrow money for current consumption. External rules are, for example, pension plans where the employer pays part of the premiums and the employee another part.

The authors declared that when the model was confronted with savings data it made valid predictions. They did not submit their model to any real test, but cited evidence from other analyses in support of their model. They culled evidence about mental accounts from an experiment of their own and from earlier analyses that suggested that people consumed wealth from different sources with different probabilities. They selected a number of problems that have been discussed in connection with the LCH such as the role of pensions for (discretionary) savings, consumption smoothing over the life-cycle (consumption after retirement), permanent income and saving, income and consumption and bonuses and windfalls. For each problem, the authors made predictions using their own model. All of these predictions clashed with the predictions of the LCH.

There is much-debated evidence (from the USA) that an increased public contribution to a pension scheme may not lead to a corresponding decrease in discretionary saving for pensions (Cagan, 1965; Katona, 1965). Shefrin and Thaler noted the fact that people continued to save money for their pensions despite the public contribution and found that this agreed with their model. The latter also predicts that consumption after retirement will be lower than before if there is not an abundance of pension means. The model, moreover, predicts that higher permanent income will lead to higher saving; there is not proportionality as Friedman (1957) claimed (but did not find). Consumption seems to track income, which is in accordance with the model.

The hypothesis about differing propensities to consume for different mental accounts leads to the prediction that there is a lower propensity to consume a bonus that is usually paid as a lump sum than to consume regular income. That it may be easier to save from a lump sum, appears in the following quotation from an interview with a twelve-year old boy in UK: 'I get £5 a month from my mum 'cos if I got say a bit each week, I'd just spend it all. This way I have to save over the month to have some money' (Webley et al., 1991, p.143). The propensity to consume a windfall is lower than the propensity to consume regular income, but higher than the annuity value of the windfall. The propensity to consume a windfall decreases with increasing size of the windfall.

The BLCH has not been tested in full, but there is plausibility in the manner in which well-known LCH problems are handled. Its primary function so far is that it provides ideas for improving the LCH using some findings from the behavioral sciences. From the vantage point of this book, it is interesting that the authors revive some psychological concepts and try to show how they can be made compatible with economic analysis, notably marginal utility analysis. There are certainly many useful ideas connected with the BLCH and those can be fruitfully explored in empirical contexts. Still, it may be argued that the deductions behind the authors' predictions are somewhat doubtful. The results that they use to support their model are known in advance and the explanations are thus after-the-fact and ad hoc. The deductions from the theory do not always seem perfectly straightforward and the reasoning is not totally transparent.

From a behavioral point of view the fact that the important concept of self-control is made dependent on two conflicting forces – the doer and the planner – is despite the authors' reference to neurophysiology something of a weakness. There must be simpler ways of describing self-control than through postulating two utility functions with time horizons varying from the current budget period to the remainder of the life cycle. What is of particular interest in the model is the addition of a term for willpower to the utility function. Empirical investigations of willpower face some questions. Can the willpower necessary in each case be measured in any meaningful way or replaced by acceptably good proxies? Can utility of consumption over the rest of the lifetime be measured?

TIME PREFERENCES

Hence the lesson of self-denial – the sacrificing of a present gratification for a future good – is one of the last that is learnt.

Smiles ([1859] 1969, p.282)

Some might interpret the low wealth accumulation as being evidence of myopia, irrationality, or a failure to enforce 'mental accounting' (Richard Thaler, 1994), while others might view the low level of wealth accumulation as evidence of high individual rates of time preference.

Hubbard et al. (1994, p.174)

New Developments in the Study of Time Preference

There is an increasing interest in the behavioral aspects of time preference. The issue is how people actually make discounts of future utility. The question whether people do discount future goods and events is usually given an affirmative answer although the term 'discount' may not be used. The concept of time preference was developed so as to describe people's tendency to undervalue the future. As described earlier, Böhm-Bawerk (1888) who was preoccupied with explaining interest rates formulated a theory of saving which became known as 'the impatience theory'. Fisher (1930) translated some of it into mathematics, added his own ideas in an elegant form and made 'impatience' a legitimate concept in economics under the alternative name of 'time preference'. The discount function was held to be exponential with a constant discount rate.

Economists had quite sophisticated views on how people dealt with the future and the views did not only involve the tendency to undervalue the future. It was stressed that the value of a future good decreased very rapidly with the first lapse of time and then more slowly. A common assumption is now that discount functions fall very rapidly at first and then level off in the long run (see also Jevons, 1871; Ainslie, 1975). Böhm-Bawerk ([1888] 1912, p.447) said that in particular when the undervaluation (or lower evaluation of the future good) was caused by defects of will, there might be a strong difference between an enjoyment which offered itself at the very moment, and one which did not. There was only a small or no difference between an enjoyment that was far away, and one that was even further away.

As mentioned before, self-control was by the early economists considered to be an important factor when explaining saving behavior. The degree of self-control can be conceptualized as rate of time preference. Persons with low self-control were assumed to have a strong preference for the present. They can be said to ask a high interest rate in their discount functions for future events or in more psychological terms be impatient.

Marshall ([1890] 1990, p.187) wrote about men who never attempted to make provision for the time of need. They could discount the future benefits 'at the rate of many thousands per cent per annum.' He hinted that preferences might change over time. People want one thing today and another thing tomorrow, which means that they may later regret earlier behavior. Trying to explain addiction, the psychiatrist Ainslie (1975) has devoted much attention to this problem which will be treated further below.

The Discounted Utility (DU) model that is used in economics and finance is based on the assumption that there is a time preference rate for each individual and that it is valid both for lending and borrowing. Loewenstein and Prelec (1992) criticized this model. They alleged that the research that had shown weaknesses in the Expected Utility model had led to much more discussion than the actually more serious flaws found in the DU model: 'the counterexamples to DU are simple, robust, and bear directly on central aspects of economic behavior.' (Loewenstein and Prelec, 1992, p.574). On the basis of behavioral research they pointed out four anomalies in the model and proposed a model that could handle those. Their model is in principle an intertemporal interpretation of prospect theory (see Chapter 6).

When the individual's subjective discount rate exceeds the interest rate at which the individual can borrow money, s/he may feel better off if s/he borrows money and spends now (Loewenstein, 1988; Maital and Maital, 1991, pp.202-3). People who have high subjective discount rates can then be expected to have debts, use credit, save little, and if they save, pay off debts. Like Shefrin and Thaler (1988) Maital and Maital (1991) suggested that people try to protect themselves against overvaluing present consumption by making precommitments and imposing limits on their purchasing behavior.

Measurement of Time Preferences

In economics, it is usually assumed that the market interest rate is the same as the average rate of time preference. Fisher's impatience schedule suggested a way of measuring time preference: simply ask people about how much they are willing to pay out of next year's income for receiving (borrowing) $100 today. By now, many studies of how people judge delaying or expediting of awards and expenditures have been reported. Thaler (1981) seems to have been one of the first to make such studies.

Both judgment scales and hypothetical choices have been used to study time preferences. In the rare case, actual choices among alternatives with consequences have been used. As always when hypothetical choices are used to measure preferences, the question arises whether such methods yield reliable and valid results. Do people really answer the questions they are supposed to answer? The use of hypothetical choices has been criticized and many authors in the field have pleaded for studies of real intertemporal choices. At the same time they have admitted the difficulty of carrying out such experiments. In an experiment on intertemporal consistency, Horowitz (1992) used monetary incentives in a lottery-type of task. Incidentally, his results indicated individual inconsistency, but aggregate consistency.

Time preferences have sometimes been studied by other means than hypothetical intertemporal choices, for example, by the use of a judgment scale. A study in the Netherlands indicated that measurements of people's time preferences contributed significantly to explaining saving (Ritzema, 1992). Time preferences were measured on a simple scale, representing different degrees of impulsiveness–thriftiness, in an interview survey of saving habits.

Reliable measures are measures that are consistent and stable between different measuring occasions. Valid measures correspond to and adequately represent concepts in a model or theory. A common criterion for validity is that the measures predict or at least correlate with a relevant observable behavior. The recent discussion of the measures has focused on what they really represent, an aspect of validity. Knetsch (1997) gave an excellent review of the problems and advice for the treatment of time preferences. He explained earlier findings in terms of gains and losses, relying on prospect theory, and noted that rates of time preference could be expected to vary considerably. The stability and consistency of time preference measures have to my knowledge not been investigated. The external validity of the measures has been little investigated. Even with the weakness of the methods used, it seems safe to say that the results clearly cast some doubts on the market interest rates used in LCH studies.

It has been suggested that time preference could be inferred from savings. Against this, it is pointed out that there are many influences on savings and that it would be impossible to extricate the influence of time preference from all other influences (Loewenstein, 1987; Benzion et al., 1989). In one study time preference was inferred from behavior. In a study of Dutch households' purchases of a consumer durable, Antonides (1988) found that people who saved differed from those who did not save. For the former, the (by Antonides calculated) monthly discount factor was 0.014 percent while it was

0.026 percent for non-savers. Non-savers with an optimistic view of the future had the highest discount factor: 0.035 percent per month.

Some Behavioral Findings on Time Preference

Thaler (1981) was probably the first to carry out an actual experiment using hypothetical choices that revealed time preferences and made it possible to calculate discount rates. He challenged the assumption that the same, constant discount rate was valid for lending and borrowing. He gave an example for a mental experiment (Thaler, 1981, p.202)

    (a) Choose between   (a1) one apple today
                             (a2) two apples tomorrow
    (b) Choose between   (b1) one apple in one year
                             (b2) two apples in one year plus one day.

While many people may prefer (a1) to (a2), very few would prefer (b1) to (b2). This neatly illustrates the type of mental experiments that earlier economists made. In Thaler's experiment, questionnaires were distributed to groups of students. The questions were about how much money the students demanded so as to make a future amount of money equally attractive as a present amount. The same thing was done for losses. As he had expected Thaler found that the rates of time preference could be several times higher for gains than for losses.

In behavioral research on time preferences, it has typically been found that people do not have any definite, subjective time preference or discount rate that holds over a wide range of situations. The rate of time preference seems to vary with a number of circumstances (Thaler, 1981; Loewenstein, 1988; Benzion et al., 1989; Nyhus, 1997); those are similar to the four anomalies that Loewenstein and Prelec (1992) described.

1. The length of the time period
2. The amount of money
3. Whether delay or speed-up
4. Whether received payment or cost (satisfaction or pain).

The findings indicate that the longer the time period and the larger the amount, the lower the requested discount rate. Basing themselves on a study by Loewenstein (1988), Loewenstein and Prelec (1992, p.578) suggested that 'the amount required to compensate for delaying receiving a (real) reward by a given interval, from t to $t + s$, was from two to four times greater than the amount subjects were willing to sacrifice to speed consumption up by the same interval, i.e. from $t + s$ to t.' Nyhus (1997) found support for this hypothesis in her analysis of VSB panel data. Her analysis did not find significant length of time period and amount of money effects which she ascribed to differences in methods used. Thaler's (1981) finding that costs are discounted at lower rates than gains has been corroborated in many other studies.

Time preferences are influenced by socioeconomic and knowledge factors. Comparing their results obtained with students trained in financial matters with those of Thaler (1981), Benzion et al. (1989) noted that their subjects on average reported much lower discount rates. Those were closer to the market interest rate, in particular for delayed reception of large amounts over long periods. In a later study, Benzion et al. (1994) tested subjective discount rates against some theories from financial economics. The questionnaire asked how much interest the subjects – Israeli students – wanted for different kinds of financial investments in Israel under varying conditions. They did not find support for any of the tested theories at the microeconomic level.

Positive time preference means impatience to spend or, in more general terms, that good things are wanted soon and negative things are welcome to a delay. To have a high rate of time preference is the same as wanting to consume now rather than later and not caring to save. Some saving may still arise if the person has a strong feeling of uncertainty of the future or has a strong precautionary motive (Browning and Lusardi, 1996; Carroll, 1997).

The common assumption that time preference affects saving raises the question of which time preference measure to use. The time preference measure that undoubtedly is closest to saving, if saving is seen as postponement of consumption, is delayed reception of payment. This leads to the question which length of period and amount of money to use as a basis for the estimate. The answer is maybe an index combining different measures.

Time Preferences and Changing Tastes

A person's desire at a certain moment may change to a later date. This common phenomenon is often referred to as 'changing tastes' or 'time inconsistency'. Taste changes cause difficulties in economic theory which has stable preferences as one of its main tenets. When a time preference has been established through a choice of a plan or an action, the individual should stick to that choice and not regret it or try to change it. If a person now prefers to spend on immediate, perhaps lavish consumption, s/he should not the next week or later regret that the money was not saved. The classical and neoclassical economists spent considerable time trying to deal with this problem. It can be formulated in many ways and there are ways of handling changing preferences in economic analyses. The economists have been grappling with the question why people sometimes or often prefer to consume today rather than save money for tomorrow.

The decreasing value of an object with increasing remoteness in future time is in economics expressed as an exponential function with a constant discount factor. From the shape of the discount function it follows that it is easier to postpone decisions that involve some pain than to put them into immediate effect. The decision 'I shall start saving next year' is easier to make than 'I shall not buy anything, but start to save as of this moment.' In economic recessions, some governments with budget deficits have few plans for immediate cuts in expenditure, but plenty of ideas for starting to save next year and the following years. Whereas their behavior is consistent with the implications of the DU model, it may not be in agreement with the recent negative time preference hypothesis (see below).

The problem of 'changing tastes' is not only puzzling to economists. It is similar to problems of addiction and to how to get rid of bad habits. People may by far prefer behavior A to behavior B, but still choose B because its utility is immediately available. This implies that the discount functions for the two acts or goods A and B cross somewhere, which they cannot do with a constant discount factor. It means a change of taste, which only with difficulty can be handled by economic theory. Elster (1986) dealt with the relation between desires and behavior in a rather formal way

> Akrasia (weakness of the will) is characterized by the following features. (1) There is a prima facie judgement that X is good; (2) There is a prima facie judgement that Y is good; (3) There is an all things considered judgement that X is best; (4) There is the fact that Y is chosen. Taking a drink against one's own better judgement is a familiar example. (Elster, 1986, p.15)

The myopia involved in excess consumption now may be explained by the fact that present utility or pleasure is weighed against a future cost. The problem of addiction like smoking, drinking, and drug consumption can be seen as an approach – avoidance conflict over time. There is a current feeling of utility and (often vague) notions of costs that are distributed over a long period of time. The costs are heavily undervalued which suggests that the discount rate is high although much lower than for future gains. There does not seem as yet to be any generally accepted theory about how people weigh present pleasure against future, distributed costs. Ainslie (1975; 1992) depicts the conflict between an immediate pleasure which is repeated a number of times and costs that are not immediate, but distributed over future time. The individual must consider every single choice in the long-term perspective to overcome the temptation.

Fehr and Zych (1996) carried out an experiment in which they tested Becker's rational addiction theory. They found that their subjects undervalued future costs relative to present benefits. They noted that present benefits were highly salient. 'In contrast, the fact that future costs per period are relatively small, distributed over time and, thus, subjectively of ambiguous size renders them much less salient' (Fehr and Zych, 1996, p.17). The authors added that their subjects despite the fact that they were students in business administration and in the experiment had special training were not able to value the future costs adequately. 'It seems that their cognitive abilities did not allow them to integrate distributed future costs into one correct number' (Fehr and Zych, 1996, p.18)

The fact that people had a tendency to change their plans over time led the economist Strotz (1956) to suggest a way of describing the phenomenon of changing tastes and also to give some advice as to how the individual could safeguard against such behavior when it was unwanted. He proposed two ways to impose self-control so that undesirable crossing of discount functions could be prevented. People could (a) precommit themselves or (b) use the strategy of consistent planning. 'Precommitment' can be exemplified by Ulysses's behavior in the episode with the Sirens; he tied himself to the mast so that he could not yield to the temptation. Strotz remarked that unluckily precommitment was more often of the negative kind. People used credit to consume immediately and were thus committed to save afterwards. 'The strategy of consistent planning' consists in choosing the best of the plans that the individual counts on actually being able to follow. This entails some protection against deficient self-control in the future.

Strotz (1956), agreeing with Böhm-Bawerk (1888) and Fisher (1930), thought that the proper discount functions were established early in life through the teaching of parents and through social pressure from the environment. Children and other (according to Strotz) 'uninstructive' groups in society were too impatient in their discounting of the future. Ainslie (1975) further expanded Strotz's ideas and related them to psychological research. Like Jevons (1871), Böhm-Bawerk (1888), and Strotz (1956), Ainslie (1975) described a discount function that strongly overvalued objects and events that were close to the present. On the basis of psychological research, among other things in animal laboratories, he suggested that impulsiveness could be described in terms of a discount function. The function did not follow the course of exponential functions with a constant exponent, but rather had the form of a hyperbola. This shape meant that the time preference was represented by the expected value of the object divided by the time before the object became available. The idea is further developed in a later paper, presented to an audience of economists (Ainslie, 1991) and in a book with the title *Picoeconomics: The Strategic Interaction of Successive Motivational States within the Person* (Ainslie, 1992).

Elster (1977), further developing Ainslie's ideas, proposed ways of overcoming the temporary superiority of the present as against objects available in the future. He accepted precommitment as one way of overcoming impatience, but pointed out that another way was also used by Ulysses, namely avoiding exposure. Ulysses put wax into his sailors' ears so that they could not hear the singing of the Sirens.

Elster systematically reviewed ways of establishing self-control. There are several ways of tying oneself or precommitting oneself as Ulysses did. Sidebets are one type: 'I'll give you a hundred dollars if I can't save enough for a trip round the world in twelve months.' The ways of strengthening self-control are part of a theory of what Elster called 'imperfect rationality', meaning that the individual contrives means of compensating for a weak will or lack of self-control. Precommitment means binding oneself so that future impulses will not prevail and avoiding exposure means giving less room for getting new impulses. The tying can be internal and refer to 'challenges' and side-bets which the individual makes to her- or himself or external so that there is some public that can take the culprit to task in case of failure to fulfill the commitment. Leading a hermit's life or avoiding environments with known temptations are examples of the second remedy. Making rules like the planner i the Behavioral Life-Cycle Hypothesis and punishing oneself for transgression is a third mean of increasing the self-command.

Although these ideas have not been tested in saving contexts, they give food for thought. They stress the value of making the saving unavoidable through commitments. They suggest that people may not actually make decisions to save money, but rather deliberate on and decide on how to avoid spending money. They do this by refraining from exposure to temptations or by precommitments, such as deductions from wages, so that it becomes more difficult to spend than to save.

Negative Time Preferences

Recent thinking and experimental work on phenomena that were in fact touched upon by some of the classical economists have produced some hypotheses of great interest in connection with the characteristics of time preferences. Time preference may be negative according to Fisher (1930), only he classified it as a rare phenomenon. He illustrated the idea with an example in which a person had a large present income and a very small future income. In such circumstances, the person might even be willing to lend money for nothing.

> and even less than nothing, simply because he would, in such a case, be so surfeited with this year's income and so short, prospectively, of next year's income

that he would be thankful to get rid of this year's superfluity, for the sake of adding even a trifle to next year's meager real income. (Fisher, 1930, p.248)

A basic idea behind the new thinking is that people in general prefer improvement to deterioration, a climax order. They tend to order things in such a way that a climax is reached rather than to put the best things first and risk an anticlimax. Keynes (1936) distinguished the desire for improvement as one of eight motives for saving money. This implies that a *negative* time preference may at least sometimes be possible as an alternative to the generally assumed positive time preference (the strength of which, however, is assumed to vary). Economic utility theory predicts that things are rank ordered from most preferred to least preferred and chosen in that order, given a budget constraint. The new thinking leads to the idea that people may postpone consumption and save money because they want future improvements – something to look forward to – in their standard of living. This again raises the question: where do people get the strength to live up to such aspirations? Is it enough to assume that if the perceptions of possibilities for improvement are clear and vivid enough, the appropriate actions will ensue? Or is it necessary to assume something more: a will (desire) that is strong enough?

According to Loewenstein (1987), there are two kinds of utility to consider. One is the utility derived from actual consumption and the other is the utility derived from anticipating future consumption (cf. Jevons, 1871). The latter, if positive, is called *savoring* and if negative, *dread*. When there is a preference for an improvement order, some preferred events will be postponed and some non-preferred events may be wanted earlier. The latter would, for example, be the case if a person is waiting for a painful operation. It feels better to get it over with.

Summarizing the research evidence – which is still rather slim – Loewenstein and Prelec (1991) stated

Savoring and dread contribute to the preference for improvement because for gains, improving sequences allow decision makers to savor the best until the end of the sequence. With losses, getting the worst outcomes over with quickly eliminates dread. Adaptation and loss aversion induce preference for improvement because, over time, people tend to assimilate to ongoing stimuli and to evaluate new stimuli relative to their assimilation level. Thus, changes in, rather than levels of, consumption are the carriers of value. Improving sequences afford a continual series of positive departures (gains) from one's adaptation level; declining sequences provide a series of relative losses. (Loewenstein and Prelec, 1991, p.348)

The authors concluded

Any operation, custom, or habit that causes the stream of purposeful activity to fragment into a series of isolated choices, each involving a simple intertemporal tradeoff, and each unrelated to a larger plan, encourages impatient choices.

> Whereas the integral sequence frame, by fusing events into a coherent sequence, promotes concern for the future, thereby creating an appearance of negative time preference. (Loewenstein and Prelec, 1991, p.351)

This thinking implies that saving acts should not be promoted as separate actions. They should be embedded in sequences that involve improvement. A similar idea was brought forward by Elster (1986)

> I believe, however, that a person who takes his future states as given, rather than something created, is fundamentally irrational. Moreover, I believe a person will be better off by striving for connectedness, since only then will he be able to form the long-term plans that are a condition for living a meaningful life, even in the present. (Elster, 1986, p.11)

In a later paper, Loewenstein and Prelec (1993) elaborated the hypothesis on negative time preference. They indicated that the evidence so far was stronger for the existence of negative time preference when painful objects or events were involved (dread) than when the objects or events were attractive. The improvement order is interpreted as meaning that individuals do not want deterioration, but rather an even spread of consumption over time. This is surprisingly similar to the main assumption of the Life-Cycle Hypothesis. The hypothesis that people do not want to be kept waiting for known negative things to happen, but may prefer to have them done with, raises doubts about the efficacy of some political measures. Social benefits curtailments that will start to operate some time in the future rather than immediately may create 'dread' that is detrimental to behavior.

A New Look at Time Preference and Saving

Behavioral research shows that how people are dealing with the future is not a simple application of a discount function to make present and future alternatives comparable. It is not only that positive and negative events are treated differently. A number of characteristics of the events are also sources of variation in the relationships between the present and the future. The treatment of costs offers special problems. A positive time preference means that future costs are discounted with some discount rate that is usually found to be lower than the rate used for future positive events. If a future good or event has benefits and costs, the costs will be overvalued in comparison with the benefits. This may strengthen the preference for the present and for the alternative 'no change'. There is the contrary observation that small, future costs that keep coming back are undervalued.

One conclusion to draw from the discussions is that negative consequences must be considered along with the positive consequences. Knetsch

(1997) drew attention to the importance of studying gains and losses. The idea of negative time preferences suggests that there are costs or more generally expressed negative events that people prefer to endure as soon as possible, because of what Loewenstein called 'dread'. Those negative events are apparently of such size that they create highly unpleasant anticipations.

Time preference is an important concept in theories of saving, but obviously there are no simple relationships. Saving could be stimulated by strong positive anticipation of future pleasures that can be attained or by the mere feeling of a secure financial position in the future. So far very few studies of the relationships between time preference and saving have been done. Empirically, there are problems of defining and measuring. It seems questionable to use a single measure of time preference (see, for example, Knetsch, 1997; Nyhus, 1997).

Economic-psychological research on time preferences and saving is still at an early stage. Much of the focus has been on exploring the nature of time preferences (see, for example, Nyhus, 1997). Some studies have indicated that people who save tend to have lower rates of time preference than non-savers (Daniel, 1997). Wahlund and Gunnarsson (1996) reported that saver groups that were characterized by different financial strategies displayed differences in time preferences, consistent with the behaviors. The field of time preference has attracted much interest and many survey studies of saving behavior include some attempt at measuring time preference rates.

Finally, proverbs can express time preference as well as uncertainty (cf. Baxter, 1993, p.234). The British say 'a bird in the hand is worth two in the bush' which, if the uncertainty of getting the birds in the bush is negligible, means a high discount rate. What about the corresponding Swedish proverb: 'a bird in the hand is worth ten in the bush'?

5. Psychological and Other Behavioral Research on Household Saving

As a normal part of life, thrift now is un-American . . . People no longer identify saving with morality.

W.H. Whyte Jr. (in *Fortune*, May, 1958) Cited from Katona (1960, p.98)

For most people saving is something positive. Subjectively it is not merely a consequence of not spending, but rather the result of substantial pressures directed toward achieving highly valued goals of life. Saving is considered most important and its absence is greatly regretted.

Katona (1960, p.101)

The high value attached to thrift has puritan undertones that persist among many people despite the much-lamented 'thing-mindedness' of our age.

Katona (1975, p.235)

THE USE OF PSYCHOLOGICAL RESEARCH ON SAVING

Psychological research has two major functions in the study of saving: (a) providing methods and techniques for collecting subjective and objective data that are otherwise difficult to obtain, (b) supplying psychological concepts and theories for use in describing, explaining, and predicting saving and savings. A third function could be to develop a psychological theory of saving with a view toward studying reactions to the future (see Chapter 8).

Many differences in saving between countries and over time periods can be explained by economic and demographic factors, but there still remains a role to play for psychological research. The fact that at every level of income there are people who save and people who do not save illustrates that economic and demographic variables may not tell the whole story. The psychology of saving was for long solely the concern of economists who attributed saving to a quality called 'thrift'. Classical and neoclassical economists devoted a lot of interest to factors that influenced thrift. It was suggested that impatience and lack of self-control were important factors and it was assumed that such factors were associated with low education, low income, and low age. Some economists provided rather elaborate psychological theories that were quite different from what the contemporary psychologists were

166

busy studying. The question 'Why do people save?' accompanied by the politician's question 'How can people be made to save more?' has been with us at least since the Middle Ages when legislation against certain consumption was introduced in the form of the so-called sumptuary laws. Saving includes postponing consumption of something so that future consumption is made possible. Uncertainty about the future and a desire to do something so as to still the uncertainty may be assumed to lie behind saving. Saving is a matter of complex behavior and the links between the perception of uncertainty and the actual saving act are not very clear. Some guidance for psychological studies of saving can be found in the writings of classical and neoclassical economists (see Chapter 3). Early interview surveys comprised questions about at least some of the saving motives that the economists had listed.

The macroeconomic focus lies on total savings in an economy. Psychology can contribute some explanation of what is hidden under the movements of aggregate savings. Many welfare societies have been suffering from too little saving. There can also be too much saving in a country which may cause or deepen a depression. The question arises which groups in the population could save more and in the second case spend more. Essentially, there are in economic psychology four approaches to the study of saving behavior:

1. Survey research on saving habits, attitudes, and motives
2. Segmentation research ('saver groups'), mostly using survey data
3. Controlled laboratory experiments
4. Qualitative research on saving as a process.

Present uses of economic-psychological research have predominantly involved collection of data for testing hypotheses that are close to observations and looking for tendencies in the data. As mentioned earlier, George Katona had a model of saving that although simple in its basic assumptions grew into a behavioral theory of saving based on cumulative, consistent research findings. Katona's contribution was that he brought back interest in willingness to consume at the side of ability and created tools for assessing the willingness.

There is relatively little theory development in economic-psychological research on saving and the question inevitably arises: Is there enough reliable knowledge to contribute to a meaningful discussion of savings problems at the national level without collecting new data? I think there is already such a possibility for certain macroeconomic issues, for example, by exploiting the Index of Consumer Sentiment or the idea of saver groups (see below). There is still, in my view, a need to structure better the psychological research on saving behavior by means of more theoretical, better specified models.

In the following, a brief review of results from empirical research with a psychological orientation will be given. Most of this research has been influenced by the work that was started by George Katona at the University of Michigan in the late 1940s and that has been pursued ever since. It has been an exemplar for survey research on saving in many countries. After that, some typical findings on saving motives are reported. Research on the economic socialization of children and the place of saving in this is discussed. A review of some findings in survey research where psychological concepts were used shows how new psychological variables besides willingness have been introduced in research. The review gives a partial answer to the question of how psychological concepts can improve saving research. Some models that open ways of reasoning about saver groups or segments will then be presented. Finally, the new developments in saving research involving experimental research and qualitative studies are presented.

KATONA'S SAVING MODEL AND STUDIES OF SAVING

The survey-based research on saving started in the 1940s and George Katona was one of the leaders of the project. The research established a paradigm for asking people about their savings, saving attitudes and saving motives that has later been adopted by economists in many countries (Klein, 1954). More recently, a number of economic psychologists have turned their attention to the study of saving behavior.

Before Keynes, economists had focused on the role of the interest rate for saving and added considerations of income, personality factors like thrift, and saving motives. While earlier economists paid some attention both to ability and willingness to save/consume, Keynes made ability the main factor. After Keynes, current income and, later, past income and future income came to dominate the saving theories. Katona's theory of saving was based on the assumption that saving was a function of two sets of factors: *ability* to save (mostly objective data) and *willingness* to save (a variety of psychological factors, in time-series analyses usually the Index of Consumer Sentiment; see below). The function, which combines economic and psychological variables, still embodies the gist of most economic-psychological theories of saving. Willingness to save is assessed through a rather broad array of psychological variables.

Although individual and household income data were usually collected in the survey interviews, 'ability' was in Katona's work typically estimated through aggregate data on total disposable income. 'Willingness' was measured through subjective data collected from households. The measure that was used was computed for the aggregate and had no exact equivalent at the individual/household level. It is called the 'Index of Consumer Sentiment' (ICS) and indicates the degree of optimism or pessimism in a population. It has shown ability to explain and predict total savings in a country (more about this later in this and the following chapter).

Katona thus reintroduced 'willingness to save/consume' and in his short-run forecasts exploited willingness alone measured as the Index of Consumer Sentiment. The importance of the willingness factor was due to the fact that many people had discretionary or supernumerary income that they could freely spend or save after they had covered their expenditures on necessities. As mentioned in Chapter 2, Katona distinguished three types of saving, based on reasons or motives for saving: (1) contractual saving, (2) discretionary saving, and (3) residual saving.

'Contractual saving' is similar to the precommitment ideas brought forth by Strotz (1956) and some later economists. Such saving may be self-imposed or imposed by others, for example, by governments. In the former case, it is often a consequence of a voluntary decision, but others then enforce the saving. Buying on an installment plan necessitates later regular saving since the debt must be paid off. Buying life insurance or a retirement pension scheme involves a contract to save regularly and usually for long periods of time. 'Discretionary saving' is an original concept and like discretionary consumption one of Katona's main theoretical contributions to behavioral economics. It relates to the room for genuine decisions that many people have in affluent societies. People may decide to save for many reasons such as wanting to purchase an expensive durable, to go on a long vacation or just desiring to have money available if opportunities for attractive spending arise. Katona's critique of Keynes's psychological law, which stipulated that consumption was in the long run tied to current income, was based on the idea of discretionary consumption. The consumer freedom to save or to spend some of the current income made it difficult to find stable relationships between income and consumption/saving.

'Residual saving' refers to money that has not yet been spent. It is saved by default rather than planning. A possible interpretation is that some, maybe a major part, of residual saving may not derive from abundant income, but rather emerge as a consequence of strict control of expenditure.

The effects of macroeconomic changes, for example, the effects of a tax cut on savings in a country, are assumed to depend on such intervening variables as the attitudes and expectations of the taxpayers. Since the pertinent attitudes and expectations can rarely be predicted on the basis of easily available objective data, the consequence is that new data on the state of the intervening variables will almost always have to be collected before the effects can be explained or predicted.

The Psychology of Saving

The Survey Research Institute at the University of Michigan was the place where the economic-psychological studies of saving behavior began. They have continued over the years. Studies of savings, relying on face-to-face interviews, were carried out in many countries in the 1950s and 1960s. They tended to follow the pattern of the University of Michigan studies that Katona participated in. The results of the early studies of saving were summarized in Katona (1960). Conclusions from studies carried out during a somewhat longer period were presented in Katona (1974, 1975).

Katona (1975) studied how discretionary saving changed with the business cycle and how income changes affected this saving. If an increase in income was followed by another increase or there was a firm expectation of further increase, consumption tended to go up and saving to decrease. If there was a decrease in income and expectation of further decrease, consumption tended to decrease and saving increase. The effect of inflation was difficult to assess since people's expectations of further price increases might induce them to buy early, but under certain circumstances make them postpone buying.

In addition to regular surveys in which data on saving were collected, special studies were also carried out. One such study was devoted to the economic behavior of the affluent (Barlow et al., 1966). A sample of affluent people were interviewed about their savings, saving motives, and investment behavior.

The saving of self-employed create a special problem since the self-employed are both private persons and enterprises. Katona (1960) remarked on the savings of the self-employed

> Entrepreneurs tend to save on average a larger proportion of their incomes than other people with similar incomes and have a unique and apparently powerful motive to save [. . .] . Many unincorporated businesses are chronically short of funds and often do not have ready and easy access to the capital market. Ownership of small business is also commonly associated with the desire to be independent and to be one's own boss. Paying off partners and creditors, who may restrict the independence of the owner, then becomes a strongly felt need. The owner may therefore reduce his personal expenditures for the purpose of plowing back more money into his firm. (Katona, 1960, pp.94-5)

Incidentally, in a Swedish study, Wärneryd et al. (1987) found that the self-employed were different from employees. Those had more money in bank accounts, presumably because they needed higher liquidity, received larger amounts of interest payments and paid more interest than a comparison group of employees. Among researchers using survey data on saving behavior it is nowadays well known that data on self-employed may be very different and require removal and special analysis as constituting outliers.

Have the USA and other economies changed so much that Katona's ideas are no longer valid and interesting? In 1980, Katona himself made the following, sober statement: 'Behavioral economics, developed in an era of spreading affluence and optimism, is confronted with new tasks in an era of limited growth and uncertainty' (Katona, 1980, p.16). The Index of Consumer Sentiment gets more attention than ever both by the mass media and by economic researchers. The basic model which states that consumption–saving is a function of ability and willingness to consume–save is still valid if both ability and willingness are interpreted in a broad sense and modern cognitive and social psychology is exploited. Close reading of some of Katona's works reveals many ideas that are still applicable and testable on consumption and saving.

STUDIES OF SAVING MOTIVES

Respondents in a large number of survey contexts have been asked questions about motives for saving. The motives elicited are usually quite similar to those listed by Keynes (1936; see Chapter 4). Katona (1975, pp.233-4) noted that most of the reasons people gave for saving belonged to one of the following categories, in order of importance: (1) for emergencies, (2) for retirement, (3) for children and family needs, (4) for other purposes such as to buy a house, to buy a business, to buy durables, or to pay for vacations and other trips. On the whole, it was uncommon in the USA to save to buy durable goods. While most Americans used installment plans for this purpose, West Germans preferred to save. Hardly any US respondents mentioned saving for the purpose of earning additional income in the form of interest or dividends, a few mentioned the motive to bequeath money to their heirs.

Table 5.1 shows data on saving purposes from some studies. The first column reports data from a Swedish study, done with a representative sample of Swedish adult men in 1978. The other two columns are based on VSB Panel data from two waves. Some of the respondents were the same in both waves, but each sample was in principle representative of the Dutch population at the time the data was collected. Many studies have shown that the protection against emergencies or the perceived need to have some capital as a buffer if something happens is the most important saving motive (cf. Fisher's 'saving for a rainy day'). This motive was dominating in the Swedish study and the most important one in the Dutch data. Katona (1975, p.235) likewise reported that saving for emergencies was the most often stated motive (45 percent in 1966), followed by saving for retirement and old age (31 percent), and for children's education and other needs (22 percent). With government-run old-age pension systems and no school fees two saving motives that are frequent in the USA and Japan have little importance in Sweden and many other European countries.

Table 5.1 Saving Motives in Sweden and the Netherlands

Purpose of saving	Lindqvist	VSB –94	VSB –96
	Percent	Percent	Percent
Car	6	18	17
House	22	19	17
Holidays, travel	14	21	20
Durable goods	8	16	18
Extra income (e.g. interest)	?	6	6
Unforeseen circumstances	46	31	33
Old age	?	11	20
My children	3	11	18
Paying off debts	?	5	4
Other purpose	7	5	3
No particular purpose	?	21	16
Did not save	14	32	36

Note: Some respondents stated more than one motive.

Sources: Lindqvist (1981b, p.165). VSB Panel data from the 1st and 4th waves.

While saving for bequests was infrequent in the Swedish study, it seems more frequent in the Dutch data, but the category 'My children' covers more than bequests. The bequest purpose was also uncommon according to the US data, except among high-income earners and wealth owners. This is clearly demonstrated in the study of the affluent by Barlow et al. (1966)

> As income increased, there was a steady decline in the proportions saving for re-
> tirement or for their children's education. Presumably at the highest income levels
> most individuals felt confident of meeting these particular needs out of the current
> income provided by the capital they had already accumulated. One might have ex-
> pected similar responses on the objective of saving to meet future emergencies, but
> this objective maintained roughly the same importance at all income levels. As in-
> come rose, the bequest motive, however, became more prominent, being men-
> tioned by about half of those with incomes over $300 000. (Barlow et al., 1966, p.32)

ECONOMIC SOCIALIZATION AND CHILDREN'S IDEAS ABOUT SAVING

In a broad sense, 'socialization' is the process in which an individual becomes a member of a social system. Children's economic socialization is the
process through which children gain knowledge, understanding, and skills in
relation to the economic environment, as consumers and at the work place.
There are many studies of children's economic socialization (see Stacey,

1982; *Journal of Economic Psychology*, Special Issue on Economic Socialization, Dec., 1990; Lunt and Furnham, 1996). The focus is restricted to what
the research has shown about children's relationships to saving: what they
know, what they think about saving, and their actual saving behavior at different ages.

Saving habits are learned early in life according to many authors (see e.g.
Böhm-Bawerk, 1888; Marshall, 1890; Fisher, 1930; Strotz, 1956; Maital,
1982). Studies of economic socialization have mostly paid relatively little
attention to children's saving behavior. They have dealt more with related
phenomena like possessions and acquiring possessions, and children's ideas
about the role of banks and shops.

'Early in the child's experience with age-mates, possessions and posses-
sive behaviour take on social characteristics involving interpersonal control
and power over possessions' (Stacey, 1982, p.171). The idea of possession
enters the mind very early and is very important according to one, often-cited source

> It is already clear that possessions are related to many areas of psychological de-
> velopment: personal possessions are often an integral part of one's self-concept,
> possessive behavior has been linked to fundamental motivational constructs such
> as effectance and competence and possessions are often a focal point in the devel-
> opment of peer relations and social transactions. (Furby, 1979, p.181)

Furby obtained her data from US and Israeli children and she warned that the
results were probably not valid for non-capitalistic countries. A few studies
of economic socialization have obtained data about children's saving behavior. A brief summary was given by Lea et al. (1987, pp.392-3). A few later
studies have had a rather broad scope and will be commented on here. Jundin
(1988) reported such data from her Swedish studies. Sonuga-Barke and Webley (1993) made a very thorough study of children's saving, employing laboratory simulation experiments and semi-structured interviews with children
and their parents. More will be said about this study in a later section on experimental studies of saving.

Jundin (1988, p.84f) summarized the findings from her own Swedish
studies of economic socialization and those of other researchers. Her conclusions were similar to those reported later by Sonuga-Barke and Webley
(1993). Children 4 to 6 years old do not seem capable of understanding the
function of saving. They may still have a high opinion of saving since they
think of saving as a norm. They adopt attitudes and imitate the behavior of
adults without question, as rules that have to be followed. They do not understand the value of money and tend to accept that change in many small coins
is worth more than a single coin with higher value.

When children are 7-8 years old they discover, in an often sudden insight,
that saving serves a purpose or is functional, a term used by Sonuga-Barke

and Webley (1993), and that saving is of value to them. Children in this age group often collect objects like stones, stamps, pictures, etc. and they become socially active. Together with peers they may even form clubs with the purpose of saving up for something (or for at least discussing the possibility). Their saving goals may be highly unrealistic like saving to buy a horse, a bicycle or a boat, but they seem capable of frequently revising their saving goals.

Older children begin to understand more aspects of economic life like the role of banks and the role of interest on bank accounts and loans. Children aged from 10 to 14 usually get more money for their own use and they may make extra money by doing a job. This gives them more experience with money and its uses in the short and the long run. Teenagers strive for independence and frequently try different life-styles, which costs money. They become less interested in saving money and their attitudes towards saving are more negative than earlier and later in life.

In one of her studies, Jundin (1988) interviewed teenagers from 13 to 18 years of age. She found that only 10 percent of them did not save at all. While among the youngest savers, two-thirds kept their savings at home, only 13 percent among the 18-year-olds did so. Savings in the bank increased correspondingly. The crucial age for the change seemed to be around 15. The younger bank savers did not themselves put money in a bank, but let their parents do this – over 50 percent of the 14- and 15-year-olds as against 4 percent of the 18-year-olds.

The most important motive for saving was related to short-run consumption goals. Table 5.2 presents data on saving motives for age groups and gender. Boys and girls differed somewhat. Girls seemed to save more for long-run goals like preparing for getting an apartment of their own. It was more common to save money so as to have it at hand, if need be, than to save for a certain goal. The differences between the age groups are surprisingly small.

The reasons given for putting savings in a bank account varied more. The most common reason was 'it is more difficult to spend the money and easier to keep track of the money if it is in a bank'. This reason was stated more often by girls (55 percent) than by boys (44 percent). The second most important reason had to do with investing – getting a profit or an advantage from the bank in the future (29 percent of the boys and 18 percent of the girls). For the youngest age groups, especially the 13-year-olds, the safe storage of money in a bank was the second most important motive. They were also more often inclined to invoke a social norm for saving in a bank. Jundin suggested that it might be important for policy makers and bank marketers to pay more attention to the time dimension of children's saving motives and reasons for putting money in a bank account.

Table 5.2 Saving Motives of Swedish School Children

	Age Group						Gender	
	13	14	15	16	17	18	Girls	Boys
	Per-cent	Per-cent	Per-cent	Per-cent	Per-cent	Per-cent	Per-cent	Per-cent
Savings give a feeling of security	20	27	29	26	33	30	26	29
I save only if there is something special I want to buy	18	16	17	19	19	18	20	16
I save money so I shall have money if I want to buy something special	35	34	35	34	32	36	29	39
I save so as to have money when I move from home	26	22	20	21	16	16	25	16

Note: The class years used by Jundin (1988) are here replaced by average age.
Source: Jundin (1988, p.104).

Traditionally, there are two theoretical approaches to socialization. One approach focuses on the role of age and maturation, often in the spirit of Piaget's theory. The other views the process as determined by social interaction and emphasizes the influence of social agents. In empirical research on economic socialization, there is now a tendency to see it as a matter both of maturation *and* social influence. It is often assumed that saving habits are learned early in life and that parents have an important influence. Even apart from everyday observation that children in one and the same family may have highly divergent consumption and saving habits, empirical research appears to indicate that there are similarities between parents and children, but that they are not overwhelmingly great.

Sonuga-Barke and Webley (1993) gave reasons for the lack of similarity

> It seems that a surprisingly large number of parents do not make any concerted effort to 'train' their children in the management of money, most relying in a rather vague way on encouraging a savings habit either by forcing or encouraging their children to save pocket money or by letting their children have nominal control of a bank account opened in their name. Like the savings institutions there is no attempt to teach the purpose of saving nor the value of thrift as a trait of character. (Sonuga-Barke and Webley, 1993, p.83)

Other researchers have found limited attempts of parents to influence their children (Ward and Wackman, 1973; Moschis and Churchill, 1975; Jundin, 1988). Studies of children becoming consumers indicate that there is little purposive consumer training by parents. They still show that parents have considerable influence on the process. The parents make purchases with their children, they discuss purchases among themselves with children as more or less engaged listeners, they discuss buying options with their children, they approve or reject their children's own purchases. They also open bank accounts for their children and act as mediators for putting their children's savings in bank accounts.

Table 5.3 Comparison of Attitudes towards Thrift between School Children and Adults in Sweden. Percent Agreeing with Statement

	Age groups						
	13	14	15	16	17	18	Adults
Thriftiness is an important quality in a person	35	25	21	23	21	13	53
It is important to have money left at the end of the month	35	34	30	39	22	30	38
Those who manage to save will do well in life	38	41	29	28	22	18	31
It is unnecessary to save when so much aid can be obtained from society	4	4	2	6	1	6	2

Note: The size of the age groups varies from 35 to 73. The adult sample comprises 429 respondents

Source: From Jundin (1988, p.98)

Table 5.3 is based on two Swedish studies of saving behavior. In those, the norm or moral dimension of saving was covered through four attitude statements, with which the respondents could agree or disagree. Jundin (1988) provided data about schoolchildren in two Swedish cities, collected in 1985 and made a comparison with 1978 data on adults, collected from a representative sample by Lindqvist (1981b). The two sets of data are not wholly comparable, but they give an interesting indication of differences between generations. Whether these will persist, so that the young people will be less appreciative of saving when they grow up, is an open question. In Table 5.3, the youngest children are around 13 and the oldest are around 18. While the younger children were more favorable towards saving than the older ones, they differed significantly from the adult population in their appreciation of saving as a desirable quality. The adult data were collected at the end of the

1970s and the school data in the middle 1980s long before the cutdowns in social benefits began. Interestingly, both children and adults rejected the idea that saving was unnecessary because of aid available from society.

While, according to a number of studies, there seems to be a certain order in which the knowledge, values and skills develop, there are clear cultural differences in when or at which age, a certain stage is reached. Using essentially the same questions as Jahoda (1979, 1981) had earlier posed to Scottish children, Ng interviewed Hong Kong children aged 6 to 12. The questions concerned knowledge about banks and about shops. It turned out that the Hong Kong children who came from varying socioeconomic backgrounds with some overweight for middle-class acquired economic knowledge much earlier than the Scottish children. 'A full understanding of the bank emerged at age 10, while that of shop profit emerged at age 6, both showing a precocity over the Scottish sample' (Ng, 1983, p.209). The author attributed the differences to the socio-economic realities that shaped the children's economic understanding. A later study (Ng, 1985) that was conducted in New Zealand confirmed an age-related progression of knowledge and reasoning about banks, but the rate of progression was different, with the New Zealand sample lagging behind the Hong Kong children by about two years.

An international group of economic psychologists carried out parallel studies of economic socialization in a number of countries. The results were published in the *Journal of Economic Psychology*, Dec., 1990. Children 8 years old (S), 11 years old (M), and 14 (L) years old were interviewed. While the interviews were not fully structured and the interviewers given some freedom, some questions appeared in the questionnaires of all the countries. The following question asked for views about savings and investment

> Suppose a person has plenty of money he doesn't need right now. What can he do with it? What else? Is there a way to increase that amount? (If the bank would give him more: Why would they do this?)

The answers were coded in the following way: (a) consume more, (b) store in a bank, retrieve the same amount in due course (including in addition to an increase in consumption), (c) invest in bank, stock exchange etc. so as to retrieve more: (interest, shares, bonds, etc.) (including in addition to an increase in consumption), (d) charity, and (e) don't know.

The Psychology of Saving

*Table 5.4   Answers to a Question about What a Person with Extra Money
Could Do with the Surplus. Proportion of Answers*

Country	Age	Consume more	Store in bank	Invest	Charity	Don't know
Austria	L	0.00	0.00	0.00	1.00	0.00
	M	0.40	0.00	0.00	0.60	0.00
	S	0.54	0.00	0.15	0.31	0.00
Denmark	L	0.13	0.00	0.76	0.11	0.00
	M	0.14	0.00	0.73	0.14	0.00
	S	0.27	0.00	0.47	0.27	0.00
Finland	L	0.06	0.00	0.80	0.00	0.14
	M	0.00	0.00	0.74	0.00	0.26
	S	0.14	0.40	0.29	0.00	0.17
France	L	0.17	0.00	0.83	0.00	0.00
	M	0.14	0.57	0.29	0.00	0.00
	S	0.00	0.25	0.00	0.00	0.75
Israel,	L	0.00	0.20	0.72	0.04	0.04
kibbutz	M	0.00	0.59	0.37	0.03	0.00
	S	0.08	0.64	0.00	0.28	0.00
Israel, town	L	0.08	0.27	0.65	0.00	0.00
	M	0.04	0.59	0.26	0.00	0.11
	S	0.21	0.43	0.07	0.00	0.29
Norway	M	0.24	0.18	0.22	0.36	0.00
	S	0.31	0.24	0.07	0.34	0.03
Poland	L	0.14	0.17	0.69	0.00	0.00
	M	0.23	0.45	0.23	0.00	0.10
	S	0.31	0.49	0.08	0.00	0.13

Source: Based on Leiser, Sevón and Lévy (1990, p.621, Table 5).

Table 5.4 shows the answers for a number of participating countries. First, it
should be noted that the younger children in some countries had difficulties
answering the question about what a person could do with money he did not
need right now. There was a tendency for younger children to answer 'consume more' more often than for older children. The most common answers
mentioned putting the money in a bank. There were two categories. The first
one comprised the answers that were restricted to the storage aspect and did
not mention interest or profit. When increasing the capital was mentioned,
the answers were coded in the second category. These categories also included an increase in consumption. The oldest children, the 14-year-olds,
gave to a much larger extent answers that were coded in the 'investing' category. In this age group, children were apparently aware of the possibility of

increasing one's wealth by investing. The 11-year-olds more often noted the storage aspect. Except in Austria, charity was an uncommon suggestion, but some of the youngest children recommended this. This study did not report any data on children's attitudes to saving and their own attempts at saving.

In a summary of the ten studies, Leiser et al. (1990) discussed age trends and cultural differences. While there were very clear differences that were attributed to cultural differences between the countries, there were also clear age differences. The trends in age differences led to the conclusion '. . . that young children conceptualize the economy from the perspective of 'social man', whereas some older children have shifted the conceptualization to that of the 'economic man'. There were cultural differences that seemed to explain when and how age group differences appeared.

There is, on the whole, agreement that there are characteristic stages in cognitive development and that, if defined broadly enough, those tend to follow a certain order. Lea et al. (1987, pp.374ff.) expressed some doubt about the stages in children's cognitive development and considered some alternative theory. They wanted more differentiation between learning physical world phenomena and learning relationships in the social world. The cultural similarities found could be caused by similarities of approaches.

DO PSYCHOLOGICAL VARIABLES IMPROVE PREDICTIONS OF SAVING?

The Index of Consumer Sentiment

The 'Index of Consumer Sentiment' (ICS) was introduced by Katona in the late 1940s. It is still, with minor modifications, used in many countries. In Europe, it is now usually called 'Index of Consumer Expectations'. In the mass media, it is known as 'consumer confidence'. The ICS is computed as the 'balance' for each of five questions, i.e. the difference between the percentage of those who report improvement and the percentage of those who report deterioration, averaging over the five questions. The ICS is a predictor of turning points in business cycles, indicating ups, downs or no change. It reflects changes in optimism-pessimism about the financial future. The proper interpretation is that the population is becoming more optimistic or more pessimistic, not that the majority is optimistic or pessimistic. The measure used is a pure macropsychological measure of change.

Katona's simple measurement of financial expectations has proved its mettle and ability to survive. On the whole, the acceptance of the Index for short-run forecasts is high. The mass media seem to have an increasing interest in the ICS measures and often report them as news about increasing or decreasing 'consumer confidence' for the general audience and not only for economic specialists. In fact, the latter may be more skeptical of ICS than are news journalists. ICS has been used as a (post hoc) predictor of total saving in many economic and econometric studies and has been found to be a significant predictor in many contexts (Juster, 1981; Williams and Defris, 1981; Biart and Praet, 1987; Vanden Abeele, 1988; van Raaij and Gianotten, 1990; Carroll et al. 1993; Berg and Bergström, 1996).

The reason for the long survival of the ICS is obviously its ability to predict in a useful manner certain economic developments related to turning points in the business cycle. In the USA, it is said to be capable of short-term predictions of changes in interest rates (as far as six months ahead), changes in the Consumer Price Index (three months ahead) and changes in the unemployment rate (nine months ahead) (Curtin, 1992). There is some divergence of opinion about the use of the ICS in time-series analysis (see Vanden Abeele, 1988). There are, however, many examples of significant contributions to explaining variance in savings and consumer durable sales, when the measures are combined with economic variables in multivariate analyses of time-series data (Biart and Praet, 1987; van Raaij and Gianotten, 1990). When ICS goes down, that is, more people become pessimistic, savings tend to increase. When people become more optimistic they tend to spend more.

Many attempts have been made to explain what factors determine ICS. First, some economic-psychological studies will be mentioned. In a Dutch study, van Veldhoven and Keder (1988) found quite high correlations between newspaper economic news and the Index of Consumer Expectations in the Netherlands. Their tentative conclusion was that there was, in particular, an influence of negative news. What constituted positive news was somewhat more puzzling. It seemed as though the absence of economic news sometimes had a positive effect on expectations.

Using the concept 'pessimistic rumination', Zullow (1991) tested media influence on consumer optimism or pessimism and on economic growth. He carried out content analyses of pessimistic themes in popular music and in *Time* magazine and found that there was a correlation with the ICS and the Gross National Product. Moreover, he traced a time sequence with popular songs as the first step or indication of growing pessimism in the USA, followed by changes in the ICS and later the GNP.

According to Katona (1975), the ICS was not supposed to be used in time series analysis since the purpose of it was to assess phenomena that lacked stability over time. In his own use of the ICS, he added information that was solicited in the interviews through follow-up questions like 'Why do you think so?'. The usefulness of the Index rested on predicting turning points in the business cycle when there was substantial change. This has not precluded its use in time-series analyses. Economists who usually shun subjective data have tried to trace the objective determinants of the ICS and to replace it with objective indicators. This presupposes a certain stability of the ICS over time. Shapiro (1972) investigated how well total disposable income, unemployment rate, a price index, and an index of industrial common stocks explained the ICS 1956–70. He found $R^2 = 0.83$ and could not reject the hypothesis of stability over time. ICS_{t-1} , the lagged ICS, played an important role in the equation.

Shapiro concluded

> The results do imply, however, that a stable model of consumer attitude formation can be isolated from readily available data on income, inflation rates and equity prices, and that for some purposes (e.g. short-term forecasting), this information may be used in models of consumer behavior in place of survey results. (Shapiro, 1972, p.378)

In spite of the fact that expensive surveys could then be dispensed with, ICS data are regularly collected. There may be two reasons: (1) the necessary data are available too late and (2) ICS is still better for short-term forecasts of turning points. Predictions made on the basis of multiple regression equations with ICS and a number of objectively measured variables have also been tried with somewhat varying success. Juster's (1981) attempt to predict the US saving rate in 1979 using such an equation was a failure. Consumers were growing pessimistic about their financial future and made anticipatory purchases in the expectation that prices would rise further.

Many econometric studies have used ICS or a similar index as an extra explanatory factor in time-series, multiple regressions for total savings. Juster (1981) presented a saving rate model based on short-run uncertainty influences and Houthakker-Taylor's zero-depreciation model of saving behavior (Juster and Taylor, 1975).

> In the long run, assuming no growth in income or in population, saving would disappear as assets become adjusted to the steady-state long-run income level. Thus saving arises because of disequilibrium between assets and income, or out of population growth. In the short run, changes in various components of income (including personal taxes and social security taxes) will produce positive or negative saving as part of the adjustment process. Finally, uncertainty about real income prospects will have an impact on short-run saving behavior, although uncertainty factors are expected to have little or no long-run effect. (Juster, 1981, p.92)

Juster found that a lagged ICS improved the explained variance of saving rates, but that price expectations contributed even more. Juster and others have in different contexts used the mean and variance of the price expectations distribution as a proxy for the 'uncertainty' of future income. Juster (1981) used a filtered ICS where the filter eliminated changes in the ICS that were neither large nor systematic. This was in accordance with Katona's view that the ICS primarily predicts turning points in the business cycle.

Using Australian data from 1973 to 1978, Williams and Defris (1981) regressed the saving rate on inflation, change in unemployment rate, survey answers to the attitude items 'inflation serious now, 'unemployment serious now', 'unemployment serious in future', and the Australian ICS. They also included a variable that indicated the net number of favorable news items. All these variables were significantly related to the saving rates. Two of them were negatively related, namely, the ICS, a result that was similar to those of other studies, and the number of favorable news items. The latter again suggests that people spend more when there is a tendency towards optimism.

Carroll et al. (1993) specifically dealt with the question whether ICS contained any information that was not available in other indicators. They wanted to answer two questions; (1) Does ICS have any predictive power of its own for future changes in consumption spending? (2) Does ICS contain information about future changes in consumer spending aside from the information contained in other available indicators? Analyzing data for the years 1955 to 1992, the authors concluded that lagged values of the ICS, taken on their own, explained 14 percent of the variation in the growth of total real consumption expenditures. The answer to the second question was less clear: 'Overall, we read the evidence as pointing toward at least some significant incremental explanatory power' (Carroll et al., 1993, p. 1397). The contribution toward explaining R^2 seemed to be between 1 and 3 percent, except that for one short period the contribution was negative.

In a Swedish study, Berg and Bergström (1996) found that there were two important determinants of the Swedish equivalent to ICS: changes in real interest rates and changes in the inflation rate. These authors split the index into two, one of which concerned the household's own financial situation and the other the general economic situation in Sweden. The former was found to be more closely related to changes in consumption than the latter. The household financial situation index standing alone explained around 37 percent of the variance in the growth rate of consumption. Even when combined with other variables in a standard consumption equation, the household financial index gave a significant contributton. It increased the explained part of the variance from about 0.69 to 0.76.

Other Psychological Measures

Ölander and Seipel (1970) presented a behavioral model of saving behavior with a highly cognitive texture. It was based on the commonly defined steps in the decision process. The primary purpose for this model was to order results from empirical studies and to note where there were major gaps in the research. The authors found that there were actually very few attempts to study any variety of psychological variables in the context of saving behavior. The second purpose was for the model to guide further research on saving. Julander (1975) and Lindqvist (1981a, 1981b) used the model as a starting point for their empirical studies of saving behavior and developed simpler versions of it.

Lindqvist (1981a) who interviewed a random sample of Swedish households with telephones (N = 429) employed as dependent variables four measures of household saving:

1. Bank savings during the last three months
2. Changes in possession of securities (shares and bonds) during the last three months
3. Repayment of debts during the last three months
4. The amount the household could withdraw from the bank ('liquidity').

He was interested in finding measures of the short-run flow of savings. The measures should be so simple that they could be inexpensively collected through telephone interviews with the household head. The interviews comprised detailed questions about bank account changes and changes in other assets. There were also questions about attitudes towards saving and financial expectations. Lindqvist tested a model that in the first place comprised the socioeconomic variables income and stage in life cycle. These variables were assumed to influence the 'intervening' variables of attitudes towards saving, financial expectations, and economic activity. The three measures of saving flow and the liquidity measure were dependent variables in the analyses. They, in their turn, influenced 'economic satisfaction'.

The index for attitudes (alpha = 0.96) comprised 14 items, representing the importance of saving. The expectations index (alpha = 0.46) was similar to the Index of Consumer Sentiment. The index for economic activity was based on the number of bank accounts and other types of saving and whether the respondents discussed saving and tried to protect themselves against inflation. First, the author ran a multiple regression analysis for each of the four dependent variables. The regression for bank saving was not significant and none of the independent variables was significant. The regressions for the other dependent variables were significant. Income, family size, and type of residence explained debt repayment. While the socioeconomic variables income, stage in life cycle and attitudes towards saving explained changes in total savings, expectations and economic activity explained liquidity (bank funds). A path analysis of the latter dependent variable showed that there were considerable effects of household income and educational level as well as of the psychological variables.

Furnham (1985) studied the determinants of saving attitudes and saving habits in Britain. He challenged the often heard idea that nearly everyone had a positive attitude towards saving and found that there were several dimensions: the existence of benefits or pointlessness of saving money, how one should save, whether saving secured wealth, and the self-denial implicit in saving. He noted that even those who found saving money pointless recognized the benefits of saving. 'That is, people's attitudes to *their* saving of money probably reflect their ability to save more than their beliefs about saving. Furthermore, this apparent paradox may occur only in times of economic depression' (Furnham and Lewis, 1986, p.176). The socio-demographic variables, except age, made no difference in what percentage of income was saved. Higher-income people seemed to save approximately the same percentage of income as lower-income people. Furnham suggested that this cast some doubt on Katona's concept of discretionary saving.

Recently, several economic-psychological studies of saving have been reported. Two British studies will be briefly summarized. They show that a combination of economic, sociodemographic and psychological variables gives better explanations than either category alone.

Lunt and Livingstone (1991) studied saving in relation to life events, coping strategies and social networks. Related to this was the assumption that saving is related to budgeting and planning. The authors used a rather small, non-random sample (N = 279) the representativeness of which is unknown, but open to some doubt. Like in many other economic-psychological studies of saving the results should be seen as tentative. The authors included a large number of variables in their study: economic, demographic, and psychological variables.

The broad set of psychological variables comprised judgments and expectations about budgeting, definitions of debt, satisfaction judgments, consumer possessions and judgments of necessities and luxuries, consumer desires and pleasures, attitudes towards debt and credit, patterns of shopping, spending and credit use, social comparison (with parents, children and peers), locus of control scale, thinking, worrying and talking about money, coping strategies for general and financial problems, life events in the past three months, values, and attributions about the causes of own financial problems. The dependent variables were based on total savings and recurrent saving.

The importance of the variables varied somewhat depending on the dependent variable analyzed. In a discriminant analysis of savers, non-savers, and non-savers with savings, the two latter groups were found to be similar. Disposable income, years of finishing education, and a number of psychological variables distinguished between savers and non-savers. The savers had higher disposable income and higher education. The most important variables were 'feel better off compared to a year ago', 'know what bills will be each quarter', and 'feel in control of finances'. Locus of control was significant, meaning that non-savers were more externally controlled (fatalistic).

The multiple regression analysis of amounts of recurrent (regular) saving indicated that disposable income was important and so was spending on clothes. The larger the amounts saved, the more was spent on clothes which probably means that those who made more money and had more wealth, could spend more on clothes. Savers tended to spend less on food than non-savers. Among the significant psychological variables were 'argue with partner', 'shop for best buy', 'discuss with friends', and 'attitude to debt as bad management'. Savers tended to be lower on 'value of enjoyment' and 'use of for sale columns'.

The authors concluded that recurrent saving and total savings were differently explained. Psychological variables had more explanatory power for recurrent saving than for total savings. The latter were best explained by economic variables. Psychological variables were important for distinguishing between savers and non-savers.

Daniel (1997) employed a number of psychological scales and questions in her study of individual differences in saving. She hypothesized that saving would be associated with low time preference, preference for delayed gratification, low impulsiveness, high consideration of future consequences and high self-control (Daniel, 1997, pp.131-2). She used a small sample from a region in Britain and analyzed in all 195 questionnaires. Reported total savings and amounts saved regularly were used as dependent variables in a series of multivariate analyses that tested different combinations of socioeconomic and psychological variables. Like Lunt and Livingstone (1991), Daniel found that socioeconomic variables contributed more toward explaining the variance in total savings than the psychological variables. Variables like time preference, impatience (measured on a psychological scale), impulsiveness, and delay of gratification were significant in some of the analyses of regularly saved amounts, but the pattern was not stable, possibly due to high correlations between some of the variables. The overall result for the psychological variables led Daniel to the conclusion that individual differences as represented by the psychological variables were important to saving behavior and worthy of notice by policy makers and financial marketers.

Van Veldhoven and Groenland (1993) treated the problems that arise in behavioral research on saving when a large number of socioeconomic and psychological variables are combined. They summed up earlier economic-psychological research on saving and arranged a variety of variables in a systematic schema. The schema encompassed a large number of factors, including many psychological. The authors pleaded for more study of the process of making allocative decisions in the household and they suggested longitudinal and cross-cultural studies.

The VSB-CentERdata Savings Project

CentER for Economic Research at Tilburg University, The Netherlands, is running a huge research project on saving, originally financed by the VSB bank. The project in this book is referred to as the VSB Panel Project, the original title. Since 1997, the Panel is known as the CentER*data* Panel. It involves annual interviews with a panel of households, with addition of new households when the original households no longer contribute. The VSB panel consists of two samples, both interviewed by means of computer questionnaires administered through modems (see Nyhus, 1996). One sample, here called 'the representative panel' (RP), is a representative selection of Dutch households, and the other sample, here called 'the high-income panel' (HIP), is representative of high-income earners with more than Dfl. 105 000 in annual income 1991. As in all survey research, in particular panel studies, there is a problem of dropouts and non-response.

All household members 16 years and over are interviewed. In the first wave, which was carried out in December 1993–April 1994, over 4 000 respondents participated. The questionnaires cover housing, employment, income, health, detailed assets lists, and a number of psychological variables. While the latter vary over the panel waves, a large set of data is now available on psychological variables such as risk attitudes, saving motives and attitudes, planning, personality, reference groups, life expectancy, and expectations of future income. For some variables there are repeated answers from the same respondents. It is a unique database that makes it possible to explore the role of psychological variables in the study of income, wealth, and saving.

In Chapter 2 some use was made of the data and in Chapters 6 and 7, some early analyses will be briefly reported. In some of these analyses, the answers of one representative of each household are used, usually those of the person who was indicated as head of the household. This makes it possible to use savings data referring to the whole household. The representative sample then counts 1 520 and the high-income sample counts 796 respondents.

THE IDEA OF SAVER GROUPS AND MARKET SEGMENTATION

Differences Among Savers

People save various proportions of their income and there are people who do not save at all. Can their behavior be explained by the same theory? In the discussion of the weaknesses of the LCH, it has been suggested that the model may be applicable on a segment of the population, but that other segments may be better described in other ways. For example, the findings of Burbridge and Robb (1985), using Canadian data, indicated that there were two groups of elderly savers. Blue-collar workers seemed to conform more to the LCH predictions than white-collar. While King (1985) found that there was evidence for questioning the validity of LCH, he thought that it was consistent with the observed behavior of a majority of households. The trouble was that there was no alternative, rigorous model. His main suggestion for remedial action was to complement the LCH with a bequest motive, which presumably would add to the explanation of differences among savers. The non-savers would be left alone.

Campbell and Mankiw (1989, 1990, and 1991) accepted the fact that LCH could explain only part of household savings and proposed that there were two groups of consumers. One group consisted of those who were liquidity-constrained or rule-of-thumb consumers who spent all of their current income. The other group comprised those who were forward-looking consumption smoothers who behaved in accordance with the LCH. The two groups were assumed to have about equal size in the USA. The authors expected that the rich would behave more like the LCH pattern prescription. They tested their model on aggregate data from the USA and a number of other countries and found support for it (Campbell and Mankiw, 1991, p.753). The proportion of LCH-savers varied considerably among the countries.

In a review of Kotlikoff (1989), Weil (1991) suggested that there could be three groups of interest: (a) non-savers, (b) forward-looking savers, and (c) the non-forward-looking savers. The very rich were likely members of the last category. Weil also recommended that more attention should be given to the value of housing. A comparatively large proportion of the elderly population in the USA held a valuable house and few financial assets. They could leave bequests of considerable value.

A French economist, André Babeau (1981) who was the leader of an institute for research on savings and who made regular surveys of French saving, launched the idea of four saver groups with very distinct characteristics. The grouping was not a direct result of data analysis, but was based on quantitative and qualitative analyses. Babeau gave the approximate size of each group and asserted that the estimates were quite accurate for those who were gainfully employed.

The first group was called 'Persons or households who only need storage of money'. They amounted to around 20 percent of the French households. They did not really save money, they had cash that they wanted to put into an easily available account, often a checking account. Katona (1975) called this 'a temporary repository'. Babeau noted that there was an increasing tendency for this saver group to put their money in a bank account. Many of the members of this group were young and unmarried.

The second group wanted storage of liquid means as well as buffers for better security against unforeseen circumstances. Immediate availability of the money was a prerequisite for their deposits. Babeau labeled them 'the cautious group'. Its size was approximately one-third of the households.

The third group, which amounted to something like 30 percent of the households, was depicted as 'households with a large variety of needs'. Most of the time, these savers owned their houses or planned to do so. They saved money both as a matter of precaution and with the decided goal to have a secure future, preferably with property that all the time went up in value.

The fourth group consisted of wealthy people who had total wealth exceeding FF 400 000 (in 1981). These savers were around 15 percent of the households. The members of these households were well informed and they put their wealth in many types of investment. In comparison to the other groups they had only a small proportion of their wealth in bank accounts, on average 15 percent.

According to Babeau (1981), persons and households could move between the groups. It was common to move from group 1 to group 2 as one grew older. Group 4 was the most stable group. Babeau's four groups of savers are quite similar to a Swedish, economic-psychological model of saver groups, which will be presented next. It was developed without knowledge of the French studies.

A Hierarchical Model of Saving Motives

Lindqvist (1981b) distinguished between four saving motives or needs that he assumed to be hierarchically ordered: (1) cash management, (2) buffer for unforeseen emergencies, (3) financial means for attaining a desired goal, (4) wealth management. The need hierarchy was based on a categorization suggested by Ferber (1973). The assumption was added that the motives formed a pyramid with the most frequent need (cash management) at the bottom and the least frequent one (wealth management) at the top. The model neatly summarized earlier findings and ideas about reasons for saving. The hierarchy implies that there is a movement upward or downward in a logical or chronological order, possibly following the household life cycle.

This model of saving motives was developed into a model of saver groups in which the groups are formed after their dominant saving motive: wealth managers, goal savers, buffer and security savers, and cash managers. Through cluster analysis the model was tested on empirical data from Swedish surveys. The analysis supported the meaningfulness of the grouping

(Wahlund and Wärneryd, 1987). The following discussion of the implications of the model is based on Wahlund and Wärneryd (1987).

The most basic need or motive is *cash management* since incomes and expenditures are not perfectly synchronized in time and place. This holds for all income earners. Cash management implies that that there is a quest for liquidity, for what Keynes (1936) labeled 'transactional motives'. The money is there to be spent within a short period of time. A typical case is accumulating money in a checking account to pay interest on mortgages. What Katona (1975) called 'residual saving' also belongs here. The members of this group may change their behavior from merely hoarding money at home to real saving in a bank account and become more willing to postpone some otherwise possible consumption, as their financial situation after some lean years improves. This category is an attractive target group for commercial activities from banks and savings institutions. The cash managers are assumed sensitive to what they perceive as immediate rewards from saving behavior. The marketing efforts of commercial banks in the USA and some other countries testify to that. Those may give prizes for the first deposit and pay interest on a daily basis.

Young families with dependents tend to worry about not having enough of a buffer capital. Many of them are cash managers with little savings. The striving to create and keep a buffer may be taken as a will to safeguard against at least some unforeseeable, but not unlikely future needs. People who spend all their income often have a feeling that they are too short of money and lead a dangerous life. Then the question arises of having some reserve for taking care of future irregularities of income and expenditure that may occur. Many people report that they save money in order to have a buffer against the possible ill consequences of events in the future. 'Saving for a rainy day' is the most common saving purpose according to many studies. Those who do not have a buffer seem to feel guilty about not having it. Katona pointed to the strength of this motive: 'But even when unemployment occurs or large medical expenses have to be paid, savings are used grudgingly, because the worse the current situation, the greater looms the need to maintain reserves for future emergencies' (Katona, 1975, p.231).

When people have some buffer they may turn their attention towards the potential acquisition of something especially attractive that cannot be purchased with available financial means. They may start saving towards a goal, pursue functional saving (Sonuga-Barke, 1993), maybe serving the down-payment motive that Browning and Lusardi (1996) propounded. Saving for better housing, for buying a motor vehicle, or for a long vacation are common examples. The 'goal savers' save for the purpose of acquiring new things that they cannot afford to buy out of a single period's income. In times of rising prices and inflation, it may pay to save after the purchase and use credit. This was the case in many Western countries during the 1980s.

The top level of the hierarchy refers to creation and management of wealth. Ferber (1973) called this category 'asset management'. This motive is not actually a saving motive in the ordinary sense of saving as postponed consumption. People who have this motive may not increase their wealth through saving since they have better means or think that they have better means of accomplishing wealth increases than saving from income. They invest their money to keep or increase its value and make a profit. 'Wealth managers' have in many cases inherited all or part of their wealth. There are studies indicating that wealth owners often have a feeling of an obligation to leave more in legacy than what they received themselves (Barlow et al., 1966; Katona, 1975). Barlow et al's study showed that the bequest motive was important in this category of savers. Since the wealth managers own a large proportion of the aggregate wealth, this motive can be important for total savings although comparatively few savers may deem it of prime importance. Modigliani (1988) discussed the bequest motive and reached the conclusion that planned bequests were not quite as important as had been suggested by some critics of the LCH. People who have the wealth management motive are more sensitive than others to differences in interest rates (Wahlund and Wärneryd, 1987) and the reactions of this category to changes in interest rates may be especially worth studying.

Saving from income – however high the income – today hardly creates a fortune unless the money is wisely invested. People who are characterized by this motive may still be savers at the cash management level in the hierarchy while some of their money is in a bank account waiting for better opportunities. With the developments in the financial markets, wealth managers now seem to have more importance than ever. They do not appear to save money in the sense of refraining from something. To the extent that the investors are 'yuppies', they rather waste money and other resources on conspicuous consumption at the same time receiving good salaries and making highly profitable investments. If they want to increase their wealth they are likely to take risks. Higher risks mean higher profits, but also greater losses. The high risks associated with some investments may backfire, especially when stock prices fall rapidly and interest rates climb. Although bank savings are usually characterized as riskless in economics there are recent examples of serious crises in savings institutions and commercial banks. The perceived security of bank savings varies over time and is probably not as high as it used to be.

A first test of the hierarchy of saver types was carried out by Wahlund and Wärneryd (1987) who found support for the idea. Wahlund (1991) later presented a more rigorous test. The original sample comprised a representative sample of around 1 700 Swedish males. In the analysis, those who did not have a monthly income over SEK1 000 (deflated to 1980) were excluded. The author used a k-means cluster analysis with nine variables as defining variables. A summary of the results is given in Table 5.5.

Table 5.5 Means of Variables Defining Four Saver Groups

	Wealth Managers	Goal Savers	Buffer Savers	Cash Managers	Total
Age	48.5	36.6	38.0	40.1	40.9
Percent family members without income	26.7	18.1	16.3	43.7	27.8
Buffer motive	3.08	1.76	3.78	2.83	2.96
Cash motive	2.31	1.72	1.52	3.46	2.36
Goal saving motive	1.80	3.24	1.80	1.15	1.85
Interest-getting motive	1.05	1.09	0.75	0.47	0.79
Bank savings (SEK)	82 183	33 322	17 143	16 390	34 920
Number of respondents	197	149	231	268	845
Percent of respondents	23.3	17.6	27.3	31.7	100

Source: After Wahlund (1991, p.347).

The cluster analysis supported the idea of the existence of saver groups, differing in terms of their main saving motives. Each group was highest on the expected saving motive. The group of wealth managers was larger than expected which may be a consequence of the fact that there was no specific, investment return motive associated with it. Wahlund (1991) noted that cluster analysis was not a robust technique and depended on the instructions given about number of clusters. In this case, the technique was instructed to yield four clusters. Further analyses indicated that it would have been possible to add more clusters.

Wahlund (1991) then tried to ascertain how these four saver groups had been affected by the tax reform that took place in the early 1980s in Sweden. He found that there were notable differences. The reform was among other things aimed at making people reduce their debts and save more. According to Wahlund, the cash managers were actually dissaving during the period and only the wealth managers increased their savings to any considerable extent. They were also the ones who to a large extent used the schemes for savings with tax incentives.

Wahlund and Gunnarsson (1996) further developed the idea of saver groups. In their sample of Swedish households (N = 503), they distinguished six groups of savers who differed in their financial strategies. The six groups were labeled (Gunnarsson and Wahlund, 1997, pp.210-11):

1. *Residual savers* (45.5 percent of the sample). They preferred saving forms with high liquidity and had fairly high debt-to-asset ratio = 1 (the financial debts divided by financial assets)
2. *Contractual savers* (22 percent). They seemed to have borrowed freely and saved through paying off debts and had a debt-to-asset ratio = 4.2
3. *Security savers* (14 percent); they were the heaviest investors in retirement-related financial instruments such as private pension plans and they had some investment in stocks and bonds mostly avoiding risky investment; the debt-to-asset ratio = 1.3
4. *Risk hedgers* (9.3 percent); they had large financial wealth, invested in risky and long-term assets (stock, mutual funds, and options); debt-to-asset ratio = 0.52
5. *Prudent investors* (3.2 percent); they had large savings and avoided risky investments, preferred bonds to shares; debt-to-asset ratio = 0.28
6. *Divergent strategies* (6 percent); they had well diversified portfolios and invested in risky, complex, and unusual assets such as options; debt-to-asset ratio = 0.50.

The authors discussed the use of this grouping as a way of segmenting the population of households and found that there were clear implications for policy and marketing strategies. The idea behind segmentation in marketing is that groups of consumers that can be revealed for example through cluster analysis are differently sensitive to marketing activities and therefore they should be treated differently.

EXPERIMENTAL RESEARCH ON SAVING

One implicit attitude concerning the significance of experiments is particularly widespread among experimental psychologists. They are prone to think of their results in extremely general terms. This generality involves both species and situations. Except as he is, from time to time, caught short in his application of experimental data, the experimental psychologist is inclined to view his findings as valid without regard to the readily apparent difference between his laboratory situations and those obtaining outside the laboratory. Indeed, he is likely not to keep in mind the great dependence that behavioral data have on the particular methods used in securing them.

Bevan (1965, p.103)

Some Characteristics of Controlled Experiments

Experiments always yield unexpected results. The issue is not whether surprises occur, but whether they are perceived.

Swieringa and Weick (1982, p.79)

Psychological research was from its beginning characterized by the use of controlled experiments that were carried out in laboratory settings. While the experiment is still the preferred approach in many branches of psychology, survey interviews and questionnaires have become important research techniques in most fields of psychology, in particular in personality and social psychology. In the 1970s and early 1980s, the prevalent use of the experiment in psychology, notably its use in social psychology, was heavily criticized (see, for example, the discussion in the *Journal of Consumer Research*, 1982–83). Laboratory settings were said to produce artifacts with little validity for explaining phenomena outside the laboratory.

At first, the critique of the laboratory experiment focused on certain problems that plagued experimental research according to then current findings and that experimenters had not paid much attention to (Rosenthal and Rosnow, 1969). Two phenomena attracted special attention: (1) demand characteristics and (2) experimenter expectancy. Since these phenomena, although less discussed today, may affect findings in both psychological and economic laboratories it seems worthwhile to say something about them.

The *demand characteristics* effect arises from the fact that subjects' thoughts about an experiment may affect their behavior in carrying out the experimental tasks. The effects are caused by the subjects' perception of the purpose with the experiment, of the settings, of the experimenter's personal characteristics and many other things that may contribute to the subjects forming an opinion and adjusting their behavior in accordance with the opinion. Studies indicate that even small details may give signals that are important to subjects. The presence of a panic button in a stressful laboratory experiment may entice subjects to experience panic while subjects with no access to a panic button do not panic. If the experimenter wears a white coat (or a tie) instead of casual wear, the different demand characteristics may lead to different results. An economist as experimenter may get different findings than a psychologist running the same experiment.

While demand characteristics emanate from the subjects' hypotheses about the experiment, *experimenter expectancy* refers to the possibility that the experimenter's hypotheses are somehow conveyed to the subjects and that they knowingly or unknowingly behave in accordance with them. A simple example is that the experimenter or interviewer (without necessarily knowing it) looks pleased at certain answers and sad at others. The experimenter bias typically arises from the treatment of subjects. Experiments in class rooms have, for example, shown that telling a teacher in advance that a class was bright and highly motivated led to better performance than when the teacher was told that the class was average.

Some remedies against these biases are now standard procedures in experimentation with humans. Instructions are, for example, given in written or tape-recorded form to avoid personal variations. The debriefing of subjects after an experiment involves telling the subjects about the purpose of the experiment and giving a chance for questions. It is usually introduced by questions that try to find out how the subjects perceived the experiment. It is recommended to provide an independent test of the effectiveness of the experimental treatment – a so-called 'manipulation check' (see Aronson and Carlsmith, 1968). Some psychologists have recommended and used deception of subjects, but there are ethical objections and the rule is that there should be informed consent for participation in an experiment.

Critics have declared that psychological laboratory experiments can only give artifactual results that say nothing about reality. Defenders of the laboratory experiment in psychology and social psychology have maintained that the purpose of the laboratory experiment is to develop and test theory and establish possibilities of relationships rather than to provide estimates of the external probabilities of relationships (see e.g. Petrinovitch, 1979; Mook, 1983). The laboratory experiment has survived as an important research tool to develop theory. Furthermore, the controlled experiment is now the major research tool in a new branch of economics, *experimental economics*.

There are some characteristic differences between experiments carried out by psychologists and by economists (see Hey, 1991; Smith, 1991). While psychologists nowadays tend to strive for experimental setups that are close to the complexity of reality and have ecological validity, economists want to create clean environments to have maximum control of the situation. Hey (1991) pictured laboratory experiments as a way for economists to test abstract theory. A certain economic theory is usually assumed to be valid 'with all other things remaining the same' (ceteris paribus). When tested against data representing reality, this condition is rarely fulfilled, something already observed by Jevons (1871). Many factors are free to play a role. In a laboratory experiment, variables that should not affect the test are in principle (not always in practice) held under control. Hey saw this as an important reason for the rapidly increasing interest in experimental economics, despite earlier resistance from mainstream economists. He suggested that experiments should also be run on more complex theories of economic behavior since he felt that it was in the handling of complexity that economic theory failed.

Economists study economic decisions and they want to make sure that the subjects are motivated to make economic decisions. This means that they tend to insist on monetary incentives that are related to the performance of the subjects. Whereas the psychologists attempt to produce subject involvement and create motivation to participate fully in the experiment through the set-up and, if possible, minor rewards, the economists are anxious to instill economic motivation, which they assume to be primarily based on monetary incentives. Hey (1991) indicated that economic experiments were most often tests of specified theory and psychological experiments primarily aimed at suggesting theory. Typically, the psychological experiments on economic behavior have been richer, with diminished control of influencing variables as a consequence and the experiments run by economists have had a tendency to be rather abstract and somewhat devoid of content. In some cases, economic experiments have been characterized as tests of the subjects' ability to make calculations rather than tests of decision making.

Psychological Experiments Related to Saving Behavior

In the history of psychology, only a few examples of studies of economic behavior can be found. Besides some learning studies relating to the psychology of money, there are some reports on so-called 'token economies'. Psychological researchers have arranged environments in such a way that economic developments could be observed under conditions similar to reality. In a token economy, people, for example the inmates of a psychiatric ward, can through their own efforts make money which they receive as 'tokens' with a given value, and then spend it on things they find necessary or just attractive. They can also save the money to the extent that they find that they want to exchange the tokens for real money at the end of the experiment (see Lea et al., 1987, Chapter 17).

In a field experiment that is unfortunately not reported in English, Julander (1975) studied the effect of feedback on saving behavior. He developed and tested a model for saving decisions, with feedback from behavior back to the decision problem and the goal that started the decision process. The study comprised detailed interviews with 215 young women between 24 and 28 with full-time, gainful employment, no academic training and living in one-person households in Stockholm. The questionnaire included questions about financial status, attitudes towards saving, and a number of scales relating to knowledge about financial matters, planning activities, satisfaction with income and standard of living. There were also measures of personality traits such as future time perspective, degree of impulsiveness, delay of gratification and internal-external locus of control scales. At the end of the first interview, half of the respondents were asked to keep records of their income, expenditures and savings for a period of 30 days and they were given four bookkeeping booklets to use. After the 30-day experimental period, another period of 30 days elapsed before the second interview was made. All respondents were then interviewed a second time.

Analysis of the first interviews yielded a significant correlation between knowledge about how the income was used on different expenditures and satisfaction with income use, which corroborated the idea that feedback was important. The experiment gave an unexpected outcome. The respondents in the experimental group became significantly more dissatisfied with their income and level of living compared to the control group. In the experimental group, those who spent too much money in relation to their disposable income before the experimental treatment decreased their variable expenditures significantly. Those in the experimental group who before the experimental treatment had very low variable expenditures and who saved a lot, increased their expenditures substantially.

Julander interpreted the results of the survey and the experiment to mean that high savers tended to have a tight control over all their variable expenditures. The bookkeeping gave them information that they could increase their expenditures considerably without jeopardizing their economy.

Webley and Lea (1993) argued that children's problem solving in a children's world should be studied rather than children's responses to the adults' conception of the world. Similar ideas dominated the work by Sonuga-Barke and Webley (1993) who in a monograph reported a sequence of laboratory studies, simulating the world of children. The authors devised a number of situations where children could display their knowledge of what was functional. Five experiments were carried out. The book also reports on some non-experimental studies, among others on parents' attitudes to their children's saving behavior.

Study 1 was based on a board game where some of the squares were empty and some were associated with symbols representing a bank, a toyshop, and a sweetshop, all of them available in the same room. A robber and a toll gate were also included on the board. The bank had money boxes with different withdrawal rules which could be used to put aside tokens for a longer or shorter period during the game. Before the board game started, the subjects, 16 girls between 4 and 12 years old, worked at a lever pressing machine to get tokens which they could spend on the attractions or lose to the robber in the board game or save. The long-term goal of the game was to save enough tokens to buy a toy from the toyshop. The children could protect their money against the robber whom they were to meet when advancing in the game. They could deposit their money in the money boxes of the bank, which they came to before the robber.

Not unexpectedly, the results showed that the older girls better resisted the temptation to buy sweets and knew better how to protect their wealth of tokens against the robber and the toll gate. Interviews with the girls showed that none of the 4-year-olds understood the role of the savings bank. Whereas all of the 9 and 12-year-olds understood that the savings box could prevent yielding to temptation and protect against the robber, none of the 6-year-olds understood the first function and two understood the second, the protection. The authors do not mention how many of the girls managed to save tokens to buy the desired toy.

In Study 2 a similar board game was used. Subjects were 24 girls, 6, 9, and 12 years old. Two squares before the sweetshop the subjects were asked to predict the number of sweets they would buy. These predictions were then compared with the size of the actual purchase. The number of predictions made decreased across age groups. There was no improvement in the accuracy of the prediction with age. The authors suggested that the older children were no better than younger children at handling temptation when they got to the sweetshop. Children from all age groups underestimated the number of sweets that they would buy. Again it was found that the older the child, the better she knew how to avoid the 'temptation-threat' and the 'theft-threat'.

The authors noted a difference in the way different age groups understood the value of economic actions. While younger children talked about actions in moral or social terms, from nine years the children started to think in terms of economic consequences. In one version of the board game in Study 3, the subjects could escape losing money to the robber by paying a few tokens for a ferry across a river. In another version they gave up more money by paying for the ferry trip than what the robber demanded. While younger children to a large extent preferred the ferry even when that was the most expensive alternative, the older children observed the economic consequences and chose the cheaper alternative. The authors interpreted this as a confirmation of the idea that the younger were more social and moral in their economic actions. This leads me to the question: Was there maybe a difference in motivation and involvement in the game between the age groups? The younger may have been more scared by the prospect of being robbed.

After summing up the results of these three studies with a board game, the authors wanted to develop a more realistic play economy. A report of this experiment was first published by Webley et al. (1991) and will be used for the account here. Boys 6, 9 and 12 years old, ten in each age group served as subjects. The boys were given token money at some intervals and they then passed through three rooms where temptations were offered at a price, along with some free activities. Before the first trial the boys were asked to select a favorite toy which they could buy at the end of the experiment if they had enough money. In all, they each received 90 tokens and the selected toy cost 70 tokens. The boys could thus spend 20 tokens yielding to temptations. The authors did not only observe how children chose to spend their allotted money on various entertainments and sweets or to save it for the selected toy available after the experiment, but also interviewed the children in a semi-structured way. They explored four issues: (1) the status of the play economy, (2) the emergence of differing saving strategies, (3) the role and conceptualization of institutionalized saving, and (4) saving as a social behavior.

The authors noted that the somewhat stricter play economy and the interviews helped them find out about what the boys in the age groups thought about saving and about putting money in a bank versus in a money box. They found clear differences between 6 and 12-year-olds in the capacity to save the money and in their views on the banks. None of the 6-year olds, seven of the 9-year-olds, and nine of the 12-year-olds reached the objective of being able to buy the selected toy at the end of the experiment. Most of the 6-year-olds saw putting money in a bank as lost money; the authors concluded that it was then 'understandable rationality' that these children preferred to spend money on sweets, drinks etc. as they went along. The social ramifications of spending and saving became clear in the interviews since the boys revealed their bargaining with their parents and other relatives.

The authors identified five types of saving strategy:

1. No attempts at saving. Half of the 6-year-olds practiced this strategy and did not worry about saving except maybe on the last day (round) of the experiment.
2. Saving by spending a little each day. Among the 6-year-olds there seemed to be a hope to have money enough for the toy if they just did not spend everything every day. In this age group, spending half the daily amount was common.
3. Saving by not spending at all over the whole game. This was practiced by two 9-year-olds.
4. Saving up until target was reached and then spending. Two boys saved 70 tokens and then started spending what they had above those.
5. Calculated saving. Most of the 12-year-olds made a plan at the beginning of the game for saving and spending, deciding in advance what activities they would spend their extra tokens on.

These experiments were run with children. The results can be seen as part of the research on the economic socialization of children. Most studies in this area have not been experimental or if experimental, with less ambition to simulate realistic conditions. Socialization studies often include questions about saving, interest, and the role of banks. Can similar simulation studies be carried out with adults and if so, do such studies really reveal anything about saving? The main purpose would be to study saving decisions in closer and richer detail. Here is a brief account of such an attempt.

In an unpublished study, carried out by two students in economic psychology at Tilburg University, an attempt was made to test some hypotheses from the Behavioral Life-Cycle Hypothesis in a rich environment (van Tilburg and Vruggink, 1994). The authors carried out a two-step experiment on saving. The first step was a regular laboratory experiment and the second, which was a follow-up with the same subjects, was a field experiment. The main idea was that the subjects carried out some work in the laboratory and received payment that they could use to buy snacks, drinks, or entertainment such as playing computer games or reading newspapers in the breaks between the tasks. The payments were either distributed over the periods or paid in lump sums. The other experimental variables were bonus versus no bonus payments and precommitment to save versus no precommitment to save. In the follow-up of the experiment the subjects were assigned to similar conditions, but opposite to the laboratory conditions they had been exposed to. Due to limited funds, the students only ran sixteen subjects who were recruited through ads in a supermarket.

What is of particular interest in this context is that the laboratory environment and the set-up seemed to work. While no significant effects were found in the laboratory, the authors distinguished some of the expected effects in the follow-up. They were themselves a bit skeptical about the laboratory setting and recommended an expanded field study as being more realistic. In my view, they demonstrated that a laboratory experiment with satisfactory realism for adults can be carried out.

Economists' Experiments on Saving Behavior

Economists have also carried out some experiments on saving. The purposes have varied somewhat. In an early study, Johnson, Kotlikoff, and Samuelson (1987; described in Anderhub et al., 1997) let subjects who by instructions knew their income and remaining lifetime decide in a number of budget periods whether to borrow to consume more than income, consume all income or save. The purpose was to test the predictions of the LCH for a deterministic environment. The authors found a number of deviations from the LCH predictions. Other experimenters have studied uncertain environments, with income and life expectancy depending on probability distributions. Hey and Dardanoni (1988) reported a computer-run experiment on consumption and saving with the following characteristics:

1. The subject is told that the experiment consists of a random number of periods and that there is a 1 in 10 chance that any period will be the last
2. In each period a randomly determined income, denominated in tokens, is given and a decision has to be made how much of the wealth should be converted into money (consumed) or transferred to the next period earning interest at 12 percent per period
3. There is a maximally permitted overdraft (borrowing) of tokens from the tokens account (the non-converted tokens)
4. Any money converted in an earlier period is lost (consumed)

5. The subject's payment is the amount of money converted in the final (randomly determined) period.

This experiment dealt with optimal consumption under uncertainty about income and remaining lifetime. The subjects who were university students from various disciplines (N = 128) should in principle maximize their (subjective) expected utility over their lifetime. It was no surprise to the authors that there were significant differences between optimal and actual behavior since the calculations required for optimal consumption were quite prohibitive.

In each period, the subject faced two problems: (a) how much to convert into money (consume), not knowing whether this might be her/his final payment and (b) not knowing whether the income in the next period would be smaller or larger. In contrast to LCH, the subject wanted to have as much wealth as possible in the last period and convert it into money. A psychologist may well ask whether this is a true experiment on saving. Did the operations used to define saving correspond to the theoretical concept of saving? There was postponement of consumption so in this sense there was saving, but did the subjects see it as saving, given the rule for final payment? The mundane realism of the experiment may have been low. I shall return a little later to the question of how realistic an experiment should be.

A similar experiment was carried out by Köhler (1996). Whereas Hey and Dardanoni checked subjects' saving decisions against the optimal consumption strategy, Köhler wanted to look more closely at the decision processes and, in particular, answer the question: did subjects look forward over all periods of the possible lifetime or did they restrict the range of time considered? British and Dutch university students (and some staff members) were subjects (N = 165). Compared to Hey and Dardanoni there were some changes in the experimental procedure:

1. The tokens given as income in each period could be converted into points or saved for conversion later, with interest being paid
2. The aim was to get the maximum possible number of points
3. The probabilities of three levels of income were given to the subject
4. There was no borrowing
5. The subjects could use a computer facility for trying out in advance different consumption strategies in each period
6. To ensure risk neutrality, the subject could win either a high or a low prize in a lottery (binary lottery technique). The more points the subject had, the greater the chance of winning the high prize.

The subjects were asked to maximize consumption over a lifetime of unknown length if the conversion to points is assumed to correspond to consumption. Saving tokens gave interest that after a number of periods could result in more points than if everything was immediately converted. The subjects could try out strategies before making their actual decisions. Analysis of such optional trials was expected to reveal important dimensions in the decision processes. Köhler distinguished three types of trial strategies. The first was a 'learning strategy' in which several trials were performed in the first one or two periods. The second was a 'rolling strategy' where there were trials all the way through the experiment. The third was a 'fixed end point strategy' where the subjects chose a single period in the future as the end point for a series of trials that they performed over several periods.

The most common trial strategy was the rolling strategy in which subjects throughout the experiment performed trials, but looked only a few periods ahead. The author concluded that people simplified savings decisions by restricting the amount of information that they took into account. 'They only look ahead for a short span of time, rather than the whole of a lifetime' (Köhler, 1996, p.12).

Anderhub et al. (1997) reported an experiment that can be seen as an extension of the two British experiments above. Since the interest here is focused on approach and design of saving experiments in experimental economics rather than on results, only a few details will be presented.

The subjects were instructed that they were to participate in 12 rounds with a number of periods in each round and that in each round they would survive at least three periods. The number of periods in a round was decided by dice to be three, four, five, or six. After each period, a dice was thrown; there were three differently colored dice with different terminal probabilities. After being used the dice was taken out. The throwing of the dice meant an update of the subject's life expectancy.

In the first period in each round the subjects were given an amount of money (S) which they were to distribute over the periods (minimum three, maximum six periods). In each period the subjects decided how much of the allotted money S to spend in the period and how much to save for later periods.

For each round of the game, the win was calculated. For one group of subjects it was a multiplicative relationship (where it was desirable to avoid 'zero' for any period of survival) and for the second group it was the sum of the square roots of the by the subject allotted amount for each period.

The experiment concluded with a questionnaire containing questions about the game and a personality inventory, Brandstätter's adjective scale version of the 16PF personality test. This inventory will be described in Chapter 7.

The departure of the study was that optimal consumption behavior is difficult to achieve, especially if the environment is stochastic. In this experiment the termination probabilities ('stopping probabilities') depended on random

events. The authors expected bounded rationality rather than optimizing behavior. The latter would have been too complex for ordinary human beings.
The main goal of the study, which is one in a series of studies, was to develop
theory about how the participants in the game perceived the game and how
they proceeded to generate their saving decisions. Since each subject went
through more than one life cycle, it is possible to study the influence of experience on saving decisions ('learning'). The ultimate aim is to develop a behavioral theory of saving, exploring experimentally dimensions of decisions
that can hardly be studied in field surveys. The authors who are economists are
interested in individual differences which is against the tradition in economics.

Experimental and Mundane Realism in Saving Experiments

The cited experiments clearly differ in their set-ups. Saving experiments run
by economists tend to be closely related to economic theory, to test specified
hypotheses, and are strictly controlled. Saving experiments run by psychologists are complex, more vaguely related to theory, and maintain less strict
control of variables. Does the degree of realism in an experiment matter?
Aronson and Carlsmith (1968) suggested that a distinction could be made
between *mundane realism* and *experimental realism*. The former has to do
with how realistic the experiment is in terms of similarity to reality and if the
events occurring in the laboratory are likely to occur in the 'real world', outside the laboratory. The latter refers to how the subjects see the experimental
setting and the experiment and their willingness to accept to work under the
given conditions. Swieringa and Weick (1982) who dealt with experiments in
finance thought that the experimental realism was more important than the
mundane. High mundane realism may even hurt the experimental realism and
low mundane realism may lead to new discoveries.

> The concern about mundane realism reflects our tendency to view experiments in
> terms of verification, hypothesis testing, and description. But experiments also can
> be used for purposes of discovery and for developing and testing theory. Experi-
> ments can be used to create conditions that do not exist now and to address 'what
> if' questions. (Swieringa and Weick, 1982, p.57)

The purpose of the experiment will then decide how much of mundane realism is desirable. When theory is developed through laboratory experiments
(including experiments run in classrooms), there should be follow-up outside
the laboratory to the extent that this is possible. Cialdini (1980) called for
'full-cycle social psychology' which meant that laboratory experimentation
should be preceded and followed by field research. A good example of what
he wanted to achieve is his best-selling book *Influence: Science and Practice*
(Cialdini, 1988). The content is based on psychological theory, specific labo-

ratory research, and the author's observations when he worked as an apprentice in trades where consumers are influenced by various means.

The first laboratory experiments described here were carried out by psychologists and had high mundane realism. Judging from the authors' reports, one must conclude that the experiments also had high experimental realism. In the experiments with children, the children were apparently highly motivated to comply with what the experimenters wanted. Obviously, the authors learned a lot about children's economic behavior and they convey these insights to the reader. Did they lose something as a consequence of the high mundane realism? This is hard to tell. Swieringa and Weick (1982) warned

> Mundane realism may lead subjects to emit familiar, overlearned routines about which they are inarticulate. The routines themselves are likely to be smoothed performances that contain shortcuts, substitutions, and cryptic versions of the acts from which they were assembled. Overlearned skills, by definition, may be less sensitive to experimental manipulations than newer skills. Furthermore, realistic settings are rich in cues that reinstate significant past events for subjects. (Swieringa and Weick, 1982, p.80)

The environments were specially designed and not perfectly mundane, but could be seen as interesting environments for playing games. In addition, Sonuga-Barke's and Webley's experiments, in particular the fourth study, were followed by careful interviewing to find out about the children's experiences and perceptions.

The experiments carried out by experimental economists are abstract and devoted to testing abstract economic theory against actual choice behavior. The mundane realism is low. What the subjects believe about what is expected of them is highly important in a strictly controlled experiment. There may be biasing on account of the demand characteristics, for example, that subjects perceive the task to be one of calculation rather than decision making. The experimental realism usually seems high and the motivation of the subjects is reported to be high. The participation involved money and something could be gained or lost as a consequence of a decision. The question is then: did the experimenters learn something that they could not have learned without the experiment and do we as readers learn something?

It should be noted that the experimental approach to the study of saving is new and what has been presented here are glimpses of on-going research. Still, I think that we already can learn from the setups of these experiments and from the observations already made. Köhler's ideas about the extent to which people try out strategies in advance seem promising and worthwhile to pursue further. The experimenters in all these cases seem to be intent on discovery and try to answer 'what-if' questions.

QUALITATIVE STUDIES OF SAVING

Anthropological studies usually employ very informal data collection methods and succeed in producing fascinating stories about consumption and other phenomena in primitive societies. In recent consumer behavior research, some formerly strict researchers have enthusiastically tried the anthropological approach. A group of well-known consumer behavior researchers adopted the idea of naturalistic research and went on a consumer behavior odyssey to meet with real consumers in many parts of the USA (Belk, 1991). The odyssey apparently yielded a wealth of new ideas for consumer research and changed the perspectives of the participant researchers.

A constructor of questionnaires often experiences frustration when facing all potentially possible answers and when grappling with the task of eliciting all relevant answers. S/he may envy those who make informal interviews with a guide for questions rather than a structured questionnaire. In an informal interview situation it seems so simple to ask the pertinent follow-up questions. Informal interviews have often been used as preliminaries and in pilot studies. Over the last decades, the number of qualitative studies that are not considered preliminary and rather representing a research approach has increased. This has not led to full acceptance of such research in leading journals. Very little qualitative research on saving behavior and savings has so far been published. Economic socialization studies are often based on informal interviewing. Sonuga-Barke and Webley (1993) interviewed their subjects in semi-structured interviews and also reported similar interviews with parents of the children and other adults.

Lunt (1996a, 1996b) argued that society and consumption had changed so much since Katona's days that new thinking about savings was necessary. While savings were earlier an insurance against future hardship to provide necessities or to gain a particular good, there was now uncertainty about the use of savings. Consumption decisions have in this analysis become more complex and more uncertain and at the same time the roles of the state and of financial institutions have changed. Lunt (1996b; Lunt and Livingstone, 1992) arranged discussions with nine focus groups with 47 members. The purpose was to find out about present-day social perceptions of the economy, including savings. The discussions indicated that the participants discerned a new, much more uncertain, not very clear function for savings. Due to the availability of financial institutions and possible attacks on savings by taxation and inflation, buying now and paying later rather than saving up in advance was a much-used alternative. In fact, the findings are not very different from what Katona discussed in *The Powerful Consumer*. Lunt's rejection of Katona may have been inspired by the assumption that the ICS was the main ingredient in the latter's theory of saving.

Despite the fact that I am in no way convinced that qualitative research would be superior or even equal to quantitative research, I definitely think there is a place for more qualitative research on saving behavior. The approaches that Groenland and van Veldhoven (1993) pleaded for often require more flexible procedures than ordinary questionnaires admit. It is true that full-fledged psychological tests can be used in some interview situations with anonymous interviewers, but, conceivably, much more could be found out, by means of subtle interviewing about the meaning of saving. Informal interviews could provide insights about what it means not to have any savings and how the financial situation of a family is related to events in life. Some attempts to do this, using videotaped interviews, have been carried out in the Netherlands. Some of the reports are in Dutch and not yet published. For example, Groenland and Bloem (1994) reported on a way of combining theory, qualitative data, and strict analysis. In a published report, Winnett and Lewis (1995) looked for different saver types in the qualitative material and described the distinguishing characteristics.

The distinction between quantitative and qualitative research is nowadays not as clear as it used to be. Qualitative research is turning to sophisticated methods for data collection and data analysis. The emerging scientific role may be compared to that of controlled laboratory experiments: the aim is to develop theory.

6. The Use of Psychological Variables in the Study of Saving: The Cognitive Concepts of Expectation, Uncertainty, and Decision Making

The purpose of this and the following chapter is to take a closer look at some of the psychological concepts that have been used in the research and discussions of saving. Also research that is not directly related to saving, but can give ideas for better understanding the psychology of saving, is reviewed. Some recent developments that appear promising and give new ideas for research are also described. The focus is on microeconomic rather than on macroeconomic psychology. A major task for research in economic psychology is to provide more detailed knowledge about economic behavior. This presupposes more use of basic research in psychology. The present chapter focuses on some cognitive concepts that to some extent have proved their value in explaining economic behavior and that can potentially turn out to be even more useful.

EXPECTATIONS

Early economists like Jevons (1871) and Böhm-Bawerk (1888) emphasized that decisions concerned the future and that the future could never be known with certainty. Classical economists talked about anticipations [of the future] with differing degrees of probability. Böhm-Bawerk stressed the role of uncertainty about the future and the importance of having ability to imagine the future, a property later referred to as 'foresight' by Fisher (1930) and Keynes (1936). Keynes brought 'expectations' of the future into focus as a capstone concept of macroeconomics and used the concept to explain business cycles. He particularly emphasized the role of expectations for investments. Loewenstein (1992) reviewed the history of what he called 'The Discounted Utility Model' and discussed economists' attempts at considering why people took the future into account and why the economists had not been overly successful in their attempts.

Expectations involve perceptions of future states. The price of a stock should reflect the present value of expected future earnings. Expectation is then equal to mathematical expectation. Financial markets are said to be efficient if the prices of assets reflect all available information. A consequence of this assumption is that past prices contain no information about future prices and stock prices follow a random walk. How can expectations then be formed? The assumption is made that (new) information is rationally used when the actors form their expectations. Even casual observation of the stock market reveals that stock rates deviate in ways that seem hard to explain.

Textbooks on financial economics often mention the occurrence of financial market 'bubbles' where the price of an asset first sky-rocketed and then plummeted. Shiller (1989, p.56) propounded that stock market operations were swayed by fads and fashions. A fad was a bubble if the contagion of the fad was spread through prices and people were attracted by observed price increases. Famous bubbles of this sort are the tulipmania in the Netherlands (Garber, 1989a and 1989b) which took place in 1634–37, and the South-Sea scandal in England around 1720 (Schachter et al., 1985). In these bubbles like in the real estate bubble that some countries have just (1998) recovered from the same pattern of expectation development seems to have occurred.

Spurred by expectations of enormous profits, many people, most of whom were ordinarily rather cautious, started investing in future options which were highly insecure unless there was continued exponential growth. Expectations apparently generated new and higher expectations up to a point when the grim reality behind the expectations was suddenly recognized. Pyramid schemes of investment and similar commercial strategies are based on engendering unrealistic expectations where people, who think that they can outdo chance by being smart, base their expectations on recent developments to a disastrous extent.

The purpose of the first section of the chapter is to review theories of expectation and to introduce a simple model of expectation formation that encapsulates ideas both from economic theory and psychology. The presentation is essentially based on Wärneryd (1997). The model is used to illustrate the differences between the economic theories of expectations and involves a reinterpretation in behavioral terms.

The Role of Expectations

Saving has two dimensions: perception of future needs and provision for the future. There are no facts about the future and all decisions and acts are based on expectations that are more or less founded on earlier facts and guesses. Still, people may feel extremely sure about certain decisions and courses of action because things have invariably turned out in a certain way. Other expectations never come true. Outcomes of actual events may satisfy the expectations or turn out to be more or less different from what was expected, whether hoped for or feared. One interpretation of uncertainty is that there is no certain knowledge about the future, only more or less well-founded guesses, which can be called expectations. Consumer, business, and government decision making is based on expectations, that is, more or less well-founded guesses about dimensions in the near or distant future.

Keynes (1936) may not have been the first economist to talk about expectations, but he was apparently the most influential. Collard (1983) noted the importance that Pigou attached to expectations; the latter was actually a precursor of rational expectations theory. Collard (1983, p.411) quoted from Pigou: 'the varying expectations of business men . . . and not anything else, constitute the immediate and direct causes or antecedents of industrial fluctuations.'

The use of expectations in economics arose with the discussion of how investment decisions were made and how those influenced the business cycle. Decisions on investments did not show any immediate results and they depended upon beliefs about the future. Keynes (1936) and the so-called 'Stockholm School' of economists devoted much thought to how business decision makers formed their expectations. Keynes used the expression 'animal spirits' to designate the optimism that characterized investment decisions. Consumer expectations did not matter in these discussions. Probably, Katona's work drew the first attention to the role of consumer expectations.

In a stable world, reliance on past experience is often the most rational use of information. In the case of producers, Keynes (1936) expressed it like this

> a large part of the circumstances usually continue substantially unchanged from one day to the next. Accordingly it is sensible for producers to base their expectations on the assumption that the most recently realized results will continue except in so far as there are definite reasons for expecting a change. (Keynes, 1936, p.51)

The expression 'definite reasons for expecting a change' is similar to what Katona (1975) called 'new information'. When people like something in past developments they are even more inclined to expect it to continue and become frustrated when changes occur.

Expectations have occupied an important place in economics ever since Keynes presented the foundations of macroeconomics in the 1930s. The new classical macroeconomic theory, which is mostly due to Robert Lucas, is even more dependent on the concept of expectations than Keynesian economics (Klamer, 1984). In economics, there is now one dominating view: expectations are formed on the basis of information which is dealt with in a rational manner. The confidence in the expectations is often seen as a matter of the credibility of the information.

Macroeconomics is founded on theories that deal with the concept of expectation as economic rather than as psychological. Expectation is mathematical expectation. The assumption is that expectations can be quantitatively derived from objective data. In behavioristic psychology, the concept is mostly replaced by 'expectancy' which means an observable tendency. Present use of 'expectation' refers to a subjective belief about future events or objects (Feather, 1982). According to Katona (1972), expectations are routinely formed and based on past experience or on important new information that leads to problem solving and restructuring of expectations. Macroeconomic psychology has adopted the view that expectations are something that people have and can express. This view made it possible to contribute subjective measures of expectations. Those are ascertained in sample surveys through sets of questions posed to consumers and business decision makers (see Chapter 5 about The Index of Consumer Sentiment).

Expectations in Economics

It is certain that a very large part of what we experience in life depends not on the actual circumstances of the moment so much as on the anticipation of future events.

Jevons ([1871] 1911, pp.33-4)

Rational Expectations Theory and other theories of expectations
In economics, three theories of expectations compete in the sense that they were earlier often seen as mutually exclusive: (1) simple extrapolation of earlier experience, (2) adaptive expectations, based on learning from differences between outcomes and earlier expectations, and (3) rational expectations. (1) and (2) are actually two different ways of dealing with past experience. Past experience usually refers to objective data on earlier development rather than to subjective experience or perception of past developments. 'Extrapolative expectations' are based on past experience, which can be weighted or unweighted. In weighted models, particular weight is usually given to the most recent experience, that is, objective data on recent developments, e.g., in the price level or incomes. 'Adaptive expectations' involve letting earlier discrepancies between expectation and outcome affect the new expectation. An expectation based on previous experience is corrected with some factor whose size is related to earlier expectation-outcome discrepancies.

The basic idea behind 'rational expectations' theory is that people use information about economic events when they form their expectations and, furthermore, that they do this using the best of economic knowledge (Muth, 1961). Like any other economic behavior, the formation of expectations is assumed rational. Some economists add a pinch of salt and think in terms of asymptotic rational expectations, i.e. expectations are formed in rational processing of information, given enough time. This is similar to Keynes's view that economic behavior was rational on average and over time. Rational is used in an economic sense and not in the way psychologists tend to think of rationality, as a process. The rational expectations theory provided a way of handling the influence of new economic information. The sophisticated discussions in economic theory of how expectations are formed have, in my view, much that psychologists and economic psychologists in particular can learn from. The big issue for both economists and psychologists is how past experience and new information are integrated by individuals when they form expectations about the relevant future.

Taking price level (inflation) expectations as an example, 'extrapolative expectations' can be defined as

$$PE_{t+1} = w_1 P_t + w_2 P_{t-1} + \ldots \; w_n P_{t-n}$$

where PE_{t+1} = expected price level in next period, assessed at time t
$\quad\quad P_i$ = realized price level at the end of period t, $t-1$, $t-n$
$\quad\quad w_1$, w_2, w_n are empirical weights.

'Adaptive expectations' involve letting earlier discrepancies between expectation and outcome affect the new expectation. It means correcting an expectation based on previous experience with some factor (a) whose size is related to earlier expectation-outcome discrepancies. 'Adaptive expectations', again using price expectations as an example, are defined as follows

$$PE_{t+1} - PE_t = a(P_t - PE_t)$$

which can be rewritten as

$$PE_{t+1} = a\,P_t + (1-a)\,PE_t$$

or

$$PE_{t+1} = PE_t + a(P_t - PE_t)$$

where $0 < a < 1$.

The latter form defines an adaptive expectation as the expectation of the last period, plus a correction of part of the last period's forecast error.

Nerlove (1983) found that the adaptive expectations theory which he called 'error-learning' theory explained surveyed expectations quite well for business firms in Germany and France. The theory of adaptive expectations can be expected to make less sense for consumers than for business decision makers. Consumers who are asked questions about their price expectations in a survey can hardly be presumed to remember what they answered six months or a year ago, unless they are especially motivated to remember or are reminded of their earlier answers. Income expectations may at least for some survey respondents be more of intentional expectations, that is, they are similar to plans that the respondent will implement. In the case of business decision makers, the answers to questions about production and sales which presumably cover intentional expectations may be based on budget data and similar records and a comparison of expectation and outcome may be easily accomplished and part of regular follow-ups.

The original rational expectations theory was in simple terms explained: 'expectations, since they are informed predictions of future events, are essentially the same as the predictions of the relevant economic theory' (Muth, 1961, p.316). The new theory referred to how businessmen formed their expectations about prices and was inspired by two conclusions from earlier studies of expectations:

1. Averages of survey expectations in an industry were more accurate than naïve models and as accurate as elaborate equation systems, although there were wide individual variations
2. Survey expectations generally underestimated the extent of changes actually taking place. There was severe criticism of adaptive expectations theory, since adaptive expectations consistently underestimated actual expectations when there was steady growth. (Muth, 1961 p. 316)

A formal definition of rational expectations looks like this, taking price level as an example

$$PE_{t+1} = E(P_{t+1} \mid I_t)$$

where PE_{t+1} = expected price level next period at t
E = the mathematical expectation (of P_{t+1} at time t)
I_t = the set of information available at t.

The rational expectation is then the mathematical expectation of the price level at time $t + 1$, conditional on all the information available at time t. Rational expectations are often defined in the following way which suggests a way of assessing whether expectations are rational

$$PE_{t+1} = P_{t+1} + u$$

where PE_{t+1} = expected price level for period $t + 1$, formed at the end of period t

P_{t+1} = realized price level at the end of period $t + 1$
u = stochastic error term.

Rationality implies that u has mean zero, that there is no serial correlation, and there is zero correlation between u and any information known at the time to the person who is forming the expectation. This involves complete, unbiased and efficient use of all information.

The theory of rational expectations is intended as a theory of how expectations of a wide range of economic variables are formed (Attfield et al., 1985, p.11). Rational expectations have been described in varying terms

> The underlying idea is simply that economic agents behave purposefully in collecting and using information just as they do in other activities. In this general form the hypothesis is a compelling one, but in practice this idea is often translated into the requirement that expectations are, in the model at hand, formed in a way that is stochastically consistent with the behavior of the realized values of the variables in question. (Nerlove, 1983 pp.1254-5)

In the Life-Cycle Hypothesis, expectations about future income are essential for the consumption/saving decision. It is assumed that expectations are revised, as new information about income becomes available. As, for example, Thaler (1990) noted, this can be a very demanding task. Rational expectations involve that earlier experience and new information are used in an optimal way which means that they are treated as in economic theory. This involves computing a kind of annuities, based on the best knowledge about current and future income.

The rational expectations theory overrides the other theories of expectation formation. While the main emphasis is on the use of new information, the optimal use of information may involve pure extrapolation and sometimes an adaptive process. So far researchers have shown only limited interest in how survey expectations are formed under the influence of external events, but a growing interest in the intricacies of survey measurements of consumer and business expectations can be noted (Nerlove, 1983; Lovell, 1986; Batchelor and Dua, 1992; Ivaldi, 1992).

Maital and Maital (1981) discussed social influence on consumer expectations and using some Israeli data found that interpersonal trust had a significant influence on inflation expectations as had also income and age. Batchelor, alone (Batchelor, 1986) and with a co-author (Batchelor and Dua, 1990a; 1990b; 1991; 1992) has paid considerable attention to inflation expectations and used some ideas from psychophysics to elucidate the formation of such expectations. Batchelor and Dua (1990a; 1990b) also studied the predictive success of US economic forecasters. They found that those who made the best forecasts worked with specified econometric models based on some ideology, in the first place Keynesian theory. The authors noted that all forecast-ers added a lot of subjective judgment to the model: they put more weight on judgment than on any formal modeling technique.

Testing the Rational Expectations Theory
The reasoning around rational expectations implies that they primarily are a macro concept. On average and over time expectations will tend to be ra-tional, when the situation is not too complex. The limited cognitive capacity of humans makes it unlikely that any human being has really rational expec-tations (Simon, 1984; 1990). Katona (1980) and Simon (1984) noted that one aim of rational expectations theory was to make measurement of expectations unnecessary, an ambition they did not share.

The original formulation of the rational expectations theory hardly admit-ted any empirical testing of its validity. In Muth's (1961) first formulation it was a theory aimed at improving descriptions of economic behavior of pro-ducers whose behavior was described through the so-called cobweb theorem. The cobweb theorem explains the production of producers who relied on ex-trapolated, most recent past experience and did not heed new information or learn from their errors. While some adherents of the rational expectations theory still think that the theory cannot (and should not) be tested directly against empirical data on subjective expectations (cf. Sheffrin, 1983), there are now several formulations of the theory that invite such testing. A weak form of test involves that the discrepancies between expectation and outcome should on average be equal to zero (unbiased). A stronger test means that there is no correlation between information available when the expectation was formed and the expectation error (Attfield et al., 1985, pp.106-9).

A simple delineation of rational expectations is that expectations are ra-tional when there is no pattern of systematic error: 'Purposeful economic agents have incentives to eliminate such errors up to a point justified by the costs of obtaining the information necessary to do so . . . The most readily available and least costly information about the future value of a variable is its past values' (Nerlove, 1983, p.1255). Extrapolation of past experience may be the only information used in some cases of expectation formation. If there is good agreement between expectation and outcome, at least one cri-terion for rationality is satisfied.

Tests of the rational expectations theory have been carried out using labor-atory experiments and in a somewhat different vein interview surveys. Brown and Maital (1981) did an early test of rational expectations. They showed that economic experts in the well-known Livingston panel of economic experts underutilized available information, particularly data on monetary growth. The experts were partly, but not fully rational. In an earlier study, Maital (1979) found that a unit change in monetary growth had the largest impact on inflation expectations of consumers. He found it unlikely, though, 'that pipe-fitters and stevedores furrow their brows over the latest figures on M_1, M_2, and excess reserves' (Maital, 1979, p.434). As noted above, forecasts differ in predictive accuracy. Batchelor and Dua (1991) found that individual forecasts were more likely to be rational if they were based on mainstream economic theory and included a substantial element of judgment. The latter part may be due to the importance of new information. Baghestani (1992) tested the inflation expectations of households collected by Institute for Social Research, University of Michigan. The test concerned the rationality of the survey expectations. He found that the survey data tended to outperform the forecasts made using objective data. Ivaldi (1992) compared business survey data with rational expectations theory and found that there was some similarity.

The primary aim of many of the tests seems to be to ascertain whether there are systematic errors when expectations and realizations are compared. The test involves that there is a correspondence between expectations at time $t - 1$ for time t and the appraisals of outcomes at time t. If there is agreement, the rational expectations hypothesis is assumed to hold. This is, of course, not really a test of the rational expectations hypothesis. It is not only a very weak test of fit, it errs in presupposing that the only way to make accurate predictions or rather to have accurate expectations is to treat the available information in an optimal way, that is, as economic theory prescribes. Arrow (1986) has emphatically stressed that there are many plausible alternatives to the rationality assumption.

Lovell (1986) reviewed many of the tests performed so far and concluded

> If the cumulative evidence is to be believed, we are compelled to conclude that expectations are a rich and varied phenomenon that is not adequately captured by the concept of rational expectations; while the predictions of some forecasters may be characterized as rational, in other instances the assumption of rationality is clearly violated. (Lovell, 1986, p.120)

Lovell cited two reasons why the theory did not seem to be borne out. One was simply measurement error and the other the possibility that shifts in the environment might necessitate transient departures from rationality. It could be added that it is not always easy, using even the best of economic theory, to know and pursue what is rational as Akerlof (1991) has amply demonstrated in a readable essay on procrastination and obedience.

Summing up the previous discussion of expectations as treated by economists one arrives at the conclusion that all three theories can at times explain expectations, but under different circumstances. The discussion hints that when the economic conditions are stable and do not vary much or vary in the same way over long periods of time, for example, a long spell of steady, but slow growth, simple extrapolation of earlier development may do well. When there is new information, implying breakdowns of earlier patterns, both extrapolative and adaptive expectations theories fall short as single explanations of actual expectations. Adaptive expectations theory presumes that there is a correction depending on earlier discrepancies between expectations and outcomes. The theory will do normatively better than extrapolation theory in times of changing patterns like what is described as the hog-cycle, but it probably still falters as a description in such cases.

Learning from earlier misjudgments may also be rational in the sense of rational expectations theory. Most so-called tests of rational expectations theory on empirical data are compatible with this idea since the crucial issue is the agreement between expectations as measured in surveys and actual outcomes (Lovell, 1986; Baghestani, 1992; Ivaldi, 1992). Depending on what periods the tests are based on, it seems possible to confirm both extrapolative and adaptive expectations theories. If the tests indicate that the expectations are unbiased, i.e. the error distribution has mean 0 and that there is no relevant new information, the criteria for rationality are fulfilled.

Expectations in Economic-Psychological Research

The extent of human intelligence involved in problem solving should not be overestimated. The formation of new expectations is not always based on a careful consideration of all facets of a situation. Problem solving makes use of shortcuts and stereotypes; the search for reasons may be superficial and inadequate.

Katona (1972, p.554)

Expectations constitute an important area of research in economic psychology. Interesting discussions can be found e.g. in Vanden Abeele (1988) and Bechtel et al. (1993). With few exceptions, there is little discussion of how economic-psychological theory of expectations can be improved. While the current focus is on the measurement of a few expectations through survey interviews and very simple indexes like the Index of Consumer Sentiment or Index of Consumer Expectations prevail, there is reason for drawing on both economics and psychology to develop economic-psychological expectations theory. It should be acknowledged that the simple indexes used have shown surprising usefulness in macroeconomic contexts (see Chapter 5).

With respect to economic-psychological research, I would like to make two main points: (1) that the *formation* of expectations measured in surveys is largely unknown and (2) the study of other economic expectations than those relating to the business cycle is undernourished. In many consumer behavior contexts, there has been an unfortunate focus on attitudes and attitude change rather than on expectations and on how expectations are formed and influenced. The formation of expectations seems to be highly relevant when new products and other innovations are to be launched in the market. In a recent paper, Johnson et al. (1995) have shown how adaptive and rational expectations can be related to customer satisfaction.

A Model of Expectation Formation

Based on economic and psychological theories of expectations that will be explained shortly, three sets of beliefs are assumed to constitute expectations. The three sets have different importance in different contexts, indicated by weights. In its simple, individual form the model looks like this

$$EXP_{t+1} = w_1 B_{Pt} + w_2 B_{At} + w_3 B_{It}$$

where EXP_{t+1} = expectation about period $t + 1$ stated at time t_0
B_{Pt} = beliefs based on extrapolation of past experience
B_{At} = beliefs due to discrepancies between expectations and outcomes
B_{It} = beliefs based on new information
w_1, w_2, w_3 are (empirical) weights which can vary from 0 to 1.

If $\Sigma w_i = 1$, the assumption is made that the components are integrated by averaging rather than summation (cf. Busemeyer, 1991). This is consistent with many findings in information integration theory (Anderson, 1991). B_{At} represents 'error-learning'. This set of beliefs operates primarily when the expectation is similar to a goal or plan, an *intentional* expectation (see Van-den Abeele, 1988). B_{It} are beliefs that can be divided into two sets of beliefs, one pertaining to the individual/household, the other to economy-wide information.

The basic idea is that expectations are formed and revised on the basis of past experience of a phenomenon (or similar phenomena, involving generalization), learning from how successful earlier, intentional expectations were, and finally, on new information in the individual's immediate or more distant environment. If the weight of one set of beliefs equals zero, the other sets are the basis for forming an expectation. If the expectation is *contingent*, i.e. the outcome cannot be affected by anything the holder of the expectation does, the weight of the error-learning beliefs is equal to zero. Many expectations are simply founded on past experience. In terms of the model this means that the other two sets of beliefs have weights equal to zero or at least very small weights. In other cases, there are no earlier experiences, but some information in the environment, which will then serve to form the expectation.

A simple criterion for rational expectations is that the discrepancies between expectations and realizations are minimal, that is, do not deviate significantly from zero. Extrapolative as well as adaptive expectations are then compatible with rational expectations provided they give good enough predictions. The third set of beliefs involves that there is new information to utilize, something that is not handled by the extrapolative and adaptive expectations theories. In some, presumably rare cases the new information will have such dominance that other sets of beliefs get zero weights. Katona (1972) said that new and dramatic information could lead to problem-solving rather than the usual routine behavior.

Expectation – A Cognitive Concept

The psychological concept of expectation belongs in cognitive theory. The basic assumption is that the individual forms expectations using past experience and available information. There may be an emotional or motivational touch to expectations implying that the informational support for the expectation may be of lesser importance. Vanden Abeele (1988) distinguished between *contingent* and *intentional* expectations. While the individual has no control or perception of control over the events or objects in the former case, in the second there is some degree of (perceived) control. Intentional expectations are then similar to plans, goals and levels of aspiration.

Feather (1982) described the current view of expectations in psychology

> People are assumed to possess cognitive structures that concern the implications of their action, both now and in the future. They also consider events that they cannot influence. These implication structures may not always be well-defined, they may be in error, and one would expect them to vary in their details from person to person. But they are assumed to exist and, along with subjective values, valences, or utilities, to be important determinants of goal directed behavior. (Feather, 1982, p.2)

Behavioristic psychology avoids cognitive and other mental concepts. *Expectancy* was the preferred concept in such theory (see Vanden Abeele, 1988). Expectancy referred to something inferred from observed behavior. It should be noted that the dominant expectancy-value theories of attitude formation and change use expectancy as synonymous to expectation. Otherwise, expectancy refers to something inferred from observations of behavior. An example of expectancy in the behavioristic sense is when a dog running down an alley is said to have an expectancy when he starts preparing for a curve which he cannot yet see. Certain changes in movements and perhaps other overt behavior can be observed and they indicate a tendency that may be called an expectancy.

It seems possible to transfer expectancy in this sense to economic behavior. Changes in economic behavior may indicate new expectancies that have import for future behavior. If there are no such indicator changes, the assumption is that the expectancy is the same as in the preceding period. A retailer may for example notice that consumers are spending more on consumer durables and take this as a sign of increased optimism, tantamount to a changed expectancy towards the future.

A behavioristic alternative to the Index of Consumer Sentiment would be to collect behavioral indicators from households and business firms rather than asking for rather general assessments of situations. The respondents would be asked to report about their behavioral changes, if any, and on their observations of changes in the environment. Whereas news reporters in the mass media have a tendency to ask consumers and businessmen about behavioral changes in connection with certain economic changes, there is no attempt to collect systematically indicators of changes in overt economic behavior.

Cognitive theory, in contrast, deals with expectation as a subjective concept that epitomizes what a person anticipates from the future in a more or less well-defined respect. An expectation is not inferred from behavior, but something that the individual can state. When expectation is more of a motivational concept and contains elements of plans or goals, i.e., is intentional, it can be compared to level of aspiration, which is a kind of goal an individual sets for her/himself. The level of aspiration is susceptible to learning from the discrepancies between goal and outcome (cf. Katona, 1975).

The Formation of Expectations according to Psychological Theories

Expectations regarding objects and events are formed in one of three possible ways (Feather, 1982, p.63): (a) memory of past experience, (b) direct observation which includes new information, and (c) inference provide the basis of expectations. These can be seen as operating together, assuming different weights for the components. The earlier presented model of expectation formation reflects exactly this thinking. The three components are similar to the economic theories of expectations, which involve extrapolated past experience, inference from past experience, and new information present in the environment.

Four types of expectations are distinguished in the psychological literature (Feather, 1982, pp.64-8): (1) situation-outcome expectation, (2) action-outcome expectation, (3) action-by-situation outcome, (4) outcome-consequence expectation. Applied to the economic context, an example of the situation-outcome expectation would be a measure of how the economic situation of the country is expected to change over the next 12 months. It is a contingent expectation. An example of an action-outcome expectation would be a plan to save money for a certain goal in the future. This is tantamount to an intentional expectation. The same example with the additional condition that the state of the economy seems appropriate for saving illustrates the third type of expectation. The fourth is finally the contingent expectation about consequences for oneself of certain things happening. The formation of expectations is assumed to vary somewhat between the four types.

In learning theories, the reinforcement of earlier behavior or of cognitive maps involving relations between means and ends is the main impetus for the formation of expectations. Learning from error, as adaptive expectations theory presumes, presupposes some kind of relation to motivation, that is, reinforcement. On a rather superficial level, it can be said that cognitive linkages that have turned out to serve in earlier situations are projected on to the future. Available new information that contradicts the earlier experience has to be strong to modify the linkages. Katona (1975) distinguished between routine behavior and problem solving. While routine or habit was the prevalent behavior, a simple repetition of earlier behavior, problem solving was brought forth by new information of some scope that required new thinking. Katona (1972) applied similar ideas to expectations. Repetition created, according to him, expectations that the same thing would happen again. Expectations involved problem solving when understanding of relationships that affected the future was required. Expectations could then derive from established principles and theories which in their turn might be the results of other people's problem solving.

If Katona's distinction between routine behavior and problem solving is applied, expectations during stable periods are mere repetitions of earlier expectations. They may be seen as habitual. If one's income has gone up steadily over the last years, the expectation for the next year will be that the income will go up with approximately the same percentage. If there has been no change, the expectation will be 'no change'. Only if there is new information of some import, the expectation will be different from last time. Overreactions to certain kinds of news may occur and incite important expectational and behavioral changes (Andreassen, 1990). The new information may come via the mass media from external sources and be shared by large masses of people. The information may be news of good or bad events of a more general scope like information about business cycles, political unrest or changes in government policies. The new information may be general and have special implications for the individual household, such as information about changes in unemployment, price level and interest rates.

The new information may also come from household internal sources, for example, involve that a family member who has not had gainful employment starts working, a family member who has had gainful employment stops working because of redundancy or retirement, or that a new family member will be born. Expected changes in family conditions influence the expectations of household financial situation in addition to possible expected economy-wide changes if the latter are seen as relevant to the household.

Bechtel et al. (1993) proposed a distinction between *sociotropic* and *personal* dimensions of expectations. The term sociotropism originated in political theory and referred to the fact that collective interests rather than personal interests could motivate a person to vote. The authors now use it in a broader sense to designate expectations that encompass the economic development of the whole economy rather than the personal or individual household financial situation. This approach makes it interesting to study more in detail the relationships between personal and sociotropic expectations. There is, for example, the possibility that the personal expectations are more loaded with affect and motivation. They may be less uncertain than the sociotropic expectations, being based on personal knowledge. They perhaps contain intentions and plans for the future and are not only passive attempts to foresee economic development for the household. Berg and Bergström (1996) found that the personal component of the Swedish ICS significantly contributed to explaining consumption growth.

The role of affect in the formation of expectations could be important. There is not room here for more than a few ideas. The degree of affect connected with different types of expectations seems to vary. For example, consequences that can be attributed to one's own actions have more emotional content and ego-involvement than consequences attributable to outside forces. Non-fulfillment of an expectation that embodies a goal or a level of aspiration is likely to induce more feelings of frustration than non-fulfillment of an expectation regarding the national economy. Expectation is a kind of social judgment and is as such apt to be influenced by emotion. Recent research has produced an interesting theory of emotion in social judgments which seems appropriate to use in this connection: the Affect Infusion Model (Forgas, 1994). This model reveals under what circumstances and how affects are infused in social judgments.

While economic theory makes no assumption about how past experience, whether extrapolative or adaptive, and new information are combined in the formation of expectations, some psychological theories handle the integration of past and present stimulation, the merging of past experience and new information into one judgment. There are essentially three theories that pertain to how earlier experience and new information are combined in a judgment: (1) *adaptation level theory* (Helson, 1964; Appley, 1971), (2) *information integration theory* (Anderson, 1991), (3) *expectancy-value theory* (Ajzen and Fishbein, 1980).

Adaptation level theory recognizes the possible influence of three types of stimuli. First, earlier experience of the stimuli, treated in such a way that the most recent occurrences are most important, influences the judgment. Secondly, the stimuli present in the situation have some influence. They serve as background stimuli. Thirdly, the characteristics of the stimulus to be judged have an obvious influence. The main point is that new stimuli are not judged in any absolute way, but are judged in relation to earlier experience and what is present in the context which may be equivalent to competing new information.

It is characteristic of both adaptation level theory and *information integration theory* that a stimulus is not judged alone since it is always compared and integrated with an existing mass. Information integration theory, which is accompanied by a special measuring method called 'functional measurement', is not a theory in the sense of comprising a set of psychological laws. It is rather an approach to the empirical estimation of how stimuli of various kinds are combined into one judgment. Information integration theory works with ratings of stimuli and scaled judgments with the purpose of finding stimulus weights that best explain the judgment.

An interesting finding is that, in many cases, the judgment is made by averaging rather than adding a new stimulus to the present state. Levin (1985) studied satisfaction with wages and prices using information integration theory. The question was which weights given to wages change and to price level change best explained the satisfaction measure. It was found that the integration followed a ratio rather than a summation principle. Earlier studies by Levin had indicated that an averaging principle obtained as in many other information integration studies.

The effects of new information in macroeconomic contexts may be widely different if an averaging principle rather than summation is used by most consumers or decision makers. If new, favorable information is integrated by averaging it may take much longer for optimistic expectations to develop than if the new good news is added. This implies that if there are many highly favorable indicators of economic growth and one more indicator, which is favorable but less so than the earlier ones, appears, the new judgment will be less favorable than before the new favorable information became available. With a summation principle, the new judgment would become even more favorable. Saving, investing and consumption may be influenced by such trivial circumstances.

Expectancy-value theory is the dominant attitude theory. It deals with beliefs, affects and behavior related to an object or event. Attitudes are often held to consist of three components: belief(s) about an object, affect towards the object, and the tendency to action towards the object (the conative component). People are assumed to have sets of salient attributes for each object to be evaluated and beliefs about how likely the object is to display or lack the desired attributes. The subjective expected utility model can be seen as a special case of expectancy-value models (Fishhoff et al., 1982).

While expectancy-value is not really a theory of how earlier experience and new information combine, some important things for the dealing with expectations can be winnowed from it. Expectations can be dealt with as a particular kind of belief that concern the future. It seems possible that the role that expectations can play for actions can be elucidated by means of expectancy-value theories. The most important expectancy-value models are focused on predicting actions and could give ideas for research on intentional expectations. They may not be applicable to sociotropic expectations.

Ajzen's (1985, 1991) Theory of Planned Behavior embraces some ideas that can be applied in the study of expectations. According to Ajzen, an attitude consists of (a) behavioral beliefs, which are assumed to influence attitudes toward the behavior, (b) normative beliefs, which constitute the underlying determinants of subjective norms and (3) control beliefs, which provide the basis for perceptions of behavioral control. Ajzen added the component *perceived control* to the well-known Ajzen-Fishbein model. The models will be treated further in Chapter 7.

A person is assumed to hold a limited number of salient beliefs about an object, eight to ten at the most. The behavioral beliefs are of two kinds: beliefs about the costs and benefits of engaging in the behavior (instrumental beliefs) and beliefs about positive or negative feelings derived from the behavior (affective beliefs). The degree of perceived control defines whether an attitude or expectation is a plan for behavior against the object. When the individual has strong control, an expectation becomes similar to a goal or level of aspiration. It is intentional and can be adaptive. From level of aspiration studies, it is well known that deviations of outcomes from expected achievements have strong motivational force (Brickman and Campbell, 1971). The setting of new levels of aspiration is influenced by earlier discrepancies. Again, this is the psychological concept of error learning.

Price Level Expectations and Saving

While some countries had high inflation and low, decreasing saving ratios, high inflation rates and high saving ratios characterized other industrialized countries during the early 1980s. Among the reasons for the positive correlation suggested by economists were mistaken notions about real prices since consumers were assumed only to find out prices of goods they were about to buy and not of goods for which they were not in the market. Another reason was that, in the face of future inflation, there could be borrowing constraints that would lead to reduced liquidity and further reduced consumption expenditures. Finally, a rise in anticipated borrowing constraints could increase precautionary saving. Koskela and Virén (1982) who used Finnish data found that there was a significant effect of price anticipations, as calculated from price level data, on the saving ratio. Some more psychologically oriented research will now be mentioned.

Whereas the ICS is based on a few questions asking about changes in the present and the future financial status of the household and of the national economy, studies of perceptions and predictions of inflation often ask for quantitative estimates. In Katona's first studies, questions about inflation were simple and asked for the direction of the expected change in prices: up, down, or unchanged. In later studies, attempts were made to ask for more detailed information (Katona, 1975). Today survey questions often ask for percentage estimates from the respondents.

On average, people seem to have a good grasp of how much prices in general have increased during the last year (Jonung, 1981; Blomqvist, 1983; Batchelor, 1986). When asked about price level changes over the next 12 months, people on average seem to be able to make reasonably good predictions. Although many respondents in a survey hesitate to make any prediction, those who do, in some cases provide an average estimate that is amazingly close to the actual development, as assessed after 12 months (Wärneryd and Wahlund, 1985). The way the questions are asked appears to be of great importance. When people are asked how much the prices of certain goods have gone up or how the price of a basket of goods has changed, the results are much less accurate than when respondents give percent estimates for the total price level.

Hudson (1989), citing Wärneryd (1986a) concluded that there were two sets of inflation expectations. One was based on direct experience of price changes and could be measured in surveys through asking questions about price changes for shopping baskets of goods. The second set was indirect and derived from information about price changes received from the mass media and from other people. It could be covered through questions about percentage changes in price levels. On average, the indirect estimates tended to be much closer to reality than the direct ones, which wildly overestimated price rises.

There are a few behavioral studies of how inflation affects saving. Katona (1975) found that the relationships were rather complex. Juster (1981) said

> The pervasive consumer reaction to general price increases during the postwar period had always (with few exceptions) been retrenchment on spending and increase in saving. But reactions to prospective price increases for specific items like houses and cars can be, and in 1978 [were], quite different. The survey data are unambiguous on this point: many consumers thought that this was a good time to buy houses and cars, mainly because they expected housing and car prices to rise substantially in future, and hence felt that it was better to buy now than wait until later. (Juster, 1981, p.89)

Table 6.1 Expected Inflation and Expected Bank Saving

Will save	Inflation less than 8 percent		Inflation equal to or over 8 percent		Total	
	n	Percent	n	Percent	n	Percent
More	230	35.0	114	23.1	344	29.9
Equal amount	287	43.7	228	46.3	515	44.8
Less	140	21.3	150	30.5	290	25.2
Total	657	100	492	100	1149	100

Source: Wärneryd and Wahlund (1985, p.334).

In a Swedish study with a representative sample of adult men, Wärneryd and Wahlund (1985) asked quantitative questions about price expectations: 'By what percentage do you think that prices in general will go up or down during the next twelve months?' Around 11 percent did not make any guesses about future inflation. The rest of the sample gave guesses that when 12 months later compared with the Consumer Price Index were on average surprisingly close to it. The respondents were also asked: 'Do you think that your household will twelve months ahead have more, an equal amount or less money in the bank than today?'

Table 6.1 shows the relationship between expected inflation and expected bank savings. Those who expected *lower* inflation significantly more often expected to save more in bank accounts during the next 12 months. A similar analysis for total savings, not only bank savings, gave the same result. This suggests that even at relatively moderate rates of inflation expectations of increased inflation may have a dampening effect on saving.

What Influences Consumer Expectations?

In public debates, it is often argued that the mass media, through reporting on ill events and ominous signs of poor prospects for the future, build up expectations, especially of an impoverished future. Katona (1975) suggested a *social learning* process in which a large number of people were at the same time reached by some important information and reacted in the same way. What the mass media reported could have great influence on such social learning. This was a reason for frequent measurements of consumer and business expectations.

Only a few studies investigate the correlation between mass media reports and economic developments. Katona's evidence was mostly indirect. Van Raaij (1989) gave an overview of the relationships between news and expectations and concluded that there was often an overinterpretation of tendencies

If reporters interpret random and/or minor deviations from the trend as structural trends attributing the deviation to internal causes, people generally will form or revise expectations based on this information. Both mass media reporters and the public at large will base their conclusions on imperfect information. (van Raaij, 1989, p.490)

An interesting study of how headlines that reported violence on the front page of the *New York Times* correlated with department store sales in New York, serves as an example of how such studies can be done although it does not directly refer to expectations. Schachter et al. (1986, p.240) found that the more violence was reported, the smaller the sales were. Having carefully checked for other possible explanations, the authors concluded 'we are inclined to accept the interpretation that reports of violence in the mass media can create a community-wide state of uneasiness sufficient to affect department store sales.' In another study they investigated fluctuations on the New York Stock Exchange and found that emotions, induced by such factors as reports on airplane crashes and presidential elections, seemed to explain certain deviations from market efficiency. Similar research was reported by Andreassen (1990).

Bechtel et al. (1993) pointed out the importance of distinguishing between the ICS questions relating to the household and those relating to the national economy. While the first type refers to the personal environment which to some degree can be influenced (intentional expectations), the second type involves contingencies and, by these authors, are called 'sociotropic'. The relationships between the two sets can be of great interest. When a recession begins, the expectations for the national economy tend to go down first and people seem to believe that they will do better than others. When the financial crisis of the early nineties turned into more positive development in some countries, there was at first more optimism about the financial situation of the nation than about the household's own situation. A tentative explanation of the differences is that sociotropic expectations are influenced by the mass media while personal expectations are more influenced by past experience and observations in the immediate environment.

While the theory of rational expectations dominates the economists' discussion of expectation formation, there are disagreements about the exact form to use and there is an increasing demand for descriptive data on expectations and expectation formation (Lindbeck, 1989). Psychological researchers can here find recognition of the utility of psychological research and a hope for clarifying, descriptive theory based on survey interviews and laboratory experimentation.

Although some rational expectations theorists say that past experience may be the best available information, the theory seems to play down the role of past experience. An intriguing problem for psychologists to tackle is how past experience and new information are integrated. This can be studied in laboratory experiments, following information integration theory (Anderson, 1991) as well as in survey research. In the latter case, questions about the evaluation of new information will have to be asked of the respondents.

UNCERTAINTY

What is undoubtedly true for rational decision makers need not be true for human decision makers.

Anderhub et al. (1997, p.3)

What Is Uncertainty?

Uncertainty means lack of assurance or conviction and is in everyday usage an imprecise and broad concept that covers all sorts of phenomena. In economics and other social sciences, a distinction that was suggested by the economist Frank Knight is often made between three decision-making situations with respect to the kind of information available (Luce and Raiffa, 1990, p.20).

1. *Certainty* is when a specific action is known to lead invariably to a specific outcome
2. *Risk* is when each action leads to one of a set of possible specific outcomes and each outcome occurs with a known probability
3. *Uncertainty* is when any or all of the alternative actions have as consequence a set of possible specific outcomes, but the probabilities of these outcomes are completely unknown or are not even meaningful.

Knight distinguished between 'measurable uncertainty', which he called risk, and unmeasurable uncertainty. Uncertainty and risk are not always kept strictly apart in research contexts. If the above distinctions are adopted, risk should be used on situations or outcomes to which a probability can be attached and in principle at least can be insured against. Uncertainty refers to outcomes where there is no probability or even any limited interval of probabilities. In Bayesian decision theory, subjective probabilities are used instead of the objective probabilities that are missing in the uncertainty case.

The *American Heritage College Dictionary* (1993) defines risk in several ways. The first sense is the possibility of suffering harm or loss. The second sense sets risk equal to hazard; a factor, thing, element, or course involving uncertain danger. The third meaning is the term used by insurers to designate the probability of a loss. The fourth sense is the investor's view: the variability of returns from an investment. These different meanings are important when people are asked about their risk taking. In everyday usage, risk is associated with fear that something unpleasant will happen and uncertainty is when you do not know (cf. Drottz-Sjöberg, 1991). Still, the strict categories can be used to discuss different decision-making situations.

Risk does not always have a connotation of fear or negative emotions. Practitioners in certain fields are all the time handling what they think of as calculated risks. Investors in put and call options may, for example, be risk takers in the eyes of the general public and also in their own eyes, but they probably feel that they have some control over the risks that they take. In the world of finance, taking high risks is connected with expectations of high profits. Uncertainty is not necessarily associated with emotions of fear, but may have different degrees of emotional loading. One has to live with uncertainty about the future, but some risks can be avoided or reduced. When no instructions for best choice can be given, as is the case in genuine uncertainty situations, the psychological consequence may be anxiety and confusion. Insurance does not reduce the risk of an ill event, but it increases the possibility of bearing the consequences if the event happens. The feeling of uncertainty may then be reduced.

Uncertainty and Its Measurement

When uncertainty is mentioned in economics, it mostly refers to uncertainty about future employment and income. In connection with the LCH, uncertainty about income, remaining lifetime and, lately, uncertainty about health have drawn much attention (see, for example, Kotlikoff, 1989; Hubbard et al., 1994). In discussions of consumption in the modern society, other types of uncertainty are also pointed out, for example, uncertainty about what will happen to the family, such as divorce and re-marriage. Social life is full of uncertainties. All these types of uncertainty may affect savings.

While the original LCH did not encompass uncertainty about future income, it is now common to use a model with uncertainty – where uncertainty is equivalent to risk since it can be calculated. This does not simplify the model, nor does it necessarily make it more realistic in a psychological sense. King (1985, p.269) cited evidence from psychological research that severely questioned the assumptions about optimal decision making. He referred to Tversky and Kahneman (1982) who argued that when constructing subjective probabilities people used a limited number of heuristic principles which sometimes led to violation of Bayes's theorem. This derived from an inability of individuals to comprehend more than a certain part of the problem at any one time. The findings showed that the probabilities used by individuals were unduly dominated by the most recent observed outcome. An alternative interpretation was that the costs of decision making under uncertainty were so great that individuals devised rules of thumb for their consumption and saving behavior.

Uncertainty about future income and uncertainty about subjective life expectancy have become crucial concepts in the discussion of the LCH. In recent years, many attempts have been made to get subjective estimates both of income and lifetime uncertainties. Economists tend to use aggregate measures of uncertainty, for example, the mean and variance of price level developments, measured as changes in the Consumer Price Index. If they use subjective data, they tend, in a corresponding manner, to use the mean and variance of the price expectations as a proxy for uncertainty about the future (Juster and Taylor, 1975; Juster, 1981; Batchelor and Jonung, 1989). Income uncertainty can be assessed by using the mean and variance of the aggregate income distribution or income realization estimates from panel data, based on answers to questions about earlier income development. Subjective data on income expectations were long rejected by mainstream economists with the argument that the measures were not consistent with theory and did not perform well in empirical tests (Sheffrin, 1983).

Consumers are in surveys asked about their income and price expectations. The typical procedure is to ask, first, whether the income increased, decreased or remained unchanged over the last 12 months. If the answer involves a change, the next question asks for a percentage estimate of the change. The same is done for the coming 12 months. The questions about the future are often accompanied by another question about how sure the respondent is with respect to the estimate. The questions eliciting price experience and price expectations are similarly phrased.

There are some interesting developments in the measurement of income uncertainty. They involve attempts to get subjective estimates of uncertainty. In an Italian survey of savings, respondents were asked to state the probabilities for income decreases and income increases of given percentages, for example, for 15 percent, 10 percent, and 5 percent increase and decrease of income during the next 12 months. Many respondents apparently found this to be a very difficult task and the rate of non-response was very high. Guiso et al. (1992) and Lusardi (1993) related the variance in these estimates to precautionary savings.

In the VSB Panel project at CentER, Tilburg University, a simplified procedure was used to ascertain income uncertainty. Instead of stating probabilities the respondents were asked to use a 7-point rating scale which was verbally anchored, running from 1 = 'highly unlikely' to 7 = 'highly likely'. The likelihood of three increases and three drops in income (15 percent, 10-15 percent, and 5-10 percent) and of no change were judged. The questionnaire also included the usual questions about income expectations, asking for percentage changes, and about how certain the respondent was. The rating scale

values can with some effort be converted to probabilities to fulfill economist's craving for probability distributions. For a psychologist it might be
natural to look for a scale of conversion from rating scale to probability
through running an experiment with subjects who are asked about the probability equivalents of the rating scale numbers.

Dominitz (1996), Dominitz and Manski (1995, p.30) reported on an elaborate procedure for assessing income uncertainty

> What do you think is the LOWEST amount that your total household income, from
> all sources, could possibly be over the next 12 months, BEFORE TAXES?
> What do you think is the HIGHEST amount that your total household income,
> from all sources, could possibly be over the next 12 months, BEFORE TAXES?
> What do you think is the PERCENT CHANCE (or what are the CHANCES OUT
> OF 100) that your total household income, BEFORE TAXES, will be less than Y?

The last question is asked for each of 4-6 income thresholds (Y) between the
lowest and highest stated values. These responses are used to estimate each
respondent's subjective probability distribution for next year's household
income. From the 1995 wave, these questions were included in the VSB
Panel questionnaire. Das and Donkers (1997) concluded that the use of these
subjective data was worthwhile. They found that the household income in the
past 12 months was a dominant predictor for future income, but less so when
there was a working spouse or partner. Income uncertainty decreased with
age up to retirement. There was more uncertainty when there was a working
spouse, in particular if the partner was unemployed and looking for a job.
The authors compared their measure of income uncertainty with similar
measures for Italy and the USA. Perceived income uncertainty was larger in
the USA than in the two European countries.

It is often assumed that the objective life expectancy can be used instead
of the subjective when the LCH is tested. According to rational expectations
theory, people use the best available information when forming their expectations. What could be better than taking one's life expectancy from a life
table? As said in Chapter 4, many people leave at their death wealth that far
exceeds what would have been necessary if objective life expectancy had
been adopted. Subjectively longer life expectancy can be part of the explanation, but it cannot explain much. On average, people may expect to live
longer than average, but they can hardly believe that they will live long
enough to bring their wealth down to zero! Additional explanations appear
necessary. A possible discrepancy between subjective and objective life expectancies may give some contribution towards explaining variance in asset
holdings at death.

Asking people about how long they expect to live is a delicate issue. In the
first waves in the VSB Panel, respondents were asked the following ques-

tions: 'What age do you think people of your age and sex reach on average?'
This was followed by: 'You answered that you think people of your age and
sex on average reach an age of . . . If you consider your situation and your
current health condition, do you expect to live longer or shorter than the average person of your age? (1) shorter, (2) about the same as the average person, (3) longer, (4) much longer, (5) no idea.' Figure 6.1 shows the results
from the first interview wave in the VSB Panel. The youngest expected to
live at least 50 years and the oldest expected to live four to five years. Taking
into consideration the respondents' answers to the question whether they expected to live longer than the average person would slightly increase the life
expectancies. There were no differences between the representative and the
high-income samples.

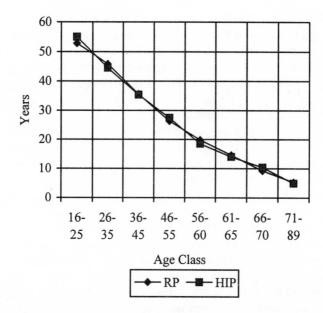

(RP = representative sample, HIP = high-income sample in VSB Panel).

Figure 6.1 Life Expectancy in Different Age Classes and Wealth Groups

The Health and Retirement Survey in the USA reports a number of questions designed to elicit information about subjective probability distributions
(Hurd and McGarry, 1995, 1996). The respondents (N = 10 575) who were
51-65 years old were asked to estimate their chances of surviving to age 75
and to age 85 in face-to-face interviews: 'Using any number from zero to ten

where 0 equals *absolutely no chance* and 10 equals *absolutely certain*, what do you think are the chances you will live to be 75 or more? . . . 85 or more?'

Hurd and McGarry (1996), using data from two interview waves reported on the predictive validity of the subjective probability distributions. During the two years between the waves, 182 people had died which agreed quite well with the life table mortalities.

> Comparing those who died with those who survived, we see that the survivors are younger by about a year on average, and they had higher income and assets reflecting differential mortality by economic status. The survivors gave considerably higher subjective survival probabilities in wave 1. This is an important validity check on the subjective survival probabilities. (Hurd and McGarry, 1996, p.3)

Risk Attitudes

Risk aversion and fear of risk

Economic decision making is assumed rational. Through the rational decisions utility is maximized; maximization of utility is one definition of rationality. Since utility refers to future outcomes nothing definitive can be known and the maximization is done over expected utility. The utility function is a fundamental concept. It determines preferences – which can only be studied through actual behavior (preferences revealed through choices) – and its shape discloses the degree of risk aversion. If utility is plotted against wealth, the function is risk averse if the curve is concave and risk loving if the curve is convex. Note that the curve and not the person is risk averse or risk loving. Saving decisions involve intertemporal utility which includes the utility of future consumption. It is well known that in reality people deviate from rationality and that the deviations sometimes seem systematic, even lawful. More will be said about this in the following pages, but here it should be noted that findings of lawfulness of some irrational behaviors do not preclude individual differences.

The popular view of the saver coincides with what many early economists thought. The saver is a self-controlled, cautious person who is risk averse, that is, abhors taking risks with money. The review of empirical research in Chapter 5 indicated that there is more than one type of saver. It does not seem likely that all saver groups have the same risk attitudes. Wealth managers may, for example, be different from buffer savers and cash managers from goal savers. Individual differences in risk attitudes may be important and well worth study.

In economic theory, people are seen as risk averse. Friedman and Savage (1948) questioned the assumption of risk aversion at all wealth levels and postulated a utility function that was risk-taking at low wealth levels and risk averse at high wealth levels. Such a function can explain the behavior of individuals who both buy lottery tickets and insurance (see Machina, 1990).

To a psychologist, the concepts of risk aversion and its converse risk seeking, by economists often called risk loving, look somewhat elusive, given the abstract quality and all the ramifications of utility theory. Risk aversion is in psychology a property of a person and can at least in principle be ascertained by making the right kind of observations of an individual, including asking questions about risk taking. Here *risk attitude* is used to designate a person's observed or reported tendencies in handling risks.

Experimental techniques for assessing risk attitudes are mostly based on some form of lottery choices. They are of great interest both to economists and psychologists who do research on decision making. The lottery choices used to elicit risk attitude or risk propensity are often of the following type. The individual makes a choice between two alternatives of the form (v, p) where p is the probability to win, v is an amount of money and $(1-p)$ is the probability to win nothing. The expected utility of such an alternative is $pu(v) + (1-p)u(0)$ where u is the utility function for money. The individual is assumed to select the alternative with the greatest expected value.

In psychology and social psychology, studies of risk perception and risk attitudes often focus on fears and perceived dangers and less on financial risk taking. Various approaches are used, including asking respondents in representative samples to make probability estimates of risks to themselves and to people in general (for a review, see Drottz-Sjöberg, 1991). It is commonly found that people tend to underestimate risks to themselves as well as to overestimate their chances of winning in lotteries (Sjöberg, 1998).

Subjective expected utility and risk attitudes

Expected utility is a combination of mathematical expectation and decreasing marginal utility. The assumption of risk aversion is a consequence of the assumed shape of the utility function. Risk aversion in a more general sense is supported by many observations of people's unwillingness to take financial risks and by the fact that people buy insurance to protect themselves against the consequences of ill events with often low probabilities. At the same time, it is obvious that many people gamble and may spend fortunes on lotteries, gambles, and risky investments.

The original idea of decreasing marginal utility came from Daniel Bernoulli who in 1738 maintained that wealth had diminishing marginal utility. He assumed that expected utility increased less than the expected value with increased amounts of money. Dfl. 1000 is subjectively worth less than ten times Dfl. 100. Bernoulli suggested that utility was a logarithmic function of value. This assumption was later generalized in psychophysics as 'Fechner's law'. Sensation was assumed a logarithmic function of physical stimulus value. The law was a dominant feature in experimental psychology towards the end of the last century and applications of it are also found in economics; Edgeworth (1881) referred to the idea (see Chapter 3).

Some facts of life are hard to reconcile with the shape of the theoretical utility function. People pay more than the expected value for insurance, but they also do so for lottery tickets. The subjective expected utility is apparently greater than the expected value in such cases. If it was not, insurance companies, casinos and national lotteries would not be profitable. The utility of insurance is probably higher than the expected value since a loss without insurance may often be ruinous. The utility of a lottery or other gambles may seem more dubious and essentially involves the utility of gambling itself. The latter is emotional and involves dreaming about winning high prizes and the thrill of sacrificing something small for an excitingly large gain albeit with often extremely low objective probability.

In psychology, the focus lies on *subjectively* expected value or utility. This involves that both the perceived probability and the perceived value may differ from objective data if such data exist. Subjective probability does not necessarily have a corresponding objective probability. The sources of the differences between expected value and (subjective) expected utility are of great potential interest to psychologists. Situational factors as well as characteristics of the individual may be expected to have explanatory power (see Lea et al., 1987, ch. 10).

Economists assume that consumers maximize subjective expected utility. Psychologists are doubtful. Although they cannot reject the idea that at the moment when a decision is made it is judged to be best (= optimal), they point out that the decision process may be so complicated that it is difficult to know what is optimal. Simon (1955) introduced the concept of *bounded rationality,* which means that consumers and other decision makers look for satisfactory, acceptable outcomes rather than optimal outcomes. To some extent, this is a question of where information seeking about alternative outcomes and their properties stops.

Prospect theory, loss aversion, and the endowment effect

Studies of decision making, mostly carried out as laboratory experiments, have shown that actual risky choices deviate considerably from what maximization of expected utility presupposes (for an overview, see Lopes, 1990, pp.267-70). The simple logarithmic relationship between objective value and utility obviously does not hold over a wide range of phenomena. *Prospect theory* which was originally presented by Kahneman and Tversky in 1979 and which was recently extended (Tversky and Kahneman, 1992), involves an attempt to reconcile theory and behavioral reality. It pays attention to gains and losses rather than to wealth, assumes that subjective decision weights replace probabilities, and that *loss aversion* rather than risk aversion is an overriding concept.

Risk aversion is in prospect theory no longer defined as a characteristic of the utility function over wealth. 'Risk aversion is defined as a preference for a sure outcome over a prospect with an equal or greater expected value . . . Risk seeking is exhibited if a prospect is preferred to a sure outcome with equal or greater expected value' (Tversky and Fox, 1995, p.269). If a person prefers $50 for certain to a 60 percent chance of getting $100 – which has a higher expected value – s/he is risk averse. If a person prefers a 40 percent chance to get $100 to $50 for sure, s/he is risk seeking

According to prospect theory, people are *risk averse* for gains with high probabilities and for losses with low probabilities, *risk seeking* for gains with low probabilities and losses with high probabilities (Tversky and Kahneman, 1992). 'Losses loom larger than gains' is a much-cited description of this phenomenon. The theory also observes the strong preference for outcomes that are certain, the so-called *certainty effect*. The pattern is explained by the weighting function for probabilities which overestimates small probabilities and underestimates moderate and high probabilities even if the latter are close to but less than 1. This is done slightly more for gains than for losses. A non-linear transformation of the probability scale prevails. The risk attitudes found in the experiments do not agree completely with the shape of the utility function, suggested by Friedman and Savage (1948).

In prospect theory, people are assumed to know precise probabilities. Einhorn and Hogarth (see Hogarth, 1987, p.101f) presented an ambiguity model in which people are assumed to assess ambiguous probabilities by first anchoring on some value of the probability and then adjusting this figure by mentally simulating or imagining other values that the probabilities could take. According to the ambiguity model, people do not know exact probabilities. You may know the cost of your automobile insurance, but not know the exact probability that you will have an accident or that your automobile will be stolen. The implication of ambiguity is that a probability distribution should be used rather than a single value.

The tendency for people to be risk seeking for gains with low probabilities is presumably enhanced with increasing amounts of money. People will accept low probabilities to win large prizes in lotteries. The existence of large prizes with low probabilities would be more attractive than the possibilities of winning smaller prizes with much higher probabilities. The most successful lotteries are then those with high prizes and such low probabilities that the cost to the gambler can be held very low.

Normatively, a person should choose in such a way that the expected utility is maximized even in a single trial. This is a recommendation made by Samuelson (1963) as well as by von Neuman and Morgenstern. The argument is, simply expressed, that if a person persistently pursues expected utility in risky choices over the life cycle, the gains will be highest. The trouble is that one may not get so many chances to make choices for a given category of events – or should small and big events be treated under one label? The reality-oriented opposition against the view points to the fact that people make a clear discrimination between cases of single and repeated gambles (Lopes, 1994). Intuitively, it certainly makes a difference if one is faced with a choice of a large gain with probability $p = 1$ and a much larger gain with probability less than 1 whether one knows that there will be many more choice occasions of the same kind and amounts or that the choice is the only chance in a lifetime.

If somebody gets a gift with a certain value, there is a tendency to ask a higher price than the value of the gift when it was received. This tendency has been called the *endowment effect* (Thaler, 1980). The effect is attributed to loss aversion; people are unwilling to part with something they have and gains have to be (often two to three times) larger to outweigh losses. It seems likely that some kinds of savings can be explained by the endowment effect. Katona (1975) noted that people rather borrowed than touched their buffer capital in temporarily difficult situations. Amateur investors tend to keep their losing shares too long and buy winning shares too late. Benartzi and Thaler (1995) used loss aversion (and short evaluation periods) to explain why people in general invested in bonds rather than in shares although shares were much more profitable over a longer period.

In both economics and cognitive psychology, the assumptions are formulated as general laws that are presumed to hold for everybody with some dispersion around the mean. The decision weights in prospect theory are subjective, but assumed to be the same or at least highly similar for all individuals. Individual differences cannot be explained by these theories, except as dispersion around the mean. In economic psychology, the interest is often focused on individual differences with a view towards looking for *segments* within the population, i.e. for groups of people who are similar within groups and different between groups (cf. Brandstätter, 1993). A distinction is sometimes made between risk averters and risk takers. It may not pay to look for segments whose members are consistently risk taking or risk averting over all situations, but rather to think of risk propensities as contingent also upon situations (MacCrimmon and Wehrung, 1986, pp.34-6).

Methods used to assess risk attitudes

Utility functions are unique to individuals and should, according to mainstream economic thinking, in principle be studied through behavior as it is revealed through actual choices. Outcomes of actual choices such as portfolios of assets are then the proper way of studying utility or preferences for assets. The composition of the asset portfolios reveals the true risk preferences. Pålsson (1996) demonstrated a way of analyzing risky wealth components using data from Swedish income tax returns. She distinguished between household portfolios containing different proportions of risky assets. Bank deposits were defined as less risky assets than stock, especially if the stock was financed through loans. Real estate was also judged more risky than bank deposits. It was usually at least to some extent financed through mortgages and loans. Pålsson found that the degree of risky investment was negatively correlated with age: older people tended to have more of their assets as bank deposits.

In the wake of game theory, ways of assessing subjective expected utility through choices have been developed. For reviews, see; for example, Farquhar (1984), Hogarth (1987) and Machina (1990). Hypothetical risky choices are the most common method of studying risk and utility both in economics and psychology. As a rule, economists are more anxious than psychologists that the choices should not be purely hypothetical, but have some monetary consequences for the subjects in terms of gains and losses. Psychologists refer to comparisons of the effects of different incentives on choices and tend to draw the conclusion that subjects can be sufficiently motivated by incentives not directly related to the outcomes of the choices. They get little support from the findings of Kachelmeier and Shehata (1992; see below). It seems reasonable to use these methods also to explore differences in risk-taking propensity among people in different situations. Such differences can be explored to define segments in the population who may be expected to react differently to certain economic stimuli, such as lottery bonds and national or state lotteries.

Psychological tests intended to measure risk propensity have not been very successful and the agreement between different tests is disappointingly low (MacCrimmon and Wehrung, 1986). While general tests for risk propensity do not seem to work well, tests of risk taking in specific areas do better. In psychology, it is common to use measures based on self-descriptions such as subjective reports on earlier acts of a certain type and on propensities to act in specified situations. Tests of this kind have, for example, been constructed for the area of financial investments (MacCrimmon and Wehrung, 1986; LeBaron et al., 1989; Roszkowski et al., 1989).

Attempts to assess risk aversion and risk seeking in economic behavior are usually based on choices between lotteries. There are several ways of eliciting the risk attitudes:

1. A choice between a certain alternative and a probable alternative
2. Choice between two probable alternatives with the same or unequal expected value

3. Request for a certain value equivalent to a probable value (certainty equivalent technique)
4. Request for a probability statement that makes the subject/respondent indifferent between two alternatives one of which is certain (lottery equivalent technique)
5. Request for a probability that makes the subject indifferent between two alternatives one of which has a known probability (cf. MacCrimmon and Wehrung, 1986, pp.58-9; Hogarth, 1987).

In the first case, the subject/respondent is presented a lottery which involves a reward with $p = 1$ and a reward with $p < 1$ and with the same or unequal expected value as the certain option. The second case is the same as the first except that both options are probable. The last three cases are different forms of the equivalent technique, which asks the subject/respondent for a probability or amount. In the third type, the subject is offered a reward (loss) with a probability p and asked to state how much s/he would want to receive (pay) with certainty to be indifferent between the lottery and the other alternative. This is also formulated as the minimum selling price (maximum buying price). In number 4, the subject is asked to state the probability that makes her/him indifferent between the two options. Case 5 is a further development of 4 and involves an attempt to avoid the certainty effect. It is often recommended to use $p = \frac{1}{2}$ rather than $p = 1$ in order to avoid the certainty effect. The task, although it may still be difficult for many respondents, is somewhat easier with a *certain* alternative (McCord and de Neufville, 1986; Hogarth, 1987, pp. 278-9).

The risk attitudes elicited through the different techniques are seldom the same. This is demonstrated by the so-called *preference reversal phenomenon* (see Tversky et al., 1990; Lopes, 1994, p.203f.). When asked to choose between two options one of which has a high probability of winning a small sum (A) and another that has a low probability of winning a large sum (B), people tend to choose (A). When asked how much they would be willing to pay for each option, people tend to pay more for (B). Such reversals of preferences were even observed in an experiment carried out in a Las Vegas casino.

There is some tendency to avoid asking subjects to handle probabilities directly and to use easier ways such as scales that are simple to understand. Many investigations of businessmen's risk attitudes have employed verbal descriptions of situations in which the options have been couched. The descriptions make the situation more interesting to the respondents, but they may give rise to associations that obscure the risk propensity measure and rather reveal risk-modifying attempts. The respondents may feel a strong urge to make qualifying statements rather than choices (MacCrimmon and Wehrung, 1986, ch. 3).

Most experiments that have embraced choices with probabilities, have been carried out with college students and other sophisticated subjects. There are a few examples of studies with other subjects. Binswanger (1981) carried out an experiment with Indian farmers. He used payoffs that were real and large in relation to the financial situation of the subjects. The choices comprised options in which a certain prize was offered together with a probable prize with the same expected value or two probable options with the same expected value, but varying spreads. The risk aversion measures used were validated against actual farm decisions. The latter were more conservative for the more risk averse farmers. Risk aversion increased with the amounts at stake in the risky choices.

Kachelmeier and Shehata (1992) carried out another series of experiments with high payoffs. They used a certainty-equivalent task to get individual risk preferences. The task comprised a dichotomous lottery with a probable prize and a request to state the lowest amount that the subject would be willing to accept in exchange for the offered prize. In the second step, a card was drawn from a stack of 100. If the amount on the card exceeded the minimum amount, the amount on the card was immediately paid. If it was lower, the subject proceeded to play a lottery with the probability to win the prize stated in the first option.

The size of the monetary incentives influenced the risk taking. The subjects in this study were less risk-seeking (more risk averse) for the high payoffs. The authors also found a high, non-linear sensitivity to win probabilities that agreed with the predictions of the revised prospect theory (Tversky and Kahneman, 1992). The procedure deviated in two ways from what is usually characteristic of the certainty-equivalent method. (1) There was not an absolutely certain prize, and (2) the subject knew that there were repeated trials. The procedure, however, guards against the certainty effect which is usually considered to be a problem in these measurements (Farquhar, 1984).

Risk attitudes, saving, and investing

It is generally assumed that the typical saver is risk averse. There may still be individual differences in actual risk taking. From a psychological point of view, it is reasonable to look for differently motivated strategies behind actual portfolios. It is conceivable that people with a propensity for risk seeking (gamblers) invest in risky assets without having recourse to other assets if they lose the gamble. It is also conceivable that more risk averse investors are willing to speculate with some of their money in order to get the higher profits that higher risks are assumed to yield and may actually yield. Their fundamental financial security is not threatened even if the high-risk investments turn out to be failures. These ideas suggest that it is interesting to look for measures of propensity to take risks, independently of actual choices and portfolio composition. Such measures can be used to explain differences in portfolio composition along with measures of other kinds such as sociodemographic data. Hypothetical risky choices that have been used to study risk attitudes have rarely been validated against actual behavior, displayed as asset portfolios or participation in various kinds of gambling.

Buying lottery tickets and participating in gambles are held to be more common in low-income groups than in high-income groups. Gambling is in this sense an inferior good. 'The vast majority simply have no legal way to procure a fortune, no matter how hard they work or how intelligent they are. Against this background, lotteries with small costs and high winnings may well seem a sensible alternative.' (Lea et al., 1987, p.271). Is participation in lotteries and other gambles reconcilable with saving? If people spend little money on gambling the gambling may not interfere with saving. As a pastime, gambling seems to be spread over all social classes, only the form, participation frequencies, and amounts at stake vary.

Risk Taking and Risky Behavior

The first VSB psychological questionnaire included eight questions that concerned hypothetical risky choices (for a description of the VSB study, see Chapter 5 and Nyhus, 1996). The questionnaire also included questions about attitudes towards taking risks in investing money and about how much the respondent participated in lotteries, played lotto etc. The questionnaire on wealth contained detailed questions about assets, which made it possible to examine portfolio composition with a view to risk taking. The following summary of a study is essentially based on Wärneryd (1996c). Two questions are in focus:

1. Risk attitudes and outcomes of risky choices compared to portfolios of assets. Do these indicators of risk propensity correlate with the risk taken in investments?
2. Risk attitudes, participation in lotteries, and saving. Do the indicators of risk propensity correlate with participation in lotteries and similar things? Does such participation have a negative correlation with saving?

The hypothetical risky choices
After some questions about purchases of lottery tickets and other legal gambling, the respondents were asked a series of questions about risk taking which involved hypothetical choices between risky alternatives. The choices

were preceded by an introduction that compared the task to some well-known TV games in which participants choose between a certainty alternative and an alternative with a probable outcome. The first risky choices to be made by the respondents involved choosing one of two options with varying probabilities. The respondent was not provided with any escape from making a choice. There was no 'don't know' alternative. Here is an example

> In the following, we present you with a number of such choices. It is a question of amounts of money. Some amounts are sure and others you may win in a lottery. We would like to know your choices. There are no right or wrong answers.
> BET1. We toss a coin once. You may choose one of the following two options:
> Option 1: You receive Dfl.1,000 with either heads or tails
> Option 2: With heads you receive Dfl. 2,000, with tails you don't receive anything at all.

In 'the lottery equivalent method', the respondent is presented with a certain ($p = 1$) prize and is asked how probable an alternative prospect with a higher prize must be to be equally valued. To avoid the certainty effect, it is advised to use $p = \frac{1}{2}$ instead of certainty (Hogarth, 1987, p.278f.). Since this makes the task even more difficult, it was decided to use a certain ($p = 1$) prize in the questionnaire.

> Imagine you have won Dfl. 200 (1 000, 5 000) in a game. You can now choose between keeping that Dfl. 200 (1 000, 5 000), or having a lottery ticket with a certain chance to win a prize of Dfl. 20 000. How high would that chance to win Dfl. 20 000 need to be such that you would prefer the lottery ticket to keeping the Dfl. 200 (1 000, 5 000) that you had already won? I would prefer the lottery ticket if the chance to win the first prize would be at least . . . %.

The respondents could avoid stating a probability by typing '0'. In the representative panel (RP), between 1/5 and 1/4 of the respondents chose the '0'-response category. Although smaller than in RP, the non-response was also quite high in the high-income panel (HIP). In all, 16 percent typed '0' for all three questions. This means that they found the procedure too difficult. A study of the non-response to the three examples shows that older, female, low-income and less educated respondents more often failed to respond.

Very few gave probabilities that were equal to or lower than the probability that was necessary to make the expected values ($p = 0.01$, $p = 0.05$, and $p = 0.25$) equal for the certainty and optional alternatives. Those were risk seeking and they were more frequent in the high-income sample. The proportion increased with increasing value of the prize. The median probabilities requested by the respondents were, however, much higher than the probabilities required for equal expected values and thus highly risk avert.

In the second wave of interviews, the respondents were asked to state probabilities for two new values of the certain outcome: Dfl. 100 and Dfl.

10 000. The value of Dfl. 1 000 was also repeated. The median probabilities for the five alternatives are given in Figure 6.2. The usual assumption was made that 0 had the probability $p = 0$ and the prize Dfl. 20 000 had the probability $p = 1$. The RP curve is more concave and thus more risk averse than the HIP curve; the latter is convex and actually reminding of a risk seeker's curve (cf. Machina, 1990, pp.94-5).

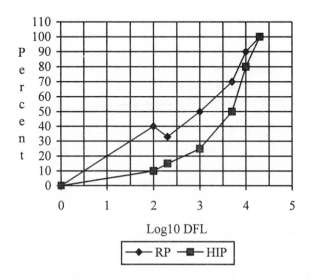

Source: Data from interview waves 1 and 2, VSB Panel.

Figure 6. 2 Desired Equivalent Probabilities (Medians) and Certain Values in Dfl

Risk attitudes and portfolios of assets

It is not easy to find a good measure of the perceived riskiness of portfolios. The Dutch tax laws have an influence on the composition of asset portfolios. Up to a limit, it is advantageous from a tax point of view to have money saved in bank accounts. After this limit, it becomes more beneficial to save money in e.g. mutual funds. A portfolio may accommodate more or less risky assets. A simple behavioral measure of riskiness is whether the household has invested in a risky asset or not. If it is assumed that there is a sort of progression in risk taking, the number of risky asset categories tried could also be a meaningful behavioral measure. It can be objected that if a portfolio consists of risky assets, it is in principle better to have a variety of assets than to have invested all the money in a single risky asset, if the assets are at the same level of risk. It may, however, be less risky to have all the money invested in shares that are risky in comparison to bonds than to have money invested in shares and in derivatives.

For the purpose here, the assets were classified according to the degree of risk in the following manner: (a) *low-risk* assets: check accounts, saving accounts, saving certificates, employer-sponsored saving schemes, (b) *middle-risk* assets: bonds, mutual investment funds, (c) *high-risk* assets: growth funds, shares, options (put and call options).

The classifications are crude and admittedly somewhat arbitrary. Buying an apartment or a house can be seen as a risky investment, especially if highly mortgaged. In general, the main purpose of acquiring an apartment or a house is not to make a profit, but rather to provide housing. It therefore seemed appropriate to leave out this wealth component in the present context. Three measures of the riskiness of portfolios were computed. The first two were based on the number of high-risk asset *categories* adopted. The first index could take values from 0 to 3 where 3 means that the respondent household had indicated investments in shares, options and growth funds. The second index is the first index adding the middle risk categories bonds and mutual funds. This index runs from 0 to 5 where the latter indicates that the respondent household has invested in all five categories. The third index is the high-risk assets as a percentage of total wealth, excluding the value of the house.

Ordered probit analyses were carried out with the two indexes indicating the degree of risk in the portfolios of assets, as dependent variables. Indicators of risk attitudes were among the independent variables. The other independent variables consisted of sociodemographic variables, some financial variables, and psychological variables relating to saving as well as two personality traits. The two indexes were quite well explained by a few variables: age, having academic training, investment risk attitude, perceived risk-taking in the respondent's own investments, and the amount of money in bank saving accounts. 'Investment risk attitude' is an index of risk propensity in investing based on six attitude statements. Keeping little track of expenditures and an active interest in saving money were highly significant for both dependent variables. Being male and thinking it important to leave a bequest seemed to increase the number of risky asset types tried. Only one risk measure based on hypothetical choices approached significance for one of the indexes and the relationship unexpectedly was negative. The results seem to suggest that investing in some assets that are more risky than savings accounts may not be seen as risk taking since the investors can afford the worst possible outcome of the risk.

The regression analysis of the third index, which involved the proportion of wealth invested in risky assets, was only based on those who owned higher-risk assets and the analysis was aimed at finding differences among those who had invested in risky assets. N was very small and included only

228 respondents. The same set of independent variables as in the earlier two analyses was used. 'Investment risk taken', gender, household income, and a time preference measure were the significant independent variables. Gender was strongly negatively related to the dependent variable, meaning that the women (who were heads of households) had higher values. Having more risky assets seemed to involve more impatience, that is, a higher subjective discount rate. 'Investment risk taken', which is the subjective assessment of actual risk-taking in investing, was negatively related to the index suggesting that those who had relatively more invested in risky assets did not think of the investments as being more risky.

An ordered probit analysis of factors assumed to correlate with the variable 'investment risk taken' was also performed. Wealthier people had taken significantly higher risks. The risk propensity measure 'investment risk attitude' was highly significant, indicating good agreement between the more general attitude towards investment risks and the subjective judgment of actually taken risks. Interest in financial matters was highly significant. The higher risk takers tended to think of bequests as less important. The desire to have a buffer was negatively related to risk taking. Men, older people, and people with a longer time horizon were more prone to judge their investments risky.

It is conceivable that people in general make somewhat riskier investments when they want extra money for some reason. The tax system seems to promote somewhat riskier investments when the optimal size of bank savings accounts has been reached. People who are already wealthy can afford to take more of a chance when they invest a small part of their assets in risky portfolios. Very few people in the two samples appeared to be highly risk taking in their investments according to the risk attitude measures and to their reports on their portfolios.

Risk Attitudes, Saving, and Participation in Lotteries

Playing lotto, buying lottery tickets etc. is usually assumed to be more common among low-income earners and people with low or no wealth, among people with lower education and among males than among females (cf. Lea et al., 1987). Sociodemographic variables are thus expected to have significant influence on participation in lotteries. Psychologically, it seems reasonable to assume that people who are carefully controlling their expenditures are less likely to spend money on anything depending on chance. A number of variables related to saving are expected to have negative correlations with frequency of playing lotto and buying lottery tickets and with the amounts involved. The utility of gambling because of the thrill it may give at a low cost should not be underestimated. Even high-income earners (who have low wealth) can be expected to play and wealthy people have been known to gamble with high stakes in casinos.

In the Netherlands, it is possible to buy a full Dfl. 25 ticket or a 1/5 ticket at Dfl. 5. It is thus possible to get five 1/5 for Dfl. 25. This gave the idea to test preferences for high prizes versus higher chances of winning. A risk seeking person is expected to prefer the first alternative whereas a risk averse person prefers the second since it gives a larger chance of winning a prize. The majority in both samples and all age classes preferred the full ticket to the five one-fifths (in RP 67 and in HIP 70 percent). The possibility of a five times greater prize dominated over the five times higher probability of winning. This confirms that people in general do not discriminate very closely between very low probabilities and rather tend to focus on the size of the prizes. Logistic regression analyses indicated that the higher probability of winning rather than the high prize was more often preferred by those who had academic training, by older people (RP), by those who had more money in the bank (HIP), and by those with low time preferences. The hypothetical choice questions that were closest to the lottery situation were highly significant. It means that those who chose the higher probability of winning in the hypothetical choices were consistent in their gambling preferences and preferred the split tickets.

Two questions covered the participation in lotteries and similar activities. One question referred to frequency of playing in lotteries and the other to how much money had been spent on lottery tickets, lotto and similar things over the last 12 months. The amounts spent on lotteries over the last 12 months were calculated as percentage of household income. In the following analyses, all respondents who had answered the questions were included.

The median amount spent on lottery tickets, lotto etc., by those who played, was Dfl. 150 over the last year, around three guilders per week. Slightly less than two percent reported that they had spent over Dfl. 1 000 on lotto etc. over the last 12 months. Judging from the answers received, slightly less than half of the sample participated often or at least several times a year in lotteries, played lotto etc. They were close to being an average of the population with few distinguishing features. People who ruin themselves on gambling are not likely to participate in surveys.

Ordered probit analysis was used for the frequency of playing and OLS for amounts spent on lotto etc. The explanatory values were low, but significant, for both dependent variables. For frequency of playing, the sociodemographic variables gender and academic training were highly significant. Women played less often than men did. People with academic training played more seldom than less educated people. Two variables pertaining to hypothetical risky choices were significant. Keeping track of the expenditures and desiring a buffer were significant. The frequency increased with the will to have a buffer. Maybe the dream of getting some extra capital that could serve as a buffer is an important motive to participate in lotteries for people with low income. 'Automatic saving transfer' was more common among those who played more often which maybe is a sign of a safeguard against overspending on lotteries etc. The attitude towards incurring debts was more negative among those who played less often. With higher propensity to save money after necessary expenditures and resisting impulses towards immediate spending, there was less frequent indulgence in playing.

For the amounts variable, 'family size' and 'academic training' had significant, negative relationships. Older people spent more money on gambling. The variable 'saving involvement' was significant which suggested that those who played more often and with larger amounts wanted to save money. Again, this may be a sign of dreams about wealth through the only possible means (cf. Lea et al., 1987). One of the measures from hypothetical risky choices was significant for this dependent variable. The frequency of gambling was negatively related to saving, measured as a dichotomous (yes-no) variable and as a subjectively estimated amount saved over the last year. The amount spent on gambling was not significant.

Binswanger (1981) reported that he used hypothetical choice questions since it was not possible to elicit valid risk attitude measures through ordinary interviews. His validation of the choice questions gave a positive answer. The results in the VSB study were somewhat equivocal. The first five choices seemed to work quite well. The respondents were not given a chance to avoid answering and the answering was probably not seen as overly difficult. The results were close to those predicted by prospect theory.

The lottery equivalent method was apparently very difficult. Many respondents used the escape response. The task is probably made easier if the prize is given with a probability and the respondent is asked to state the equivalent certain value (minimum selling or buying price). For those who answered, there was a very strong certainty effect shown by the fact that many respondents for all three prizes preferred the certain prize to a probable prize unless the probability was close or equal to 1.

The research questions concerned the usefulness of risk attitudes, that is, their relationships to possession of risky assets, to lottery participation, and the relationship between participation in lotteries and saving behavior. The fact that a household had tried investing in more risky assets was quite well explained by the independent variables introduced. The risky proportion of investment was less well explained. The measures yielded by the hypothetical risky choices did not come out significantly in any of these regression analyses. In contrast, the self-descriptive measures of risk propensity were highly significant. One of the risk attitude measures from hypothetical choices was significantly related to self-assessed riskiness of investments.

The self-descriptive measures which were closely related to the field of interest were superior to more general tests of risk-taking propensity for explaining portfolio composition. It is a common experience in psychological research that tests that are specifically adapted to the situation do better than more general tests. The situational factors are often of primary importance. This is a potential cause of disagreement between psychologists and economists. The latter are looking for more general relationships among variables and tend to dislike the situational contingencies that psychologists (love to) bring in.

The second question concerned factors explaining lotto playing and similar activities. Such playing seems to be well spread over socioeconomic groups. In the data, some tendencies seemed to agree well with what is generally supposed. There was less playing in high-income, wealthy groups, among women, among those with higher education, but these differences explained little of the total variance.

It appears as though the hypothetical risky choices had little import for explaining the riskiness of investment portfolios. They displayed some explanatory value for recreational gambling, but also here the contribution to explaining the variance was small. Investing in shares, growth funds and options and playing lotto etc. were apparently activities that under certain circumstances did not involve much risk taking. The important thing seems to be whether one can afford to indulge in these chances of getting higher dividends and prizes.

If one is a low-income earner and has little or no wealth, one plays in lotteries with modest amounts and does not really gamble as long as the stakes are low. As Lea et al. (1987) pointed out there may be little other hope for accumulating the extra capital that one needs for extra consumption or for a buffer against unforeseen circumstances. Moderate playing on lotto and lottery tickets does not involve much expenditure and many people seem regularly to indulge in such gambling. Judging from the regression analyses, there is some braking power in good control of expenditures. Risk taking is not really a concern. Playing in lotteries on a small scale seems to be compatible with saving and a well-regulated life.

If one is a high-income earner and/or has some wealth, one tends to invest in risky assets if one thinks that higher dividends are important. The risks taken are well within the scope of what the investor can bear. It was not possible to study investors who had taken great risks. Only very few respondents used the highest category when answering the question about the riskiness of their investments. Those who make risky investments may have preferences for gambles that differ somewhat from those of lower-income earners. The VSB data do not make it possible to elucidate what activities were actually included in the estimates made by the respondents. The phrasing of the question suggests that gambling activities that can be pursued with great regularity and at a relatively low cost such as buying lottery tickets in the National Lottery and playing lotto, were considered in answering the questions, rather than betting on horses or playing poker.

If the 'lottery' techniques can be applied with reasonable success, the question remains as to what they measure. The measures did not correlate with portfolio composition and only in a limited way with playing in lotteries. This may throw some doubt on the general use of these techniques to assess risk attitudes, but it appears likely that many investors can harbor considerable risk aversion and at the same time invest in e.g. shares. Their wealth is large enough to survive even large losses. The probabilities and values used in the questions may in accordance with what psychological researchers often have found work better if they are clothed as problems in investing rather than gambling. If risky choice questions are employed, it may be interesting to focus more specifically on people who really speculate in their investing. The differences relevant to understanding investment behavior may be between (a) those who take very small risks (play safe), (b) those who take risks the ill outcomes of which they can well bear, and (c) those who take risks that may be ruinous.

Prospect theory (Kahneman and Tversky, 1979) encompasses a phenomenon called *framing*. In a psychological dictionary, the framing effect is defined: 'The effect of irrelevant aspects of the context on reaching a conclusion or making a decision' (Sutherland, 1995). When a person faces a situation, the first step consists in editing the situation, which involves describing it and establishing a frame for the decision. According to prospect theory it is very important whether a situation is framed in terms of gains or losses: 'losses loom larger than gains'. Framing includes the selection of a reference point that decides whether something is a loss or a gain. Thaler (1985), and Thaler and Johnson (1990) explored the editing or framing of gains and losses and the influence of prior outcomes. The latter found a 'house money effect' which meant increased risk seeking in the presence of a prior gain. They found 'break-even effects' in the presence of prior losses. Outcomes that offered a chance to break even were especially attractive.

SOME ASPECTS OF DECISION MAKING

In addition to more or less elaborate, explicitly rational procedures, economic choices in reality are frequently made by trial and error, imitation, following an authority, habit, thoughtless impulse, and hunch.

Pingle and Day (1996, p.191)

Are Decisions Really Made?

In reality, genuine decisions are quite rare. A decision is both in business and in households frequently a summing up and sanctioning of a number of acts that have already been carried out and that have limited the number of alternatives. Some important outcomes result from not making any decision. Only on rare occasions can it be said that a decision has been made at a certain point in time when all information about alternatives and outcomes has been scrutinized and weighed. Katona (1974, 1975) pointed out that most, perhaps 90 percent, of consumer decisions were routine, habitual behavior, just doing more of the same. Still, it seems convenient in theory to talk about consumption and saving decisions. What is in the theory modeled as a decision to save can in reality be a series of failures to do anything with available money!

Mental Accounting and Other Categorization

When the Behavioral Life-Cycle Theory was presented in Chapter 4 the concepts of framing and of mental accounts were mentioned. In the terms of the theory, income from different sources is framed into different mental accounts and is not fungible as economic theory implies. The propensity to consume or to save an income is assumed to depend on the source of the income and how this source is perceived. When the concept of mental accounting was introduced by Thaler (1980) and Kahneman and Tversky (1984) no attempt was made to explain the phenomenon.

There is a clear resemblance between mental accounting assumptions and the assumptions behind psychological *categorization theory* (Henderson and Peterson, 1992). Categorization is a fundamental process and involves how information that is being processed or in the memory is organized. This is a classical philosophical problem and psychological research on categorization has been much influenced by the philosophical discussion. While there are several theories, using concepts like script or schema rather than category, there is some agreement about the characteristics of categorization. The following is mostly based on Henderson and Peterson (1992). They noted that the only difference between mental accounting and categorization seemed to be that the former specifically dealt with money. They distinguished the following seven principles for categorization:

1. Knowledge of elements which can be objects, people, or events, is organized into groups
2. The grouping of elements is spontaneous and can occur very quickly with minimal thought and effort. This is due to prior learning or frequent repetition
3. Cognitive efficiency is improved through categorization. This is true for all kinds of cognitive processes such as recall, evaluation of new elements and it leads to rapid formation of expectations

4. The groupings provide expectations about the nature of an element. In a category or class there are members that are more characteristic (prototypical) than others and they serve as reference
5. The elements activated in a category are often context-dependent
6. An element may be a member of more than one category. This is referred to as 'graded membership'
7. Categories are ordered in hierarchies and they therefore differ in their degree of inclusion or abstraction.

Despite intensive research, the theories of categorization do not explain in a wholly satisfactory way how categories emerge and are changed and how new objects, people and events are compared with existing categories. They provide a number of interesting ideas that make it possible to understand how mental accounting may function and give a stimulus for new research on mental accounting. The idea that people tend to sort changes in wealth into different categories and that different categories mean different propensities to consume is in clear contrast to the LCH and economic theory. There is as yet little research on mental accounts. The present support for mental accounting derives from anecdotal evidence, a few tests on propensity to consume different types of income using aggregate data, and hypothetical questions about what experimental subjects would do with incomes from different sources.

To what extent do the categories actually used by consumers correspond to the three categories proposed by Shefrin and Thaler (1988)? The ideas are provocative, but should be further explored before they inspire policy makers to plan wealth changes (payments as lump sums or distributed over time) in such a way that saving is stimulated (if that is wanted) or discouraged. It seems clear that consumers have different propensity to consume wealth changes deriving from different sources, but there is little detailed, empirical knowledge. Consumers may use other mental accounts of potential interest to researchers and decision makers than those suggested so far. An interesting question is how people react to changes in wealth components and not only to income changes. Is a dollar always a dollar?

Keynes (1930, p.197) was sure that the paper losses when shares dropped in value made people inclined to save while gains in paper value could instigate increased spending on consumption. Shefrin and Thaler (1988) suggested that incomes from different sources were treated differently since they were looked at as belonging to different mental accounts. Winnett and Lewis (1995) hypothesized that the propensity to consume would be lower for a non-realized increase in share value than for an increase in dividend. Testing the idea on data from the VSB panel, they found that all income from capital tended to be seen as non-spendable, irrespective of the form in which it accrued.

The concept of mental account involves that the consumer puts distinct labels on amounts from different sources. It has been supplemented with the concept of 'mental budgets', under the assumption that separate mental budgets are made for different expenditures (Heath and Soll, 1996).

> [B]udget setting leads people to overconsume some goods and underconsume others. Because budgets are set before consumption opportunities arise, they sometimes overestimate or underestimate the money required for a particular account . . . expense tracking implies that some expenses are more likely to produce over- or underconsumption. As people track their expenses, expenses that are relatively easy to categorize – those that are more typical examples of their categories – will be the most subject to the rigors of budgeting. (Heath and Soll, 1996, p.40)

The authors' hypothesis that those items that are most typical for a category of expenditure are most controlled through a budget is interesting. It was supported by their data. The authors then described two steps in the mental budgeting process

> We suggest that people generate two kinds of labels that affect their decisions as consumers. First, people label money as relevant for a certain class of goods, and second, they label the goods as relevant for a certain pool of money. We refer to these processes, respectively, as the budget-setting and the expense-tracking processes. (Heath and Soll, 1996, p.41)

Other studies and anecdotal evidence indicate that many consumers practice a special kind of budgeting procedure which makes sure that there is money for different expenditures and also provides a check on expenditures. Such budgeting can be illustrated by some anecdotal evidence. Many years ago an economist friend of mine told me that when he received his monthly salary payment, which was always in cash, the money was split up in expenditure categories and for each category a special envelope was used. Limited borrowing between envelopes was permitted. This was a way for a young family to control and keep track of expenditures. Later, informal interviews carried out by researchers in my research group revealed that some respondents practiced different techniques for making sure that money was available and used for the right purposes. I also found that some researchers in their questionnaires had included questions about pigeonholing money for different purposes.

Rainwater et al. (1979) found that working-class wives performed 'tin can accounting'. The women kept monies apart for different expenses, in tin cans or labeled envelopes. One receptacle was for paying mortgages, another for food and groceries, a third for entertainment and so on. Zelitzer (1993, p.199) noted: 'The wives in Bakke's landmark study of unemployed workers in the 1930's [. . .] used china pitchers to segregate different types of income earmarked for particular expenses: the rent of an extra room, for instance, might serve to pay off the mortgage, while a child's earnings were designated to purchase school clothes.' Hussein (1985, cited from Webley and Lea, 1993, p.470) reported 'a variety of practical ways in which people partition their money between different budget headings: some kept it in jam-jars, some distributed it around a variety of pockets while one carried it around in plastic bags.' Winnett and Lewis (1995, p.445) found in their analysis of qualitative data that 'accounts have labels and purposes and there is evidence of non-fungibility.'

Money received from social welfare is not the same as money received from wages (Zelitzer, 1993)

> To further support official notions of proper spending, charity organizations sponsored a large number of thrift institutions, ranging from stamps savings to fuel clubs and vacation savings clubs, all designed to earmark dependents' money into 'proper' expenses [. . .]. How successful were they? My preliminary evidence suggests a sort of contest between official and private earmarks as people found strategies to subvert bureaucratic restrictions on the uses of their money, often spending in ways that outraged middle-class observers, paying, for instance, for burial insurance with money allocated for food purchase. (Zelitzer, 1993, p.206)

A dollar is not always a dollar! The examples above show that prescriptive mental accounts may not coincide with those of the consumer. It should be a task for researchers to investigate which mental accounts people have and whether and how those mental accounts affect saving.

7. The Use of Psychological Variables in the Study of Saving: Attitudes, Motives, Personality and Social Influence

Simple industry and thrift will go far towards making any person of ordinary working faculty comparatively independent in his means. Even a working man may be so, provided he will carefully husband his resources, and watch the little outlets of useless expenditure.

Smiles ([1859] 1969, p.294)

The purpose of this chapter is to take a closer look at some non-cognitive, psychological concepts that have been used in research and discussions related to saving behavior. People's attitudes towards saving tend according to many researchers to be favorable. Katona (1975) said that many people regretted that they saved too little. If this is true, the predictive value of attitudes towards saving will be low. Modern attitude theory is reviewed and some data from the VSB Panel are presented. The saving motives that have been discussed in many contexts – the precautionary, the bequest, the profit motives, and habit formation – are scrutinized. 'Habit formation' is translated into something called 'control of expenditures' which draws attention to keeping track of expenditures rather than to saving acts.

Classical economists were concerned with a personality characteristic that they called 'thrift' and that was related to self-control and willpower. Modern psychology employs related concepts in dealing with volitional problems and new personality theory has something to say about factors related to thrift. Finally, the discussion of Duesenberry's relative income theory, which was begun in Chapter 4, continues with more theory about group influence on consumption and saving.

The Use of Non-Cognitive Psychological Variables in Economic Analyses of Consumer Behavior

Whereas cognitive psychological variables made their real debut in economics with the use of decision theory which in turn derived from game theory, psychological variables that were close to personality psychology entered the

252

economic discussion much earlier. This does not mean that they are nowadays more accepted by economists. Psychological variables, such as saving motives, if they are discussed at all in economic theory contexts, are usually considered to be stable over long periods of time and not likely to have any influence on economic development in the short run. Even if they change, they are mostly seen as functions of more fundamental economic phenomena and are replaced by such functions. Price expectations may, for example, be treated as functions of past price level development. Consequently, there will be little need for assessing such price expectations through approaching consumers and business decision makers who possess the expectations, if data on past price developments are readily available.

Rational expectations theory stresses the importance of new information for the formation of expectations. It does in principle not require measurement of individual expectations since the holders of expectations are assumed to use the best available information in an optimal way, that is, the way economic theory prescribes. In spite of the fact that mass communication research has found that access to information is unevenly spread and that people differ in their capacity to receive and handle information, the assumption is made that the same information is available to everybody at the same time and at little or no cost. Psychological mass communication research indicates that reception of information in a certain field is often related to attitudes towards the field. Positive attitudes facilitate reception and negative attitudes make reception less likely.

In economic contexts, the main impetus for attitude measurement is the prospect of finding attitude change that can predict change in an economic variable. Using changes in an aggregate psychological variable to predict changes in economic variables is the principal application of psychology at the macroeconomic level. Morgan (1967) who was involved in developing the Index of Consumer Sentiment maintained that *changes* in psychological states, notably in attitudes, were of use to economists. Economists were not concerned with what was stable, but with what reactions followed changes in prices, exchange rates, incomes and tax legislation. Personality factors that remained stable over long periods of time could not predict changes in economic variables. Attitudes that were stable over long periods would then be of little consequence to economic analysis.

As a psychological concept, personality refers to consistency over time and represents a presumably stable pattern of behaviors (Ozer and Reise, 1994; Revelle, 1995). It can still be useful in economic contexts if population groups (segments) rather than the whole population or total aggregate are considered. Tobin and Dolbear (1963) suggested that psychologists could help economists find stable relationships between personality characteristics and economic phenomena like saving. Katona (1975) found, for example, that people with substantial liquid assets tended to add more to their total assets than people whose existing stocks were low. Tobin and Dolbear (1963) said that this tendency might derive from the fact that people with a thrifty disposition had saved more in the past and continued to do so. Or it might be that the greater the initial holdings of liquid assets, the greater the savings increases would be. The implications were said to be important, for example, when there was high liquidity in times of inflation. Studies of relationships between personality and economic behavior could then have implications for economic policy. The thrifty population segment could be expected to react differently from the non-thrifty segment.

ATTITUDES TOWARDS SAVING

Do Attitudes Predict Behavior?

So far, short-term attitude changes have been the focus when psychological variables have entered macroeconomic analyses. The Index of Consumer Sentiment (ICS) which reflects expectations or attitudes towards the future predicts short-run changes and turning points in business cycles. The use of attitude measures to predict individual behavior is a complex question that has aroused much debate in social psychology and in applied contexts such as in marketing. Economists have often found the attitude concept to be of little use. Meyer (1982) remarked that psychologists were simplistic to believe that behavior could be predicted from attitudes alone. According to him and other economists, attitude researchers had a tendency to disregard the cost or sacrifice aspects that were so important in 'two-valued' (cost-benefit) economic theory and to focus solely on measuring attractiveness.

The direct relationships found between attitudes and behavior have generally been weak. Some of the difficulties derive from differences in definition and measurement of attitude, but some convergence of the thinking about defining and assessing attitudes can be noted. Some remedies have shown promise. The more specific the attitude is, the better are the chances of finding a substantial correlation with behavior if behavior is also defined as a specific act (Fishbein and Ajzen, 1975; Ajzen and Fishbein, 1980). There is also evidence that goes in the other direction, without necessarily being incompatible. Prediction of behavior is improved if both the attitude and the behavior are aggregated over people, time or situations (Katona, 1979; Epstein, 1980; Ajzen, 1991, p.180). The Index of Consumer Sentiment is a case illustrating this (see Katona, 1979).

At best, the attitude measures explain only a small proportion of the variance in behavior. Many attempts to improve explanations and predictions have been made, making attitude theory more elaborate and putting attitudes into a context by adding variables to the attitude models. While attempts to predict purchases of new products based on attitude measures have been notoriously unsuccessful, opinion polls have often predicted outcomes of political elections with amazing precision. Even if attitudes towards new products are as specific as political party or candidate sympathies, situational influences may prevail in the former case. This calls for models that put attitudes into a context of other influences on behavior.

With stable attitudes towards saving, people keep their positive or negative attitudes towards saving whether they save or not. If the saving attitudes are not stable, but vary between people and for the same people over time, they seem more interesting as potential predictors of change in saving. In macroeconomic studies of saving where psychological variables have been included, the focus is usually on financial expectations rather than on attitudes towards saving. In the regular EU surveys of consumer expectations, two questions relate to saving. These questions were also included in the VSB Panel questionnaires. One question concerns plans to save during the next 12 months (scale 1-4) and another question asks whether it is meaningful to save money (scale 1-4) at present. Time series analyses have shown that these data have some, though not very high predictive value for aggregate saving (van Raaij and Gianotten, 1990). The question whether it is meaningful to save given the present financial situation can presumably be answered independently of positive or negative attitudes. It seems possible to find it meaningless to save money even with a generally positive attitude towards saving and vice versa.

The low correlations commonly found between attitudes and behavior depend not only on the possible deficiencies in attitude definitions and measures, but also on the behaviors used as dependent variables. Studies of saving attitude and saving behavior relationships tend to find significant positive correlations and small contributions towards explaining variance. The significant correlations are typically found when the saving measures are based on verbal reports. It is not easy to find good measures of saving. Intuitively, measures of saving should be close to what people think of as saving if psychological variables are to be related to saving. If something that is not seen as saving is included, the correlation between attitudes and saving can be expected to be low. This need, however, not necessarily be so. It may be possible to find strong relationships between a psychological variable and saving defined independently of subjective definitions. While studies at the aggregate level have found such relationships, attempts at the household level do not seem to have been successful.

Models of Attitudes

Most attitude models focus on attitude formation and change rather than on the model's ability to predict behavior. Fishbein and Ajzen (1975) as an exception concentrated on the predictive ability of attitudes and presented models that especially considered prediction of behavioral acts. Ajzen and Fishbein (1980) proposed a comprehensive model of attitude-behavior relationships, called the *Theory of Reasoned Action*, with certain distinguishing features:

1. The attitude pertained to performing an act towards an object and comprised belief components and evaluation components that were multiplied and summarized over salient attributes
2. The act against which the prediction was tested was specific
3. The main focus was on predicting 'intent' which was assumed to be close to actually performing the behavior
4. Intent was a function of attitude towards the act *and* social norms/ social motivation.

The Theory of Reasoned Action is an example of so-called 'expectancy-value models' which in principle are quite similar to subjective expected utility (SEU) theory. In experimental settings, there is often a difference between the decision theory approach to SEU and social-psychological approaches to expectancy-value based attitudes. While the former studies clean-cut problems in strictly controlled environments, the attitude studies are usually complex and less controlled (Fishhoff et al., 1982).

The Theory of Reasoned Action was aimed at predicting and explaining human behavior in specific contexts (Ajzen, 1991, p.181). The model inspired much research in the 1980s. While the results usually showed that the specificity of both the attitude and the act to be predicted as well as the social norms are important, the variance explained was still in many cases quite small (Ajzen, 1991).

Ajzen changed the model into the *Theory of Planned Behavior* by including perceived behavioral control. He argued that the predictive value could not be expected to be high when there was a low degree of volitional control. Voting for a political candidate or a party involves high behavioral control and an attitude towards voting for a candidate would have high predictive value according to this theory. Low perceived behavioral control means that the predictive value is low unless the other components in the model, notably attitude towards the act and social norms/social motivation are correspondingly stronger. Perceived behavioral control is assumed to influence the intention to perform the act. A direct path from perceived behavioral control to behavior is expected to emerge only when there is some agreement between perceptions of control and the person's actual control over the behavior (Beck and Ajzen, 1991, p.287). Many studies have indicated that the predictive ability of attitudes has been improved by including perceived behavioral control in the model (Ajzen, 1991; Tesser and Shaffer, 1990; Madden et al., 1992). Sjöberg (1998) questioned perceived control and suggested that the control could be perceived after the act rather than before. The model has the following structure

$$Intent_a = \sum_{i=1}^{n} b_i e_i + \sum_{i=1}^{o} n_i m_i + \sum_{i=1}^{p} c_i p_i$$

where $Intent_a$ = intention (probability) of performing act_a

$\sum b_i e_i$ = attitude towards performing the act; b_i is a salient belief, that is, the subjective probability that the behavior will produce the outcome in question and e_i is the evaluation of that outcome

$\sum n_i m_i$ = (salient) normative beliefs and motivation to comply with those; n_i is what important individuals or groups think of performing the behavior, m_i is the person's motivation to comply with a referent's opinion

$\sum c_i p_i$ = beliefs about control of resources (c_i) and the power (p_i) of a resource to facilitate or inhibit performance of the behavioral act.

The main dependent variable is intention. The behavior or behavioral act is assumed to be directly proportional to the behavioral intention

$$Act_a \propto Intent_a$$

The concept of intention is somewhat ambiguous. In the earlier Theory of Reasoned Action, intention was set approximately equal to the behavioral act. Ajzen (1991) seemed a little more cautious and rather visualized a probability relationship between intention and act. He stated

> Intentions are assumed to capture the motivational factors that influence a behavior; they are indications of how hard people are willing to try, of how much of an effort they are planning to exert, in order to perform the behavior. As a general rule, the stronger the intention to engage in a behavior, the more likely should be its performance. (Ajzen, 1991, p.181)

If there is an independent measure of intention that is highly predictive of a behavioral act, why bother about attitudes and subjective norms? This measure should by itself be enough for predictive purposes. The rationale for the more complex model is the zeal to explain intention and behavior. If the model is borne out, it divulges how intentions are formed and can be influenced. In marketing, it is, for example, important to know how product attributes are perceived and evaluated by consumers. Purchase intentions are not enough. In the same vein, factors influencing intentions to save may be interesting even if the intention is by itself a good predictor of saving.

Habits and attitudes are sometimes treated as equivalent, but usually a clear distinction is made. Habits are seen as routines that are learned through rewarded, earlier experience and they are assumed to have predictive power. The prevailing conception is 'more of the same', that is, that people tend to behave in new situations the way they behaved in earlier, similar situations. A popular assertion is 'past behavior is the best predictor of future behavior' (Ajzen, 1991, p.202). This seems valid both for habits and personality, with the notable exception that circumstances may change and the whole situation become radically new. New information then overrides past experience in the way both Katona (1972) and rational expectations theory assume.

The Theory of Planned Behavior has been criticized for not sufficiently taking past experience into account. Ajzen (1991, p.203) rejected the argument that only habit represented past behavior and should be considered in the model. He argued that residues of past behavior were already in the model and that habits also depended on other things than just past behavior. He did not preclude completely that past behavior could be useful in the model. Katona (1975) noted that most behavior was routine behavior and that changes were made when there was important new information. Rational expectations theory has drawn attention to the importance of new information for economic behavior. Past experience is not a sufficient guide for behavior when the situation involves a radically new structure. Attitudes may also be inadequate and even wrong for coping with a new financial situation. Deep-lying attitudes that do not easily change may then have a role for explaining persistence and resistance to change in behavior.

In a study involving financial behavior, East (1993) tested Ajzen's theory and found that it gave good predictions of actual behavior. He interviewed people about their attitudes and intentions towards buying shares two weeks before they had to file applications to participate in the British Government's privatization of three companies. The measures of intention gave a good prediction of applications for shares. Intention was explained by attitude, subjective norm, perceived control, and past experience.

According to Brandstätter (1993, 1995), the predictive value of attitudes is increased if attitudes are treated as (partly) determined by personality. Personality is a broad concept and the direct relationships between personality and specific acts cannot be expected to be very high. Motives and attitudes, according to this view, mediate the effects of differences in personality.

Many studies have shown that most people have positive attitudes towards saving (Lea et al. 1987; Wärneryd, 1991). In a somewhat jocular vein, Lea et al. (1987) suggested that saving might be held in high regard because saving was difficult and gave some pain. Thaler and Shefrin (1981) and Shefrin and Thaler (1988) pictured saving as the outcome of a conflict between the long-run utility and the impelling force to spend for immediate utility. Those who find it most difficult to save money and do not save may think more of saving than those who save by routine. There is no doubt a moral tinge to saving and there may be differences between moral principles and actual behavior. If attitudes towards saving are assessed on the basis of broad, general statements indicating that saving is a good (bad) idea and touching on moral aspects, the attitude measures cannot be expected to contribute much to explaining differences in saving and changes in total saving.

Even if, by themselves, the saving attitudes fail to explain or predict saving behavior, Ajzen's model may have predictive power provided the other components are important. Subjective norms to save or not to save may be strong and they may change over time. During the recent recession (in some countries depression), there may have been more group pressure towards saving, not only for financial reasons, but also because ostentatious behavior seemed more inappropriate than in good times. Perceived behavioral control is in the case of saving tantamount to the individual's financial situation. At least for some households there is considerable variation in this component of the model. Changes in the perceived financial situation or perceived control may be the important determinants of saving.

Specific questions or attitude items relating to saving are an alternative to the broad and general statements. Saving can be seen as consisting of more than one specific activity and each one is connected to a specific attitude (towards performing the specific saving act). The predictive power of such specific attitudes would be expected to be good and at least better than the predictive power of general attitudes towards saving. Measures of more general attitudes towards saving will find their primary use in the description of segments in the population.

Saving money for a short-term goal, say a vacation trip or a consumer durable like a PC, involves putting money away for a time and then using it up. Both the saving and the expenditure can take place within the same budget period, which is usually assumed to be 12 months, more or less coinciding with the calendar year. Such saving does not affect in any way the wealth of the household unless the money saved is at hand over the end of the year. While the respondent who saved and spent the money during the same year should answer 'no' to the question about saving over the last 12 months, the respondent who still had the money at the end of the year should say 'yes', on the proviso that this was the only type of saving. Probably, both types of respondents answer 'yes' in the usual interview surveys. It is, however, often possible to distinguish between them because of their answers to a follow-up question that asks about the saving goal(s).

The role of general attitudes towards saving can for saving behavior be:

1. Directly determining, that is, the attitudes are positively correlated with and predictive of behavior
2. Indirectly influential, that is, the attitudes serve to give a direction in which the holder of the attitude tends, but may not always succeed
3. The attitudes have no influence on actual saving and saving may even determine attitudes.

In the first case, it is likely that the attitude as well as the saving behavior is specific or aggregated at a high level. Two types of attitudes or rather expectations have proved their value in predicting aggregate saving. One is the Index of Consumer Sentiment which reflects financial attitudes and the other type is questions about plans to save, accompanied by a question whether it is meaningful to save. Specific attitudes and saving acts would involve questions about putting money in saving accounts, buying bonds, shares etc.

In the second case, the attitudes may predict the behavior when the situation changes. If people at a certain point in time cannot save, a positive attitude towards saving will probably lead to saving when the financial situation becomes better. When there is forced saving, a negative attitude would lead to discontinued saving once the obligation to save is over.

With respect to the third case, it is easy to think of cases where attitudes towards saving and saving behavior do not agree. Money may be saved as a forced compliance with an installment buying plan, retirement pension scheme or some other contractual arrangement and the saver may be fundamentally negative towards saving and think of it as an imposition, but unfortunately necessary. Somebody who is highly positive towards the idea of saving may have difficulties to save because of the financial situation, a deficiency in ability rather than in will. When saving attitude statements are not composed in the way prescribed by Ajzen but are rather broad, they seem to capture more long-term values (Rokeach, 1973) that do not always correlate with short-run behavior.

How are saving attitudes acquired? The usual assumption is that attitudes are learned and that the learning is based on reinforcement. A common additional assumption is that saving habits are learned early in life (cf. Sonuga-Barke and Webley, 1993). There may be two types of reinforcement of saving, one having to do with the act of saving and the other having to do with the outcome of saving, the expected future utility. Recognizing the fact that there is money saved opens up possibilities of action that the holder of the attitude appreciates (cf. Jevons's 'anticipated utility', [1871] 1911). Even for ordinary people and not only for misers, every instance of putting money away or non-spending of money may give a feeling of happiness or accomplishment. This is similar to what Gordon Allport called 'functional autonomy of motives' and what is now often called 'intrinsic motivation'. It is habit formation where the habit has lost its original purpose.

A Model of Attitudes Towards Saving

The theory of planned behavior suggests a model for relating attitudes to reported saving behavior. The model presented here is close to the theory of planned behavior, with attitudes towards saving, subjective norms, perceived control of behavior, and past behavior as the main determinants of intention to save and reported saving (Figure 7.1). Perceived Control takes care of the financial dimension in the two-valued logic of economics (Meyer, 1982).

The expectation is that saving attitudes overall will be positively related to saving intentions. In certain cases, attitudes that are more positive can be expected among people who do not save. Not having enough of a buffer and not being able to save for a buffer may be such a case. Positive attitudes, strong social motivation for saving and perceived control of financial situation are expected to lead to higher saving.

The model has been tried out on Dutch data from the VSB Panel (Wärneryd, 1996b). The measures used were rather proxies than exact equivalents of the concepts in Ajzen's model. Three saving measures were used. They were based on whether the respondent household had saved over the last two years, on subjective reports on amounts saved during the last year, and the ratio of saved amounts to household incomes.

The proxies for subjective norms significantly affected intention to save. The 'perceived control', measured as the perceived financial situation of the household, significantly influenced saving, but not intention to save. This corroborates Katona's postulate that both ability to save and willingness to save are necessary for saving to take place. Saving attitudes had a strong, *negative* influence on saving intention, which is surprising. This relationship is partly explained by age since older people had attitudes that were more positive and had less frequent saving plans, and partly by the fact that respondents who most wanted a buffer could not save towards one. When 'past saving' was introduced into the analysis, it turned out to have a large influence on saving and to change the role of perceived control in such a way that the picture became rather confusing.

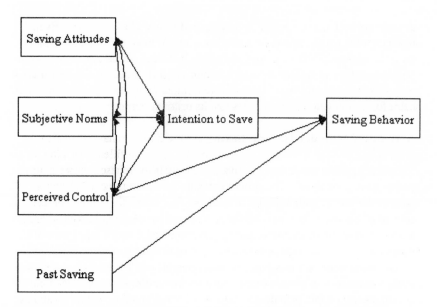

Figure 7.1 A Model of Saving Inspired by Ajzen's Theory of Planned Behavior

The Use of Attitude Measures

The concept of attitude is used widely and in varying senses. In Ajzen and Fishbein's (1980) Theory of Reasoned Action and in Ajzen's (1991) Theory of Planned Behavior it has a relatively precise definition. It is defined in terms of salient beliefs and evaluations about performing an act towards an attitude object. Due to the complex nature of the attitude-behavior relationships, broadly defined saving attitudes may not seem to be of much use at the aggregate level. It can, however, be useful for policy makers and marketers to know how much saving is more or less forced upon households through various arrangements such as paying off debts and mortgages, paying premiums on pension schemes and life insurance. It may be interesting to know to what extent the forced situation is self-imposed, such as fixed deductions from salaries/wages. The reason for such self-impositions is apparently that it is unpleasant and requires efforts to save. Binding precommitments help (Strotz, 1956). This is a fundamental tenet of the Behavioral Life-Cycle Hypothesis (Shefrin and Thaler, 1988) that was described in Chapter 4. Negative attitudes towards saving and a high saving rate are then evidently compatible.

It may be useful for different purposes to know about the attitudes towards saving in population segments. The attitude measures can primarily be used for making distinctions between segments of the population. Population segments with positive attitudes towards saving may be expected to save more than those with negative attitudes when the ability to save increases and they may be more willing to continue to save if the financial situation is deteriorating.

Realization of Saving Plans

It is interesting to note that in the case of purchase plans retrospective interviews always show that there have been more purchases than planned for. Those who stated in the first interview that they had purchase plans, to a large extent, but in far from a 100 percent of the cases, fulfilled their plan to purchase a consumer durable. The majority of actual purchasers came from among those who said that they did not have any plans. In the case of saving, it seems to be the other way round. Plans to save were rarely fulfilled to a full extent according to Katona (1975). As a rule, people planned to save more than what they were actually able to live up to. Plans to save were not good predictors of actual saving. On the other hand, answers to the EU survey questions whether people plan to save and whether it is a good time to save money give better predictions of total savings in the Netherlands (van Raaij and Gianotten, 1990).

With VSB Panel data from three waves of interviews, it is possible to follow up plans to save at the household level (Wärneryd, 1996b). When the saving intention questions are used in EU surveys, the answers serve as macroeconomic indicators. The plans in the VSB Panel seemed to have good predictive value at the individual level, but the correlation was far from perfect. Some plans were not fulfilled and in other cases, there was saving that had not been planned. A saving plan may to some extent be a question of hope rather than an actual plan. Positive attitudes may breed intentions that are not fulfilled. The important determinant of whether the intention is attained is maybe the (perceived) financial situation. Those who had planned to save had a better financial situation than those who had not planned. Those who saved without having planned to save had as a rule an improved financial situation compared to those who had persisted in their plans not to save. A possible explanation is a positive income change during the last 12 months.

The results confirmed that those who did not save although they had planned to save had on average a worse development of income than those who had planned to save and actually saved. Those who saved although they had not planned (or expected) to save had the same favorable income development or a better income development than those who had not expected to save and did not save. There was some agreement between expected and achieved income change. More saving occurred among those who had more favorable income development. Those who expected an income increase and had an increase were more often savers than those who had expectations of higher income and had worse income development than expected. Many of those who expected a decrease in income and had the worst income development still saved money.

SAVING MOTIVES

It is will – force of purpose – that enables a man to do or be whatever he sets his mind on being or doing.

Smiles ([1859] 1969, p.230)

Saving Goals, Saving Motives and Saving Behavior

Many economists again focus their attention on (enduring) motives or persistent goals for saving. Commonly, three saving motives are distinguished: (1) the precautionary motive (see Hubbard et al., 1994), (2) the bequest motive (see Bernheim et al., 1985), and (3) the investment or profit-making motive (Keynes, 1936). All three of them are of psychological interest. In economics, the assumption seems to be that such motives are stable over long periods. Rather little interest has been devoted to the possibility that saving motives and saving goals may change over time and be tied to age cohorts. Some discussion of the possible changes over the life cycle can be found in the literature about the saving of the elderly (see, for example, Hurd, 1990).

Motives are in behavioristic psychology measured and experimentally manipulated through 'antecedents', that is, observable behavior that precedes a learning situation, such as hours of hunger or of not smoking or physiological measures. Motives are seen as forces influencing behavior; they can become drives that push behavior in a certain direction. It is often assumed that there are a few basic drives such as hunger, thirst, sex and that new, learned drives could be acquired because of those (primary versus secondary drives). The list of basic drives varied among authors. Based on findings regarding what could motivate monkeys (in a cage), a curiosity drive was added to the basic drives. Psychological learning theories assume that *reinforcement* is fundamental to learning new behavior. Behavior that is positively reinforced takes on a higher probability to occur again. Behavior that is punished takes on a lower probability of being executed again.

Cognitive learning theory that was for many years the main competitor to behavioral learning theory dealt with means-ends relationships. The behaviors were seen as a means to reach a desired goal (end). The subjects (animals and humans) were assumed to learn such linkages and establish cognitive maps of their environment with such linkages inscribed. The theory drew attention to goals rather than to reinforcement effects. In market research, the so-called *laddering technique* was developed to elicit information about means-ends chains that were pertinent to the marketing of goods and services

(Gutman, 1982). As far as I know, the technique has not yet been used to elicit saving goals and motives. There are few similarities between cognitive learning theory, which deals with the learning of means-ends chains, and modern cognitive psychology, which is focused on information processes, and the theories should not be confused. Cognitive science, a much broader concept created by Herbert Simon (see Simon, 1979), is even more different and refers to all sciences researching the human mind, preferably with the computer as a model, for example, cognitive psychology, linguistics, and artificial intelligence.

Saving motives as they have been suggested by economists over the centuries have had little to do with the drive theories of behavioristic psychology. They have been closer to cognitive learning theory since purposes rather than drives are stressed. The proponents of saving motives usually got their ideas from their own observations and insights. Interpreted in terms of psychology, the saving motives are related to goals since they express wishes to accomplish some objective. A goal is more specific than a motive and has an external reference.

Next, four motives for saving will be discussed. They could also be called goals for saving or even reasons. The first reason for saving is similar to what economists call 'habit formation'. It will be argued that the habit formed typically, but not always, involves keeping track and good control of expenditures. The bequest motive and the precautionary motive have been much discussed in critiques of the Life-Cycle Hypothesis. Some psychological reflections are added to this discussion. Finally, the profit motive is considered.

The four motives are not mutually exclusive. A person or a household can very well save money for more than one of the reasons at the same time. It seems likely that someone who carefully controls her/his expenditures would also like to leave some bequest because that belongs to the idea of what is proper behavior. It is likely that the saving motives may vary over the individual's and the household's life cycle.

Saving as a (Continued) Habit: Control of Expenditure as a Major Goal

Economic saving theories picture savings as something that remains after consumption and the theories are related to the consumption function. Intuitively, it makes sense to treat consumption as primary and saving as residual. It means that there may be money over at the end of the budget period, say, a calendar year, without a clear decision to save. Katona (1975, p.232) talked about 'money that the owner failed to spend'. A related interpretation of savings that is again not applicable to all savings is that the individual has goals implying proper levels for the consumption of goods of different kinds. The goals may be attained without spending all the available resources and residual saving follows as a consequence. The goals are probably often related to what the income permits and it is possible that the goals for consumption are set at a level that admits saving. Is it appropriate to talk about decisions to save in such cases?

In survey studies of saving, a sizable group of people who say that they save money are not willing to state any goal for their saving. When given the choice between a number of goals, with the possibility of adding a goal that is not in the list, and the category 'no specific goal', they prefer the latter. If there are questions about earlier saving, they tend to indicate that they have saved and plan to continue to save. In such cases, it seems appropriate to talk about well-established saving habits that are not aimed at any goal. Future consumption is not specifically involved.

In economics, habit formation stands for 'a psychological stock of habits' whose presence affects the utility to be obtained from current consumption (Deaton, 1992, p.17). In psychology, habit implies a tendency towards repetitive and routine behavior. Learning theories assume that the behavior has somehow been reinforced which increases the probability that it will be repeated. One way of looking at this is to call saving that is repeated over a long time a well-established habit. Why do people build up and keep such saving habits? My favorite answer is that they have learned to control their consumption expenditures. The choice of consumption level may be the primary factor and the saving thus residual rather than discretionary. Duesenberry (1979) saw the level of consumption of a household as the primary factor determining saving and attributed the choice of level to social influence.

For some people who have been saving money all or most of their life, giving up saving may seem like breaking a good habit and may create concern that they are overspending even if there is no longer a need to save. Breaking a well-established habit usually involves pain since resistance to change seems more in line with human nature. Loss aversion and endowment effects may play a role. The habit of saving may be reinforced through a feeling of satisfaction, a reduction of fear of the future or something similar.

One of Keynes's eight saving motives, which he called 'independence', was described as follows: 'To enjoy a sense of independence and the power to do things, though without a clear idea or definite intention of specific action' (Keynes, 1936, p.108). An activity may give satisfaction in itself. Well-known examples are activities that are performed because they give fun. Saving may be such an activity and generate what is called 'intrinsic motivation'. Anecdotal evidence and everyday observation suggest that putting money in a bank account can give pleasure to people. Some saving accomplished through severe control of expenditures means overdoing the thrift and is equivalent to avarice.

Psychological research on learning and breaking habits reveals that the art of dissaving may not be so easy to learn. When capital is available because of inheritance or lottery winnings or something else that has nothing to do with saving, but is closer to windfall income, there can easily be dissaving or rather waste of money. If somebody has saved money and accumulated wealth over a number of years, gross dissaving is highly unlikely unless there are special circumstances such as ill events or the indefatigable saving has been dictated by a specific goal, like sailing round the world at the age of 55.

There are then several possible interpretations of continued saving habits. The gist may be that a pattern of saving acts is repeated or it may be that there are habitual restrictions on consumption or a mixture of both. Earlier commitments to save, such as automatic transfers from salary account or in-surance saving may have effect after they have ceased to apply and after re-tirement. They may be treated more or less like unavoidable expenditures. If before retirement old-age pensioners have been paying in to pension schemes and they no longer have to make these payments, the habit of reserving some income for future use may still persist, even though the after-retirement in-come means a decline in disposable income (cf. Katona, 1975). Restrictions on consumption may become a life style that is upheld even when restraint is no longer necessary. In terms of the behavioral LCH (Shefrin and Thaler, 1988), this involves a continued use of the rules and precommitments prac-ticed by 'the planner' (the long-run maximizer) to control the myopic maxi-mization of utility by 'the doer' (the short-run maximizer).

Marshall suggested that much of saving was explained by the fact that people who had earlier been careful with their money continued to econo-mize even when it was no longer necessary. 'The greatest savings are made by those who have been brought up on narrow means to stern hard work, who have retained their simple habits, in spite of success in business' (Marshall [1890] 1990, p.190).

Marshall's explanation is similar to the idea that control of expenditure is primary to saving. It deviates from the common assumption that people save because they want to accomplish something that makes life easier for them in the future: more money, more certainty of being able to pay debts or buying something desired, or more pleasure. There may be different motives for be-ing restrictive with expenditures. Some, probably rather few, people may feel that resources are scarce and refrain from spending because they do not want to dissipate. Religious beliefs, environmental concerns and other ideological concerns may serve to inhibit expenditure. The role for saving of such ideo-logical concerns has apparently never really been investigated. In his book *The Protestant Ethic and the Spirit of Capitalism* Max Weber explained capital accumulation and thrift as determined by Puritan religion. It is con-ceivable that many or at least some people have a feeling that they have to observe an appropriate level of consumption and that a heightened level would be unseemly. Anecdotal evidence seems to bear this out. This could be a question of lifestyle, which may also be inspired by other ideologies than Calvinist religion, or just be something privately developed, perhaps under some social and mass media influence. Life styles are presumed to be influenced by peer groups who react in similar ways to fashions.

To some extent, the saving habit may consist in not consuming above a certain level. Maybe many people decide on or rather have a feeling about what is their appropriate level of consumption and save the money that is not used for consumption. Restriction of consumption prevails over saving. Eating habits, the types of clothes worn, type of accommodation, and recreational activities tend to persist over long periods of time. Consumption often presupposes other efforts than just money. Since some consumption requires physical fitness, increasing age may mean a natural reduction in expenses for consumption and saving may be possible even with a reduced after-retirement income. Against this, it may be said that there are always consumption possibilities that claim little physical fitness and this speaks for other reasons for not consuming. Market research for charity organizations indicates that those contributing most to collections of money are (female) low-income or low-middle income earners who do not consume very much themselves and who feel that they can spare something for a good purpose (cf. the widow's mite). At any rate, it cannot be excluded that an appropriately low level of consumption is of primary importance to some people and that saving is a consequence rather than a goal in itself.

Classical and neoclassical economists observed and discussed such tendencies to build up and continue savings habits. In a world that was always characterized by scarcity, saving in the sense of refraining from consumption was necessarily a virtue. While ancient sages like Aristotle and Cicero had views on how to manage property with a (reasonable) dividend, the interest in accumulation of wealth came with the rise of industrial capitalism. At the beginning of capitalism, the process of accumulating wealth and the uses of the saved money became interesting to thinkers as is, for example, demonstrated by Adam Smith (1776) and John Rae (1834).

Restraining consumption through law, which was the purpose of the so-called sumptuary laws in the late Middle Ages, was according to Smith unnecessary since frugality was a characteristic of the human (Smith [1776] 1981, p.441). Frugality means restrictions on consumption and control of expenditure. Saving is then a consequence rather than a goal even if the residual is wanted. Mandeville (1729) had seen frugality in a nation as something arising out of necessity and not a virtue at all. Smith saw frugality as a characteristic that was more or less part of human nature and operative under most circumstances. Smith was influenced by Mandeville's idea that it was important that the individual served his/her self-interest, but he praised individual thrift.

The immediate consumption and dissaving of the poor may be explained by the fact that postponed consumption could be followed by loss of means rather than consumption in the future. Marshall pointed out a factor that inhibited saving, namely, the possible insecurity of money saved (Marshall [1890] 1990, pp.187-8). Nowadays, taxes on wealth, inflation, and turmoil in financial and real estate markets may also deter from saving.

Bounded rationality theory assumes that people do not practice maximization, but satisficing. Alternatives are compared to a level of aspiration and when the first acceptable alternative is at hand, a choice is made and the search process stops. Control of expenditure may involve that people have some level of aspiration for consumption, based on earlier experience. If they do not maximize short-term utility, but look for satisfactory alternatives, they may have some money over.

In my view, saving habits include control of expenditures as a major component. The control may be the primary goal and the saving a secondary outcome. Or the saving may be the primary goal and the control of expenditures the means. While there is for all people an ultimate limit as to how much they can spend, the control of expenditures would seem to be more important for those with low and middle incomes. Weber's theories of the middle classes contain elements of a frugal lifestyle with the implication that the middle classes keep strict controls on consumption patterns and expenditures. With respect to saving, three groups seem to emerge from this thinking:

1. One group has plenty of money and members do not necessarily impose any conscious restrictions on their consumption (they may still feel restricted by keeping the same level as their reference groups). They have a surplus because their income is high enough. They may impose the restriction that they should not squander all their wealth, especially if much of it was inherited

2. One group saves for some kind of goal and members control their expenditures so as to be able to save

3. One group creates a surplus by maintaining restrictions on consumption.

An expected difference between groups two and three should be that the latter to a larger extent do not state any particular purpose for their saving.

The Precautionary Motive

The uncertainty about the future and the consequent attempts to reduce the uncertainty by providing for the future has been stressed by many economists, like Jevons, Böhm-Bawerk ([1888] 1912), Marshall ([1890] 1990), and Fisher (1930). Keynes (1936) mentioned the precautionary motive as one of the three motives for liquidity preference. The other two were the transactions motive (necessary to have cash for business transactions) and the speculative motive (to make profit). The precautionary motive was

> To provide for contingencies requiring sudden expenditure and for unforeseen opportunities of advantageous purchases, and also to hold an asset of which the value is fixed in terms of money to meet a subsequent liability fixed in terms of money, are further motives for holding cash. (Keynes, 1936, p.196)

The unforeseen opportunity to buy something cheap is usually not related to the precautionary motive, but it is still worthy of attention. For those who want to control their expenditure, such preparedness may be essential.

Essentially, the precautionary motive is inferred when a budget period receives more savings than it would require based on LCH annuities. The motive can be important for consumption and the accumulation of wealth. Deaton (1992) made a distinction between permanent income consumers and prudent consumers. Through a simulation study, he found that there could be considerable differences in wealth between the two types. He concluded: 'Utility gains from additional consumption now are more than offset by the value of having assets if bad luck strikes in the future' (Deaton, 1992, p.191). He noted that it might not pay for poor people to accumulate wealth considering the social benefits they might lose.

Uncertainty is in economics mostly measured as the variance in the income distribution and precautionary saving is aimed at providing against future drops in income. Dynan (1993) pointed out that self-selection made it difficult to study relationships between uncertainty and saving because of a third factor. Risk averse people could be assumed to choose professions with less variation in income as well as to save more, which would obfuscate the relationships.

Uncertainty is in psychology frequently associated with a feeling of fear, in the same way as risk. Insurance may remove the feeling of uncertainty, but not the reasons for the uncertainty itself. A better way of expressing this is that insurance is a remedy against the feeling of uncertainty in the sense that there is preparedness for facing the consequences of the ill outcomes that uncertainty may embody. From this point of view, precautionary saving relieves the feeling of not being able to overcome future difficulties. Recent research on risk perception is opening new ways for psychology to grapple with the problem of studying phenomena that are related to the precautionary motive. Economic risks have been included at the side of other risks in some interview surveys. An interesting result is that people, even when they are pessimistic about their own economic future, are more pessimistic about the future of people in general (Sjöberg, 1998, p.107).

It is common to distinguish between two types of precautionary saving. One type is saving to have a buffer for short-term income shocks. The motive strongly resembles what has been called 'saving for a rainy day' or saving for a buffer that enables a person to meet unforeseen ill events. The other type covers long-run variations in income over the life cycle. Saving for retirement or old age may be considered as long-run precautionary saving in which case the LCH can be seen as an adequate explanation.

Lacking a direct way of assessing the precautionary motive, economists tend to look for the precautionary motive in data on income uncertainty, which is commonly measured as income variability over time. If there is a positive correlation between income uncertainty and additions to wealth, this is interpreted as precautionary savings. Income uncertainty is inferred from earlier income growth or, if household panel data are available, from earlier realizations of income. Dynan (1993) used consumption variability from a consumer survey rather than income variability as a measure of risk. She used a formula that gave an estimate of the precautionary motive and found 'a small precautionary motive; in fact, the estimate is too small to be consistent with widely accepted beliefs about risk aversion' (Dynan, 1993, p.1113).

Beside income uncertainty, other possibly pertinent uncertainties, for example, uncertainty about remaining lifetime and health have also received due consideration (Kotlikoff, 1989, chapters 5 and 6; Hubbard et al., 1994; Browning and Lusardi, 1996). The three most important sources of uninsured idiosyncratic risk facing households are: uncertainty about earnings, medical expenses, and length of life (Hubbard et al., 1994, p.174). Kotlikoff (1989) discussed the role of increased insurance coverage for the US decrease in saving ratios since the 1960s. With good insurance cover, there was less need for people to save for precautionary reasons (cf. Hurd, 1987). Bernheim (1991), in contrast, concluded that even with a perfect insurance market, the typical household would prefer to maintain a positive fraction of its resources in bequeathable forms. Kotlikoff (1989) who simulated health expenditures and precautionary savings varying a number of assumptions found that health uncertainty could have effects on savings.

Much of the discussion about the precautionary motive has focused on old age failure to dissave and it is used as a possible explanation of why the elderly save or do not dissave money. They may be afraid of running out of money before they die. Since they do not know exactly how long they will need the money they tend to keep more than they need and consequently leave considerable wealth to posterity.

From a psychological point of view the interpretation of the precautionary motive mainly involves the perceived risk of running out of money some time before life expires. Anecdotal evidence indicates that even people who are quite well-to-do may have such fears. Americans who were born in the early 1920s and who grew up during the Great Depression in the 1930s kept the fear of going bankrupt for many years (Elder, 1974). Subjectively, there may be an implicit assumption of a long, almost eternal life behind the fear of running out of money.

Many studies have over the years shown that the protection against emergencies or the perceived need to have a buffer is the most often stated saving motive (cf. Fisher's 'saving for a rainy day'). Katona (1975) reported that saving for emergencies was the most often stated motive, followed by saving for children's education and other needs. He made the observation that people hesitated to use such buffers and if they actually used the buffer felt as if they borrowed from it and had to repay it as soon as possible. Hubbard et al. (1994, p.178) noted in a similar vein: 'Should a household experience low wealth because of an unusually bad draw [of income], the household is careful to rebuild the buffer stock.' Carroll (1997) used the observation that in surveys the most used response alternative to a question about motives for saving was 'being prepared for emergencies'. In developing a new hypothesis, he made the assumption that consumers were faced with important income uncertainty and were prudent, that is, they had a strong precautionary motive and engaged in buffer-stock saving behavior.

In a consumer survey, those respondents who have adequate buffers may put high value on this reason for saving, but for them it should have little importance as a motive or goal for present saving. Those who do not have a buffer may feel the strongest need for it and also value this motive highly. If their finances improve, they should have a high probability of starting to save for a buffer. More penetrating studies of what people mean by 'unforeseen circumstances', how much money there should be in an adequate buffer, and whether they think that they have reached this limit are lacking.

The Bequest Motive

Since life span is uncertain, individuals choose a level of bequests at each point in their lives; that is, there is not a single planned terminal bequest but rather age-specific bequests contingent on dying at that age.

Kotlikoff (1989, p.28)

The bequest motive for saving was by the classical and many neoclassical economists advanced as a main motive for saving money. Now its importance is questioned by e.g. Modigliani (1986 and 1988) who was the main originator of the LCH. This motive creates some difficulty for the theory since the individual is assumed to consume all income during the life span and altruism is not fully compatible with the rationality concept. A question, puzzling to the economist way of thinking, concerns why people do not buy annuities to a larger extent so as to maximize their lifetime utility and avoid leaving considerable amounts of money at their death. Annuities are defined as 'survival-contingent income' or 'actuarial contract' (Bernheim, 1991, p.900).

The alternative to planned or intended bequests is that they are accidental. Ando and Modigliani (1963) assumed that the individual neither expected to receive nor desired to leave any inheritance. They suggested two ways of relaxing this assumption, but they provided no micro-level hypothesis about the bequest motive

> First, we may assume that the utility over life depends on planned bequests but assume that it is a homogeneous function of this variable as well as of planned consumption. Alternatively, we may assume that the resources an individual earmarks for bequests are an increasing function of the individual's resources relative to the average level of resources of his age group, and the relative size distribution of resources within each age group is stable over time. It can be shown that either of these generalized assumptions implies an aggregate consumption function similar in all essential characteristics to the one obtained from the stricter assumptions stated here. (Ando and Modigliani, 1963, pp.56-7)

Hurd (1990) pointed out that, particularly in a society with economic growth from one generation to the next, people with heirs might not care to leave bequests and still, more or less by accident, leave money. He suggested that one way to test for a bequest motive was to compare the consumption level of someone who had children or close relations with the consumption of someone who did not. Economists tend, in the first place, to estimate the bequest motive indirectly. Is it then not possible to ask people about a possible bequest motive and get reliable data? In fact, such data are now collected in a number of interview surveys, for example, AHEAD and the VSB Panel.

In the current economic discussion of LCH and saving, the role of the bequest motive for saving seems to be arousing a growing interest. Some authors like Kotlikoff (1989) ascribe great importance to this motive. According to estimates made by him and Summers, intergenerational transfers appear to be the major element determining wealth accumulation in the USA, maybe four-fifths. Other attempts at estimating intergenerational transfers have arrived at lower figures (cf. Bernheim, 1991). Modigliani (1988) who tried to play down the importance of bequests arrived at a figure close to one-fourth of total wealth. The argument was that bequests were after all not very important, that the illiquidity of assets like real estate made it impossible to do away with all property, and finally that uncertainty about remaining life time made precise calculations of how much to spend each year indeterminate. The fact that people leave bequests is attributed mainly to their wish to have enough money while they are still alive. Saving for this purpose is called precautionary saving.

The illiquidity argument focuses on the fact that many people may have their assets tied up in such a way that they cannot easily provide liquid funds. Many elderly still have houses of their own and they may have invested in other property that is expected to increase in value in the long run rather than give immediate dividends. Further mortgaging may be a way to free money for consumption, but most people are probably reluctant to what they think of as borrowing money for immediate consumption purposes. The so-called reverse mortgages have so far not been successful. The idea is that house equity is released through increasing mortgage loans towards the end of the lifetime. The failure may be a cohort effect or a question of the form of the mortgage (life annuity or not) or a general fear of incurring more debt. No one wants to die poor!

In his *Theory of Justice* Rawls (1973, p.284ff) talked about the problem of justice between generations. How far is the present generation bound to respect the claims of its successors?

> each generation, except possibly the first, gains when a reasonable rate of saving is maintained. The process of accumulation, once it is begun and carried through, is to the good of all subsequent generations. Each passes on to the next a fair equivalent in real capital as defined by a just savings principle . . . This equivalent is in return for what it received from previous generations that enables the later ones to enjoy a better life in a more just society. (Rawls, 1973, p.288)

Marshall ([1890] 1990, pp.189-90) thought that most saving arose out of family affection. This involved saving money for the well-being of the family both before and after one's death. In surveys, when questions are asked directly about motives for saving, typically 3 or 4 percent answer that they save to leave legacies (Katona, 1975; also see Chapter 5). In a study of the affluent, over 30 percent stated this as a reason for saving (Barlow et al., 1966). Saving for bequests was uncommon, except among high income earners and wealth owners. The affluents do not save in the sense of refraining from consumption, but rather by managing their assets in such a way that the value of those is kept and potentially increased. Behind this there may be some motive of the type hinted at by Rawls: a feeling of obligation to leave to the next generation at least as much as one received from the previous generation.

It certainly makes psychological sense that people want to leave something when it means protection for beloved ones. 'A couple (or individual) gains utility from the knowledge that if both die, someone whose welfare they care about will receive their bequeathable wealth as a bequest' (Hurd, 1990, pp.606-7). Concern for the welfare of a possible single survivor who will have less income can be a motive for the elderly to save. Concern for the welfare of young children may be a motive for saving in some form, for example insurance, when people are of young or middle age.

There may not be a causal connection between a bequest motive and saving. The prevailing idea may be to keep the wealth undiminished or not to reduce it below a certain minimum level. If so, there should be no direct bequest motive for saving, except in the sense that the individual avoids overspending. This again reverts to the control of expenditures. People who have some wealth do not necessarily want to add to it in order to enable them to bequeath more. People who do not have any assets are hardly likely to save for this particular reason unless there is a special reason like a disabled child.

Saving inspired by a pure bequest motive has no correspondence in terms of future utility. Rawls (1973) pointed out that bequests deviated from the general rule of reciprocity. The inheritors are not obliged to do anything in return.

> Normally this principle [of reciprocity] applies when there is an exchange of advantages and each party gives something as a fair return to the other. But in the course of history no generation gives to the preceding generations, the benefits of whose saving it has received. In following the savings principle, each generation makes a contribution to later generations and receives from its predecessors. (Rawls, 1973, p.290)

Recent attempts to explain de facto inheritance have led to the idea that there may be an exchange relation between bequeathers and potential inheritors (Bernheim et al., 1985). Those who are able to leave legacies can, in a way, buy favors now from relatives and other potential inheritors by giving or retracting promises of legacies. To explore this possibility, four attitude statements were included in the VSB Panel questionnaire. The statements represented exchange, altruism, self-interest, and rejection as possible attitudes towards inheritors. The respondents who had children were instructed to select the statement closest to their own view about bequests. The attitudes refer to the will to leave bequests, not to motives for saving. Although the project involves a panel, due to dropouts the samples do not overlap completely. Replacements of respondents made each sample a representative sample of Dutch households.

Table 7.1 shows the results. Judging from the answers, most respondents thought of their own enjoyment rather than of providing utility for the next generation and the tendency apparently increased over the years. The tendency was, however, much lower in the upper age classes and among those who were better off. Among those who were over 65, the altruism statement attracted many choices and came much closer to the third statement in popularity than in the younger age groups. In 1993, the altruism item was chosen by those over 65 in 43 percent of the cases as against 45 percent for the self-interest item. In 1995, the corresponding figures were 36 and 59 percent. The results give rise to a suspicion that for ordinary people who do not have considerable wealth leaving bequests is a secondary matter. They may not want to die poor and they are confident that something, at least a house or an apartment will be left.

Table 7.1 Motives for Leaving Bequests

Statement	1993		1994		1995	
	N	Per-cent	N	Per-cent	N	Per-cent
If our children take good care of us when we are old, we would like to leave them a considerable bequest (exchange motive)	93	4.3	85	3.7	72	3.5
We would like to leave our children a considerable bequest, regardless of whether they will take care of us when we are old (altruism motive)	478	22.3	447	19.7	375	18.3
We have no advance plans for leaving a bequest to our children because we want to enjoy our own lives (self-interest)	1 524	70.8	1 684	74.1	1 556	76.0
We don't intend to leave a bequest to our children, because we don't think it is desirable (rejection)	58	2.7	56	2.5	45	2.2
Total	2 153	100	2 272	100	2 048	100

Source: Data from the VSB Panel, 1st, 3rd, and 4th waves.

Marshall said about men who had worked hard and accumulated wealth: '[they] desire to be found at their death richer than they had been thought to be' (Marshall [1890] 1990, p.190). A desire to die wealthy may not be a bequest motive at all, but rather mean that leaving some legacy connotes that you have accomplished something in your life. It may be a shame to die poor, in particular if you were born rich. Psychological study of the bequest and the precautionary motives could perhaps clarify the issues. Collecting data from individuals on this matter requires subtly and skillfully designed survey questionnaires that may need to be supplemented by informal interviews.

The Profit Motive

Because of a lack of relevant psychological knowledge, security analysts have all too often been forced to become amateur psychologists themselves.
Slovic (1972, p.780)

Adam Smith and John Rae talked about saving or capital accumulation in terms that implied a growth in resources if those were saved. Saving money involved a gain. The speculative motive was one of Keynes's proposed motives for holding cash. It involved the expectation that interest rates would change. If the expectation was that interest rates would fall, it paid to buy bonds and do away with cash. If interest rates were low, it paid to keep cash and wait for higher rates on bonds. Business firms are assumed to maximize profits, consumers are assumed to maximize utility.

When consumers in surveys are asked about saving goals, one of the response categories is often 'extra income (e.g. interests)'. If one may judge from Dutch data (see Table 5.1), this goal is not frequently applicable. This can probably be interpreted as a sign that for most savers other goals are more important. Few ordinary savers save money because they think they can prosper on the bank interest rates. Pareto ([1909] 1971, p.323) noted that people might save even with negative interest rates. Even in times of high inflation, considerable savings are usually not protected against depreciation. This does not mean that there is no concern about profit. Many examples show that savers are ready to move wealth to some extent when more profitable investments with low perceived risk become available. When Swedish real interest rates were very high, many people who otherwise saved in bank accounts apparently started saving money in bonds to make a higher profit. Profit appears to be related to what Keynes (1936) designated as the second part of time preference, namely, the form in which savings are placed.

For those savers who are primarily investors, the prospect of profit is more important than for ordinary savers. It is well-known from studies in many countries that investors, if by investors is meant those who have put money into shares and similar securities involving more risk taking than putting money in savings accounts, are rather neglectful about their portfolios. They make few changes, buy more rather than sell and if they sell, they sell late in the downward cycle when prices have gone down too far. Conversely, they may, stimulated by climbing share rates buy when prices are too high.

Are business leaders more than other people dominated by the idea of maximizing profit also in their own private economic sphere? From time to time, in many countries a discussion arises of the compensations that business leaders get. Popular opinion as reflected in the mass media seems to be that they are overpaid. Asking for high compensation may be greediness, but it is more likely that it is a matter of price. The compensation reflects the business leader's value in the eyes of the market place and who would not want to be highly valued? It is not easy to distinguish between the profit motive and the value of profit as a symbol of success. The symbolic value of riches was stressed by Scitovsky: 'Money is sought and valued, not only for its purchasing power but also as a symbol of achievement, of success, of society's appreciation of one's services; and this other function of money does not fit into the economist's model of rationality' (Scitovsky, 1986, p.71). A good review of the symbolic value of money can be found in Lane (1991, chapter 6).

SELF-CONTROL AND SELF COMMAND

One of the greatest human fears is losing control, and one of our strongest motivations is to have control over our lives. The quality of our lives, the lives of those around us, and ultimately the well-being of our planet may be determined by where and how we, as individuals and species, seek to maintain a sense of control.

Shapiro et al. (1996, editorial introduction)

Declining Saving Ratios and Declining Self-Control?

The staple conversation on the farms around was on the usefulness of saving money; and smock-frocked arithmeticians, leaning on their ploughs or hoes, would enter into calculations of great nicety to prove that parish relief was a fuller provision for a man in his old age than any which could result from savings out of their wages during a whole lifetime.

Thomas Hardy (*Tess of the D'Urbervilles* [1891] 1993, pp.54-5)

Saving ratios (total saving in relation to total disposable income) have been declining in most Western industrial countries over the last decade. Smoothing the income over the life cycle leads to saving at certain life-cycle stages and to dissaving at other stages according to the LCH. If there is no growth, what one age group saves is spent by another age group. While Keynesians see savings as a potential threat to economic growth, most economists seem to believe in a positive relationship between savings and growth and to think that there may be a causal relationship from savings to growth. Declining saving ratios are then of concern.

Economic rationality interpreted as an attempt to maximize life-cycle income does not necessarily lead to saving. In a welfare society, it is conceivable that an individual may reach a higher life-cycle income by not saving money, but by depending on the social benefits to the utmost (like in Hardy's famous novel). Certain benefits become available on the sole proviso that the receiver has no wealth or savings of his or her own. Rather than dissaving from earlier saved buffers, the individual can rely on temporary aid from social security systems if there is a need. Hubbard et al. (1994, p.175) formulated the problem in strong terms: 'many households face a high implicit tax on saving should they become eligible for AFDC, Medicaid, or Food Stamps. These social insurance programs with asset-based means-testing alter in significant ways the incentives to save.' These authors provided evidence to the effect that social security systems may remove some important incentives to save. AFDC is, by the way, Aid to Families with Dependent Children and Medicaid is a US health care program reimbursing hospitals and physicians for care of those needing financial assistance.

Another way of interpreting the downward tendency is to depict a decreasing need for self-control. Maital and Maital (1991) suggested that in welfare societies there has been a decrease in self-control and that this decrease may be responsible for the decline in savings. The reason was that there was less need for self-control in the old sense since the public sector (and employers) provided maximum security whatever ill events occurred. Why should people then save? In a paper that presented an elaborate, psychological model of self-control, Hoch and Loewenstein (1991) suggested that a closer study of consumer self-control might lead to a better understanding of low saving rates.

Hirschman's assumption that capitalism had a dampening effect on passions may be valid for saving behavior in the sense that if people learn to save money, it means better control of their impulses and a better planned living. This may be treated as a learning process. If it is possible directly to reward the act of saving, more people could learn this type of self-control.

Self Command

> *This expression [temperance the same as master of himself] . . . seems to me to mean that there is in the man himself, that is, in his soul, a better and a worse, and when the better has by nature control of the worse, then, as we say, the man is master of himself; for the expression is one of approval. When, on the other hand, in consequence of bad training, or the influence of associates, the better is weaker than the worse, and is overcome by its superior numbers, this is condemned as something disgraceful, and the man who is in this condition is called slave to himself, and intemperate.*
>
> Plato (*The Republic*, p.117)

In his *Theory of Moral Sentiments*, Smith wrote about self command as enhancing prudence, a main component of virtue

> The man who lives within his income is naturally contented with his situation, which, by continual, though small accumulations, is growing better and better every day. He is enabled gradually to relax, both in the rigour of his parsimony and in the severity of his application; and he feels with double satisfaction this gradual increase of ease and enjoyment, from having felt before the hardship which attended the want of them. He has no anxiety to change so comfortable a situation, and does not go in quest of new enterprises and adventures, which might endanger,

but could not well increase, the secure tranquillity which he actually enjoys. (Smith [1759] 1982, p.215)

Smith saw prudence as the union of the two qualities of reason and understanding, on the one hand, and self command on the other. He said that, although the principles of common prudence did not always govern the conduct of every individual, they always influenced that of the majority of every class or order. Smith seems to advise people with entrepreneurial spirits to be careful rather than enterprising. As an entrepreneur, a person with self command in this sense would be risk averse! Entrepreneurs do not, however, see risks where others might and they are usually found moderate risk-takers.

To Smith, self command was the ability to take the view of the impartial, objective spectator who could see both the present and the future situation. The more a person was able to adopt the way of thinking of an objective spectator, the more s/he had self command. Smith more or less recommended that a person had dual selves, one self more impartial and objective than the other. The relationship between self command and the other components of virtue – prudence and benevolence/justice – was that self command was a prerequisite for their pursuit. Here is a resemblance to the Behavioral LCH.

Schelling (1984) spoke of self-command in a somewhat different sense. To him it signified deliberate choice to accept pain in order to gain something. He assumed that men were characterized by alternating preferences and that there might be a wish to do away with some of the alternatives in a binding way and well in advance. He called the problem 'anticipatory self-command' since it consisted in finding ways of excluding future behaviors that are not wanted (with the preferences extant now). Schelling's examples derived from a variety of fields and often referred to everyday experiences. He gave a number of recommendations for strengthening the self-command like enlisting the help of others, refraining from exposure to attractive stimuli, and blocking possibilities of yielding. In many ways, these measures are similar to those that Elster (1977) proposed. They can be translated into rules for behavior that decrease spending and thus increase savings.

Self-Control, Willpower, and Provision for the Future

It is will – force of purpose – that enables a man to do or be whatever he sets his mind on being or doing.

Smiles ([1859] 1969, p.230)

Rae (1834) used the expression 'prompt to action' to explain why the universal desire for effective accumulation did not always materialize in capital accumulation. Other economists talked about 'will' or rather 'lack of will-power'. 'Will' entails the notion of overcoming something difficult. If it is not difficult, it does not take much will to do it. A dictionary definition of will (*American Heritage Dictionary*, 1979) runs as follows: 'The mental faculty by which one deliberately chooses or decides upon a course of action; volition: *"Will is the sustaining, coercive, and ministerial power – the police officer* [in man]." (Emerson).' Another, to me less fascinating, definition in the same dictionary puts will equal to *determination, diligent purposefulness*. This dictionary definition lays more emphasis on deliberation than on the difficulty of undertaking the action, but the quote from the poet Emerson who was a contemporary of the psychologist William James neatly illustrates that there is more to will than just deliberation.

In *The Principles of Psychology*, William James began the chapter on will with the following definitions

> Desire, wish, will, are states of mind which everyone knows, and which no definition can make plainer. We desire to feel, to have, to do, all sorts of things which at the moment are not felt, had or done. If with the desire there goes a sense that attainment is not possible, we simply *wish*; but if we believe that the end is in our power, we *will* that the desired feeling, having, or doing shall be real; and real it presently becomes, either immediately upon the willing or after certain preliminaries have been fulfilled. (James, [1890] 1983, p.1098)

In other contexts, James stressed even more the fact that will involved difficulties which could be overcome with some effort, but he has been criticized for underestimating the required amount of effort (Sjöberg, 1998). James's definition of will is quite similar to Aristotle's delineation of choice: 'Since, therefore, an object of choice is something within our power at which we aim after deliberation, choice will be a deliberate appetition of things that lie in our power. For we first make a decision as the result of deliberation, and then direct our aim in accordance with the deliberation' (Aristotle, *Ethics*, p.120). With this interpretation, it is patent that choice is not equivalent to an observable act or some particular revealed behavior. It is a process with several steps leading in a certain direction, often requiring effort.

The essential characteristic of will is thus that we believe that the desired end is in our power and that we expect to be able to overcome the difficulties. What is missing is that exercising will is a drawn-out process. 'To have a strong will means being able to stick to an initial well-balanced decision under various forms of pressure' (Sjöberg and Johnson, 1978, p.150). James's discussion of will implies that there is a force involving resistance that requires some effort to master. In their economic theory of self-control, Thaler and Shefrin (1981) pictured the problem as one of conflict between a short-term maximizer (the doer) and a long-term maximizer (the planner). Some effort is assumed necessary for the desire to save to materialize in actual saving. There are differences between a positive attitude towards saving, the will to save, and the actual saving behavior, even though, as James suggested, there may be a belief that the end to save is in one's power.

In everyday usage, will is apparently mostly used in expressions related to willpower such as having a strong will (usually not in a flattering sense) or having a weak will (which is even less flattering). Willpower designates an assumed personality trait with some stability. To some extent, this is equivalent to self-control. Will has not been a popular concept in psychology ever since psychology became an experimental science in the 1870s and especially after functionalism and behaviorism came to dominate psychological thinking. There is now again room for concepts related to will and an increasing willingness among psychologists to explore suchlike phenomena. The recent upsurge in research on self-regulation and related phenomena illustrates this (Kuhl and Beckmann, 1985; Karoly, 1993; Shapiro et al., 1996; Sjöberg et al., 1998).

When asked to explain saving, psychologists tend to mention ability to delay gratification as a possible explanation of individual saving. Most studies of 'delay of gratification' have been done with children as subjects. Psychologists have studied children's capacity to defer gratification and have found that age, social status, and education are positively related to the ability to postpone satisfaction as Böhm-Bawerk and other economists had surmised (for a review of findings, see Mischel et al., 1992). Serious criticisms have been directed against many of these studies (see Gurin and Gurin, 1970). Experiences of opportunities or rather lacking opportunities may explain why immediate rewards are largely preferred: future rewards may be highly insecure in environments with limited opportunity sets.

In the writings of the classical economists, discussions of cognitive factors such as perception of uncertainty as well as conative factors such as desire and will can be found. Some of the economists rather focused on the cognitive aspects than on desire or will or goals. One example is Jevons (1871). He did not pay much attention to the psychological problems of saving when he developed Bentham's theory of pain and pleasure which became the foundation of his utility theory. He talked about the uncertainty about the future and what pain or pleasure the future could bring. While he stressed the importance of anticipation, he recognized that, depending on age, income, and social class people had different power of anticipation (Jevons, [1871] 1911, p.35).

It is interesting to note that Jevons picked out the cognitive part of the complex behavior of saving. The ability to anticipate was the important prerequisite for saving. The underlying assumption behind this must be that to a rational person anticipation and uncertainty necessarily lead to the appropriate actions. If the anticipation exceeds a certain level of vividness, this may apparently be enough to tilt behavior.

Among the reasons given by Böhm-Bawerk for people's tendency to overvalue the present good as against the future good, his suggestion of a consistently undervaluing perspective of the future is of particular interest here. He propounded that three circumstances lay behind the undervaluation: (1) erroneous beliefs on account of lack of imagination and ability to understand, (2) weakness of will, making people prefer a smaller utility now to a larger utility later; (3) uncertainty about the future.

Böhm-Bawerk thus distinguished between cognitive factors and volitional factors; the latter were factors impeding or expediting the saving act. He carefully pointed out that a person might 'decide on the smaller present good although he knows well enough and at the moment of choice even specifically thinks that the future payment ('Einbüsse') is larger and that therefore his choice for his welfare on the whole is unfavorable' (p.447). The reason for such behavior was thus not cognitive (having to do with 'Wissen', knowledge) but rather a lack of will ('Willensfehler'). Böhm-Bawerk demonstrated some hesitation about the necessity of the concept of will and intimated that the psychologists desired a cognitive explanation in terms of the vividness and potency of the cognition.

Marshall (1890) stressed the cognitive aspects of the motivational forces. Talking about the definition of interest (as a reward for waiting), he said that the accumulation of wealth was dependent on man's *prospectiveness*: that is, his faculty of realizing the future. (p.193). Both Böhm-Bawerk and Marshall replaced will with the power of *vividly* imagining the future. There is support for this idea in some modern psychological research. Self-relevant scenarios that involved vividly imagining a future activity turned out to influence compliance with a request (see Gregory et al., 1982).

James ([1890] 1983, p.1182) formulated a similar problem in somewhat different words: 'Since a willed movement is a movement preceded by an idea of itself, the problem of the will's education is the problem of how the idea of a movement can arouse the movement itself.' Presumably, the more vivid the idea, the more likely the movement. If movement is replaced by 'saving act', James neatly describes the problem of stimulating individual saving behavior, how the 'prompt to action' is achieved. Sjöberg (1998) proposed that the amount of mental energy necessary to translate a decision into action should be explicitly considered.

Marshall seemed to believe in the varying power of cognitive habits rather than in will. Interestingly he thought that there had been a development towards more prospectiveness. 'The habit of distinctly realizing the future and providing for it has developed itself slowly and fitfully in the course of man's history' (Marshall, [1890] 1990, p.186). Nevertheless, it had developed.

Fisher (1930) made a distinction between foresight and self-control: 'Foresight has to do with *thinking*; self-control, with *willing*. Though a weak will usually goes with a weak intellect, this is not necessarily so, nor always. The effect of a weak will is similar to the effect of inferior foresight' (Fisher,

1930, p.83). The last sentence indicates that there is some hesitation about the actual role of will; the more cognitively oriented concept of foresight may do the job. With foresight you note the possibility of a future adverse condition, with self-control you decide to do something about it. It takes something more than a feeling of uncertainty to spur saving.

The behavioral LCH emphasizes self-control as a means to postpone consumption. People implement self-control by means of self-imposed rules and precommitments. An important reason for the saving of the elderly is that elderly persons keep the same rules and precommitments and do not break their consumption and saving habits. Self-control is assumed to involve a cost in terms of effort, but it also takes extra effort to engage in new habits. A change may breed feelings of insecurity, given the uncertainty about what will happen in the future. 'Even though it makes sense for the retired to relax their rules that restrict access to savings, many households appear to have trouble making this transition (Footnote: To paraphrase a well-known expression, it is hard to teach an old household new rules.)' (Shefrin and Thaler, 1988, p.632). The concept of self-control is one of the major aspects of this new model.

Fisher generalized his observations of individual characteristics to whole nations. A degeneration in the bonds of family life is again launched as an explanatory factor for non-saving behavior. Without such bonds there were no educational tendencies that instilled the habit of thrift from childhood. Modern Western societies have been characterized by such dissolution of family bonds for some time. Fisher did not tell what could be done to make the population of a whole country less impatient to consume, but presumably he counted on the individual remedies as being efficient also at the aggregate level.

The Psychology of Self-Control

Among the terms used (often interchangeably) to denote a capacity for self-regulation are freedom, autonomy, agency, responsibility, maturity, ego-strength, willpower, self-control, choice, purposiveness, self-direction, voluntary action, self-sufficiency, morality, consciousness, free will, independence, conscientiousness, self-discipline, intentional action, self-intervention, intrinsic motivation, self-determination, and volition.

Karoly (1993, p.24, footnote)

The above quotation from a review article, indicates that there is no overwhelming consensus about what self-control actually amounts to. Rae ([1834] 1905) spoke of factors that 'prompt to action' so that the desire of accumulation is fulfilled. Using similar expressions, classical economists usually ended up by referring to will and willpower. Willpower was seen as the factor that made a difference between passively accepting the status quo or doing something to remedy it. Psychologists like William James were pre-occupied with the role of will. New schools in psychology, in the first place behaviorism, led to serious criticism and later total rejection of will and voli-tional concepts (Kuhl and Beckmann, 1985). Gradually, 'volition' came back, mostly disguised as 'motivation'. Today, the processes that involve management of actions are again in focus.

Mischel (1984) pictured self-control as the mechanisms that helped per-sons overcome 'stimulus control' – the power of situations – and achieve increasing volitional control over their behavior even when faced with com-pelling situational pressures. He studied

> one fundamental human quality – the ability to purposefully defer immediate grati-fication for the sake of delayed, contingent but more desired future outcomes. These investigations seek to clarify the ability to defer gratification both as a psy-chological process and as a basic human competence. They analyze the mecha-nisms that allow self-control [ ] both in terms of the psychology of the situation and of the person. (Mischel, 1984, p.353)

Mischel and his co-workers carried out a number of studies of children's ability to delay gratification and focused on the interplay between person and situation. With preschoolers (mean age about four years) Mischel ran ex-periments in which the children could have a desired object, for example, a marshmallow immediately or two marshmallows after a delay. When the awards were unavailable for attention by being obscured during the delay, the children waited more than ten times longer on average than when the rewards were exposed and available for attention. Thinking about the rewards when instructed to do so, the children found waiting for them just as difficult as if they were in view. The temptation of the visual presence was overcome when there was a distraction in the form that the children were told to 'think fun'.

The researchers aimed at understanding what made delay acceptable

> how people ideate about the outcomes (rather than what they face in the situation) is crucial. The more the children focus on the arousing qualities of the blocked goals, the more frustrating and aversive the choice conflict and the delay seem to become and the sooner they terminate the situation. Conversely, cognitive repre-sentations of the same objects that focus on their nonconsummatory (more abstract, less arousing) qualities appear to facilitate the maintenance of goal-directed be-havior, presumably by allowing the person to keep the goal in mind without be-coming too aroused and frustrated to continue to wait for it. (Mischel, 1984, p.353)

Hoch and Loewenstein (1991) discussed the roles of proximity and vivid representation for time-consistent behavior. The research showed that in-structing subjects to think of future rewards could increase their willingness to delay, but that proximity and physical presence were dominant. They un-derlined the importance of treating an event of transgression (yielding to the temptation of immediate pleasure) not as a single event but as an event in a long series of transgressions. Incidentally, making events isolated is used in some practical marketing as a technique for reducing the customer's feeling of cost. An example is a focus on the (low) down-payment and not on the future installments.

It seems safe to conclude that self-control is at least to some degree a matter of having the right kind of ideation and to maintain it over time (cf. Elster, 1977; Schelling, 1984; Sjöberg and Johnson, 1978). This brings to mind what Böhm-Bawerk and Marshall asserted about the importance of the vividness of imagination.

From a cognitive-psychological point of view, self-control is a matter of *cognition-behavior consistency* (Kuhl, 1985). Saving comprises perception of future problems, by economists and decision theorists called uncertainty and risk, *and* some kind of act involving provision for the future. How do the mechanisms that mediate between perception of future needs and actual provision for the future work? In modern psychology, the concept of self-control has found limited acceptance, except maybe in some personality theories. The cognition-behavior consistency is dealt with under such labels as self-regulation (Karoly, 1993), and action control (Kuhl, 1985). While these two approaches focus on *processes* that end in actions, self-control is a more static, enduring characteristic of a person. The concept of self-control implies that persons can be characterized by ways of controlling such processes that are stable over time and situations.

Willpower was assumed necessary in the face of difficulties, and self-regulation usually refers to situations in which people have to engage in aversive activities like working on boring tasks or refraining from some pleasurable activity (Kuhl, 1985). Kuhl's own concept of action control has a somewhat broader scope and encompasses the enactment of seemingly simple intentions like reading a letter or opening a window. Action control is used 'to denote those processes which protect a current intention from being replaced should one of the competing tendencies increase in strength before the intended action is completed' (Kuhl, 1985, p.102).

The individual is assumed to have knowledge about her/his own strategies for managing intentions. Such strategies are: (1) selectively attending to information supporting the current intention, (2) selectively encoding goal-related features of incoming information, (3) activating positive emotions and enhancing the motivational basis of the current intention by manipulating (4) the internal or (5) the external incentive structure, and (6) avoiding overlong decision making. These strategies may be used more or less automatically. Studies of children's ability to delay gratification have confirmed that also children can use them. Children may learn to maintain an experimentally induced intention against a seducing action alternative by closing their eyes or otherwise avoid visual contact with the source of distraction, for example, a very attractive toy. Delay-of-gratification studies have shown 'that the amount of attention directed to a "tempting" stimulus is an important determinant of a child's ability to delay gratification. Strategies that limit the levels of this attention facilitate "self-control" (Sonuga-Barke and Webley, 1993, p.20).

The strategies suggested by Kuhl resemble those proposed by Strotz (1956), Schelling (1984) and Elster (1977). They discussed ways of resisting temptation and avoiding disturbing changes of taste. Similar thinking is found in Akerlof's concept of *procrastination*. 'Procrastination occurs when present costs are unduly salient in comparison with future costs, leading individuals to postpone tasks until tomorrow without foreseeing that when tomorrow comes, the required action will be delayed yet again' (Akerlof, 1991, p.1). While the main purpose of Akerlof's paper was to explain unlimited obedience, Akerlof briefly noted that procrastination could explain why people did not save enough for retirement unless there were pension plans. His emphasis on the salience of present costs can be compared to Ainslie's (1975, 1991) hypothesis about the strong preference for present utility in relation to distributed future disutility and costs.

Hoch and Loewenstein (1991) dealt with the problem of changing consumer preferences. 'We believe that time-inconsistent preferences are due to sudden increases in desire brought about by a shift in the consumer's reference point' (Hoch and Loewenstein, 1991, p.494). They framed self-control as a struggle between two psychological forces, desire and willpower. They distinguished two classes of self-control strategies: (a) attempts to directly reduce desire, and (b) overcoming desire through a variety of willpower tactics. Three strategies were possible: avoidance, distraction, and substitution. The authors added that precommitment and entitlement (feeling that you are entitled to a reward for working hard or 'everybody else is doing it') also affected economic cost assessment. They particularly stressed long-term goals that influenced preferences and they tried to accommodate emotional behavior (unpredictable changes in moods and tastes causing changed reference points) in their desire-willpower model of self-control.

There are several psychological scales for assessing self-control. Kuhl (1985) presented very elaborate scales for studying action control. Another scale that has been used for similar purposes is the self-monitoring scale (Briggs and Cheek, 1988). The difficulty with using such scales is often that the statements that the respondents are asked to use to describe themselves are broad and sweeping. Kuhl's scale is tied to rather concrete actions and is preferable to many alternatives. Commonly, it is found that when self-control aspects of a certain type of behavior are investigated the results are improved if content-specific scales rather than general scales are employed.

PERSONALITY AND SAVING

Saving and Thrift

Thrift was for a long time the foremost psychological concept used by economists to explain why certain individuals, households, and nations saved while others did not. Thrift was never measured or assessed in any other way than looking at savings statistics. When saving ratios dropped, the verbal explanation was that people were probably less thrifty which was just another way of describing the fact of diminished savings in the absence of independent observations of decreased thrift. In recent attempts to explain the decreased saving ratios, ideas of changes in some psychological variables have again been revived. Developments over the last few years have led to increased saving ratios in a number of countries that had notoriously low and even negative saving ratios in the late 1980s. Have consumers again become thriftier in any way that can be assessed independently of the savings data? Or do cognitive variables like expectations of the future contribute more towards explaining the variance not explained by LCH variables? Expectations are volatile and can be counted on to change more than thrift.

In earlier economics, thrift was treated as an enduring and important characteristic similar to a personality trait. If there are no changes in personality, except in the very long run, data on personality will not contribute towards better predictions of savings. A counterargument is that personality may change and that the distribution of personality types in the population may change over time. There may be segments in the population that are characterized by different personality traits and they may react differently to economic changes and policy measures. Thus, the interpretation of long-term tendencies may be served by data on personality traits and enduring thriftiness.

Thrift and its converse extravagance are similar to personality traits in the sense that they are assumed persistent over long periods. Everyday observation seems to suggest that there are stable differences among people and among households. Some households save money regularly, manage their finances well while others with similar incomes use up all their cash, and may even incur debts that they cannot afford to pay back. While personality was earlier described in terms of traits that were similar to everyday notions and often were tinged with moral evaluations, modern psychological trait descriptions are usually based on personality theories. These theories exhibit personality traits that do not exactly correspond to thriftiness, but may be related to it.

Assessment of Personality

Personality generally stands for behavioral consistency of long duration. The concept is used to explain individual differences in behavior and refers to sets of characteristics, called factors or traits that do not easily or quickly change. In psychology, the interest in personality has varied greatly over time and again seems to be increasing (Revelle, 1995). The research on personality is very comprehensive. The fundamental questions are (Revelle, 1995, p.296): (1) What are the relevant dimensions of individual differences in personality? (2) How do genetic mechanisms lead to individual differences? (3) Does personality have a biological basis? (4) How does personality develop? (5) What are the social determinants of personality?

Many psychologists, especially those in cognitive psychology, pay little attention to the concept of personality. The prevailing conception is 'more of the same', i.e., that people tend to behave in new situations the way they behaved in earlier, similar situations. 'Past behavior is the best predictor of future behavior' (cf. Ajzen, 1991, p.202). Transaction theories of personality focus on the interplay between persons and situations. The dominant theory in the personality trait tradition is *the five-factor model*, which has assumed somewhat varying shapes with some fundamental agreement. Despite wide acceptance, there are also solid criticisms of the five-factor model. It is said that it is only a classification and that there is no theory of personality behind it (Ozer and Reise, 1994).

The five-factor model of personality is based on descriptive traits that can be seen as residues of past behavior. When respondents are filling out personality assessment scales, they ideally abstract or distill a number of self-observations and what they have heard from significant others. Five dimensions are held to be fundamental: *extraversion, agreeableness, conscientiousness, emotional stability*, and *intellect*. None of those seems to incorporate completely the personality traits that have been supposed to promote saving. It may, however, be possible to trace an influence of at least some of the five personality factors on motives for saving and attitudes towards saving. Brandstätter (1993) argued that personality affected attitudes and that explanations of behavior could be improved if personality and attitudes were jointly used. This again suggests that attitudes must be put into a context to contribute more to explaining behavior.

Brandstätter (1988, 1995) has developed a five-factor model, with dimensions similar to those above, but based on Cattell's 16PF test, and has provided a personality test in the form of an adjective scale version that is easily administered. The test consists of 32 polarities of adjectives, two for each of the original 16 dimensions. The test was translated into Dutch and used in the VSB Panel study.

In the first and second waves of the VSB panel, 32 adjective polarities were included in the questionnaire. A principal components analysis yielded five personality factors that were similar to the well-known five-factor model of personality. Together with a number of socioeconomic and psychological variables, the five personality factors were included in multivariate analyses with 'intention to save' and reported saving as dependent variables. The two factors 'conscientiousness' and 'inflexibility' turned out to have significant indirect influence on intention to save and saving behavior. The more conscientious and the more inflexible the respondent, the more likely s/he was to report saving. This influence was mediated via saving attitudes. The latter were also influenced by saving motives which had no direct influence on saving. Conscientiousness and inflexibility are related to the early concepts of self-control and will power. (Wärneryd, 1996a)

SOCIAL INFLUENCE ON SAVING

for that we have such an extraordinary Concern in what others think of us, can proceed from nothing but the vast Esteem we have for our selves.
Mandeville ([1729] 1924, p.67)

The Role of Social Influence

On the basis of cognition alone, without the language of the market and ongoing social interaction with other agents, rational decision is frustratingly illusive.
Smith (1991, p.894)

Individual preferences are according to prevalent economic theory assumed to be independent and unique to the individual. Economists have been accused of neglecting the fact that consumers are not independent of one another and that consumers influence consumers. Tarde (1902) complained that economics was not based on social interaction, but on the individual pursuit of self-interest, and that it disregarded the importance of the social environment for the individual. Veblen (1899) emphasized the social influence on consumption of certain goods, 'conspicuous consumption' or 'conspicuous waste', which was aimed at impressing others. Other critics of economic theory as well as many adherents have raised questions about the neglected role of social interdependence among consumers and business decision makers. The possible importance of social influence and the interdependence of preferences is becoming more and more of a concern in economics (see e.g. a number of articles in Gilad and Kaish, 1986).

Leibenstein (1950) distinguished three types of social effects on consumption: bandwagon, Veblen and snob effects. The *bandwagon effect* involved that when more people adopted a product, the pressure to adopt increased for the consumers who had not yet adopted. The *Veblen effect* referred to the circumstances connected with status motives and conspicuous consumption in that a higher price was assumed to increase the consumption of certain goods, what the economists call a backward-sloping demand curve. The *snob effect* was opposed to the other two in its effect on consumption: a product could become more attractive when fewer consumers possessed it: the fewer the possessors, the more attractive the good. These effects all seem to have a negative effect on saving since they incite consumption.

Social influence is assumed strongest when there are visible signs of following or not following the norm. Veblen pointed to the importance of 'conspicuous' consumption. The social influence is low or non-existing when there is no signal to relevant others that a person or household is saving. Lavish consumption in relation to the social environment means non-saving and waste and it is often highly visible. The weight of the social influence can be assumed to fall on consumption rather than on saving per se. Saving has low visibility. Can there be direct social influence on saving and savings? When I was a child, the savings banks opened a savings account for every seven-year-old and in many schools (mine at least) the pupils were encouraged to put a coin in a savings box with individual slots every week in front of the other children.

Consumption is to an important extent visible and can more easily than saving be observed by others. There may be some visibility for saving, but probably often in the negative sense of meanness. People may, however, be observed to be restrained in their consumption habits and judged as thrifty. When money that must obviously have been saved is spent, say, on a luxurious vacation trip, other people may observe the happy consequences of saving. Advertising from savings banks and other financial institutions have sometimes made use of this theme.

When an excess of income over expenditure is produced as a consequence of controlling expenditure, the nature of social influence may be different from the case when it results from a pursuit of a definite saving goal. If a saving goal is primary and holding down expenditure is secondary, the social influence is probably smaller. The pressure of a definite saving goal may lead to attempts to increase income as well as to cutting down expenditure.

Social Norms and Saving

Perhaps saving is seen as moral just because it is difficult

Lea et al. (1987, p.216)

Cultural and social norms have usually worked in favor of saving. A social norm is any behavior, belief, attitude, or emotion that occur so often that they are held to be correct and acceptable within a society. Saving money seems to have many features of a social norm in many Western societies. Thrift was for many centuries held to be a virtue and considered very important for the economic growth of a nation. Saving was one of the long-term values that characterized many Western economies (see Lea et al., 1987, pp.214-6). The intrinsic value of saving money was spread through religious teaching, through education of children and various popular attempts to enlighten people about the importance of being frugal (within limits). Examples are Benjamin Franklin's pamphlets about Poor Richard and Samuel Smiles's books about self-help (1859) and thrift (1875).

Thrift was part of a cultural norm which was also supported by the dominating religions. Deviations from the norm were self-righteously declared to lead to poverty and destitution. Without savings and supporting relatives there was little of a security net which could catch and assist those who were without money. As noted in Chapter 3, some thinkers deviated from the received norm. The Mercantilists had serious doubts about the usefulness of savings that involved hoarding. Mandeville spoke in favor of spending for those who could afford to spend. Keynes (1936) warned that too much saving led to unemployment. The Mercantilists and Keynes probably had more influence on politicians than on social norms.

Economists have pondered on why people adhere to norms and applied cost-benefit thinking. Kreps (1997, p.359) suggested the following reasons:

1. Adherence is costless relative to isolation and so – why not?
2. Adherence is immediately, personally beneficial because it permits coordination (e.g. bear to the right in a crowded walkway)
3. Adherence, while immediately costly, leads to better treatment by others than will violation
4. Adherence is desirable per se.

The fourth reason seems difficult to address in such utility terms that it fits in the basic utility function.

Lindbeck (1997) discussed the influence of social norms in three areas: work incentives, the non-acceptance of underbidding, and saving. He added to the utility function a term whose size was determined by the number of people (perceived) to observe a certain social norm. The idea is similar to Leibenstein's (1950) concept of bandwagon effect. In the case of saving, the emergence of the welfare state may have lessened the social norms favoring savings. When the welfare systems, as has happened in some countries, have run into serious economic difficulties, characterized as budget deficits and incurring of public debts, the social norm of saving may again be strengthened.

The establishment of security nets that could insure against unemployment, ill health and, of course against deficiencies in thrift may have contributed to relinquishing the norm of thrift. Modern welfare systems have reduced the need for buffer capital or other extra assets that could be employed in cases of need and floors for social benefits may punish income increases. Maital and Maital (1991) and Hoch and Loewenstein (1991) referred to decrease in self-control as a possible cause of diminished saving rates. This is another way of expressing the lessened need for restraint and thrift. Although the social norm of thrift may be less prevalent in many Western countries now, there are social norms pertaining to social groups. Certain groups or segments of the population may have norms, that is, expectations that those who want to claim to belong to the group, do not display extravagant consumption which perhaps also involves saving money. In social psychology, such phenomena are described as 'reference group' influence.

Reference Groups and Saving

In Chapter 4, Duesenberry's theory of saving, 'the relative income hypothesis', based on the demonstration effect, was presented. Duesenberry applied the concept of reference group on consumption and saving. The concept was at that time newly created and used to explain influence on voting behavior and on consumer behavior. People have an innate tendency to compare themselves with others according to Festinger (1954). It is generally accepted as a fact that people try to evaluate their attitudes and capacity with other people as a comparison object, in particular when there are no objective, non-social objects to compare with. The probability that a person compares herself or himself with another person decreases with increasing difference between them with respect to the dimension that the comparison involves.

Reference group theory systematizes the determinants and consequences of the evaluation processes in which the individual takes over values or standards from other individuals and groups. In the first uses, reference group was applied to groups of which the individual was not a member, or to other individuals who did not necessarily form a group of any kind (Merton and Kitt, 1952). Later, the concept has been allowed to include also membership groups on the proviso that the individual compares her/himself with the group members in some respect. A distinction can be made between two functions of the reference group (Kelley, 1952). The *comparison* function is primarily informative. The reference group serves as a source of information about possible attitudes and behaviors. This aspect is perceptual-cognitive. The *normative* function imposes values on the individual who is subject to power exertion from the group. This aspect is motivational. The same group can serve both functions.

Some reference groups may be aspirational (positive) reference groups, which leads to special conformity to the group. Other reference groups are negative reference groups. The attitudes and behaviors of the latter provoke opposing beliefs and behaviors. Since poverty may be a more visible aspect of a person or a group than having savings accounts, some reference group influence on savings may be of the negative kind. Swedish savings banks used to show negative referents in their advertising campaigns. For many years, Swedish school children received a magazine with both a positive referent girl, christened 'Save' (in Swedish 'Spara'), and a negative referent girl, called 'Waste' (in Swedish 'Slösa'). Many Swedes over 50 still associate to this magazine when they hear the word 'save'.

The concept of reference group nowadays seems to be less used in empirical studies, probably because reference group influence has been hard to measure in practice. It is difficult to establish which persons serve as referents for different behaviors. Mainly three types of approaches are used. The *first* approach involves asking which groups respondents compare themselves with, for example, neighbors, friends and acquaintances, colleagues at work, people with the same level of education, of about the same age and people having the same job as the respondent or people known from the newspapers or from TV. The questions typically refer to spending patterns or standard of living, not to saving.

The *second* approach means asking about selected sociodemographic characteristics of circles of acquaintances: 'people you see often such as friends, neighbors, acquaintances or perhaps people at your place of work'. The typically requested characteristics are average age, education, annual income, average working hours per week, and types of occupation for both spouses. Questions like those have been used in the Socioeconomic Panel of the Dutch CBS and in the VSB Panel. The answers to these questions can be used for different purposes, such as testing hypotheses about group similarities and saving. If the income of the respondent household is lower than the average for the circle of friends, lower than average savings would be expected in accordance with Duesenberry (1949). The *third* approach uses attitude statements of the type 'Most people in my environment are saving money', 'When I compare myself with my friends I find that I am better off'.

While there are many studies of social influence on consumption or rather on the composition of consumption and the use of branded goods, few studies have concerned social influence on saving and other financial behavior. Those who endorse attitude statements implying that they have many friends who save usually also report more saving (see Lunt and Livingstone, 1991). East (1993) found that there was great influence of friends and relatives on the making of applications for shares in British companies that were to be privatized.

Reference groups influence *level of aspiration*, that is, one type of reference points or goals that people set for themselves with respect to some behavior. A person's own earlier experience seems to be the most important determinant of the level of aspiration, but, in particular when the person is lacking in personal experience, reference groups appear to be influential. Reference group effect is similar to what Duesenberry (1949) called 'the demonstration effect'. The concept of *relative deprivation* is related to reference group. This concept indicates what happens when the level of aspiration which has been set in accordance with what characterizes referent individuals, is not attained. Continued comparison with the same reference group will then give the individual feelings of being deprived in relation to the level of the reference group members. With a less than judicious choice of reference group a person can feel relative deprivation despite having access to many by others desired gifts. Clark and Oswald (1993) tested the hypothesis that happiness depended on income relative to a comparison or reference level in a study of satisfaction and comparison income. They found that workers' reported satisfaction levels were negatively related to their comparison earnings levels. The savings rate was shown to depend on the ratio of income to comparison income, which supported Duesenberry's relative income hypothesis.

Critics of the market efficiency hypothesis like Shiller have pointed to the role of social influence: 'Investing in speculative assets is a social activity. Investors spend a substantial part of their leisure time discussing investments, reading about investments, or gossiping about others' successes or failures in investing' (Shiller, 1989, p.7). Shiller reported a number of empirical studies that showed the social dynamics of financial markets and cast some doubts on the explanatory power of market efficiency theory. Keynes neatly formulated the fact that investors have other investors in mind when they make their investment decisions. He had made the following observation:

> professional investment may be likened to those newspaper competitions in which the competitors have to pick out the six prettiest faces from a hundred photographs, the prize being awarded to the competitor whose choice most nearly corresponds to the average preferences of the competitors as a whole; so that each competitor has to pick, not those faces which he himself finds prettiest, but those which he thinks likeliest to catch the fancy of the other competitors, all of whom are looking at the problem from the same point of view. It is not a case of choosing those which, to the best of one's judgment, are really the prettiest, nor even those which average opinion genuinely thinks the prettiest ... we devote our intelligences to anticipating what average opinion expects average opinion to be. (Keynes, 1936, p.156)

Keynes (1936, p.158) added: 'Worldly wisdom teaches that it is better for reputation to fail conventionally than to succeed unconventionally.' The last statement has some resemblance to attribution theory. According to this theory, people who fail tend to attribute the failure to external circumstances such as the difficulty of the task and use the fact that others have also failed as a confirmation of this. When there is success, it is primarily ascribed to one's own merits (see Weiner, 1985; Bettman and Weitz, 1983).

Influences on investors have been confirmed by other studies. In Barlow et al.'s (1966) study of the affluent, it was apparent that investors frequently used information from personal sources, but made the decisions themselves. In a study made immediately after the 1987 October Stock Market crash, Shiller (1989) found that both institutional and individual investors reported 'gut feeling' rather than technical analysis as reason for their actions. Answering the questionnaires with open-ended questions

> They often wrote 'gut feeling' as their forecasting method, and often seemed to say that they were guessing about the psychology of other investors. Investors appear to believe they have some internal sense of magnitude or direction for the market, and investors are highly divided on this sense of direction. (Shiller, 1989, p.399)

Apparently, expectations about how other investors would react to the initial price drops played a role in bringing about the crash. Part of the expectation was based on the belief which investors knew that also other investors had had for a long time, that stocks were overpriced. So-called 'portfolio insurance' which usually involves setting limits for acceptable prices using computers, had little influence according to Shiller.

Having developed an economic model for herd behavior, Scharfstein and Stein (1990) suggested that the model could explain the October 1987 stock exchange crash. They noted: 'By mimicking the behavior of others (i.e. buying when others are buying, and selling when others are selling) rather than responding to their private information, members of a herd will tend to amplify exogenous stock price shocks' (Scharfstein and Stein, 1990, p.477). The general assumption behind the authors' concept of herd behavior is that it is rational for decision makers to attempt to enhance their reputation as decision makers: 'correlated prediction errors lead to the "sharing-the-blame effect" that drives managers to herd'.

8. An Integrative Framework for the Psychology of Saving

Vieles ist bekannt, aber leider in verschiedenen Köpfen (Much is known, but unfortunately in different heads)

German proverb, quoted from Gullberg (1964)

THE PURPOSE OF THE CHAPTER

Except for the work of George Katona, psychological research has contributed little to the psychology of saving. Economists produced most of the thinking in this area, but today's economists seem to have lost some worthwhile details in their theories of saving. The chapter sums up the state of the art in the psychology of saving and presents an attempt to integrate 'thrift', 'forward-looking' (expectations) and action, relying on economics and psychology. The purpose is to create a better foundation for empirical, economic-psychological and psychological research on saving. My intention is not to suggest new microeconomic theory, but to investigate whether some potentially useful psychological thinking can be fitted into the economic thinking and whether the psychology of saving can profit from some recent economic thinking.

The primary purpose of economic-psychological research on saving is to provide descriptions and explanations of saving that are detailed and close to reality (cf. Katona, 1975; Simon, 1986; Lea et al., 1992). This enterprise is in no way in conflict with the economic approach nor is it a competitor. It will be a source of ideas which can in the long run become something more: a good descriptive and explanatory theory of savings and saving behavior. We are not quite there yet.

The last part of the chapter is devoted to presenting a conceptual schema for psychological research on saving behavior. The schema summarizes some earlier presented thinking about the psychology of saving and elaborates some of the ideas. It is an attempt to translate the psychological concepts used by classical and early neoclassical economists into terms that are compatible with modern psychology.

297

WHAT ARE THE PROBLEMS WE NEED THEORY FOR?

*Political oeconomy, considered as a branch of the science of a statesman or legis-
lator, proposes two distinct objects; first, to provide a plentiful revenue or subsistence for the people, or more properly to enable them to provide such a revenue or
subsistence for themselves; and secondly, to supply the state or commonwealth
with a revenue sufficient for the publick services. It proposes to enrich both the
people and the sovereign.*

Smith ([1776] 1976, p.428)

Why do people save? Why do people not save? Who is interested in these
questions? Let me take the second question first. An answer that is often
given by respondents in survey interviews (maybe in an exasperated tone of
voice) is that there is not money enough in the household. A second type of
answer is that it is not necessary or even desirable to save money. Apart from
political views that are based on interpretations of Keynes, the latter answer
means access to plentiful assets or total confidence in the social security net
or a heedless lack of concern about the future. Behind the 'no-money-to-
save' answer, there is often a fear of the uncertainties of the time to come, but
also of some certainties spelling a need for more money. Some reasons for
saving are known, but little is known about how these reasons vary among
population groups and over time, about what saving means to people and
whether there are changes in meaning over the life-cycle and over generations. Why is it that some people want to and manage to save while others in
almost exactly the same situation do not care or do not manage to save?

When the aim is to influence consumers to increase their savings or to dissave as the case may be, detailed knowledge about consumers seems desirable. Such knowledge may explain and predict reactions to financial policy
changes and it can help in the dissemination of information about saving
matters. Research on saving and savings has had three major tasks or problem areas as starting points:

1. Government and other political interest in capital accumulation and
    the factors influencing it
2. Financial institution and financial market interest in savings and in
    factors influencing saving behavior, in particular those that can be
    acted upon by the institution
3. Theory building as part of economic and economic-psychological
    theories for better explanations and predictions of savings in the short
    run and the long run.

A fourth task could be mentioned if it were not for its low profile so far: contributing to the development of psychological theory on forward-looking that could be helpful in discussions at the micro and the macro levels.

It is not likely that the theory developed under the third point will be satisfactory for all aspects of the first two problem areas. The above vignette from Adam Smith illustrates the economists' involvement with problems in society at a high level. With the developments of macroeconomics and welfare economics, economists' preoccupation with societal problems has become even more pronounced. Psychologists have rather focused their interest on issues related to individuals. In a presentation of economic psychology as a field of study, three major functions for economic psychology at the societal level were distinguished (Wärneryd, 1988, p.37)

1. Reporting on 'the psychological state' of the economy at regular intervals. The studies of optimism-pessimism among consumers and business decision makers are good examples. More in-depth analyses are desirable and possible.
2. Providing analytic foundations for the planning of policy measures. This involves strategy considerations as well as providing ideas for contents of actions intended to change the course of events in some respects.
3. Encouraging considerations of behavioral aspects in economic decision making; this is not necessarily a normative function, rather dissemination of knowledge.

'The psychological state' of the economy is since 1972 regularly investigated in the EU countries, except for the newly joining member states. In addition to questions relating to the Index of Consumer Sentiment, there are questions about the present financial situation (from making debts to having money over), intention to save, and whether it is meaningful to save now. There are also questions about satisfaction with life and happiness. These data offer, in principle, possibilities of combining socioeconomic data and some psychological data at the micro level for each country. So far very few advanced analyses of data relating to saving have been carried out, whether for lack of interest among researchers or restricted access to data.

The second point involves that psychological analyses are produced as preparation for policy decisions. Such analyses are exceptional and psychological consequences are either disregarded or merely speculated about. There could be more attention to the fact that Katona kept pointing out, namely, that psychological variables have a place between economic stimuli and effects. The reactions to an enormous rise in the discount rate, say, to 200 percent, may e.g. reduce confidence in the power of the Central Bank rather than reinforce perceptions of resourcefulness. This is not to say that there are good tools available for suchlike psychological analyses, only that it is often desirable to try to find out something about the psychological preconditions qnd possible reactions. This is the implication of the third point.

The overriding government and policy problem has most of the time been that there is too little saving in a country and that economic growth may be hampered by lack of funds for investing. Nevertheless, especially during depressions, economists have warned against too much saving and underconsumption that seemingly lead to unemployment and other detrimental effects.

The main purpose of research on saving is to provide means of predicting savings for a reasonable part of the near and more distant future. The research should provide data and analysis to macroeconomic models that can explain and predict savings and relate savings to other macroeconomic magnitudes. In addition to foreseeing development, there may be an interest in trying to influence saving. The means are economic policy measures such as providing tax incentives for saving, something that has been common in many Western countries. When changes are made in the tax system, the effects on savings are usually discussed and closely followed. Governments have run information campaigns to stimulate saving. Such campaigns presuppose knowledge about target groups and creative ability to create effective messages.

Financial institutions like banks and building societies actively develop products which are offered to the public and which they try to influence members of the public to embrace. Banks market their services and seek information about their target groups. They do market research, which to some extent at least relies on more basic research on saving. The market research collects data on bank customers and usually employs methods and theories from the behavioral sciences and sometimes econometrics.

A large number of economic researchers are today busy with constructing and developing economic theories of saving. Special effort is devoted to extending and improving the dominant theory of saving, the LCH. An increasing number of economists are utilizing and elaborating concepts and measurement techniques originating in psychological research. Questionnaires and other techniques for gathering data are taken over and concepts that can preferably be made compatible with economic theory are borrowed from psychology and other behavioral sciences.

WHAT HAPPENED TO PSYCHOLOGY IN CURRENT THEORIES OF SAVINGS?

How is the psychology of saving, as it was summarized at the end of Chapter 3, represented in modern saving theories? The dominant economic model of saving is the Life-Cycle Hypothesis and the interest here will be confined to that theory. It has had great success, but it obviously, despite increasing sophistication over the years since its inception, has weaknesses and it fails to explain much of savings. It explains according to some critics much less than, for example, the 75 percent of savers that King (1985) calculated with. The young seem to save more than they are expected to and the elderly rather save than dissave. Some studies have not distinguished the hump-shaped life-cycle saving predicted by the LCH.

The Basic Formula

As a basis for the discussion of the psychology of saving, the (slightly modified) basic formula of LCH is again given (Ando and Modigliani, 1963):

$$c_t = g_t v_t$$

$$v_t = a_{t-1} + y_t + \sum_{t+1}^{N} \frac{y_t^{e\tau}}{(1 + r_t)^{N-1}}$$

where c_t is a household's total consumption in year t; a proportion of total lifetime resources

v_t is total lifetime resources at their present value

a_{t-1} is the sum of net worth carried over from the previous period

y_t is current income

$y_t^{e\tau}$ is what the household expects to earn in year t

N stands for the earning span, end of lifetime

r_t is the rate of return on assets, the discount rate

Savings are what remains after consumption. The above formula does not reveal the subtleties that have been added to LCH, in the first place the assumption of uncertainty and the debated bequest motive, but the simple form suffices for the discussion here. Excellent discussions of the various saving theories and of many problems and their attempted solutions can be found in Deaton (1992) and Browning and Lusardi (1996).

The LCH formula suggests a number of reasons for changes in savings: changes in wealth, in current income, in expected income, in the discount rate, and in life expectancy. Changes in family composition can of course also be handled within the model. Government can manipulate some of these variables. The value of assets can be effected through tax changes and changes in interest rates. Income can be influenced through taxes. Income expectations can be affected both by economic and non-economic factors. The latter are primarily studied through subjective data (which is not synonymous to introspection). Changes in the discount rate which are more or less a Central Bank concern remain the main, short-run way to influence savings according to Thaler (1994). Browning and Lusardi objected to Thaler's assessment: 'The remark by Thaler (1994) that in the standard life cycle framework 'the only policy variable [to increase the U.S. saving rate] is the after-tax rate of return' ignores the theoretical developments of the past ten years.' (Browning and Lusardi, 1996, pp.1847-8). They may be right, but is it then 'the standard life-cycle framework'?

Social and psychological changes can achieve effect only through changes in the aforementioned variables and must be somehow captured by those. The potential role for psychological research is to provide data not only on income and other financial expectations, but also on changes in received information, learning and habit formation, intentions, and social influences. Such data are indispensable if policy attempts are to be made to stimulate or discourage saving and may be desirable for predictions of future developments.

Psychology in the Study of Saving So Far

A psychologist can naturally find much to raise questions about in the micro-level LCH, but it seems likely that many psychological findings have little importance at the aggregate level. A common assumption is that individual differences cancel out in the population. It may still be true that some short-run or long-run changes or tendencies can be better explained by adding psychological variables when economic variables do not suffice. Lunt (1996a) proposed that economists who wanted to remedy deficiencies in economic theory should stop looking at basic psychological phenomena at the most detailed micro level, such as the neurophysiological bases of behavior, and rather consider social and environmental influences on economic behavior. According to Lunt, the sociological changes in consumption over the past decades have been so radical that consumption and savings theory should be reconsidered.

Except in economic-psychological research, few psychological studies have concerned problems directly related to saving (for overviews, see Ölander and Seipel, 1970; Lea et al., 1987; Lane, 1991; Lunt and Livingstone, 1991; Sonuga-Barke and Webley, 1993). There is nonetheless the possibility that some existing theory is applicable to saving. The few psychological variables that have been tried so far in econometric models contribute something to the explanation of variance, but usually much less than the socioeconomic variables. In time series analyses of savings, savings a year earlier appear to be the most influential single variable (see, for example, Juster, 1981; King, 1985; Kotlikoff, 1989). Time series data for psychological variables used to be available only to a very limited extent and only for the Index of Consumer Sentiment. The regular EU surveys in all member countries now contain more psychological data that could be used in time series analysis. There are data on saving intentions, qualitative data on individual household saving, some data on health, and data on satisfaction with life and happiness.

The main importance of the psychological variables lies in their contribution to better understanding of saving behavior which may be a prerequisite for selecting appropriate means to influencing saving and provide an understanding that may be useful to forecasters.

A Summary of Psychological Issues in Connection with the Life-Cycle Hypothesis

On the surface, the dominant saving theory bears few traces of the earlier psychology of saving. The originators and most followers have carefully avoided psychological concepts. Browning and Lusardi (1996) linked modern saving theory to Keynes's list of saving motives and found that those were reasonably well covered. There are certainly psychological assumptions underlying the theory. Some are openly stated and others are hidden behind the formulas. Each psychological assumption is motivated by the overriding rationality assumption and made compatible with it. The psychologist's questions about the LCH can perhaps help clarify some problems with the theory. For economic-psychological research on saving, it seems essential to use developments in modern scientific psychology to arrive at better explanations. Such work is being pursued as reported in Chapter 5.

The psychological assumptions in the LCH may not be wrong, but they can be elaborated with the help of modern psychology. Psychological science may not be able to present relevant hypotheses in such a way that they can be directly integrated into economic savings theory, but they may still be useful. Application of psychological thinking leads to better descriptions and explanations of saving. While such applications may not lead to better quantitative predictions of saving ratios, they contribute to a better understanding of processes in saving. At any rate, it should be permitted for psychologists to participate in the search for complements to the theories and for new avenues in research on saving.

Chapter 3 ended with a summary of psychological concepts used by early economists in their discussions on saving. The most important psychological insights to take back from the brief historical review are:

1. The prevalent desire for effective accumulation and improvement
2. The assumed importance of thrift and thrifty habits
3. Self-control and willpower as determinants of thrift
4. Uncertainty of (about) the future and the role of expectations
5. Selective perception and limited cognitive capacity
6. Time horizon or attitude towards the future.

What has happened to these psychological issues in modern economic saving theory? The answer is that some of them are there, covered by assumptions that do not have to be tested, some are recognized as problematic and attempts at developing theory and finding proxies are made, and a third type is left out.

The desire for effective accumulation and improvement

The first item is not only part of saving theory, but it embodies the funda-mental assumption in economic theory. Adam Smith called it 'the desire of bettering our condition'. John Rae talked about 'the effective desire of accu-mulation' or the preference for a greater to a less which served as a prompt to action. John Stuart Mill used Rae's terms and laid them down as the founda-tion of the rationality postulate. While the postulate means maximization of utility, the original thinking encompassed the idea that people wished to get improvement over their whole life cycle. The LCH proposes that people want to smooth consumption and have largely the same level of consumption at all stages of the life cycle. Keynes had a deviant view and formulated one saving motive: 'To enjoy a gradually increasing expenditure, since it gratifies a common instinct to look forward to a gradually improving standard of life' (Keynes, 1936, p.108). The motive was called 'improvement' and it is hardly covered by the LCH in any new shape (cf. Lusardi and Browning, 1996).

The assumption that consumers strive to ensure the same level of con-sumption over the life cycle is questionable according to some recent find-ings in psychological research. Keynes's motive of improvement gets sup-port. Marshall ([1890] 1947, p.225) made a pertinent observation: 'In India, and to a less extent in Ireland, we find people who do indeed abstain from immediate enjoyment and save up considerable sums with great self-sacrifice, but spend all their savings in lavish festivities at funerals and mar-riages, they make intermittent provision for the near future, but scarcely any permanent provision for the distant future'. An interesting hypothesis says that people constantly want improvement, a climax order. They are willing to sacrifice for some time to get a better position later – maybe this is what makes certain religions so attractive when they promise rewards in heaven for accepting a poor life on earth. The implication is that consumers want improvements rather than smoothed consumption over the life-cycle. Kahneman (1994) and Kahneman and Thaler (1991) applied the ideas to wage systems and suggested that wages and salaries should be constructed in such a way that there was stepwise improvement. A life income distributed to give continuous improvements would give more satisfaction than an even distribution of the same total income over the life cycle.

Goal-directed saving may not be fixed on the end period in life as an ulti-mate climax, but rather be limited to certain periods that are followed by periods of dissaving. New periods of saving are instigated in new attempts to reach a desired high level of consumption later. Economizing for some years to become able to buy an attractive automobile, make a long journey, or get better housing is quite common. Everyday observation and anecdotal evidence support the hypothesis of an improvement order, which originates from laboratory experiments with simple, hypothetical choice situations. The improvement order may result in saving for being able to indulge in 'peak experiences' or simply to have more room for enjoyment in the future.

The psychological assumption of a climax order is open to some doubt and objection since the research evidence is rather new and slim. Part of the evidence for the preference of a climax order emanates from research on time preferences. It has been found that people may have negative time preferences, that is, want to postpone positive experiences and enjoy the anticipation of attractive consumption ('savoring', see Chapter 4) and face unavoidable, negative (non-fatal) events as soon as possible to get it over with ('dread') (see Loewenstein and Prelec, 1993).

The role of thrifty habits

The second point addresses the role of habits. Habit formation is a well-established concept in saving theory. In psychological learning theory, habit means that a certain behavior or pattern of behavior is repeated as a consequence of earlier rewards or punishments. Habit generally stands for learned responses. In economics, habit formation means that preferences in one budget period depend on the preferences in other periods. According to Deaton (1992, p.16), there are several ways of dealing with such problems in saving theory. The problem involved in the durability (non-additivity) of preferences over budget periods is handled in the same way as a stock of durables.

Survey findings that people who had saved for retirement continued to save the same or larger amounts after they had other coverage of future pensions aroused debate among economists (Katona, 1965; Cagan, 1965). 'Saving habits' were used as an explanation. It was assumed that having saved money by self-imposed obligation for many years, people had saving habits that they did not wish to break. As mentioned in Chapter 4, Shefrin and Thaler (1988) suggested that people kept the same rules, that is, 'the planner' still prevailed. The continued saving can be viewed as people keeping the same level of consumption after the introduction of the pension plan. They were thus able to save more. Economic-psychological research on saving has often focused on the regularity of saving acts, which is one way of picturing habits (Lunt and Livingstone, 1991; Daniel, 1997). In this context, psychology can contribute some theory on how habits are formed as a complement to the economists' focus on the consequences of habits for consumption and saving.

Self-control and willpower as determinants of thrift

While the third point lacks equivalents in the LCH, it refers to one of the basic elements in the Behavioral Life-Cycle Hypothesis (Shefrin and Thaler, 1988). In the preceding chapter, self-control and self command were treated in some detail. At the level of the individual and the household, the concept seems potentially important in the study of saving. Volition is coming back in psychological science albeit under varying names. This is part of a tendency towards more complex explanations in psychology and some moving away from simple behavioral laws. Browning and Lusardi (1996, p.1850) proposed a study of psychological factors like self-control as ways of modeling the heterogeneity (which can be seen as dispersion or unexplained variance) that was allowed in standard saving models. The introduction of scales of self-control in saving surveys may before long yield new findings on the role of self-control. Daniel (1997) used such scales with some success and the VSB Panel interviews contained such scales in some interview waves.

Uncertainty of (about) the future and the role of expectations

The fourth point is receiving continued attention in saving theory. The LCH now includes uncertainty in the model. Uncertainty was treated in Chapter 6 and the ideas will be summarized here together with some new ideas. People are assumed to be uncertain about future income, health, and remaining life-time (Kotlikoff, 1989; Hubbard et al., 1994). The variance of earlier income distributions, aggregate or individual, is often used as a proxy of income uncertainty (Dynan, 1993). The uncertainty is translated into the precautionary motive. The existence of this motive has usually been demonstrated through correlations between the variance in the income distribution, over time or over income classes, and savings. The implication is that a precautionary motive exists if there is income variability and more saving in a budget period than is warranted by the LCH annuity. The period gets less than its legitimate consumption share of the lifetime consumption. The proxies used may not capture the uncertainty of future employment. Recently, interesting attempts have been made directly to measure uncertainty about future income (see Guiso et al., 1992; Lusardi, 1993; Dominitz, 1996; Das and Donkers, 1997). It may be assumed that the probability distributions obtained include consideration of both income variation when the respondent is employed and the effects of possible unemployment.

The concept of risk is assigned to situations or outcomes where there is a probability attached. Uncertainty refers to outcomes where there is no probability or even any limited interval of probabilities ('ambiguity'). This implies that people actually calculate risk in some situations, employing probabilities. Many studies, notably inspired by prospect theory, have found that people handle probabilities in rather peculiar ways (Kahneman and Tversky,

1979; Kahneman and Tversky, 1984; Tversky and Kahneman, 1986; Hogarth, 1987; Lopes, 1994). Even if risk can be calculated, it may be underestimated or overestimated. Practitioners in certain fields are all the time handling what they think of as calculated risks. Investors in futures and other derivatives may, for example, be risk takers also in their own eyes, but they probably feel that they have some control over the risks that they take, due to their assumed expertise. They may be wrongly mistaken about their control. 'An illusion of control is defined as an expectancy of a personal success probability inappropriately higher than the objective probability would warrant.' (Langer, 1982, p.232). Gamblers seem to think that luck is a matter of skill – which it sometimes appears to be for a while. Modern cognitive research on risk perception and risk attitudes has many interesting findings that can be of importance to research on the psychology of saving (see, for example, Lopes, 1990; 1994, for overviews).

Savers seem to be risk averse and tend to be cautious in the sense that they do not overdo their consumption. Investors may be more or less risk seeking. If a saver has considerable wealth s/he may find it desirable and even necessary to invest in more risky assets. The risks taken by such investors are mostly well within the boundaries of what they can afford to lose if something goes wrong (Wärneryd, 1996c). They do not invest all their money and they avoid incurring debts to finance investments, except that they mortgage house equity. There are some indications that younger investors are more willing to take risks than older investors.

Psychological prospect theory stresses loss aversion rather than risk aversion. While prospect theory has not been applied in saving studies, the theory and accompanying concepts like the endowment effect sound useful to this study (Thaler, 1980; Tversky and Griffin, 1991). The endowment effect involves that once you have acquired something, the price you ask for parting with it is much higher than what you paid (and would be willing to pay for it). It is well known that many people who own shares are unwilling to part with the shares and keep them longer than they should if they want to optimize their gain. They buy and sell shares at the wrong time because they abhor losses. Benartzi and Thaler (1995) used 'myopic' loss aversion and high frequency of evaluation (noting every drop in share values) to explain why long-term investors often favored investments in bonds rather than higher-yielding stock.

Uncertainty about remaining lifetime is important in the LCH, which presumes that the individual knows her/his remaining lifetime – N in the basic function. In line with general economic reasoning, it is rational to use objective data on life expectancy in estimates of subjective life expectancy. Even if it is admitted that people may be wrong in their estimates, the estimation errors should cancel out in a population so that the average of the subjective estimates should be very close to actual life expectancy. Are people really conscious about their life expectancy and do they think at all about when they will die? Not thinking about or wanting to predict a reasonably exact date for one's own death does not preclude that one may be prepared for death. A guess based on research in other areas of psychology, indicating that a majority always tend to think that they are better than average and less susceptible to risks than other people, would be that people tend to overestimate their remaining lifetime. Suppose then that people have a tendency to believe that they will live longer than their objective life expectancy and the spouse is perhaps expected to live even longer. The annuity calculations specified in LCH would then lead to lower spending and more wealth left at death. Conversely, if people underestimate their remaining lifetime the calculations of annuities would lead to more spending and less wealth at death.

The issue of subjective life expectancy is the object of intensive research (see Chapter 6). Various ways of ascertaining the subjective life expectancies of middle-aged and old people have been tried out. The results of recent research indicate that on average people tend to be rather realistic about their remaining lifetime. If it is found that there is good agreement between actual and subjectively estimated life expectancy, it can be argued that other issues are more important when trying to improve the LCH performance. Still, life expectancy is highly intriguing with respect to its role for individual saving.

Selective perception and limited cognitive capacity

Point 5 summarizes insights that, for example, Adam Smith commented on in his *Theory of Moral Sentiments* and later Böhm-Bawerk and Marshall pointed out as limiting factors in people's rational dealings with the future. The preference for present consumption was partly a consequence of limited capacity to process information and especially to do the necessary calculations. In addition, there could be a lack of the imaginative powers that could give the right vividness to the present representation of future experience. Selective perception applies to the fact that people attend to and process limited amounts of all the information that they are exposed to. Differences in knowledge and information are to a large extent a consequence of selective perception. Information has simply not been received by all in the same way. Psychologists tend to object to the rationality assumption, involving maximization of utility, for three main reasons: (a) human lack of cognitive capacity which makes the necessary calculations unlikely, (b) only economic considerations enter into the utility function, and (c) changes in tastes do occur and can be legitimate from the consumer point of view.

Time horizon and attitude towards the future

Time horizon has to do with how far in advance people imagine future periods and plan their consumption. The LCH sets time horizon equal to life expectancy. People are assumed to include the rest of their lifetime in their planning of consumption and saving. Friedman (1957) found in his analyses of consumption data that people seemed to reckon with time horizons of three to four years. Respondents in surveys of consumption and saving are usually asked questions about the extent of planning and what they think of as a proper planning horizon. Sometimes specified questions are asked about appropriate advance planning periods for different activities. According to the studies, time horizons vary for different decision areas and for different people. Many people have time horizons of less than one year. Respondents who plan more and have longer planning horizons typically tend to save more and have less debt (Julander, 1975; Lea et al., 1995; Lunt and Livingstone, 1992).

Does a person's time horizon stop with death or do people think about what will happen after their death? The bequest motive which was treated in some detail in the preceding chapter implies a time horizon beyond one's own lifetime. The time horizon is extended beyond life expectancy when the well-being of possible survivors is considered. The most accepted version of the LCH today seems to include the assumption of a bequest motive (King, 1985). 'Since life span is uncertain, individuals choose a level of bequests at each point in their lives; that is, there is not a single planned terminal bequest but rather age-specific bequests contingent on dying at that age' (Kotlikoff, 1989, p.28). For those who do not have close relatives whom they care about, there may be some purpose which they want to promote whether for altruistic reasons or for being remembered.

Attitude towards the future encompasses time preferences. Although the micro model behind the LCH contains individual discount rates, in practice, the market interest rate is used in empirical studies and the same rate is used for lending and borrowing. The assumption of constant, exponential discount rates has been questioned (Strotz, 1956; Thaler and Shefrin, 1981; Shefrin and Thaler, 1988). Psychological research may supply subjective measures that are closer to reality. There are many attempts to estimate subjective discount rates and time preferences. The results indicate that there is considerable variation depending on the time delay of the future utility, the size of the amount involved, and person characteristics (see Chapter 4). Knetsch (1997) has discussed the findings of different subjective discount rates and proposed a model for bringing theoretical structure to the area. The model is based on prospect theory.

If preferences change over time they constitute a serious problem for economics. The fact that there are changes of taste and of preferences for alternative actions over time speaks for varying discount rates. Some classical economists, in the first place Böhm-Bawerk, asked a fundamental question: Why do people so often prefer a good with small utility today to a good with much higher utility in the future? Ainslie (1975) applied the thinking to problems of addiction and has later developed it further. Ainslie (1975, 1991) and Ainslie and Haslam (1992) proposed a hyperbolic discount function that has some empirical support:

$$Y = 1/X$$

where Y is the object and X is the distance in time or space.

Some further psychological considerations

Economists are interested in simple behavioral laws that in principle are valid for all humans. In many contexts, individual differences are assumed to cancel out in a population since people react differently. It is characteristic of economic theory of saving that individual differences are not considered. Do they always cancel out in the aggregate or is it necessary to distinguish between different segments of savers in the population? Individual differences are recognized, but they are treated as dispersion around the mean. As Katona (1975) showed, it happens that people in large numbers, owing, for example, to mass media influence, react in the same unexpected manner at the same time, and the reactions do not balance out. While experimental psychologists in particular often look for behavioral laws they are mostly attentive to contingencies and try to specify the circumstances under which different versions of a behavioral law operate. The contingencies often involve differences in values, attitudes, motives, or personality traits and suggest that there may be population segments with differing properties and different dispositions to react to economic stimuli.

The saving theories deal with consumption or decision units and individuals and households/families are treated as equivalent units. Research on household decision making has clearly shown that there can be varying household member influence on decisions, depending on family structure and what the decision is about. A few deep-reaching studies of household decision making have been made (see Kirchler, 1988). Little is known about how family members interact in consumption decisions and how family habits of controlling expenses and saving money emerge out of potential conflicts. Katona (1975) suggested that women had more influence on saving in bank savings accounts and that men more often looked after investments. The problem also involves the question of whom to interview in a household. There is no obviously superior way of selecting a respondent in a household or in weighting the influences of different members. What is household saving and what is individual saving is difficult to disentangle. Measures of savings often pertain to households while psychological measures refer to individuals. Whose psychological characteristics should be used when household saving habits are studied? More than one analysis appears desirable.

THE RELATIONSHIPS MICRO AND MACRO

In economics, the received view is that criticisms of micro-level assumptions in LCH lack significance unless the assumption leads to wrong explanations and predictions at the macro level. Mainstream economists maintain that there should be agreement between micro and macro. When a macroeconomic analysis and a microeconomic model do not agree in the sense that the macroeconomic explanations and predictions made based on the microeconomic model fail, there is reason to have a look at the relationships between micro and macro. If there is poor prediction at the macro level, a change in the micro model may solve the problem. Very few economists are inclined to reject the basic rationality assumption that governs all microeconomic models and adopt some behavioral theories in its place (Scitovsky, 1976; Alhadeff, 1982; Maital, 1982). Others propose changes in the utility function, usually involving the addition of terms. Modifications of the utility function will be treated in the next section of the chapter. There may also be other ways of solving the problem at the micro level.

Some macroeconomic models do not have microeconomic equivalents or assumptions as a foundation. This is, for example, true of balance of payment theory and the quantity theory of money. The quantity theory of money may be used to illustrate the problems to relate macroeconomics and psychology. Ever since the time of David Hume, the theory describes the relationship between the quantity of money and the price level, essentially as a positive correlation. It implies that if the money supply increases, the price level index will also go up. It has strong empirical support when long periods are considered. It is not derived from microeconomic theory and explications at the micro level are still being sought. Psychological research has primarily devoted interest to money as a symbol and can as yet hardly contribute to the theory.

Lucas (1986) who is well known for his work on the new classical macroeconomics which is based on rational expectations theory demonstrated how the quantity theory of money can be reconciled with the idea of adaptation and learning *without* psychology. His general view of the relationships between psychology and economic theory emerges in the following statement (Lucas, 1986, p.S403): 'the aggregative character of macroeconomic problems serves to emphasize the distance between much of economics and the concerns of individual psychology.' Maybe a macroeconomic theory of savings could do without any microeconomic foundation for a while. Maybe econometric models of savings over time and in cross sections could be developed without microeconomic assumptions that inhibit some thinking. Economic savings theory may be possible *without* microeconomic theory and *without* psychology of the individual.

One way of improving the power of a model is to restrict its use to a defined domain rather than to apply it to the whole population of consumers (cf. Musgrave, 1981). This was suggested by, for example, King (1985). Campbell and Mankiw (1989, 1990, 1991) estimated that about half the US population seemed to behave in accordance with the Life-Cycle Hypothesis. This implies that more than one model should be developed. The models should preferably be related to one another. It should be possible to order them along some dimension. The implication of a general model is that either all savings can be explained or that a set of variables, in the limiting case one variable, can be used to discriminate among groups of savers and that the total explanation and prediction will be improved by treating each group separately.

THE POTENTIAL ROLE OF PSYCHOLOGY

Adding Psychological Variables to the Life-Cycle Hypothesis

An improved microeconomic model seems to be what those economists who are dissatisfied with the present performance of the LCH are looking for. The microeconomic model has been altered in some fundamental ways over the years since its birth. Uncertainty has, for example, been added, replacing the original assumption of full information about future income and remaining lifetime. The LCH is constructed on the basis of a forward-looking, rational economic unit (possibly a human being) and so are the proposed additions to the theory. Browning and Lusardi (1996) said that there was no real alternative to LCH except behavioral models. The Behavioral Life-Cycle Hypothesis (Shefrin and Thaler, 1988) is the only behavioral model, based on an elaborated theory. It has inspired innovations in survey questionnaires, but unfortunately, its predictions have hardly been tested yet.

Can LCH be remedied by means of further psychological thinking? The proposed additions to LCH such as a bequest motive, a precautionary savings motive, and habit formation have psychological implications. The proxies that represent these concepts in empirical studies may work satisfactorily, but there is still the question whether superior psychological measures could be a complement so that saving processes could be better understood. Whether the assumptions behind the LCH are realistic may in the present context be a secondary consideration; the main question is whether the explanatory and predictive power can be improved through modifications in terms of psychological variables.

Psychology deals with individuals and does not possess any special competence for aggregating micro data to the macro level. There is as yet not much of a macropsychology (cf. Katona, 1979). When psychological concepts are introduced into economic analysis they are only a starting point. This implies that they do not mean the same in psychology and in economics. The psychological concepts discussed here have to be converted to economic concepts for at least mainstream economists to accept and apply them. They must be expressed in such a way that the concepts are compatible with the rationality postulate and related to the utility function. Leibenstein (1979) recognized this dilemma and propounded the use of psychological techniques rather than theory.

There are naturally limits to the use of psychological measurements. Psychological research usually involves collecting new data about individuals in controlled experiments or survey studies (correlational studies). People may refuse to submit to the procedures used in an experiment, openly by refusing to participate or covertly by faking answers. Survey studies of saving are faced with many difficulties. Intended respondents are quite often not inclined to participate. This is shown by huge non-response rates and among those who in principle participate, failure to answer certain questions. The data quality is improved through attempts to restore the representativeness of the samples by weighting. In both experiments and surveys, there are limits to what people can be asked to do so as not to exceed limited cognitive and memory capacity or to ask questions about things people rather keep secret. These potential deficiencies are something the researchers will have to live with. The psychological data may still be better than the so-called hard data that economists often prefer to work with. Data from income tax returns are not always superior to survey data on income. In fact, differences between income tax returns and survey data on income have been used to estimate amounts of tax evasion.

In microeconomics, the focus is on decisions to consume: consume now or later, that is, in the next or later budget periods. Decisions to save simply mean that consumption is postponed from the current to a later period. A genuine decision to save would be to commit oneself to put a certain amount in a bank account once or repeatedly. This decision may then be followed by a decision on how to finance the commitment, to what extent by curtailing consumption and to what extent by increasing income. Apart from precautionary savings, the ultimate goal is assumed to be consumption at some point in time. If there is a bequest motive, the time horizon stretches beyond the life expectancy (or the maximum possible life-length).

A direct focus on saving behavior rather than on consumption is conceivable, but it may be too much of a revolution in economics to try and construct a proper theory of saving in which saving is an activity of its own and not a residual after consumption. Savings are not assumed to give utility unless they are spent. From a psychological perspective, the idea is intriguing. The saving act and the existence of savings can certainly give rise to subjective utility. Some attempts to outline behavioral theories of saving have been made (see Katona, 1974, 1975; Groenland and van Veldhoven, 1993; Lunt and Livingstone, 1992; Daniel, 1997).

Somebody may be dissatisfied with an aspect of the microeconomic model and look for possible hints in fields like cognitive and social psychology. A potential role for psychology could then be to suggest changes in the microeconomic model better to accommodate deviant findings at the macroeconomic level and to furnish ideas for improved explanations and predictions at this level. Later in the chapter, I shall draw together some psychological concepts most of which have appeared in the economists' discussion of the psychology of saving and try to relate them to one another in a framework or schema. These concepts and their suggested relationships are aimed at inspiring more psychological research on saving and they may be seen as suggestions for possible elaboration of the microeconomic model.

The Economic Utility Formula and Psychological Variables

The main tenet of rationality is tied to the utility function: rationality is to maximize utility. The maximization of utility is subject to obvious constraints, for example, that total consumption cannot exceed total lifetime income (wealth). A second constraint is that consumption should be about equal in all budget periods. When the annuity income increases, more consumption is possible in each period, not only in the current period. According to the original LCH, the saving of one period is consumed in later periods so that all wealth is consumed during one's lifetime. There is no utility in savings or wealth. There is utility only when the wealth is consumed. There is no utility in work, rather disutility, but utility in leisure. The consumption unit is assumed to maximize the expected utility of lifetime consumption

$$Max \; EU(C_t, C_t...C_T)$$
$$subject \; to \; \sum_{i=1}^{T} C_i$$
$$and \quad C_t \approx C_2 \approx C_i$$

where $EU(.)$ is expected utility
   C_i is consumption at time$_i$
   T is end of lifetime
   LW is lifetime wealth, i.e., the sum of incomes and gifts received.

From a psychological point of view certain assumptions behind this model can be discussed

1. The assumption of maximizing behavior
2. Subjective expected utility and uncertainty
3. The role of past consumption.

The assumption of maximizing behavior

The basic economic assumption is that consumers maximize consumption utility over their life cycle. All that gives utility is consumption and nothing else gives rise to utility. The rationality assumption is so efficient that it can hardly be displaced by any contrary evidence from empirical analysis of actual behavior. There is a debate whether the utility function should be strictly defined and restricted to pure economic dimensions or could encompass psychic revenues and costs (see Sen, 1979; Simon, 1990)).

Proposing micro-micro economic theory for the study of firms, Leibenstein (1979) expressed it like this

> A position frequently taken is that maximization is invariably true if only we take into account (a) the right considerations and/or (b) enough considerations. Thus if on the basis of some consideration it appears that maximization has not taken place, then it is only because an additional consideration has not been taken into account. Thus if an economic agent has not appeared to have maximized profits, it is only because leisure has not been considered. If it had been, it would be reasonable to presume that the agent would have maximized the utility of a function made up of both profits and leisure. (Leibenstein, 1979, p.494)

With some sleight-of-hand, the utility function may accommodate additions of psychological concepts. The trouble with such concepts is that they obfuscate the elegant algorithm. Typically, it is difficult to find useful proxies and this means that there will be a need for special data. The use of psychological variables mostly presupposes special collections of data and special measuring techniques, which are expensive and often time- and labor-consuming.

In contrast to Scitovsky (1976, 1986) and Alhadeff (1982) who rejected the maximization of utility altogether, Leibenstein wanted to reduce the importance of the postulate of rationality in favor of exploring in more detail what happened in the firm and the household. He proposed that the best postulate 'would be one under which maximizing behavior is a special case, but non-maximization is accommodated for as a frequent mode of behavior' (Leibenstein, 1979, p.494). The essence of micro-micro theory is the focus on the individual and on what decides the individual's behavior. This means that individual differences are recognized and considered important.

An alternative to maximizing utility is to decide on the first acceptable alternative, Simon's satisficing principle, which is known as 'bounded rationality' theory. The following updated definition is given in a psychological dictionary (Reber, 1985):

> 1. A particular characteristic of human decision-making under conditions of extreme complexity. 2. A theory of cognitive processes as they are displayed under such conditions. In either usage, the reference is to the notion that in the face of complexity one cannot behave in a totally rational manner, simply because one's information-processing capacities are too limited to encompass all the knowledge required for such ideal decision-making. The theory of bounded rationality describes man as a decision-maker who circumscribes the situation by limiting (or 'bounding') the amount of information to be dealt with – often in creative and imaginative ways – and then behaving in a rational fashion with this limited knowledge base. (Reber, 1985, p.611)

The definition above is exclusively based on cognitive, information-handling processes which is in line with Simon's more recent predilection for cognitive science. In its early shape, the theory was more distinctly tied to searching and stopping at the first alternative with satisfactory properties rather than maximizing utility. The theory of bounded rationality has been found useful in many research contexts and there is now an enormous literature (for an overview, see Conlisk, 1996)

Simon (1990) conceded that the rationality concept as used by economists to describe and prescribe human adaptiveness had some advantages. 'Accepting this assumption [of rationality] enables economists to predict a great deal of behavior (correctly or incorrectly) without ever making empirical studies of human actors' (Simon, 1990, p.6).

Simon (1990) recommended the use of a few cognitive principles, such as recognition processes, heuristic search, and serial pattern recognition. Those are together equivalent to intelligence and can be used instead of optimality as the unifying principle. Just as in economics, the focus will then be on the environment: given an intelligent human being, the behavior in a certain environment should be predictable without empirical study. This raises the interesting question whether such individual behavior will be so well-defined and well-contained that it can be aggregated without empirical frequency studies of individual differences. Interestingly, Simon (1990) declared that in the long run the rationality concept in economics will have to take account of emotions

> But we are just beginning to see that, because of the strong dependence of intelligence on stored knowledge, cognitive and social psychology must be brought much closer together than they have been in the recent past. When we have made these new connections solid, the challenge will remain of bringing affect and emotion more centrally into the picture. (Simon, 1990, p.18)

In descriptions of how consumers grapple with financial problems, psychologists increasingly use something called *coping*. By coping is meant that an individual uses rational, conscious ways for dealing with anxiety-arousing situations. Whereas defensive strategies are directed at the anxiety itself rather than at its source, coping strategies are aimed at behaving in such a way that the anxiety is bridled. Worries about future finances can, for example, be checked through saving money. The meaning of the concept as it is actually used seems to vary and to involve, in the first place, the degree to which a household can cope with unexpected expenditure. Walker (1996) regarded financial coping as a subjective perception of being able to deal with life financially. She distinguished coping from *coping strategy*, which she saw as a reaction to feelings of poor coping.

Subjective expected utility and uncertainty

Economists prefer to use behavior in the market place as the sole indicator of preferences and of utility. They often find it difficult to accept measures of preferences where no actual choice behavior is involved. They have a general tendency to employ proxies based on objective data on market behavior rather than subjective measures. The interpretations of the behavior and consequently the proxies may be mistaken as Zeckhauser (1986) warned

> we should also consider how to extrapolate from what we observe to what we believe about individual's behavior. For example, if we mistakenly assume an individual is deciding under nature's uncertainties, when in fact he believes himself to be in a hostile world, we will interpret his behavior incorrectly. (Zeckhauser, 1986, p.S443)

The utility that the economist distinguishes may be totally different from the utility the individual experiences. The latter is what Kahneman (1994) called hedonic, 'experienced' utility. Zeckhauser (1986) gave a good overview of the opposing views of 'rationalists' and 'behavioralists' in economics, at the occasion placing himself in an intermediate position

> AXIOM 1. For any tenet of rational choice, the behavioralists (e.g. Amos Tversky) can produce a laboratory counterexample.
> AXIOM 2. For any 'violation' of rational behavior discovered in a real world market (e.g. the fact that hardware stores do not raise snow shovel prices shortly after a storm), the rationalists (e.g. Gary Becker) will be sufficiently creative to reconstruct a rational explanation.
> AXIOM 3. Elegant abstract formulations will be developed by both sides, frequently addressing the same points, but because there are sufficient degrees of freedom when creating a model, they will come to quite different conclusions. (Zeckhauser, 1986, p.S438)

There was a corollary to each axiom. The essence was that behavioralists should run laboratory studies on real world problems (rather than abstractions) and that rationalists should define the domains where their views seem to hold. Kahneman (1994, p.18) gave a succinct and proper summary of the problems of rationality and utility theory in the face of behavioral research: 'Research indicates that people are myopic in their decisions, may lack skill in predicting their future tastes, and can be led to erroneous choices by fallible memory and incorrect evaluation of past experience.'

Kahneman's conclusions suggest that the subjective expected utility of outcomes may be important to ascertain from participants in a decision situation. The fact that people do not recall their tastes in the past and are unsure about their future tastes is worth observing, but it does not exclude the possibility that outsiders can predict future tastes better than the person her- or himself. Kahneman proposed more research on the complexities of rationality, on when maximization was feasible, and on what deviations from maximization were most common.

The criticism that in reality people do not make decisions in the rational manner and that their time horizon is ordinarily limited to less than the remaining years of the life cycle is hardly valid if the questioned assumption is a fruitful way of modeling the decision process and no other better way can be found. This agrees with Friedman's (1953) positive economics. Lucas (1986, p.S402) further explained the position: 'technically, I think of economics as studying decision rules that are steady states of some adaptive process, decision rules that are found to work over a range of situations and hence are no longer revised appreciably as more experience accumulates.' These decision rules seem to resemble habits in psychological thinking. An implication of this reasoning is that people must be given a chance to learn in experimental situations. A common criticism of prospect theory and other cognitive psychology theory that goes against economic axioms is that the subjects are not given a chance to adapt (cf. Smith, 1991).

Lane (1991) gave an excellent review of the psychological research on money and presented constructive ideas on the role of money in market economies, including the function of money as a symbol. His purpose with the book was to replace utility with happiness and satisfaction with life or human development. Satisfaction and happiness are not necessarily the same. Lane (1991, p.9) proposed that subjective well-being had 'two overlapping measures, happiness and satisfaction with life-as-a-whole. More than a temporary mood, happiness is defined as a more or less enduring and comprehensive emotional state, whereas life satisfaction is more of a judgment, a cognitive appraisal of one's life.' A number of EU survey reports provide data on opinions and on reported satisfaction with life and happiness in life (see, for example, Commission of the European Communities, 1993). In a few cases, some analyses of what factors correlate with these two subjective measures have been made. They indicate that happiness and satisfaction with life in the first place are related to health and social life and that income has great, but not dominating importance.

The role of past consumption

Currently, Duesenberry's relative income hypothesis is often interpreted as the highest past consumption level. This idea is not taken up in LCH. When Duesenberry launched his hypothesis for consumption and saving, the focus of interest changed from current income to past experience. PIH and LCH extended the income concept to future income, i.e., permanent income and life-cycle income. Earlier income was not given any explicit role, except maybe what is captured in the formation of income expectations.

Extrapolation of earlier income changes is a commonly used way of estimating income expectations. When there is no new information, extrapolation of earlier experience may give the same results as rational expectations theory presumes. Income uncertainty is often measured as the variability of earlier income. Earlier income dominates in expectations of future income unless there is shocking new information. The utility of earlier consumption is presumably important for future consumption. It may be represented by current preferences through habit formation, but more attention to how rewarding consumption under earlier stages of the life cycle has been may give important insights into saving. Habits or routines make up most of behavior.

Some Examples of Extended Utility Functions

Below are some examples of how psychological or similar concepts have been made compatible with the rationality assumption. The first example stems from the use of dissonance theory. Akerlof and Dickens (1982) made the assumptions of dissonance theory commensurate with the rationality postulate and used the new theory to explain seemingly irrational behavior in situations where physical safety was at issue. Behavior influenced by cognitive dissonance was seen as rational and predictable. A prerequisite was that people were assumed to have preferences not only for different world states which is the usual utility function, but also for their own beliefs about world states, that they could choose their beliefs at least up to a point and that the beliefs once chosen were stable over time. Incidentally, dissonance theory is in psychology a rather controversial theory.

Shefrin and Thaler (1988) showed an example of introducing psychological variables into the utility function. They distinguished between the utility of a short-run maximizer, labeled the doer, and the utility function of a long-run maximizer, labeled the planner. If the planner prevails and there is no cost for exercising willpower, the Behavioral LCH is identical to LCH. The predictions of the two models diverge because this condition is not likely to be met. If there is no doer with short-run utility maximization, the planner rules and there is no extra need for exerting willpower. The authors maintain that in reality there is typically a conflict between short-run and long-run interest. What is of particular interest in this context is the addition of a term for willpower to the utility function.

The willingness to refrain from consumption is assumed to decrease with consumption level and income. In order to minimize the effort for each choice situation the planner works with internal and external rules. The internal rules are self-imposed and require more willpower than the external rules. An example of the former is a self-imposed defense to borrow money for current consumption. External rules are, for example, pension schemes where the employer pays part of the premiums and the employee another part.

Lindbeck (1997) handled the influence of social norms on willingness to work in the following inequality by introducing a term for disutility

$$u\,[(1-t)w_i] > u(T) + \mu - v(x)$$

where $u(.)$ is the utility from income
   t is the tax rate
   w_i is the wage rate of individual i
   T is a lump-sum transfer available to individuals who do not work
   μ is the difference between the utility derived from leisure and the intrinsic utility of work (including social interaction with colleagues at work)
   $v(.)$ is the disutility from deviating from the social norm
   x is the population share of transfer recipients.

Similar reasoning was applied to social norms and savings. The social influence is analogous to what Leibenstein (1950) referred to as 'the bandwagon effect'. The inequality captures what Hardy's laborers discussed in 1891 (see p.278).

Smith (1991) argued that the market, that is, appropriate institutions could compensate for the lack of rationality of individuals who had limited cognitive capacity and he showed experimental evidence in support of his view. Pingle and Day (1996) who also presented experimental evidence introduced another line of thought. They demonstrated that deviations from rationality in decision making could be a way of avoiding decision costs (use of resources like time, energy, costs of information search), what they referred to as *economizing*.

Pingle and Day (1996) distinguished six alternatives to economic rationality which all involved avoiding decision costs (and which could have been taken from almost any textbook in social psychology): (1) trial and error, (2) imitation, (3) following an authority, (4) habit, (5) unmotivated search, (6) hunch. Whereas the first four are self-explicatory and close to common sense, the last two are a little difficult to interpret. Number 5 seems to be to follow impulses and sometimes to yield to curiosity. Hunch is the capacity to economize – in some situations – without consciously reasoning and it is as-sumed to be based on intuition that can be sharpened by experience. These ideas which are similar to those in psychological research on problem solving are not explicitly related to the utility function and rather serve as explanations of deviations from maximizing utility. The consideration of decision costs resembles Robbins's sober note: 'The marginal utility of not bothering about marginal utility is a factor of which account has been taken by the chief writers on the subjective theory of value from Böhm-Bawerk onwards' (Robbins [1935] 1979, p.42).

These examples illustrate some ways of making psychological concepts compatible with the rationality assumption. As said before, some economists find the additions to the utility function to be too permissive. The consistency criterion that Lionel Robbins emphasized may allow such modifications, but the additions may be seen as too ad hoc.

A PSYCHOLOGICAL SCHEMA FOR SAVING BEHAVIOR

Apparently, the psychology of saving that emerged in the historical overview did not directly influence the development of the leading savings theory. Additions to it of the uncertainty concept, the precautionary and bequest mo-tives have brought it closer to the earlier psychology of saving albeit mathe-matized almost to invisibility. When possible modifications of the theory are discussed, it seems appropriate to ask whether more of the earlier insights could be exploited, in the first place to give better descriptions of saving be-havior. A prerequisite is that the concepts and relationships between concepts can be subjected to measurement, direct or by good proxies. Modern psy-chology can supplement with theory and techniques for data collection.

A summary of what psychology can offer to explain saving behavior is presented as a box-and-arrow schema (Figure 8.1). It shows how the concepts found in the economic literature can be related to one another. While it can be seen as an attempt at making a LISREL or EQS type of model whose fit can be assessed against empirical data if such are available for all variables, it is primarily aimed at suggesting variables and relationships for potential use in empirical analyses of saving that are more elaborate than has been the case so far.

The schema starts with an individual realizing that there will be future needs that presuppose some restraint on current consumption. This can alter-natively be called expectation formation. The schema uses *perceived goals* rather than motives to designate what characterizes future needs. The future needs or goals are here restricted to four: *cash management*, *security*, *non-poverty status*, and *bequest*.

The *cash management* goal embodies a desire to have money to pay fore-seeable expenditures. It is close to Keynes's 'transaction motive' and involves that people know that they have to make future payments, such as installment payments, interest and amortization payments on mortgages and that they put money aside to cope with the obligations. The money is before long withdrawn from the account and then a new accumulation process starts. On average, a household or an individual can have considerable amounts of interest-bearing money in order to have adequate, liquid resources for paying foreseen debts.

The *security* goal, which corresponds to the precautionary motive in economics, is the short-run need for buffer capital and the long-run need for retirement funds. The precautionary motive is much discussed and is often seen as an inevitable addition to LCH. It is used to explain why many people leave considerable wealth at their death. They are assumed not to want to run out of money and they misjudge how much is needed. The two dimensions of security, the desirability of having a buffer amount for unforeseen ill events and concern about old age clearly vary over the life cycle. Young households with children, facing immediate, unforeseen expenditures, may rather rely on a promptly available buffer account in the bank than on asking for welfare contributions. Upper middle age people may in the first place think of what they need for a pleasurable old age and restrain their consumption now to have more to enjoy later. Security considerations may involve concern for the lone survivor's consumption. Such considerations are not included in the bequest motive according to Hurd (1990). When old-age pension systems are shaky in modern welfare societies, the consequence is a rise in savings.

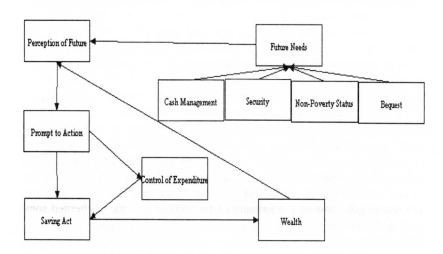

Figure 8.1 A Psychological Schema for the Study of Saving Behavior

The *nonpoverty status* goal involves the desire to have adequate means for status reasons and to avoid dying poor; the minimum amount is what is enough for a decent funeral. Marshall pointed to the importance of the status wealth gave even after death: '[Men] who nourish a contempt for showy expenditure and desire to be found at their death richer than they had been thought to be' (Marshall [1890] 1947, p.229). In the 19th century and probably also earlier, it was a shame to live in a poorhouse and be buried at a poor man's funeral. It may be a middle-class phenomenon and not compatible with welfare state thinking to restrain consumption so as not to die in poverty. As distinguished from the security goal, the nonpoverty status goal is a status goal that can also be expressed in this way: 'Money is sought and valued, not only for its purchasing power but also as a symbol of achievement, of success, of society's appreciation of one's services; and this other function of money does not fit into the economist's model of rationality' (Scitovsky, 1986, p.71). Status-seekers may indulge in conspicuous consumption in Veblen's sense. This is apparently in conflict with some aspects of the nonpoverty status goal. Conspicuous consumption that is not ruinous may, however, mean visible signs of having money and being non-poor. Fisher (1930, pp.87-8) recognized this: 'The most fitful of the causes at work is probably fashion. This at the present time acts, on the one hand, to stimulate men to save and become millionaires, and, on the other hand, to stimulate millionaires to live in an ostentatious manner.' Fisher noted that fashion was hard to predict and could involve that it became disgraceful for the millionaires to die rich (as Carnegie had expressed it).

The *bequest* goal is the wish to contribute something to survivors, a saving motive that Rae, Marshall and Fisher strongly emphasized. Parents want to provide as well as they can for their offspring as long as they themselves are alive and after their own death. This may keep them from dissaving and may even motivate continued saving after retirement. Potential bequests can be used to manipulate expectant inheritors according to the bequest-exchange hypothesis (Bernheim, 1991; Bernheim et al., 1985). The prospect of a bequest can be used to buy favors now. Gifts and bequests may be something more or less imposed by the offspring who can put a lot of pressure on their parents not to waste money on themselves and strictly to control their expenditures. Children can be imagined to withhold their love and care if they cannot obtain gifts now and inheritances later. People who have inherited some wealth often seem to have a feeling of obligation to leave at least as much as they themselves inherited (Barlow et al., 1966). Rawls (1973) applied the general principle of reciprocity in this case. Some people deviate from the norm and waste their wealth or like the philosopher Ludwig Wittgenstein give it away to purposes considered better than their own use.

The four goals are not mutually exclusive and they may operate together. A time dimension can be added to the perception of future needs. What Marshall said about the importance of imagining the future is worth noting: 'that his [the person's] willingness so to wait depends on his habit of vividly realizing the future and providing for it' (Marshall, 1890, p.233). The *time horizon* varies for different persons and may for the same person vary for the different needs. While the time horizon for cash management is probably often less than a year, it may be many decades for security needs. The importance of these needs naturally varies over age, with family composition and socioeconomic status (cf. Fisher, 1930).

The recognition of future needs and possibly inadequate future resources (the arrow from wealth signifies a comparison) does not always or for every person trigger a *prompt to action*. Here the willpower or self-control or some other volitional concept comes in. If self-control is an enduring characteristic of a person, it is a personality trait. The self-control can be measured and used as an indicator of a prompt to act, singly or in combination with other measures.

The individual may feel that current expenditures are too high and start *controlling expenditures*, thus opening a possibility for saving money. Keeping consumption at a certain level that is lower than the available resources permit, may be a primary goal and saving rather a consequence, a kind of residual saving (Katona, 1975). Or the individual makes a decision to save, for example, by committing her-/himself to transfer some amount of money every month to a savings account either by fixed deductions from wages/salary or by personal delivery to the financial institution. A conceivable curtailing of expenditure is then a consequence. Or the decision may be to create a surplus for the future by increasing income through working more overtime, getting an extra job, or having more members of the household working.

The *saving act* is something specific like putting money in a bank account, buying stock or mutual funds or bonds. What in economics is subsumed under the single label of saving, in the saver's mind seems to be divided into more than one mental account. Shefrin and Thaler (1988) suggested that for income and wealth there were three common mental accounts with differing probabilities of being spent: (a) current spendable income, (b) current assets, and (c) future income. The temptation to spend a marginal dollar is assumed to vary for the three types of mental accounts. Current income is the most tempting to spend, that is, it is characterized by the highest propensity to consume. It is followed by current assets, and then future wealth.

People apparently distinguish between different components in savings (as defined by differences in net worth) and these components may be said to be different mental accounts. When respondents are asked about what they count as saving, they generally agree that certain categories like increases in bank savings accounts are saving (see Tables 2.2 and 2.3). They also agree in rejecting the increased sales value of home equity as saving. There is some disagreement about the change in share values, but overall changes in 'paper' values do not seem to be counted. This evokes the idea that each household should be presented with a specified calculation of net wealth change during a year and asked about each item whether they would classify it as saving or not. In fact, people have been asked what of a list of acts they include in 'saving' (the VSB Panel) and which activities they found most typical of saving (cf. Groenland et al., 1996).

More variables can be added to the schema. Values which are long-run, stable phenomena can be assumed to influence the prompt to action and so can personality traits. In fact, the 'prompt to action' in the schema can be enlarged into a psychological model based on Ajzen's Theory of Planned Behavior (Ajzen, 1991; also see Figure 7.1) or on Katona's ability-and-willingness-to-save model. The prompt to action can be viewed in various ways. It can be seen as decision making based on expected utility or the value function of prospect theory. It can be seen as a question of volition, the amount of effort required to link cognition and behavior, 'vividly realizing the future' (Marshall, 1890), ideation in Mischel's (1984) terms that strengthens or weakens self-control.

The prompt to action has often been interpreted as self-control, which is assumed to be a stable characteristic of a person and thus equal to a personality trait. Shefrin and Thaler (1988) viewed self-control as disutility since effort was necessary to exert willpower. The trouble is that there can also be disutility in consuming so much that there is no room for saving, giving birth to a perpetual, bad feeling of neglecting future needs. The utility of consumption may have a maximum that is lower than the budget period's (annuity) share of the life-cycle income.

The concepts used in the psychological schema are psychological, not economic. The uncertainties of economic theory do not exactly correspond to the perception of future needs in the model. Economists focus on three uncertainties, those of income and employment, health, and length of life. The psychological model relates the uncertainties to household or individual goals whose attainment can be more or less threatened. The attainment of the goals is affected by the three economic uncertainties, but the attention is drawn to consequences rather than to causes.

The Schema as a Basis for a Behavioral Theory of Saving

The schema provides an integrative framework for psychological studies of saving and savings. It shows relationships among the concepts that appear meaningful given the present state of knowledge. It is not meant to be exhaustive and leaves room for additions. The basic idea is that saving is a function of both perception of some need and of provision for the future. The vital link between the perception and the provision has hardly been investigated at all in spite of the fact that John Rae as early as 1834 drew attention to the 'prompt to action' that mediated between the desire for accumulation and actual saving.

The schema is not a model in itself. It can be used to select psychological variables for inclusion in psychological and economic models. Economists can select sets of concepts from the schema, if desirable make them compatible with economic theory in ways that have been tried before, and thereby possibly enrich the theory and improve explanation and prediction.

Pure psychological models can in principle be constructed using the schema. As far as I know there are as yet no such models of saving behavior. Present reactions to foreseen or expected future events and preparations for the future have rarely been studied in human psychology. For economic-psychological research, the schema comprises psychological variables that can supply elements of models in which subjective concepts are combined with economic and demographic variables. Economic indicators such as unemployment rates and Consumer Price Indexes can be combined with the psychological variables. They can also be subjectively assessed as threats or promises. At any rate, it is feasible to combine objectively assessed socio-economic variables with subjective psychological variables in the same models. From detailed and valid descriptions of saving and savers, a behavioral theory of saving can emerge in the long run. The intensive and comprehensive research on revising the LCH can give a stimulus to such an undertaking.

In my view, there are two good reasons for a psychology of saving that does not necessarily involve economics, but that could give new insights to economists as well as to psychologists. In the first place, the schema suggests certain questions of fundamental psychological interest: How do people perceive the future and when does perception lead to action? What processes are involved? There is no escape from dealing with volition and self-control.

Secondly, more attention should be given to the hedonic aspects of saving. This means that saving (and non-saving!) as a process and the significance of the savings to the individual/household should be studied. Fisher (1930) made a distinction between *enjoyment income* and *money income*. This means that a difference is made between a hedonic income concept, which is close to the one used by utilitarians, and a pure economic concept with objective indicators. Studying the former is the task of the psychologist who at least today can rely on subjective scales that have been developed after Fisher wrote his book. The link to hedonism is reflected in recent discussions of the psychology of utility. Kahneman (1994) maintained that there are several kinds of utility and suggested that psychologists should pay more attention to what he calls 'experience utility'. It refers to the hedonic quality of choice alternatives and is distinguished from 'preference utility' which is revealed in actual choice behavior. Kahneman's 'experience utility' is clearly related to Fisher's enjoyment income. Kahneman pointed out important consequences of the differences between the two types of utility. This leads to the question of what the hedonic utility of saving is. After all, there are psychological methods for finding out about the meaning of things and events.

Why are researchers in basic psychology so inattentive to the psychology of saving? In their research, they invent stimuli and response categories from many fields of human endeavor, but hardly ever anything directly related to saving behavior. Part of the answer probably lies in the behavioristic approach that long dominated. The future could only be predicted by interpolation of observable behavior and this limited the researchers' interest in reactions to the future. The new cognitive psychology focused on information processing as a present event rather than as formation of expectations. Attitude researchers have been busy studying all conceivable aspects of consumption, except the time dimension, and never paid any attention to postponement of consumption and other dimensions of saving. Volition, whether it is called 'self-control', 'self-regulation', or 'action control' is again becoming an acceptable area of research and the area seems to be expanding (Kuhl and Beckmann, 1985; Sjöberg, 1998). Why are questions relating to controlling expenditures and saving rarely or never included in the questionnaires used to study self-regulation? More basic research on the psychology of saving could contribute significantly to theory in cognitive psychology, personality and motivation theory, and social psychology, the area depending on which problems are studied.

Concluding Remarks

The common economic definition of savings as the excess of income over consumption expenditure and similar definitions implying that saving is what is left after consumption are strictly speaking not consistent with the idea of independent decisions to save. While these definitions are passive, the popular view of saving which is also found in classical economic texts associates saving with refraining from consumption, postponing consumption to a later date. This view of saving entails other measures of individual household saving than differences in net worth.

There are good arguments for more psychological study of the saving process, something that is more in line with what Lea et al. (1993) recommended (and actually practiced) in the study of debt-making. Savings have a meaning to the individual. What savings mean to different persons and households, to what extent and how they are related to certain future goals is a significant task for research. The results could be useful for those who want to understand saving and contribute to the economic theory of saving.

Maximizing consumption is not necessarily the long-run aim in life for most people. Satisficing refers to finding an acceptable level of consumption that may presuppose control of expenditure. If people want improvement over the life-cycle, they will probably be prepared to postpone some consumption in order to enjoy more in the future. Saving is then not felt to be negative, a matter of now imposing pain on oneself in order to exult later, but rather something that admits savoring of the future pleasure (Loewenstein and Prelec, 1993). The idea was well expressed by the classical economist Jevons: 'It is certain that a very large part of what we experience in life depends not on the actual circumstances of the moment so much as on the anticipation of future events. As Mr. Bain says, "The foretaste of pleasure is pleasure begun: every actual delight casts before it a corresponding ideal."' (Jevons [1871] 1911, pp.33-4). Mr Bain was the leading British psychologist whom Jevons often referred to when he developed marginal utility theory.

9. Implications for Studying and Influencing the Consumer

While savings unaided by luck will ultimately enrich the saver, the process is slow as compared with the rapid enrichment which comes from the good fortune of those who assume risks and then happen to guess right. Likewise, while millions of people lose their small properties by thriftlessness, the more rapid impoverishment comes from guessing wrong. This will often turn a rich man into a poor man within a few years and sometimes within a few days.

Fisher (1930, p.336)

THE PURPOSE OF THE CHAPTER

This last chapter spells out implications of the psychology of saving in three respects:

1. Implications for policy makers and marketers of financial products and services
2. Implications for consumers who want to save more
3. Implications for research, basic as well as applied.

The chapter starts with some implications for practitioners who want to influence saving behavior whether for economic policy reasons or for attempts to steer savings into certain institutions. The state of the art of the psychology of saving may still leave something to be desired, but some implications can already be useful to consider for government policy makers, financial marketers, and even consumers who think about provision for the future. The second part of the chapter deals with continued research on saving behavior. It underlines some of the main ideas in earlier chapters. The central points concern research on how people become more or less forward-looking and build up expectations and on how volitional factors turn expectations into consistent actions. This means continued exploration of how thrift affects the outcomes of forward-looking.

WORK AND CONSUMPTION AS THE CITIZEN'S MAJOR LINKS TO THE ECONOMY

Saving is a question of the balance between income and spending on consumption. The individual household has two major links to the economy of a country: work and consumption; consumption includes leisure. Lea (1992) stressed that both links were of great interest for research in economic psychology. Saving behavior is closely related to both links since it depends on how much of income is consumed. Employment conditions, in the first place wages but also workplace conditions, affect consumption. Consumption may affect employment, e.g. the willingness to do overtime and extra work in order to buy a new car. Even in economies where unemployment is high which is at present the case in many EU countries, those who have employment often have a chance to work overtime or do extra work. Providing for the future is usually thought of as postponing consumption, which presupposes that expenditures are held down. Not spending all the money at present has an alternative: to increase the income. That can be accomplished by working extra hours, take overtime work, and moonlighting, having more than one job. Some people save extra income and spend only the regular income (see Table 2.5).

The proportion of women who have gainful employment has increased in many countries over the last decades. This means more affluence in many households at the same time as certain expenditures may go up such as costs for childcare. It is not clear how the fact that there are two income-earners instead of one affects savings. So-called double career couples may be a special case. In these couples, both parties are not only gainfully employed, but actually strive for promotion.

Over the last decade or so unemployment has become an increasing problem in many countries, the USA and Japan being among the exceptions. Many people and, in particular, young people face very high probabilities of being unemployed at least for some time. Good schooling decreases the probability. The effect of unemployment on a household's consumption and way of living is important. Little is known about the saving of the unemployed. Apparently, people who have saved earlier still try to save. There is anecdotal evidence from bank managers that some savers keep up automatic saving even when unemployed. Expectations or fears of unemployment are forceful motivators to save. Unemployment usually means such a reduction of income that little or no saving is possible. How unemployment develops seems decisive for some saving, but the effects may be mixed. On the one hand, the fear of losing employment encourages saving. On the other hand, less financial resources as a consequence of being unemployed tend to decrease savings.

CHANGING ECONOMIC CONDITIONS

In comparison with abstract economic theory, detailed empirical theory runs a greater risk of becoming obsolete as the economic environment changes. Katona's work is still seen as fundamental in economic psychology. Have the US and other economies changed so much that Katona's ideas are no longer valid and interesting? In 1980, Katona himself made the following sober assessment: 'Behavioral economics, developed in an era of spreading affluence and optimism, is confronted with new tasks in an era of limited growth and uncertainty' (Katona, 1980, p.16). Criticisms against Katona's use of simple expectation and attitude models have been raised by Lea et al. (1987) and more recently by Lunt (1996a, 1996b). In both cases, a broader use of modern psychology is requested, in Lunt's critique primarily social psychology and in Lea et al.'s critique a wider array of economic and psychological variables.

In Katona's defense it can be said that the ICS gets more attention than ever both by the mass media, decision and policy makers and by economic researchers. The basic model for consumption–saving stating that consumption–saving is a function of ability and willingness to consume/save is still valid if both ability and willingness are interpreted in a broad sense and thinking from modern cognitive, volitional, and social psychology is used. Close reading of some of Katona's works reveals many ideas that are even now applicable and testable on consumption and saving. No doubt, there is plenty of room for new, more elaborate theory that incorporates more of modern psychology.

In recent years, saving ratios have become positive and increased in many countries that had negative or low positive saving ratios before. Changing age composition in the populations is one suggested cause. If there is an increase in the relative weight of the age group 45 to 65, an increase in savings is expected on the basis of the LCH, that is, the hump-shaped curve of lifetime saving. Another cause behind the changed ratios is the inverse of one suggested reason for low saving ratios. The introduction of social security nets encompassing retirement pensions, social welfare benefits, and health insurance meant that the potency of some earlier instigators to saving decreased. Now that the welfare systems are being overhauled and shrunk in many Western countries, people begin to feel that they have to save for future needs. While this in economic terms can be called increased uncertainty, to a psychologist it appears to be perceived risk that causes fear unless something is done.

In countries like the United Kingdom and Sweden the market for private retirement pension schemes has expanded as faith in public pension schemes has declined. An interesting aspect of saving for old age is the form of saving. Bank interest rates on savings and other bank accounts have decreased to a low level and even if the low interest rates are accompanied by low inflation, the real dividend may be discouragingly low. The development involves that the borderline between saving and investing is becoming increasingly blurred. First, the bond market and now the stock market attract new customers many of whom have little experience of investment and are slow to learn. This has implications for financial institutions and possibly for consumer policy makers.

Tax reforms usually involve lower taxes for middle- and high-income earners since they pay more tax and suffer more from high marginal tax rates. The propensity to save is normally higher in these categories (middle-class mentality) and such tax reforms tend to increase total savings. The Swedish tax reform of 1991 which meant a decrease in income tax (and increase in most other taxes) is a case in point. It was followed by a considerable increase in the savings ratio (see Figure 2.1) and research suggests that the income tax cut had a significantly stimulating effect (Agell et al., 1995).

In a somewhat speculative vein, I think that much seems to speak for increased total savings in many countries in the near future. A combination of factors that influence saving will tend to increase saving in the next few years and probably much longer:

1. Wavering public old-age pension systems. The insecurity is due to earlier over-optimism of continued growth and to larger aging population segments with longer life expectancy
2. Reduced social benefits which will not be paid out as promptly and certainly as earlier
3. Reduced compensation schemes in sickness insurance and unemployment insurance
4. Attractive investment possibilities, used by new population groups
5. Increased political and consumer attention to environmental problems which will involve restriction on consumption of certain commodities.

In accordance with psychological theory, people will act on expectations of reduced benefits and faltering general pension systems. Rational expectations theory would certainly make the same prediction.

Against higher saving the following conditions speak:

1. Taxes on savings, including reduced compensations because of income- and asset-related floors for social benefits (Hubbard et al., 1994)
2. Low interest rates
3. Spending habits are hard to break
4. People may expect that future consumption will be much more expensive and hurry to buy and consume when the commodity is still comparatively cheap and within reach.

If savings increase, it becomes even more important than now to follow up where the money goes. Banks, insurance companies, and savings societies like building societies in the UK compete for deposits. They are active in marketing their services (see Sonuga-Barke and Webley, 1993, for a study of financial advertising). Banks and stock brokers market bonds, shares, and mutual funds. Savers who have experienced inflation and want to save for retirement in a rather distant future are likely to become interested in investing money in securities rather than just keep it in bank accounts. This is an important area for research since many of the new investors may be bewildered due to lack of knowledge and experience. They will need good advice.

A FEW SIMPLE RECIPES FOR STIMULATING (OR DISCOURAGING) SAVING

The modified LCH contains ideas that are essential for a psychological understanding of saving in spite of the fact that the specific psychological content is inadequate. The assumption that the consumer is forward-looking and has a time preference are such ideas with many implications. A deficiency in the theory is the lack of differentiation between people. If the existence of individual differences is acknowledged this leads to the question whether groups with similar characteristics can be distinguished and whether market segmentation is desirable. Different segments in the population may behave differently, have varying time horizons and time preferences.

The LCH is not a good description at the household/individual level. Just adding components to the utility function appears ad hoc and a savior in need (Leibenstein, 1979). The theory tends to make the consumer too sophisticated. 'The problem seems to be that while economists have gotten increasingly sophisticated and clever, consumers have remained decidedly human. This leaves open the question of whose behavior we are trying to model' (Thaler, 1990, p.203). The use of mathematics to express psychological processes may have gone too far. There is probably an end to what can be squeezed out of the rationality assumption, using increasingly advanced mathematics.

The verbal explanations of saving behavior given by some of the early economists when they explained thrift, can, combined with modern cognitive, motivational and social psychology bring forth a number of ideas that might be worth considering by financial marketers and policy makers. The suggestions in the following may seem vague, but they should be viewed as starting points for planning of relevant applied research rather than recipes for direct action. In many ways, increasing people's propensity to save involves a change of life-style and is a long-term proposition unless strong environmental factors drastically change and incite immediate changes in behavior.

Increase the Vividness of the Image of the Future

such pleasures as may now be enjoyed, generally awaken a passion strongly prompting to the partaking of them. The actual presence of the immediate object of desire in the mind, by exciting the attention, seems to rouse all the faculties, as it were, to fix their view on it, and leads them to a very lively conception of the enjoyments which it offers to their instant possession. The prospects of future good, which future years may hold out to us, seem at such a moment dull and dubious, and are apt to be slighted, for objects on which the daylight is falling strongly, and showing us in all their freshness just within our grasp.

Rae ([1834] 1905, p.54)

The first comments here are applicable to market communication and may not suggest any new product development. Among the reasons given by Böhm-Bawerk for people's tendency to overvalue the present good as against the future good, his suggestion of a constantly undervaluing perspective of the future is of particular interest here. One of the reasons why people tended to underestimate the value of a future good was the fact that its image was not so vivid: 'roughly in the way that the momentary weaker feeling vanquished the future stronger feeling only because the latter, although present, is not vivid and potent enough so as to be able to occupy our mind for itself' (Böhm-Bawerk, [1888] 1912, p.448). Juxtaposing this with Böhm-Bawerk's ideas about the circumstances lying behind the undervaluation suggests that lack of imagination and ability to understand and uncertainty about the future can explain the lack of vividness.

Marshall ([1890] 1990, p.233) said that the accumulation of wealth was dependent on man's *prospectiveness*: that is, his faculty of vividly realizing the future. The growth of wealth involved in general a deliberate waiting for a pleasure which a person had the power of commanding in the immediate present. The willingness so to wait depended on the habit of 'vividly realizing the future and providing for it'. Prospectiveness resembles imagination with the particular addition that the imagination refers to the future and does not include the past. It is striking that Marshall like Böhm-Bawerk stressed the vividness of the image. This carries over to Mischel's (1984) findings on the role of ideation in delay of gratification studies.

In my youth and even more in my parents' youth at the beginning of the century there was a lot of propaganda for saving, primarily disseminated by the savings banks. The savings banks were very active in their marketing to school children. The themes used were vividly, even dramatically expounded and the moral tinge was clearly articulated. If these activities were influenced by the thinking of Böhm-Bawerk and Marshall, present-day marketing efforts rather bear a taste of Keynes. Saving is not wholly appropriate according to this thinking and both financial marketers and politicians feel apologetic about recommending it. Bank advertising seems to put the main emphasis on the monetary profit aspect of saving and be more directed towards the inves- tor-minded than towards small savers. I may be wrong but I have a strong feeling that there is much more advertising for borrowing than for saving and that the ads give a very vivid image of what can be acquired by means of a loan. My impressions are of course based on limited observations, primarily in the Netherlands and Sweden. In most of the many editions, Samuelson's famous textbook on economics displayed much of a Keynesian position on the detrimental effects of saving, but it has in recent editions paid more re- spect to saving (*The Economist*, August 23rd, 1997, p.60).

It seems obvious that it is important to make the images of the utility of savings and future consumption rather than of immediate consumption vivid and clear to people. In social psychology there is some evidence that asking people to imagine the experience they will get if a certain act is performed facilitates conversion (Gregory et al., 1982; cf. Kahneman and Varey, 1991: experience utility and preference utility). Fisher (1930) was confident that the impatience to spend money rather than invest could be mitigated by means of education and training. He prescribed remedial actions for cognitive as well as for volitional deficiencies.

Segmentation and Saver Groups

In marketing, segmentation theory occupies an important position. The gen- eral idea behind this concept is that the total population of a country is het- erogeneous with respect to certain behavior, usually related to the demand for a good, and that it is possible to distinguish population segments that include people who are similar in this respect. Typically, in the first applications the segments were based on what benefits consumers thought that they got from the good. The distinguishing characteristic is still often psychological.

What individual differences count? To an economist economic differences such as those in income and wealth, and age and possibly gender differences are taken into account when data permit. The psychologist adds differences in terms of personal characteristics like information-processing skills, attitudes, values and personality traits. In my thinking, differences in expectations can be of great interest for segmentation purposes.

Whether one particular segment or a set of segments is chosen for further work, the idea is that the marketer is concerned with the desires of each seg- ment in terms of service development and market communication. If the ex- isting product already fulfills the needs of the segment, the main task is to fit the market communication to the characteristics of the target group. The economists' limited access to data was and still is to some extent due to qualms about data that are collected from individuals through any type of questioning (an exception is the reliance on data from income tax returns). Even if the data are accepted, an often insurmountable difficulty is that the collection of such data tends to entail expenses that may seem high.

My contention is that explanations and predictions of saving can be improved if the population is divided into groups – which like in marketing could be called 'segments' – and that the groups are analyzed and treated separately. Suppose that self-control is fundamental to saving. People with a high degree of self-control save more than people with low self-control. It is perhaps possible to squeeze a preference for controlling oneself and expenditures into the common utility function and thus distinguish segments. Shefrin and Thaler (1988) proposed two utility functions, one dominated by long-term self-control, the other by myopic lack of self-control. The subjective discount rate or time preference expresses much the same idea as self-control, only it is hardly likely that a single discount rate could catch the important differences among people. The population can be divided into a number of segments, say, three or four, on the basis of degree of self-control. The propensity to save or to consume could be studied for each segment and the variations in size of the segments be observed over time. In principle, it should be possible to assess time preferences in the population from time to time and notice changes which could then be represented in forecast equations.

In Chapter 5 the idea of saver groups was introduced. The four saver groups used in some Swedish studies (Wahlund and Wärneryd, 1987; Wahlund, 1991) are not the only conceivable groups. Gunnarsson and Wahlund (1997) reported on seven groups of investors who differed in their risk propensity and in the kind of investments. The four groups of savers will now be used to illustrate how different characteristics can evoke ideas about possible reactions to economic policy measures and marketing efforts.

The wealth managers are those who are really intent on capital accumulation. Most of them want as a minimum to preserve the value of their assets. They seem to be moderate risk takers in the sense that they appreciate the higher risk involved in more profitable investments and they keep the risk taking within the bounds they can well afford (Wärneryd, 1996c). This should be a reminder to financial advisors some of whom have been responsible for advising clients to invest into risky assets, with worst outcomes beyond the means of the client. A few of the wealth managers are gamblers. Many of them save for retirement years with something extra.

The goal savers appreciate safety in their placement of money and a reasonably high interest rate. Long-term goal savers accept savings accounts with restrictions on withdrawal if it is combined with higher interest rates. Investing in securities may be possible, but only if the risk is low.

While buffer savers praise capital with high liquidity they want some safety rules that keep them from using up the capital. Katona (1960, 1975) found that buffer capital was considered to be off limits and that withdrawals were considered as temporary loans that had to be paid back as soon as possible. The last argument may serve to explain why people to some extent persist in saving money even when the real interest rate is negative because of inflation and capital income taxation. A lowered interest rate may even lead to increased individual saving, for example, if someone saves in order to have a certain level of income in the future (Pareto [1909] 1971, p.323). Marshall saw interest as a reward for waiting, although conceding that saving could in some cases be so important that people were even willing to pay for having the security of being able to make future payments. People's sensitivity to changes in interest rates appear to depend on their saving motives.

Cash managers who primarily want safe repositories for money that they will sooner or later have to pay out may later in their life cycle turn into savers as buffer and goal savers. Some of them will end up as wealth managers.

In the psychological schema for saving behavior, I suggested four goals for saving: cash management, security (short- and long-run), nonpoverty status, and bequest. Suppose that research shows that there is good empirical support for the existence of these goals; right now, the evidence is not overwhelming for the existence of the nonpoverty status goal and it is mixed for the bequest goal. The goals can be related to existing financial services and to existing incentives for saving. The result may be that existing services provide adequate means to reach the desired ends. Then the question arises whether the potential target groups have enough information and reminders about the services or incentives offered. If there is no relevant service the goals could become objects for developing new or improved services for better satisfying one or more of these goals. It should be admitted that financial institutions like commercial and savings banks have tried many things that are related to these goals and have not always been overly successful and some services have been abolished after some trial periods. Maybe the decision makers have not thought about the role of goals in the whole process of saving behavior.

The Influence of Expectations

Decisions depend on expectations and expectations may be based on past experience or on other information. Thus one way to influence individual saving is to change expectations. Rather than trying to influence saving behavior decision makers in government bodies and financial institutions may do well noticing conditions that tend to change saving behavior and be prepared for such changes. If the policy makers want to stimulate saving, they might do one or more of the following (and encounter ethical problems)

- scare people of the future financial conditions in the economy
- forecast increased unemployment
- remove or lower taxes on wealth and income from wealth; it is essential to keep savers optimistic about the future value of assets and pessimistic about receiving future value without saving
- reduce social benefits, suggest decreased pensions, payments from sickness, and unemployment insurance
- introduce fees on children's education.

For all of those, it is true that starting a discussion may be enough for a while at least to stimulate saving (mere discussion usually costs less than actual change). If it becomes known that a government deliberately tries to instill fears of the future this will of course lead to political protest, but there are many examples of the effects of such influences on expectations. Even if expectations are influenced there is still an important step from expectations to economic behavior. To discourage saving, the following could be done to influence expectations (again risking ethical controversy)

- promise people wage increases, better financial conditions
- increase generosity in all kinds of social benefits
- levy increased taxes on savings and wealth
- introduce other punishments of savings like reduced social benefits if a household has assets above a certain limit
- impose new taxes on various expenditures, especially on durables
- spur inflation (somewhat ambivalent in its effects; 'now is time to buy' effect seems common if expected inflation is high, cf. Katona, 1975).

Again, mere discussion of the policy measures may have a stimulating effect on consumption for a while. Attempts to influence expectations by information may not be successful if there is a multitude of earlier experience that tells another story. The credibility of the information is important and a government may have used up most of its credibility in earlier promises of better financial conditions.

Training Consumers to Save?

An interesting idea for consideration in financial service development was given by Thaler (1994). Thaler has repeatedly criticized LCH for leaving the discount rate as the only means to influencing savings. He suggested that the ideal savings program, based on psychological considerations, should have the following characteristics:

1. It provides an *immediate* reward to saving
2. It is simple to use and understand
3. The money is perceived as 'off-limits' to current spending
4. Experts consider the program 'a good deal' (Thaler, 1994, p.189).

The first point builds on psychological reinforcement theory. Savings banks that have competed for savers have given gifts for opening of new savings accounts. For some time, I received almost every week an offer from a commercial bank or insurance company bank, promising me a calculator or a TV remote control if I opened an account within ten days. That may be overdoing the idea. Saving that gives a chance or preferably repeated chances of winning prizes has been popular in Sweden in the shape of premium bonds and savings accounts with lottery chances of winning a large sum of money.

The second point is probably in general true, but there can be important modifications. A little complexity may not hurt and can even increase attention and interest. People have different levels of optimal complexity and what is too simple may be boring and unchallenging according to psychological studies. People who look for a change may appreciate and believe more in something that is a little more complex. Too much simplicity may mean low credibility in some segments of the population.

The third point suggests precommitments and self-imposed rules. Fixed deductions from salaries and deposits in accounts where there is some punishment for withdrawing more than a small part of the money and for frequent withdrawals are examples of arrangements that can be made.

The fourth point probably means that impartial expert advisers consider the saving scheme a good deal. Many advisers who are assumed to be experts may have a commercial interest that colors the advice given. They may also miss important new information and rely too much on earlier developments, something that is characteristic when a financial bubble is developing.

The third point can be expanded. Other authors, for example, Strotz (1956) and Elster (1977) have directly or by implication advocated the use of rules as means of vanquishing volitional difficulties. Precommitments of an interpersonal or purely internal nature may help to some extent (if the difficulty of making the initial decision of precommitment is somehow overcome). Removing possibilities through avoiding exposure to certain temptations is another way (putting wax into the crew's ears the way Ulysses did). A difficulty not mentioned earlier is that household saving is often a matter of interaction between two or more family members who may disagree more or less vocally about immediate and future uses of money. One family member's preference for a precommitment may not be shared by other family members.

Earlier the savings banks in Sweden and probably also in other countries took a great responsibility in inculcating the importance of saving in school children. Early saving habits are according to some research important for adult saving (Maital, 1982; Sonuga-Barke, 1993). Are school children now exposed to such influence in favor of saving? Unfortunately, this seems to go against the grain in welfare societies.

Refraining from consumption was by many economists considered painful. Rae, Senior, Fisher, and Keynes, all saw saving as painful. Katona (1975) objected to this view, criticized Keynes for the latter's negative view of saving and described the positive attitudes towards saving among American consumers. Low age, low income and low social class were characteristics that tended to decrease the propensity to save, but there were also personality characteristics that involved more or less impatience to spend according to Fisher (1930). The characteristics leading to high impatience could according to Fisher (1930, pp.504-5) be systematically influenced:

1. Training that gives insight into the need for providing 'for the proverbial rainy day'
2. Education in self-control
3. Building up habits of frugality, on one hand avoiding parsimony, extravagancies on the other
4. Better hygienic habits and health care which lead to a longer and healthier life
5. Incentives for taking better care of children and future generations
6. Modification of fashion in favor of less ostentatious and harmful expenditures for lavish living.

Growing up in a welfare society means a different kind of learning about finances than growing up in an economy where average income is low and the income distribution more highly skewed. Children and youngsters may become used to looking to public sector agencies for support rather than accruing and using savings. With old-age pensions for all, there is no absolute necessity for savings of one's own, except for the extras that somebody may want. Hubbard et al. (1994) maintained that asset-based means testing of welfare programs was a strong reason for persistently low levels of wealth.

The existence and tightness of the social security net is no doubt important for saving and spending. If there are quick reactions from the public sector and high generosity in administering social welfare contributions to those who fulfill the conditions of a defined need (maybe vaguely defined and dependent on the personal judgment of the administrator/social worker), there will be little need for saving for a buffer. Now that welfare systems are being cut down and pension payments tend to outgrow what the working population can afford because of a larger proportion of aged people in many countries, the need for buffer capital would seem to increase. An important task for those who work with social welfare and for others who want to stimulate saving is then to convince and help people to hold down their expenditures so much that some buffer capital can be accrued.

There are people who save for the sake of saving, similar to what psychologists in the 1930s called 'functionally autonomous motives' and what would today probably be classified as 'intrinsic motivation'. 'They are prompted partly by the instincts of the chase, by the desire to outstrip their rivals; by the ambition to have shown ability in getting the wealth and to acquire power and social position by its possession' (Marshall [1890] 1990, p.189). The chief motive for saving is, however, according to Marshall family affection. With the decreased respect for the traditional family, this affection may have lost some of its meaning and the bequest motive may have been modified (see Table 7.1).

IMPLICATIONS FOR APPLIED AND BASIC RESEARCH

Three issues are worth special consideration:

1. Psychological differences and similarities between nonsavers, savers, and investors
2. The hedonic value of saving
3. Individual strategies for accomplishing to save.

The psychology of saving as it stands today has something to say about the three circumstances and there are implications for attempts to influence saving behavior. Under each point, some psychological concepts are particularly relevant. The first point comprises differences in future orientation, which can be seen as a comprehensive concept encompassing time horizon, time preferences, expectations and habits. The second point refers to the meaning to the individual and the household of having or not having money saved and the amount of money saved. The third point has to do with volitional problems and stratagems for overcoming resistance to postponing consumption, to the near or distant future or indefinitely. This includes how much control of expenditure is exercised and how such control is achieved or not achieved.

Psychological Similarities and Differences between Nonsavers, Savers and Investors

Individual and household reactions to economic-policy measures as well as to marketing efforts of financial institutions are usually not easy to explain and predict without recourse to psychological concepts. Detailed knowledge about the underlying psychological processes facilitates the task of influencing saving. In Chapter 8, a summary of the psychology of saving was given in the form of a schema. The schema picked up ideas that were discussed by classical and neoclassical economists over the last century. They were introduced in a historical context in Chapter 3 and commented on from a psychological perspective in Chapters 6 and 7. The schema embodies goals, perceptual-cognitive phenomena, prompt to action (values, motivational and volitional constructs), control of expenditure and saving acts. The possibilities of influencing saving can be discussed in those terms.

It is obvious from the presentations in earlier chapters that the psychology of saving leads to more focus on individual differences than on general behavioral laws. Cognitive capacity limitations, motivation, attitudes and volitional control vary between people. It seems appropriate to distinguish between segments of people who are similar in each segment and different between segments. Even apart from psychological differences as reason for segmentation, research findings indicate that there are considerable differences in economic behavior between groups classified on other grounds. The self-employed are, for example, apparently different from others. An interesting distinction, which has not been much observed in saving research, is between investors and savers. So far, only a few studies have dealt with the differences (Lunt and Livingstone, 1991; Wahlund and Gunnarsson, 1996 and 1997; Daniel, 1997), but the field is open for more intensive research. For one thing, there is an international tendency that more households acquire such assets as bonds and shares, often through mutual and growth funds. Regular savers become investors, possibly when they have already plenty of money in low-yielding bank savings accounts. At the same time, there are investors that with little or no capital of their own invest in risky assets in the hope of making quick profits.

Economists have clarified many aspects of saving. They have developed a theory that is quite powerful at the same time as it is elegant. Without the economists, especially without the classical and early neoclassical economists, there would be no psychology of saving to speak of. Psychologists have devoted very little attention and effort towards studying phenomena that are related to saving. They may have missed some of the mechanisms that are most significant for human survival! Economists discovered at an early stage that human reactions toward the future were important determinants of economic behavior. The PIH and the LCH are based on the forward-looking individual who has largely remained unknown and unstudied in psychology. Keynes and the members of the Stockholm School brought attention to the role of businessmen's expectations. Later savings and consumption theorists have explored the role of consumer expectations.

It should be appealing and fascinating for psychologists to study further how people deal with the economics of the future. That will involve how they grapple with foreseeable economic problems, how they may react to economic conditions and economic stimuli, how they expect to earn and spend money, what they get out of their spending and the feelings and emotions that accompany economic behavior. Expectation is a largely neglected area in psychology, which is probably a consequence of an earlier prevalent focus on observable behavior and current preoccupation with information processing. Decision-making studies have paid little attention to how expectations are formed and concentrated on uncertainty in terms of probabilities that are not anchored in future events. Time preferences have entered psychology more or less through a back door. When addiction is treated as a series of choices that have consequences in the future, it becomes interesting to try to find out why addicts make the wrong choices and prefer pleasure now without thinking of future costs. Ainslie (1975) explored this line of thinking and has continued ever since. A product of his thinking is the hyperbolic discount curve which has aroused a growing interest among economists.

When psychological researchers look for problems to study in the laboratory or in correlational research, they could more often than now turn to economic behavior for proper problems. Attitudes towards saving and towards taxes may be quite as interesting as political or religious attitudes. The study of the use of rewards to reinforce behavior may in some cases need only slight changes to uncover essential aspects of economic behavior.

It seems clear that here are differences between savers and nonsavers in terms of how long their time horizons are and the amount of actual planning that is done by the household. The rate of time preference has a less clear relationship to saving, but there is some evidence pointing in the direction that nonsavers have much higher discount rates and are more impatient to spend now. Well-established saving habits are important and it can be speculated on some existing evidence that they are initiated early in life. For researchers, it is impelling to study more closely how saving habits are inspired and formed. Expectations about future needs and utilities appear to have crucial importance for the choice between spending now and spending later. Such expectations are probably more essential than attitudes towards saving. Market research for financial institutions would profit from devoting more effort to studying expectations rather than attitudes.

The Hedonic Value of Saving(s)

According to Marshall, an analysis of saving involves the relations between present and deferred gratifications. He was a forerunner of the life-cycle model of saving. He talked about 'A prudent person who thought that he would derive equal gratifications from equal means at all stages of his life' would save money for a future date. He would do that even if savings would not increase in his hands, but he thought they would diminish' (Marshall [1890] 1990, p.192). Marshall used gratification instead of 'utility'. His choice of term suggests that he was well aware of the fact that emotions could be involved. This aspect was lost when revealed preference theory switched the interest from subjective feeling to observable behavior.

Kahneman (1994) attacked the concentration in economics on revealed preferences. The observable behavior might not reveal the utility that was expected when the decision was made. If the hedonic consequences that were expected do not materialize a discrepancy arises between expected utility and preference utility as measured by observed behavior. Kahneman proposed that more attention should be given to the expected hedonic consequences of a decision and less to the logical, consistency aspects that dominated economic thinking. He pointed out that people are often mistaken about the exact nature of the future hedonic consequences since memory is fallible, information is inadequate, and things may happen between the decision and the occurrence of the consequences. The distinction between the formal decision utility which is based on consistency and experienced or hedonic utility seems very important for the psychological study of saving. To what extent do people think about hedonic consequences when they save money? According to classical economists like Jevons and Böhm-Bawerk, the anticipation of future pleasure was a prevalent characteristic of postponing consumption.

Despite the fact that there is insufficient supporting evidence, it is conceivable that the present enjoyment of the saving act and the accompanying expectations may be important and should be studied. There may be at least three components in the satisfaction. (a) saving money may give a feeling that a moral commitment has been fulfilled; it is still a common norm that one should not waste money, (b) the main satisfaction may arise from the fact that the future is reasonably secure with respect to what may become necessary; the feelings may encompass complacency as well as anticipation of future pleasures, (c) there is the possibility of a feeling of independence and maybe even power over a limited space, i.e., expectations of being able to make discretionary choices ('independence' in Keynes's list of saving motives).

The question about what benefits people get from saving money (and other resources) is essential if one wants to know something of the effects of economic policy measures and other factors on savings. If attempts are being made to stimulate saving it is necessary to know something about behavior at the micro level, i.e. individual and household behavior. Quite apart from these macro purposes, there is the possibility that, as Smiles said, direct individual well-being can be increased through individual savings, provided there are alternatives on which money can be spent.

Much research in economic psychology has been devoted to questions of well-being, see Strumpel (1974; 1976); for a report on a program of research, see Groenland (1989). A particular aspect is consumer satisfaction or rather dissatisfaction, since many studies have focused on consumer complaints (Hunt, 1991). Recently, Fornell (1992; see also Johnson and Fornell, 1991) has shown that it is possible to construct an index of consumer satisfaction for various industries. The Consumer Satisfaction Barometer (CSB) is a measure at the aggregate level. It has so far not been related to macroeconomic issues, but could conceivably develop into something similar to the Index of Consumer Sentiment (consumer expectations). The CSB has been tried out in Sweden and reports on customer satisfaction in over 30 industries and over 100 corporations (Fornell, 1992). It involves measuring the *quality* of the marketing of goods and services and captures (1) general satisfaction, (2) confirmation of expectations about the properties of goods and services, and (3) the distance from the customer's hypothetical ideal product. The analysis reported shows how the CSB is related to customer loyalty and market share. An index of household satisfaction with savings would be desirable additional information about saving.

From a welfare point of view, it may not seem desirable to tell people to save to increase their well-being. It is assumed that the welfare state already assures the individual enough well-being through social security involving retirement and unemployment insurance, disability and health insurance schemes. Moreover, some politicians may see savings as a threat to strivings towards equal wealth distribution. Such views, if they exist, miss the point that savings increase the amount of freedom of an individual and may thus be essential to individual and family well-being.

Rawls (1977) treated saving as a relationship between generations. Leaving one's savings as inheritance to the young of the family, according to him, does not involve reciprocity, which is otherwise characteristic of relationships among humans. Hedonic utility is something that can be enjoyed now and the reassurance that one provides for the future security of kin or cherished charity purposes may be a motivator for saving and not dissaving. It can be argued that present generations have a responsibility to later generations: they should leave wealth rather than debts to be paid. Another demand is that they should not use up too much of natural resources for coming generations. Pigou (1920) who saw a relationship between thrift and careful use of resources indicated this. He lamented that 'Our telescopic faculty is defective and . . . we, therefore, see future pleasures, as it were, on a diminished scale.' The defective telescopic faculty may also make us undervalue what future generations will have to pay for the debts we have left.

Individual Strategies for Accomplishing to Save

'Control of expenditure' has at least two dimensions. It may refer to a level of consumption that a person finds appropriate for her/himself. A person has a 'norm' that probably is influenced by what other people think and do. The second dimension is more concrete and encompasses precommitments and rules for holding the expenditures down to a certain level, either because it is necessary or because the person wants to save money.

The research on the first dimension is linked to sociology and anthropology and maybe to cultural psychology. In the literature, there are many ideas to select from and some work has been done, for example, by Douglas and Isherwood (1996). Before regular survey questions to cover this aspect can be framed it is desirable to make some intensive studies to appreciate possible relationships between saving and the level of consumption that is perceived 'appropriate' by a person (and perhaps by different household members).

The second dimension is covered by research some of which was reviewed at the end of Chapter 6 under the subheading 'Mental Accounting'. The VSB Panel questionnaires specifically asked respondents about the stratagems they used to avoid spending money. The questions comprised such things as keeping records of expenditures, avoiding having too much cash on hand when shopping, making monthly deductions of an amount for saving, and not using credit cards. The data have not yet been analyzed.

The role of 'control of expenditure' is intriguing. It may be primary and more or less a goal in itself or it may be a means to ensure that saving goals are reached. Possible segments in the population are (a) those who have little control of their expenditures, (b) those who have good control of their expenditures, and (c) those who have a tight control over their expenditures .

Those who have little control over their expenditures are least likely to save. Over the centuries, it has generally been assumed that they have low income and are poor. They may as an alternative belong to the upper end of the income distribution and be high-income earners who do not have to worry about expenditures. In fact, they may be found at all income levels. The majority of the savers are probably recruited among those who have good control of their expenditures. Some of those who have good control over their expenditures may not be able to save because of insufficient income. The third segment, finally, consists of those who are most pervaded by strivings to minimize consumption.

The Use of Psychology

If, for a change, a psychologist is invited to participate in a panel discussion concerning current economic problems such as the so-called stock exchange crises, that have occurred in recent years, he or she will probably find that the participating economists freely use psychological explanations. The explanations do not derive from analysis of data, but may seem plausible enough. The typical psychologist will have a tendency to be very guarded in her/his attempts at explanation and will refer to paucity of research for an excuse. The psychologist looks for clear empirical data and fails to use a model based on earlier research to elucidate similar phenomena. New situations give rise to demand for new data that refer specifically to the new situation. In my view, many psychological models can already be of great help in discussions of practical problems if the models are judiciously used.

It has been and still is characteristic of much of psychological research that it is reported with little attempt at abstraction, at making it more generalizable and generative (cf. Gergen, 1982). Cialdini (1988) gave an excellent example of what psychologists can do to achieve such purposes. He distilled six general principles of influence that can be used to analyze compliance situations (from the victim's vantage point). He vividly demonstrated how they operated in practical situations

Economic psychology is a new discipline with highly limited resources. Still, I would like to assert that there is a place for approaches combining psychology and economics and these approaches do not have to observe 'the economic approach to the study of human behavior'. Instead they will provide a descriptive richness and better explanations. To be sure, research using approaches similar to the joint approach advocated here has been done and more is underway. Something can still be added: more concerted efforts and more efforts among psychological researchers to contribute to the understanding of saving.

Do we need a new type of psychology of saving because the world has changed so much since the classical and neoclassical economists used their observational power and wisdom to explain why saving occurred? In a society where there were both extreme poverty and extremely rich people and a middle class with certain characteristics the preconditions for saving may have been quite different from what can be expected in modern welfare societies with the kind of social security that is assured every citizen (except for certain pathological cases) and with easy access to financial markets with great opportunities for gains and losses. Reading the classical economists gives a feeling of recognition that suggests that fundamental human characteristics tend to remain the same and that what they thought often gives a good start in the psychology of saving research.

The Ethics of the Research

Psychological research on economic behavior is sometimes questioned. Whereas it is clear that research on consumption may give rise to ethical problems if the findings are used in attempts at influencing consumers, it is less likely that research on saving can be accused of creating such problems. If one believes Keynes and his forerunners who warned against saving too much especially in a depression, one can see a possible ethical conflict at the macroeconomic level. There can also exist ethical problems in connection with attempts to influence saving behavior.

Lea et al. (1987, pp.541-3) asked a pertinent question: 'Do we want our governments to be able to control with accuracy how much we will save, rather than spend, and how much of our tax bills we will pay rather than avoid or evade?' Their own answer was: 'The object of the disinterested study of economic psychology should be to make a knowledge of the subject as widely available as possible, so that individuals can understand the pressures they come under, understand the effects their behavior will have on the economy, and act accordingly.' This is similar to my own view.

Political Views of Saving

> *Every act of saving involves a 'forced' inevitable transfer of wealth to him who saves, though he in his turn may suffer from the saving of others. These transfers of wealth do not require the creation of new wealth – indeed, as we have seen, they may be actively inimical to it.*
>
> Keynes (1936, p.212)

While saving at the individual level is held to be virtuous, aggregate savings may be seen as damaging. This is called the composition error or in Keynes-orientated language 'The Paradox of Savings'. This idea has been spread in the leading textbooks on economics during the last 40 years, but it is less often mentioned in more recent versions. Keynes's negative view of saving seems to be shared by many politicians. In 1991, Sweden got a non-socialist government. The liberal minister of finance in her speeches repeatedly pronounced that people should save so much money that they had at least a year's income in savings. She was ridiculed in the mass media and by many politicians on the socialist side. From a welfare point of view, it may not seem desirable to tell people to save in order to increase their financial security and other aspects of well-being. It is assumed that the welfare state already assures the individual enough well-being through income policy, social security and health insurance schemes. Moreover, savings may be seen as a threat to strivings towards a more equal wealth distribution. Such views, if they exist, miss the point that savings increase the amount of freedom of an individual and may thus be essential to individual and family well-being. They also fail to observe that savings may mean increased equality of wealth.

Doubting the blessings of savings is not new. Aristotle condoned capital accumulation if it was done with moderation. The mercantilists were skeptical about households withholding money from the market (see Chapter 3). They attacked hoarding rather than saving that was invested. Keynes (1936) cited a number of writers who had questioned saving. Wealth accumulation has been appreciated by many thinkers about economic life, but often only up to a point. While the Protestant religion was, as noted by Weber (1930), an instigator of diligent and thrifty behavior, there were some doubts about the rightfulness of accumulating great wealth.

A view with some nuances seems called for. It appears more appropriate that political attitudes towards saving vary with the business cycle than that they are always negative. When there is recession or depression there may be macroeconomic reasons why people should not withhold their money from consumption and act in the spirit of Keynes and Mandeville. When there is recovery, more saving may again need to be encouraged. The individual need for buffer capital remains unchanged over the business cycle.

The politicians may think in terms of what they believe to be best for the national economy. The individual saver thinks in terms of what gains the family or the household may get from saving. What politicians enact, sometimes merely mention as possible actions, influences consumer expectations and actions. Common people may have become suspicious of the intentions behind the sumptuary laws in the Middle Ages and consequently refrained from saving. Marshall (1890) emphasized that security is a condition for saving. 'The laborious and self-denying peasant who had heaped up a little store of wealth only to see it taken from him by a stronger hand, was a constant warning to his neighbours to enjoy their pleasure and their rest when they could' (Marshall [1890] 1990, p.188). Marshall asserted that such insecurity had steadily diminished and that while the growth of the money-economy gave new temptations to extravagance, there was a new certainty that savings would actually provide what was wanted in the future.

Adam Smith (1776) asserted that only statesmen could bring a country to ruin. Left alone, people could on the whole be trusted to be frugal and to display only a few, limited extravagancies. If that is so, maybe the way to try to decrease the probability of national diseconomies is to make sure never to vote for a political candidate who does not have a savings account with regularly made deposits. Such a candidate has at least shown an appreciable degree of thrift and self-control. Maybe the politician should ponder Machiavelli's advice ([1513] 1995, p.51) to the prince: 'There is nothing so self-defeating as generosity . . . A prince must try to avoid, above all else, being despised and hated; and generosity results in your being both.'

References

Adams, F.G. (1965), 'Prediction with consumer attitudes: the time-series-cross section paradox', *Review of Economics and Statistics*, **4**, 367-378.

Agell, J., L. Berg, and P.-A. Edin (1995), *Tax Reform, Consumption, and Asset Structure*, Stockholm: National Institute of Economic Research. Economic Council, Tax Reform Evaluation Report No. 16.

Ainslie, G. (1975), 'Specious rewards: a behavioral theory of impulsiveness and impulse control', *Psychological Bulletin*, **82**(4), 463-96.

Ainslie, G. (1991), 'Derivation of "rational economic behavior" from hyperbolic discount curves', *American Economic Review*, **81**, AEA Papers and Proceedings, May, 334-40.

Ainslie, G. (1992), *Picoeconomics. The Strategic Interaction of Successive Motivational States within the Person*, Cambridge: Cambridge University Press.

Ainslie, G. and N. Haslam (1992), 'Self-control', in G. Loewenstein and J. Elster (eds), *Choice Over Time*, New York: Russell Sage Foundation, 177-211.

Ajzen, I. (1985), 'From intentions to actions: a theory of planned behavior', in J. Kuhl and J. Beckmann (eds), *Action-Control: From Cognition to Behavior*, Heidelberg: Springer, 11-39.

Ajzen, I. (1991), 'The theory of planned behavior', *Organizational Behavior and Human Decision Processes*, **50**, 179-211.

Ajzen, I. and M. Fishbein (1980), *Understanding Attitudes and Predicting Social Behavior*, Englewood Cliffs, NJ: Prentice-Hall.

Akerlof, G.A. (1991), 'Procrastination and obedience', *American Economic Review*, Papers and Proceedings, **81**(2), 1-19.

Akerlof, G.A. and W.T. Dickens (1982), 'The economic consequences of cognitive dissonance', *American Economic Review*, **72**(3), 307-19.

Albou, P. (1984), *La psychologie économique*, Paris: Presses Universitaires de France.

Alhadeff, D.A. (1982), *Microeconomics and Human Behavior. Towards a New Synthesis of Economics and Psychology*, Berkeley, CA: University of California Press.

Allen, R.L. (1993), *Irving Fisher. A Biography*, Cambridge, MA: Blackwell.

Anastasi, A. (1964), *Fields of Applied Psychology*, New York: McGraw-Hill.

Anderhub, V., W. Güth, W. Härdle, W. Müller, and M. Strobel (1997), *On Saving, Updating and Dynamic Programming. An Experimental Analysis*, Faculty of Economics, Humboldt-University. Unpublished manuscript.

Anderson, N.H. (ed.) (1991), *Contributions to Information Integration Theory. Volume I: Cognition,* Hillsdale, NJ: Lawrence Erlbaum Associates.

Ando, A., L. Guiso, D. Terlizzese, and D. Dorsainvil (1992), 'Saving among young households. Evidence from Japan and Italy', *Scandinavian Journal of Economics,* **94**, 233-50.

Ando, A. and F. Modigliani (1963), 'The "life cycle" hypothesis of saving: aggregate implications and tests', *American Economic Review,* **53**, 55-84.

Andreassen, P.B. (1990), 'Judgmental extrapolation and market overreaction: on the use and disuse of news', *Journal of Behavioral Decision Making,* **3**, 153-74.

Antonides, G. (1988), *Scrapping a Durable Consumption Good.* Doctoral dissertation, Erasmus University Rotterdam.

Appley, M.H. (ed.) (1971), *Adaptation-Level Theory. A Symposium.* New York, NY: Academic Press.

Aristotle ([undated] 1988), *The Politics.* Cambridge: Cambridge University Press.

Aristotle ([undated] 1976), *The Ethics of Aristotle. The Nicomachean Ethics,* Harmondsworth, Middlesex, UK: Penguin Books.

Aronson, E. and J.M. Carlsmith (1968), 'Experimentation in social psychology', in G. Lindzey and E. Aronson (eds), *Handbook of Social Psychology,* Vol. 2, Reading, MA: Addison-Wesley, 1-79.

Arrow, K.J. (1963), 'Utility and expectation in economic behavior', in S. Koch (ed.), *Psychology: Study of a Science,* Vol. 6. New York: McGraw-Hill, 724-52.

Arrow, K.J. (1982), 'Risk perception in psychology and economics', *Economic Inquiry,* **20**, 1-9.

Arrow, K.J. (1986), 'Rationality of self and others in an economic system', *Journal of Business,* **59** (4, Pt 2), S385-S399.

Atkinson, J.W. (1957), 'Motivational determinants of risk taking behavior', *Psychological Review,* **64**, 359-72.

Atkinson, J.W. (1964), *An Introduction to Motivation,* New York: American Book/ Van Nostrand/Reinhold.

Attfield, C.L.F., D. Demery, and N.W. Duck (1985), *Rational Expectations in Macroeconomics. An Introduction to Theory and Evidence,* Oxford: Basil Blackwell.

Azuelos, M. (1996), 'Banishing idleness: Attitudes to work, leisure and unemployment in pre-industrial England', in C. Roland-Lévy (ed.), *Social & Economic Representations.* IAREP-Paris 96. Université René Descartes.

Babeau, A. (1981), *Diversité des motivations et évolution des comportements d'épargne,* Audition devant la Commission de l'Épargne, Paris: Centre de Recherche Économique sur l'Épargne (CREP).

Baghestani, H. (1992), 'On the formation of expected inflation under various conditions: some survey evidence', *Journal of Business,* **65**(2), 281-93.

Baida, P. (1990), *Poor Richard's Legacy. American Business Values from Benjamin Franklin to Donald Trump,* New York: William Morrow and Co., Inc.

Bannock, G., R.E. Baxter, and R. Rees (1984), *Dictionary of Economics,* 3rd ed., Harmondsworth, UK: Penguin Books.

Barlow, R., H.E. Brazer, and J.N. Morgan (1966), *Economic Behavior of the Affluent,* Washington, D.C.: The Brookings Institution.

Barro, R.J. (1989), 'The Ricardian approach to budget deficits', *Journal of Economic Perspectives,* **3**(2), 37-54.

Batchelor, R.A. (1986), 'The psychophysics of inflation', *Journal of Economic Psychology,* **7**, 269-90.

Batchelor, R.A. and P. Dua (1990a), 'Forecaster ideology, forecasting technique, and the accuracy of economic forecasts', *International Journal of Forecasting,* **6**(1), 3-10.

Batchelor, R.A. and P. Dua (1990b), 'Product differentiation in the forecasting industry', *International Journal of Forecasting,* **6**(3), 311-16.

Batchelor, R.A. and P. Dua (1991), 'Blue chip rationality tests', *Journal of Money, Credit and Banking,* **23**(4), 692-705.

Batchelor, R.A. and P. Dua (1992), 'Survey expectations in the time series consumption function', *Review of Economics and Statistics,* **74**(4), 598-606.

Batchelor, R.A. and L. Jonung (1989), 'Cross-sectional evidence on the rationality of the mean and variance of inflation expectations', in K.G. Grunert and F. Ölander (eds), *Understanding Economic Behavior,* Kluwer Academic Publishers: Dordrecht, 93-105.

Baxter, J.L. (1988), *Social and Psychological Foundations of Economic Analysis,* London: Harvester Wheatsheaf.

Baxter, J.L. (1993), *Behavioural Foundations of Economics,* London: The MacMillan Press Ltd.

Bechtel, G.G., P. Vanden Abeele, and A.M. DeMeyer (1993), 'The sociotropic aspect of consumer confidence', *Journal of Economic Psychology,* **14**(4), 615-33.

Beck, L. and I. Ajzen (1991), 'Predicting dishonest actions using the theory of planned behavior', *Journal of Research In Personality,* **25**, 285-301.

Becker, G.S. (1976), *The Economic Approach to Human Behavior,* Chicago, IL: The University of Chicago Press.

Belk, R.W. (ed.) (1991), *Highways and Buyways: Naturalistic Research from the Consumer Behavior Odyssey,* Provo UT: Association for Consumer Research.

Benartzi, S. and R.H. Thaler (1995), 'Myopic loss aversion and the equity premium puzzle', *Quarterly Journal of Economics,* **110**, 73-92.

Benzion, U., A. Granot, and J. Yagil (1994), 'An experimental test of the IRP, PPP and Fisher theorems', *Journal of Economic Psychology,* **15**, 637-49.

Benzion, U., A. Rapoport, and J. Yagil (1989), 'Discount rates inferred from decisions: an experimental study', *Management Science,* **35**(3), 270-84.

Berg, L. (1982), *Konsumtion och sparande – en studie av hushållens beteende*. (Consumption and Savings – A Study of Household Behavior), Doctoral dissertation, Uppsala, Sweden: Uppsala University.

Berg, L. (1994), 'Household savings and debts: the experience of the Nordic countries', *Oxford Review of Economic Policy*, **10**(2), 42-53.

Berg, L. and R. Bergström (1996), *Consumer confidence and consumption in Sweden*, Working Paper 1996:7, Uppsala: Department of Economics, Uppsala University.

Bernheim, B.D. (1991), 'How strong are bequest motives? Evidence based on estimates of the demand for life insurance and annuities', *Journal of Political Economy*, **99**(5), 899-927.

Bernheim, B.D., A. Shleifer, and L.H. Summers (1985), 'The strategic bequest motive', *Journal of Political Economy*, **93**(6), 1045-76.

Bettman, J.R. and B.A. Weitz (1983), 'Attributions in the board room: causal reasoning in corporate annual reports', *Administrative Science Quarterly*, **28**, 165-83.

Bevan, W. (1965), 'On the approach of the experimental psychologist', in B. Wolman (ed.), *Scientific Psychology. Principles and Approaches,* New York: Basic Books, 88-113.

Biart, M. and P. Praet (1987), 'The contribution of opinion surveys in forecasting aggregate demand in the four main EC countries', *Journal of Economic Psychology*, **8**(4), 409-28.

Bilkey, W.J. (1951), 'The vector hypothesis of consumer behavior', *Journal of Marketing*, **16**, 137-51.

Binswanger, H.P. (1981), 'Attitudes toward risk: theoretical implications of an experiment in rural India', *Economic Journal*, **91**, 867-90.

Blomqvist, H.C. (1983), 'On the formation of inflationary expectations: Some empirical evidence from Finland, 1979–1980', *Journal of Economic Psychology*, **4**, 319-34.

Böhm-Bawerk, E. von ([1888] 1912), *Positive Theorie des Kapitales*. Dritte Auflage. Zweiter Halbband. Innsbruck: Verlag der Wagner'schen Universitäts-Buchhandlung. (First published in 1888).

Borgatta, E.F. and D.J. Jackson (eds) (1980), *Aggregate Data. Analysis and Interpretation*, London: SAGE Publications.

Boring, E.G. (1950), *A History of Experimental Psychology*, 2nd ed. Englewood Cliffs, NJ: Prentice-Hall.

Boulding, K. (1972), 'Human betterment and the quality of life', in B. Strumpel, J.N. Morgan, and E. Zahn (eds), *Human Behavior in Economic Affairs,* Amsterdam: Elsevier, 455-70.

Bouwen, R. (1977), 'Anticipation and realization: attitudes and buying plans in the future time orientation of consumer behavior', *Psychologica Belgica*, **17**, 113-34.

Bowie, N.E. (1994), 'Economics and the Enlightenment. Then and now', in A. Lewis and K.-E. Wärneryd (eds), *Ethics and Economic Affairs*, London: Routledge, 348-66.

Brandstätter, H. (1988), 'Sechzehn Persönlichkeits-Adjektivskalen (16PA) als Forschungsinstrument anstelle des 16PF, [Sixteen personality adjective scales as a substitute of the 16PF in experiments and field studies], *Zeitschrift für Experimentelle und Angewandte Psychologie*, **35**, 370-91.

Brandstätter, H. (1993), 'Should economic psychology care about personality structure?', *Journal of Economic Psychology*, **14**, 473-94.

Brandstätter, H. (1995), 'Saving behavior related to personality structure', in S. Troye and E. Nyhus (eds), *Frontiers in Economic Psychology*, Vol. 1. 20th IAREP Conference Bergen, Norway, August 2-5, 1995, 60-78.

Brickman, P. and D.T. Campbell (1971), 'Hedonic relativism and planning the good society', in M.H. Appley (ed.), *Adaptation-Level Theory. A Symposium*, New York, NY: Academic Press, 287-304.

Briggs, S.R. and J.M. Cheek (1988), 'On the nature of self-monitoring: problems with assessment, problems with validity', *Journal of Personality and Social Psychology*, **54**(4), 663-78.

Brown, B.W. and S. Maital (1981), 'What do economists know? An empirical study of experts' expectations', *Econometrica*, **49**(2), 491-504.

Browning, M. and A. Lusardi (1996), 'Household saving: micro theories and micro facts', *Journal of Economic Literature*, **34**, 1797-1855.

Burbridge, J.B. and A.L. Robb (1985), 'Evidence on wealth-age profiles in Canadian cross-section data', *Canadian Journal of Economics*, **18**(4), 854-75.

Busemeyer, J.R. (1991), 'Intuitive statistical estimation', in N.H. Anderson (ed.), *Contributions to Information Integration Theory. Volume I: Cognition*, Hillsdale, NJ: Lawrence Erlbaum Associates, 187-215.

Cagan, P. (1965), *The Effect of Pension Plans on Aggregate Savings*, New York: National Bureau of Economic Research.

Caldwell, B.J. (1986), 'Economic methodology and behavioral economics: An interpretive history', in B. Gilad and S. Kaish (eds), *Handbook of Behavioral Economics*, Greenwich, CT: JAI Press, 5-17.

Campbell, J.Y. and N.G. Mankiw (1989), *Consumption, Income and Interest Rates: Reinterpreting the Time Series Evidence*, National Bureau of Economic Research, Working Paper No. 2924.

Campbell, J.Y. and N.G. Mankiw (1990), 'Permanent income, current income, and consumption', *Journal of Business and Economic Statistics*, **8**(3), 265-79.

Campbell, J.Y. and N.G. Mankiw (1991), 'The response of consumption to income: a cross-country investigation', *European Economic Review*, **35**(4), 723-67.

Camphuis, H. (1993), *Checking, Editing and Imputation of Wealth Data of the Netherlands Socio-Economic Panel for the Period '87–'89*, VSB-CentER

Savings Project. Progress Report 10, Tilburg: CentER for Economic Research, Tilburg University.

Caporael, L.R, R.M. Dawes, J.M. Orbell, and A.J.C. van de Kragt (1989), 'Selfishness examined: cooperation in the absence of egoistic incentives', *Behavioral and Brain Sciences*, **12**, 683-739.

Carroll, C.D. (1997), 'Buffer-stock saving and the Life-Cycle/Permanent Income Hypothesis', *Quarterly Journal of Economics*, **112**(1), 1-55.

Carroll, C.D., J.C. Fuhrer, and DW. Wilcox (1994), 'Does Consumer Sentiment forecast household spending? If so, why?', *American Economic Review*, **84**(5), 1397-1408.

Cialdini, R.B. (1980), 'Full-cycle social psychology', in L. Bickman (ed.), *Applied Social Psychology Annual*, **1**, Beverly Hills, CA: Sage Publications, 21-47.

Cialdini, R.B. (1988), *Influence. Science and Practice*, 2nd ed., Glenview, IL: Scott, Foresman and Co.

Cicero ([undated] 1991), *On Duties*, Ed. by M.T. Griffin and E.M. Atkins, Cambridge: Cambridge University Press.

Clark, A.E. and A.J. Oswald (1993), *Satisfaction and Comparison Income*, Discussion Paper Series No. 419, University of Essex, Department of Economics.

Coats, A.W. (1976), 'Economics and psychology: the death and resurrection of a research programme', in S.J. Latsis (ed.), *Method and Appraisal in Economics*, Cambridge: Cambridge University Press, 43-64.

Coats, A.W. (1988), 'Economics and psychology: A resurrection story', in P. Earl (ed.), *Psychological Economics. Development, Tensions, Prospects*, Dordrecht, The Netherlands: Kluwer Academic Publishers, 211-25.

Collard, D. (1983), 'Pigou on expectations and the business cycle', *Economic Journal*, **93**, 411-14.

Commission of European Communities (1993), 'Trends 1974-1992', *Eurobarometer*, April.

Conlisk, J. (1996), 'Why bounded rationality?, *Journal of Economic Literature*, **34**, 669-700.

Corry, B.A. (1962), *Money, Saving, and Investment in English Economics 1800-1850*, London: MacMillan & Co. Ltd.

Courant, P., E. Gramlich, and J. Laitner (1986), 'A dynamic micro estimate of the Life-Cycle Model', in H.G. Aaron and G. Burtless (eds), *Retirement and Economic Behavior*, Washington, D.C.: Brookings Institution, 279-313.

Curtin, R.T. (1992), 'An interview with Richard Curtin', *ISR Newsletter*, Institute for Social Research, The University of Michigan, **17**(3), 8, 10.

Cyert, R.M. and E. Grunberg (1963), 'Assumption, prediction, and explanation in economics', in R.M. Cyert and J.G. March (eds), *A Behavioral Theory of the Firm*, Englewood Cliffs, NJ: Prentice-Hall Inc., 298-311.

Dahlbäck, O. (1991), 'Saving and risk taking', *Journal of Economic Psychology*, **12**(3), 479-500.

Daniel, T.R. (1997), 'The economic psychology of saving: the role of individual differences associated with intertemporal choice', Valencia: PRO-MOLIBRO. Proceedings, IAREP 22nd Conference, University of Valencia, September, 1997, 127-155.

Danziger, K. (1990), *Constructing the Subject. Historical Origins of Psychological Research,* Cambridge: Cambridge University Press.

Danziger, S., J. van der Gaag, E. Smolensky, and M.K. Taussig (1982), 'The life-cycle hypothesis and the consumption behavior of the elderly', *Journal of Post-Keynesian Economics*, **5**, 208-27.

Das, M. and B. Donkers (1997), *How Certain Are Dutch Households about Future Income? An Empirical Analysis,* CentER for Economic Research, Tilburg University, The Netherlands. VSB-CentER Savings Project. Progress Report 44.

Davis, H.L. (1976), 'Decision making within the household', *Journal of Consumer Research*, **2**, 241-60.

Dawes, R.M. (1980), 'Social dilemmas', *Annual Review of Psychology*, **31**, 169-93.

Deaton, A. (1991), 'Saving and liquidity constraints', *Econometrica*, **59**, 1221-48.

Deaton, A. (1992), *Understanding Consumption,* Oxford: Clarendon Press.

de Marchi, N. and M. Blaug (eds) (1991), *Appraising Economic Theories. Studies in the Methodology of Research Programs,* Aldershot, UK and Brookfield, US: Edward Elgar.

Dollard, J. and N. Miller (1950), *Personality and Psychotherapy,* New York: McGraw-Hill.

Dominitz, J. (1996), 'Empirical models of income uncertainty and precautionary saving', Paper presented at Workshop on Saving, Tilburg University, CentER for Economic Research.

Dominitz, J. and C.F. Manski (1995), *Using Expectations Data To Study Subjective Income Expectations,* Tilburg: Tilburg University, CentER for Economic Research, VSB-CentER Savings Project, Progress Report 31.

Douglas, M. and B. Isherwood ([1979] 1996), *The World of Goods. Towards An Anthropology of Consumption,* London and New York: Routledge.

Drottz-Sjöberg, B.-M. (1991), *Perception of Risk. Studies of Risk Attitudes, Perceptions and Definitions,* Stockholm: Center for Risk Research, The Stockholm School of Economics.

Duesenberry, J.S. (1949), *Income, Saving and the Theory of Consumer Behavior,* Cambridge, Mass.: Harvard University Press.

Dynan, K. (1993), 'How prudent are consumers?', *Journal of Political Economy*, **101**(6), 1104-13.

Earl, P. (ed.) (1987), *Psychological Economics. Development, Tensions, Prospects*, Dordrecht: Kluwer Academic Publishers.

East, R. (1993), 'Investment decisions and the theory of planned behaviour', *Journal of Economic Psychology*, 14(2), 337-75.

Edgeworth, F.Y. ([1881] 1967), *Mathematical Psychics. An Essay on the Application of Mathematics to the Moral Sciences*, New York: Augustus M. Kelley Publishers, (Reprints of Economic Classics).

Edwards, W. (1954), 'The theory of decision making', *Psychological Bulletin*, 51, 380-417.

Ekelund, R.B. Jr. and R.F. Hébert (1990), *A History of Economic Theory and Method*, 3rd edition, New York: McGraw-Hill Publishing Co.

Ekman, G. (1970), 'Quantitative approaches to psychological problems', in P. Lindblom (ed.), *Theory and Methods in Behavioural Sciences*, Stockholm: Läromedelsförlagen, 53-72.

Elder, G.H. (1974), *Children of the Great Depression*, Chicago, IL: University of Chicago Press.

Elster, J. (1977), 'Ulysses and the Sirens: A theory of imperfect rationality' *Social Science Information*, 16, 469-526

Elster, J. (1986), 'Introduction', in J. Elster (ed.), *Rational Choice*, Oxford: Basil Blackwell, 1-33.

Endres, A.M. (1988), 'Subjectivism, psychology, and the modern Austrians: A comment', in P. Earl (ed.), *Psychological Economics. Development, Tensions, Prospects*, Dordrecht: Kluwer Academic Publishers, 121-4.

Engel, J.F., R.D. Blackwell, and P.W. Miniard (1986), *Consumer Behavior*. 5th ed., Chicago, IL: The Dryden Press.

Epstein, S. (1980), 'The stability of behavior. II. Implications for psychological research', *American Psychologist*, 35, 790-806.

Etzioni, A. (1988), *The Moral Dimension. Toward a New Economics*, New York: The Free Press.

Farquhar, P.H. (1984) 'Utility assessment methods', *Management Science*, 30, 1283-1300.

Feather, N.T. (1982), 'Actions in relation to expected consequences: an overview of a research program', in N.T. Feather, (ed), *Expectations and Actions*, Hillsdale, NJ: Lawrence Erlbaum Associates, 53-90.

Fehr, E. and P.K. Zych (1996), *Do Addicts Behave Rationally?*, Institute for Empirical Economic Research, University of Zürich and Institute of Economics, University of Vienna. Discussion Paper.

Ferber, R.A. (1973), 'Family decision making and economic behavior', in E.B. Sheldon (ed.), *Family Economic Behavior: Problems and Prospects*, Philadelphia, PA: Lippincott.

Ferber, R.A. and F. Nicosia (1972), 'Newly married couples and their asset accumulation decisions', in B. Strumpel, J.N. Morgan, and E. Zahn (eds), *Human Behav-*

ior in Economic Affairs. Essays in Honor of George Katona, Amsterdam and New York: Elsevier Scientific Publishing Company, 161-87.

Festinger, L. (1954), 'A theory of social comparison processes', *Human Relations,* **7**, 117-40.

Fishbein, M. and I. Ajzen (1975), *Belief, Attitude, Intention, and Behavior: An Introduction to Theory and Research,* Reading, MA: Addison-Wesley.

Fisher, I. (1930), *The Theory of Interest,* London: Macmillan.

Fishhoff, B., B. Goitein, and Z. Shapira (1982), 'The experienced utility of expected utility approaches', in N.T. Feather, (ed.), *Expectations and Actions,* Hillsdale, NJ: Lawrence Erlbaum Associates, 315-39.

Fletcher, G.J.O. (1984), 'Psychology and common sense', *American Psychologist,* **39**, 203-13.

Florence, P.S. (1927), *Economics and Human Behaviour. A Rejoinder to Social Psychologists,* London: Kegan Paul, Trench, Trubner and Co. Ltd.

Forgas, J.P. (1994), 'The role of emotion in social judgments: An introductory review and an Affect Infusion Model (AIM)', *European Journal of Social Psychology,* **24**, 1-24.

Fornell, C. (1992), 'A national Customer Satisfaction Barometer: the Swedish experience', *Journal of Marketing,* **56**, 6-21.

Franklin, B. (undated), *Poor Richard's Almanack.* Mount Vernon: The Peter Pauper Press.

Friedman, M. (1953), *Essays in Positive Economics,* Chicago, IL: University of Chicago Press.

Friedman, M. (1957), *A Theory of the Consumption Function,* Princeton, NJ: Princeton University Press.

Friedman, M. (1992), 'Old wine in new bottles', in J. Hey (ed.), *The Future of Economics,* Oxford: Blackwell Publishers, 33-40.

Friedman, M. and L.J. Savage (1948), 'The utility analysis of choices involving risk', *Journal of Political Economy,* **56**, 279-304.

Frowen, S.F. (ed.) (1990), *Unknowledge and Choice in Economics: Proceedings of a Conference in Honour of G.L.S. Shackle,* Basingstoke: Macmillan.

Furby, L. (1979), 'Inequalities in personal possessions: explanations for and judgments about unequal distribution', *Human Development,* **22**, 180-202.

Furnham, A. (1985), ' Why do people save? Attitudes to, and habits of saving money in Britain', *Journal of Applied Social Psychology,* **15**, 354-73.

Furnham, A. and A. Lewis (1986), *'The Economic Mind, The Social Psychology of Economic Behaviour,* Brighton, Sussex: Wheatsheaf Books.

Garber, P.M. (1989a), 'Tulipmania', *Journal of Political Economy,* **97**(3), 535-60.

Garber, P.M. (1989b), 'Who put the mania in Tulipmania?', *Journal of Portfolio Management,* **16**(1), 53-60.

Gergen, K.J. (1982), *Toward Transformation in Social Knowledge,* New York: Springer-Verlag.

Gilad, B. and S. Kaish (eds) (1986), *Handbook of Behavioral Economics,* Vols. A and. B, Greenwich, CT: JAI Press.

Granovetter, M. and R. Swedberg (eds) (1992), *The Sociology of Economic Life,* Boulder: Westview Press.

Gregory, L.W., R.B. Cialdini, and K.M. Carpenter (1982), 'Self-relevant scenarios as mediators of likelihood estimates and compliance: Does imagining make it so?', *Journal of Personality and Social Psychology,* **43**, 89-99.

Groenewegen, P. (1995), *A Soaring Eagle: Alfred Marshall 1842–1924,* Aldershot, UK and Brookfield, US: Edward Elgar.

Groenland, E..A.G. (1989), *Socio-Economic Well-Being and Behavioral Reactions: A Panel Study of People Drawing Benefits from the Dutch National Social Security System,* Tilburg, The Netherlands: Tilburg University Press.

Groenland, E.A.G. and J.G. Bloem (1994), 'Bancaire dienstverlening op basis van psychologische behoeften van consumenten', [Bank services based on consumers' psychological needs], Department of Economic Psychology, Tilburg University. Unpublished manuscript.

Groenland, E.A.G., J.G. Bloem, and A.A.A. Kuylen (1996), 'Prototypicality and structure of the saving concept for consumers', *Journal of Economic Psychology,* **17**(6), 691-708.

Guiso, L., T. Jappelli, and D. Terlizzese (1992), 'Earnings uncertainty and precautionary saving', *Journal of Monetary Economics,* **30**, 307-37.

Gullberg, I. (1964), *Svensk-engelsk fackordbok för näringsliv, förvaltning, och undervisning och forskning,* [Swedish-English Dictionary for Business, Administration, Teaching and Research] Stockholm: Norstedt.

Gunnarsson, J. (1996), *Use of Spouse Data in Analysis of Couple Household Financial Behavior: The Case of Attitudes Towards Financial Risk Taking,* Tilburg: CentER for Economic Research, Tilburg University. VSB-CentER Savings Project. Progress Report 35.

Gunnarsson, J. and R. Wahlund (1997), 'Household financial strategies in Sweden: an exploratory study', *Journal of Economic Psychology,* **18**, 201-33.

Gurin, G. and P. Gurin (1970), 'Expectancy theory in the study of poverty', *Journal of Social Issues,* **26**, 83-104.

Gutman, J. (1982), 'A means-end chain model based on consumer categorization processes', *Journal of Marketing,* **46**(2), 60-72.

Hardy, Thomas ([1891] 1993), *Tess of the d'Urbervilles,* New York: Barnes and Noble.

Hausman, D.M. (ed.) (1988), *The Philosophy of Economics: An Anthology,* Cambridge, MA: Cambridge University Press.

Hausman, D.M. (1991), 'On dogmatism in economics: The case of preference reversals', *Journal of Socio-Economics,* **20**(3), 205-25.

Hayek, F.A. von ([1978] 1985), *New Studies in Philosophy, Politics, Economics and the History of Ideas,* Chicago, IL and London: The University of Chicago Press and Routledge & Kegan Paul Ltd.

Heath, C. and J.B. Soll (1996), 'Mental budgeting and consumer decisions', *Journal of Consumer Research,* **23**, 40-52.

Heckscher, E. ([1935] 1994), *Mercantilism,* With a new introduction by Lars Magnusson, Vol. 2, London and New York: Routledge.

Helson, H. (1964), *Adaptation-Level Theory: An Experimental and Systematic Approach to Behavior,* New York, NY: Harper.

Henderson, P.W. and R.A. Peterson (1992), 'Mental accounting and categorization', *Organizational Behavior and Human Decision Processes,* **51**, 92-117.

Herrnstein, R.J. (1990), 'Rational choice theory. Necessary but not sufficient, *American Psychologist,* **45**, 356-67.

Herrnstein, R.J. and D. Prelec (1992), 'Melioration', in G. Loewenstein and J. Elster (eds), *Choice over Time,* New York: Russell Sage Foundation, 235-63.

Hey, J.D. (1992), 'Experiments in economics – and psychology', in S.E.G. Lea, P. Webley, and B.M. Young (eds),.*New Directions in Economic Psychology. Theory, Experiment and Application,* Aldershot, UK and Brookfield, US: Edward Elgar, 85-98.

Hey, J.D. and V. Dardanoni (1988), 'Optimal consumption under uncertainty: an experimental investigation', *Economic Journal,* **98**, (Conference Supplement), S105-S116.

Hirschman, A.O. (1965), 'Obstacles to development: A classification and a quasi-vanishing act', *Economic Development and Cultural Change,* **13** (July), 385-93.

Hirschman, A.O. (1977), *The Passions and the Interests. Political Arguments for Capitalism Before Its Triumph,* Princeton, NJ: Princeton University Press.

Hoch, S.J. and G.F. Loewenstein (1991), 'Time-inconsistent preferences and consumer self-control', *Journal of Consumer Research,* **17**, 492-507.

Hogarth, R. (1987), *Judgement and Choice. The Psychology of Decision,* 2nd ed., Chichester: John Wiley and Sons.

Holzman, M. (1958), 'Theories of choice and conflict in psychology and economics', *Journal of Conflict Resolution,* **2**, 310-20.

Horowitz, J.K. (1992), 'A test of intertemporal consistency', *Journal of Economic Behavior and Organization,* **17**, 171-82.

Hubbard, R.G., J. Skinner and S.P. Zeldes (1994), 'Expanding the life-cycle model: Precautionary saving and public policy', *American Economic Review,* **84**(2) (Papers and Proceedings), 174-9.

Hudson. J. (1989), 'Perceptions of inflation', in K.G. Grunert and F. Ölander (eds), *Understanding Economic Behavior,* Dordrecht: Kluwer Academic Publishers, 77-91.

Hunt, K. (1991), 'Consumer satisfaction, dissatisfaction, and complaining behavior', *Journal of Social Issues,* **147**, 107-19.

Hurd, M.D. (1987), 'Savings of the elderly and desired bequests', *American Economic Review*, **77**(3), 298-312.

Hurd, M.D. (1990), 'Research on the elderly: economic status, retirement, and consumption and saving', *Journal of Economic Literature*, **28**, 565-637.

Hurd, M.D. and K. McGarry (1995), 'Evaluation of the subjective probabilities of survival in the Health and Retirement Study', *Journal of Human Resources,* **30**, S268-S292.

Hurd, M.D. and K. McGarry (1996), 'The predictive validity of the subjective probabilities of survival in the Health and Retirement Survey', Paper presented at Workshop on Saving, Tilburg University, CentER for Economic Research.

Hursh, S.R. and Bauman, R.A. (1987), 'The behavioral analysis of demand', in L. Green and J.H. Kagel (eds), *Advances in Behavioral Economics, Vol. 1*, Norwood, NJ: Ablex Publishing Corporation, 117-65.

Hussein, G. (1985), 'An examination of the psychological aspects of money', Unpublished M.Phil. Thesis, University of Exeter, UK.

Ivaldi, M. (1992), 'Survey evidence on the rationality of expectations', *Journal of Applied Econometrics*, **7**(3), 225-41.

Jahoda, G. (1979), 'The construction of economic reality by some Glaswegian children', *European Journal of Social Psychology*, **9**, 115-27.

Jahoda, G. (1981), 'The development of thinking about economic institutions: the bank', *Cahiers de Psychologie Cognitive*, **1**, 55-73.

James, W. ([1890] 1983), *The Principles of Psychology,* Cambridge, MA: Harvard University Press. (First published in 1890).

Jevons, W.S. ([1871] 1911), *The Theory of Political Economy*, 4th ed., London: Macmillan and Co. Ltd. (First published in 1871).

Johnson, M.D., E.W. Anderson, and C. Fornell (1995), 'Rational and adaptive performance expectations in a customer satisfaction framework', *Journal of Consumer Research*, **21**, 695-707.

Johnson, M.D. and C. Fornell (1991), 'A framework for comparing customer satisfaction across individuals and product categories', *Journal of Economic Psychology*, **12**(2), 267-86.

Jones, L.V. (1959), 'Prediction of consumer purchase and the utility of money', *Journal of Applied Psychology*, **43**, 334-37.

Jonung, L. (1981), 'Perceived and expected rates of inflation in Sweden, *American Economic Review*, **71**, 961-68.

Julander, C.-R. (1975), *Sparande och effekter av ökad kunskap om inkomstens användning,* [Saving Behavior and the Effects of Increased Knowledge of Income Use], Doctoral Dissertation, The Stockholm School of Economics: Stockholm. (English abstract).

Jundin, S. (1988), 'Ungdomars konsumtion och sparande', [Youth Consumption and Saving], in K.-E. Wärneryd, S. Jundin, and R. Wahlund (eds),

Sparbeteende och sparattityder, [Saving behavior and Saving Attitudes], Stockholm: Allmänna Förlaget, 77-114.

Juster, F.T. (1981), 'An expectational view of consumer spending prospects', *Journal of Economic Psychology,* **1**(2), 87-103.

Juster, F.T. (1986), 'What do we know about saving behavior?', *Economic Outlook USA,* **13**, 17-19.

Juster, F.T. and L. Taylor (1975), 'Toward a theory of saving behavior', *American Economic Review,* **65**, Papers and Proceedings, 203-9.

Kachelmeier, S.J. and M. Shehata (1992), 'Examining risk preferences under high monetary incentives: Experimental evidence from the People's Republic of China', *American Economic Review,* **82**, 1120-41.

Kahneman, D. (1994), 'New challenges to the rationality assumption', *Journal of Institutional and Theoretical Economics, JITE,* **150**, 18-36.

Kahneman, D., J.L. Knetsch, and R. Thaler (1991), 'The endowment effect, loss aversion, and status quo bias', *Journal of Economic Perspectives,* **5**(1), 193-206.

Kahneman, D. and R. Thaler (1991), 'Economic analysis and the psychology of utility: applications to compensation policy', *American Economic Review,* Papers and Proceedings, **81**, 341-6.

Kahneman, D. and A. Tversky (1979), 'Prospect theory: An analysis of decision under risk', *Econometrica,* **47**, 263-91.

Kahneman, D. and A. Tversky (1984), 'Choices, values, and frames', *American Psychologist,* **39**, 341-50.

Kahneman, D. and C. Varey (1991), 'Notes on the psychology of utility', in J. Elster and J.E. Roemer (eds), *Interpersonal Comparisons of Well-Being,* Cambridge: Cambridge University Press, 127-63.

Karoly, P. (1993), 'Mechanisms of self-regulation: A systems view', *Annual Review of Psychology,* **44**, 23-52.

Katona, G. (1940), *Organizing and Memorizing. Studies in the Psychology of Learning and Teaching,* New York: Columbia University Press.

Katona, G. (1942), *War without Inflation. The Psychological Approach to Problems of War Economy,* New York: Columbia University Press.

Katona, G. (1951), *Psychological Analysis of Economic Behavior,* New York: McGraw-Hill.

Katona, G. (1953), 'Rational behavior and economic behavior', *Psychological Review,* **60**, 307-18.

Katona, G. (1960), *The Powerful Consumer,* New York: McGraw-Hill.

Katona, G. (1965), *Private Pensions and Individual Saving,* Ann Arbor: University of Michigan Press.

Katona, G. (1972), 'Theory of expectations', in B. Strumpel, J.N. Morgan, and E. Zahn (eds), *Human Behavior in Economic Affairs. Essays in Honor of George Katona,* Amsterdam and New York: Elsevier Scientific Publishing Co, 549-82.

Katona, G. (1974), 'Psychology and consumer economics', *Journal of Consumer Research* 1, 1-8.

Katona, G. (1975), *Psychological Economics,* New York: Elsevier..

Katona, G. (1979), 'Toward a macropsychology', *American Psychologist,* 34, 118-26.

Katona, G. (1980), *Essays on Behavioral Economics,* Ann Arbor, MI: Institute for Social Research, University of Michigan.

Kelley, H.H. (1952), 'Two functions of reference groups', in G.E. Swanson, T.M. Newcomb, and E.L. Hartley (eds), *Readings in Social Psychology,* New York: Henry Holt and Co., 410-14.

Kelley, H.H. (1992), 'Common-sense psychology and scientific psychology', *Annual Review of Psychology,* 43, 1-23.

Kessler, D. and A. Masson (1987), 'Personal wealth distribution in France: Cross-sectional evidence and extensions', in E.N. Wolff (ed.), *International Comparisons of the Distribution of Household Wealth,* New York: Oxford University Press, 141-76.

Kessler, D., S. Perelman, and P. Pestieau (1993), 'Saving behavior in 17 OECD countries', *Review of Income and Wealth,* 39(1), 37-49.

Keynes, J.N. ([1917] 1988), 'The scope and method of political economy', in D.M. Hausman (ed.), *The Philosophy of Economics,* Cambridge: Cambridge University Press, 70-98.

Keynes, J.M. (1930), *A Treatise on Money,* Vol. 1 and 2, London: Macmillan.

Keynes, J.M. (1936), *The General Theory of Employment, Interest and Money,* London: Macmillan.

King, M. (1985), 'The economics of saving: A survey of recent contributions', in K.J. Arrow and S. Honkapohja (eds), *Frontiers of Economics,* Oxford: Basil Blackwell Ltd., 227-94.

Kirchler, E.M. (1988), 'Household economic decision making', in W.F. van Raaij, G. van Veldhoven, and K.-E. Wärneryd (eds), *Handbook of Economic Psychology,* Dordrecht: Kluwer Academic Publishers, 258-92.

Kirchler, E.M. (1989), *Kaufentscheidungen im privaten Haushalt. Eine sozialpsychologische Analyse des Familienalltages,* [Purchase Decisions in Private Households. A Socialpsychological Analysis of Family Everyday Life], Göttingen: Verlag für Psychologie. Dr. C.J. Hogrefe.

Kirchler, E.M. (1995), *Wirtschaftspsychologie: Grundlagen und Anwendungsfelder der Ökonomischen Psychologie,* [Economic Psychology: Basics and Fields of Application], Göttingen and Bern: Hogrefe. Verlag für Psychologie.

Klamer, A. (1984), *The New Classical Macroeconomics. Conversations with the New Classical Economists and Their Opponents,* Brighton Sussex: Wheatsheaf Books Ltd.

Klein, L. (ed.) (1954), *Contributions of Survey Methods to Economics,* New York: Columbia University Press.

Knetsch, J. (1997), 'A reinterpretation of time preference findings: some implications and evidence', Paper delivered at the TMR/Savings Workshop, CentER for Economic Research, Tilburg University, July 1997.

Köhler, J. (1996), 'Making saving easy. An experimental analysis of savings decisions', Paper delivered at Savings Workshop, CentER for Economic Research, Tilburg University, July 1996.

Koskela, E. and M. Virén (1982), 'Inflation, tight money and household saving behavior: Finnish evidence', *Scandinavian Journal of Economics,* **84**(3), 483-92.

Kotlikoff, L.J. (1989), *What Determines Savings?,* Cambridge, MA: The MIT Press.

Kreps, D.M. (1997), 'Intrinsic motivation and extrinsic incentives', *American Economic Review,* **87**, May, Papers and Proceedings, 359-64.

Kuhl, J. (1985), 'Cognition-behavior consistency: self-regulatory processes and action versus state orientation', in J. Kuhl and J. Beckmann (eds), *Action Control: from Cognition to Behavior,* Berlin: Springer, 101-28.

Kuhl, J. and J. Beckmann (1985), 'Historical perspectives in the study of action control', in J. Kuhl and J. Beckmann (eds), *Action Control: from Cognition to Behavior,* Berlin: Springer, 89-100.

Lakatos, I. (1978), *The Methodology of Scientific Research Programmes,* ed. by J. Worrall and G. Currie, Cambridge: Cambridge University Press.

Lane, R. (1991), *The Market Experience,* Cambridge: Cambridge University Press.

Langbein, L.I., and A.J. Lichtman (1978), *Ecological Inference,* Sage University Paper Series on Quantitative Applications in the Social Sciences, 07-010, Beverly Hills, CA: Sage Publications.

Langer, E.J. (1982), 'The illusion of control', in D. Kahneman, P. Slovic, and A. Tversky (eds), *Judgment Under Uncertainty: Heuristics and Biases,* Cambridge: Cambridge University Press, 231-38.

Lansing, J.B. (1954), 'Concepts used in surveys', in L. Klein (ed.), *Contributions of Survey Methods to Economics,* New York: Columbia University Press, 9-48.

Latsis, S.J. (ed.) (1976), *Method and Appraisal in Economics,* Cambridge: Cambridge University Press.

Lea, S.E.G. (1978), 'The psychology and economics of demand', *Psychological Bulletin,* **85**, 441-66.

Lea, S.E.G. (1981), 'Animal experiments in economic psychology'. *Journal of Economic Psychology,* **1**, 245-71.

Lea, S.E.G. (1992), 'Editorial: On parent and daughter disciplines: Economic psychology, occupational psychology, and consumer science', *Journal of Economic Psychology,* **13**, 1-3.

Lea, S.G., R.M. Tarpy, and P. Webley (1987), *The Individual in the Economy. A Survey of Economic Psychology,* Cambridge: Cambridge University Press.

Lea, S.E.G., P. Webley, and B.M. Young (1992), 'Economic psychology: A new sense of direction', in S.E.G. Lea, P. Webley, and B.M. Young (eds), *New Directions in Economic Psychology. Theory, Experiment and Application,* Aldershot, UK and Brookfield, US: Edward Elgar, 1-12.

Lea, S.E.G., P. Webley, and R.M. Levine (1993), 'The economic psychology of consumer debt', *Journal of Economic Psychology,* 14, 85-119.

Lea, S.E.G., P. Webley, and C.M. Walker (1995), 'Psychological factors in consumer debt: Money management, economic socialization, and credit use', *Journal of Economic Psychology,* 16, 681-701.

LeBaron, D.G., G. Farrelly, and S. Gula (1989), 'Facilitating a dialogue on risk: A questionnaire approach', *Financial Analysis Journal,* May-June, 19-24.

Leibenstein, H. (1950), 'Bandwagon, snob, and Veblen effects in the theory of consumer demand', *Quarterly Journal of Economics,* 64, 183-207.

Leibenstein, H. (1979), 'A branch of economics is missing: Micro-micro theory', *Journal of Economic Literature,* 17, 477-502.

Leiser, D., G. Sevón, and D. Lévy (1990), 'Children's economic socialization: summarizing the cross-cultural comparison of ten countries', *Journal of Economic Psychology,* 11(4), 591-614.

Levin, I.P. (1985), 'How changes in price and salary affect economic satisfaction: information integration models and preference processes', *Journal of Economic Psychology,* 6, 143-55.

Lewin, S.B. (1996), 'Economics and psychology: lessons for our own day from the early twentieth century', *Journal of Economic Literature,* 34, 1293-1323.

Lewis, A., P. Webley and A. Furnham (1995), *The New Economic Mind. The Social Psychology of Economic Behaviour,* New York and London: Harvester Wheatsheaf.

Lindbeck, A. (1989), 'Remaining puzzles and neglected issues in macroeconomics', *Scandinavian Journal of Economics,* 91, 495-516.

Lindbeck, A. (1997), 'Incentives and social norms in household behavior', *American Economic Review,* 87, May, Papers and Proceedings, 370-7.

Lindqvist, A. (1981a), 'A note on determinants of household saving behavior', *Journal of Economic Psychology,* 1(1), 37-59.

Lindqvist, A. (1981b), *Hushållens sparande,* [The Saving Behavior of Households], Stockholm: Doctoral dissertation, The Stockholm School of Economics.

Livingstone, S.M. and P. Lunt (1992), 'Predicting personal debt and debt repayment: Psychological, social and economic determinants', *Journal of Economic Psychology,* 13(1), 111-34.

Loewenstein, G. (1987), 'Anticipation and the evaluation of delayed consumption', *Economic Journal,* 97 (September), 666 - 84.

Loewenstein, G. (1988), 'Frames of mind in intertemporal choice', *Management Science*, **34** (February), 200-14.

Loewenstein, G. (1992), 'The fall and rise of psychological explanations in the economics of intertemporal choice', in G. Loewenstein and J. Elster (eds), *Choice Over Time*, New York: Russell Sage Foundation, 3-34.

Loewenstein, G. and D. Prelec (1991), 'Negative time preference', *American Economic Review*, **81** (May), Papers and Proceedings, 347-52.

Loewenstein, G. and D. Prelec (1992), 'Anomalies in intertemporal choice: evidence and an interpretation', *Quarterly Journal of Economics*, **109**, 573-97.

Loewenstein, G. and D. Prelec (1993), 'Preferences for sequences of outcomes', *Psychological Review*, **100**(4), 91-108.

Lopes, L.L. (1994), 'Psychology and economics: perspectives on risk, cooperation, and the marketplace', *Annual Review of Psychology*, **45**, 197-227.

Lopes, L.L. (1990), 'Re-modeling risk aversion: a comparison of Bernoullian and rank dependent value approaches', in G.M. von Furstenberg (ed.), *Acting Under Uncertainty: Multidisciplinary Conceptions*, Dordrecht: Kluver Academic Publishers, 267-99.

Lovell, M.C. (1986), 'Tests of the rational expectations hypothesis', *American Economic Review*, **76**(1), 110-24.

Lucas, R.E. (1986), 'Adaptive behavior and economic theory', *Journal of Business*, **59**(4), Part 2, S401-S426.

Luce, R.D. and H. Raiffa (1990), 'Utility theory', in P.K. Moser (ed.), *Rationality in Action. Contemporary Approaches*, Cambridge: Cambridge University Press, 19-40.

Lunt, P. (1996a), 'Rethinking the relationship between economics and psychology', *Journal of Economic Psychology*, **17**, 275-87.

Lunt, P. (1996b), 'Discourses of savings', *Journal of Economic Psychology*, **17**, 677-90.

Lunt, P. and A. Furnham (eds) (1996), *Economic Socialization. The Economic Beliefs and Behaviours of Young People*, Cheltenham, UK and Brookfield, US: Edward Elgar.

Lunt, P. and S.M. Livingstone (1991), 'Psychological, social and economic determinants of saving: Comparing recurrent and total savings', *Journal of Economic Psychology*, **12**(4), 621-41.

Lunt, P. and S.M. Livingstone (1992), *Mass Consumption and Personal Identity. Everyday Economic Experience*, Buckingham: Open University Press.

Lusardi, A. (1993), *Precautionary Saving and Subjective Earnings Variance*, CentER for Economic Research, Tilburg University, VSB-CentER Savings Project, Progress Report 16.

MacCrimmon, K.R. and D.A. Wehrung (1986), *Taking Risks. The Management of Uncertainty*, New York, NY: The Free Press.

Machiavelli, N. ([1513] 1995), *The Prince*, Harmondsworth: Penguin Books.

Machina, M.J. (1990), 'Choice under uncertainty: Problems solved and unsolved', in K.S. Cook and M. Levi (eds), *The Limits of Rationality*, Chicago: University of Chicago Press, 90-132.

Madden, T.,J., P.S. Ellen, and I. Ajzen (1992), 'A comparison of the Theory of Planned Behavior and the Theory of Reasoned Action', *Personality and Social Psychology Bulletin*, **18**(1), 3-9.

Maital, S. (1979), 'Inflation expectations in the monetarist black box', *American Economic Review*, **69**(3), 429-34.

Maital, S. (1982), *Minds, Markets, and Money*, New York: Basic Books.

Maital, S. (1986), *International Conference on Economics and Psychology: Choice and Exchange*, Kibbutz Shefayim, Israel, July 9-11, 1986.

Maital, S. and S.L. Maital (1981), 'Individual-rational and group-rational inflation expectations. Theory and cross-section evidence', *Journal of Economic Behavior and Organization*, **2**, 179-86.

Maital, S. and S.L. Maital (1984), *Economic Games People Play*, New York: Basic Books.

Maital, S. and S.L. Maital (1991), 'Is the future what it used to be? A behavioral theory of the decline of saving in the West', in G. Antonides, W. Arts, and W.F. van Raaij (eds), *The Consumption of Time and the Timing of Consumption: Toward A New Behavioral and Socio-Economics*, Amsterdam: North-Holland, 195-214.

Mandeville, B. ([1729] 1924), *The Fable of the Bees: or, Private Vices, Publick Benefits*. With a Commentary Critical, Historical, and Explanatory by F.B. Kaye. Vols. 1 and 2, London: Oxford University Press. (First published 1714 to 1729).

Manicas, P.T. (1987), *A History and Philosophy of the Social Sciences*, Oxford: Basil Blackwell.

Marshall, A. ([1890] 1990), *Principles of Economics: An Introductory Volume*, 8th ed., London: Macmillan. (First published in 1890).

Marx, K. ([1859] 1990), 'Capital and other writings', in M.C. Spechler (ed.), *Perspectives in Economic Thought*, New York: McGraw-Hill Publishing Co., 116-47.

Maslow, A. (1954), *Motivation and Personality*, New York: Harper and Row.

McClelland, D.C. (1961), *The Achieving Society*, Princeton: van Nostrand.

McCord, M. and R. de Neufville (1986), 'Lottery equivalents: reduction of the certainty effect in utility assessment', *Management Science*, **32**, 56-60.

McDougall, W. (1908), *An Introduction to Social Psychology*, 3rd ed., London: Methuen & Co. Ltd.

Menger, C. ([1871] 1923), *Grundsätze der Volkswirtschaftslehre*, Vienna: Hölder-Pichler-Tempsky: (First published in 1871).

Merton, R.K. and A.S. Kitt (1952), 'Contributions to the theory of reference group behavior', in G.E. Swanson, T.M. Newcomb, and E.L. Hartley (eds), *Readings in Social Psychology,* New York: Henry Holt and Co., 430-44.

Meyer, W. (1982), 'The research programme of economics and the relevance of psychology', *British Journal of Psychology* , **21**, 81-91.

Mill, J.S. ([1836] 1988), 'On the definition and method of political economy', in D.M. Hausman (ed.), *The Philosophy of Economics. An Anthology*, Cambridge: Cambridge University Press, 52-69.

Mill, J.S. ([1848] 1985), *Principles of Political Economy: with Some of Their Applications to Social Philosophy,.* Harmondsworth: Penguin Books.

Mischel, W. (1984), 'Convergences and challenges in the search for consistency', *American Psychologist*, **39**, 351-64.

Mischel, W., Y. Shoda, and M.L. Rodriguez (1992), 'Delay of gratification in children', in G. Loewenstein and J. Elster (eds), *Choice Over Time*, New York: Russell Sage Foundation, 147-66.

Modigliani, F. (1986), 'Life cycle, individual thrift and the wealth of nations', (Nobel Lecture delivered in Stockholm, Sweden, December 9, 1985), *American Economic Review*, **76**, 297-313.

Modigliani, F. (1988), 'The role of intergenerational transfers and life cycle saving in the accumulation of wealth', *Journal of Economic Perspectives*, **2**, Spring, 15-40.

Modigliani, F. and R. Brumberg (1954), 'Utility analysis and the consumption function. An interpretation of cross-section data', in K.K. Kurihara (ed.), *Post-Keynesian Economics*, New Brunswick, NJ: Rutgers University Press, 388-438.

Mook, D.G. (1983), 'In defense of external invalidity', *American Psychologist*, **38**, 379-87.

Morgan, J.N. (1967), 'Contributions of survey research to economics', in C. Glock (ed.), *Survey Research in the Social Sciences.*, New York: Russell Sage Foundation, 217-68.

Moschis, G.P. and G.A. Churchill, Jr. (1975), 'Consumer socialization: a theoretical and empirical analysis', *Journal of Marketing Research*, **15**, 599-609.

Münsterberg, H. (1913), *Psychology and Industrial Efficiency*, Boston: Houghton-Mifflin.

Murphy, G. (1951), *Historical Introduction to Modern Psychology*, New York: Harcourt, Brace and Co.

Musgrave, A. (1981), 'Unreal assumptions in economic theory. The F-twist untwisted', *Kyklos*, **34**, 377-87.

Muth, J.F. (1961), 'Rational expectations and the theory of price movements', *Econometrica*, **29**, 315-35.

Nagel, E. (1963), 'Assumptions in economic theory', in A. Ryan (ed.), *The Philosophy of Social Explanation*, Oxford: Oxford University Press, 130-8.

Naish, H.F. (1993), 'The near optimality of adaptive expectations', *Journal of Economic Behavior and Organization*, **20**(1), 3-22.

Nerlove, M. (1983), 'Expectations, plans and realizations in theory and practice', *Econometrica*, **51**, 1251-79.

Ng, S.H. (1983), 'Children's ideas about the bank and shop profit: developmental stages and the influence of cognitive contrasts and conflict', *Journal of Economic Psychology*, **4**, 209-21.

Ng, S.H. (1985), 'Children's ideas about the bank: a New Zealand replication', *European Journal of Social Psychology*, **15**, 121-3.

Nyhus, E.K. (1996), *The VSB-CentER Savings Project. Data Collection Methods, Questionnaires and Sampling Procedures*, Tilburg: CentER for Economic Research, Tilburg University, VSB-CentER Savings Project: Progress Report 42.

Nyhus, E.K. (1997), 'On the measurement of time preferences and subjective discount rates', Paper presented at TMR/Savings Workshop, CentER for Economic Research, Tilburg University, The Netherlands.

OECD Economic Outlook 58 (1995), Paris: OECD.

Ölander, F. (1990), 'Consumer psychology: not necessarily a manipulative science', *Applied Psychology*, **39**, 105-26.

Ölander, F. and C.M. Seipel (1970), *Psychological Approaches to the Study of Saving*, Studies in Consumer Savings, No. 7, Urbana-Champaign, IL: The Bureau of Economic and Business Research, University of Illinois.

Ozer, D.J. and S.P. Reise (1994), 'Personality assessment', *Annual Review of Psychology*, **45**, 357-88.

Pålsson, A.-M. (1996), 'Does the degree of relative risk aversion vary with household characteristics?', *Journal of Economic Psychology*, **17**, 771-87.

Pareto, V. ([1909] 1971), *Manual of Political Economy*, New York: Augustus M. Kelley.

Petrinovich, L. (1979), 'Probabilistic functionalism: a conception of research method', *American Psychologist*, **34**, 373-90.

Pigou, A.C. ([1920] 1952), *The Economics of Welfare*, London: Macmillan.

Pingle, M. and R.H. Day (1996), 'Modes of economizing behavior: experimental evidence', *Journal of Economic Behavior and Organization*, **29**, 191-209.

Plato ([undated] 1980), *The Republic*, Canada: Fitzhenry & Whiteside.

Popper, K. (1959), *The Logic of Scientific Discovery*, London: Hutchinson

Poterba, J.M., S.F. Venti and D.A. Wise (1994), 'Targeted retirement saving and the net worth of elderly Americans', *American Economic Review*, **84**, May, Papers and Proceedings, 180-5.

Praet, P. and J. Vuchelen (1984), 'The contribution of EC consumer surveys in forecasting consumer expenditures: an econometric analysis for four major countries', *Journal of Economic Psychology*, **5**, 101-24.

Radnitzky, G. and P. Bernholz (eds) (1987), *Economic Imperialism. The Economic Method Applied Outside the Field of Economics*, New York: Paragon House Publishers.

Rae, J. ([1834] 1905), *The Sociological Theory of Capital*, New York: Macmillan.

Rainwater, L, R.P. Coleman, and G. Handel (1959), *Workingman's Wife,* New York: Oceana Publications.

Rawls, J. (1973), *A Theory of Justice*, Oxford: Oxford University Press.

Reber, A.S. (1985), *The Penguin Dictionary of Psychology,* Harmondsworth: Penguin Books.

Revelle, W. (1995), 'Personality processes', *Annual Review of Psychology,* **46**, 295-328.

Ritzema, J. (1992), 'An extended and behavioral life cycle model', Unpublished manuscript, Rotterdam: Dept. of Economic Sociology and Economic Psychology, Erasmus Universiteit.

Robbins, L. ([1935] 1979), 'The nature of economic generalizations', in F. Hahn and M. Hollis (eds), *Philosophy and Economic Theory*, Oxford: Oxford University Press, 36-46, (First published in 1935).

Robertson, T.S. and H.H. Kassarjian (eds) (1991), *Handbook of Consumer Behavior*, Englewood Cliffs, NJ: Prentice-Hall.

Rokeach, M. (1973), *The Nature of Human Values*, New York: Free Press.

Rosenberg, N. (1976), *Perspectives on Technology,* Cambridge: Cambridge University Press.

Rosenthal, R. and R.L. Rosnow (eds) (1969), *Artifact in Behavioral Research*. New York: Academic Press.

Roszkowski, M.J., G.E. Snelbecker, and S.R. Leimberg (1989), *The Tools and Techniques of Financial Planning*, Cincinnati OH: The National Underwriter Company.

Samuelson, P.A. (1963), 'Risk and uncertainty: a fallacy of large numbers', *Scientia*, **98**, 108-13.

Samuelson, P.A. and W.D. Nordhaus (1992), *Economics*, 14th ed., New York: McGraw-Hill.

Schachter, S., W. Gerin, D.C. Hood, and P. Andreassen (1985), 'Was the South Sea Bubble a random walk?', *Journal of Economic Behavior and Organization*, **6**(4), 23-9.

Schachter, S., D.C. Hood, P.B. Andreassen, and W. Gerin (1986), 'Aggregate variables in psychology and economics: Dependence and the Stock Market', in B. Gilad and S. Kaish (eds), *Handbook of Behavioral Economics*, Vol. B, JAI Press: Greenwich, CT, 237-72

Scharfstein, D.S. and J.C. Stein (1990), 'Herd behavior and investment', *American Economic Review*, **80**(3), 465-79.

Schelling, T. (1984), 'Self-command in practice, in policy, and in a theory of rational choice', *American Economic Review*, **74**, May, Papers and Proceedings, 1-11.

Schmölders, G., R. Schröder, and H.St. Seidenfus (1956), *John Maynard Keynes als 'Psychologe*, [J.M.K. as Psychologist], Berlin: Duncker & Humblot.

Schönpflug, W. (1993), 'Applied psychology: newcomer with a long tradition', *Applied Psychology*, **42**(1), 5-30.

Schumpeter, J.A. (1954), *History of Economic Analysis*, New York: Oxford University Press.

Scitovsky, T. (1976), *The Joyless Economy: An Inquiry into Human Satisfaction and Consumer Dissatisfaction*, New York: Oxford University Press.

Scitovsky, T. (1986), *Human Desire and Economic Satisfaction. Essays on the Frontiers of Economics*, New York and London: Harvester Wheatsheaf.

Selten, R. (1991), 'Evolution, learning, and economic behavior', *Games and Economic Behavior*, **3**, 3-24.

Sen, A.K. (1979), 'Rational fools: A critique of the behavioural foundations of economic theory', in F. Hahn and M. Hollis (eds), *Philosophy and Economic Theory*, Oxford: Oxford University Press, 87-109.

Sen, A.K. (1987), *On Ethics and Economics,*. Oxford: Basil Blackwell.

Senior, N. ([1836] 1938), *An Outline of the Science of Political Economy*, London: George Allen & Unwin Ltd. (First published in 1836).

Shackle, G.L.S. (1955), *Uncertainty in Economics and Other Reflections*, Cambridge, UK: Cambridge University Press.

Shapiro, D.H. Jr., C.E. Schwartz, and J.A. Astin (1996), 'Controlling ourselves, controlling our world: Psychology's role in understanding positive and negative consequences of seeking and gaining control', *American Psychologist*, **51**, 1213-30.

Shapiro, H.T. (1972), 'The Index of Consumer Sentiment and economic forecasting: a reappraisal', in B. Strumpel, J.N. Morgan, and E. Zahn (eds), *Human Behavior in Economic Affairs. Essays in Honor of George Katona,*. Amsterdam and New York: Elsevier Scientific Publishing Co., 373-96.

Sheffrin, S.M. (1983), *Rational Expectations*, Cambridge, UK: Cambridge University Press.

Shefrin, H.M. and R.H. Thaler (1988), 'The Behavioral Life-Cycle Hypothesis', *Economic Inquiry*, **26**, 609-43.

Shefrin, H.M. and R.H. Thaler (1992), 'Mental accounting, saving and self-control', in G. Loewenstein and J. Elster (eds), *Choice Over Time*, New York: Russell Sage Foundation, 287-330.

Shiller, R. (1989), *Market Volatility*, Cambridge, MA: MIT Press.

Simon, H.A. (1955), 'A behavioral model of rational choice', *Quarterly Journal of Economics*, **69**, 99-118.

Simon, H.A. (1979), 'Information processing models of cognition', *Annual Review of Psychology*, **30**, 363-96.

Simon, H.A. (1984), 'On the behavioral and rational foundations of economic dynamics, *Journal of Economic Behavior and Organization*, **5**, 35-55.

Simon, H.A. (1986), 'Preface', in B.Gilad and S. Kaish (eds), *Handbook of Behavioral Economics*, Vol. A., Greenwich, CT: JAI Press, xv-xvi.

Simon, H.A. (1990), 'Invariants of human behavior', *Annual Review of Psychology*, **41**, 1-19.

Sjöberg, L. and T. Johnson (1978), 'Trying to give up smoking: a study of volitional breakdown', *Addictive Behaviors*, **3**, 149-64.

Sjöberg, L. (1998), 'Will and success – individual and national', in L. Sjöberg, R. Bagozzi, and D.H. Ingvar (eds), *Will and Economic Behavior*, Stockholm: The Economic Research Institute, The Stockholm School of Economics, 85-119.

Sjöberg, L., R. Bagozzi, and D.H. Ingvar (1998), *Will and Economic Behavior*, Stockholm: The Economic Research Institute, The Stockholm School of Economics.

Skinner, B.F. (1974), *About Behaviorism*, New York: Alfred A. Knopf.

Slovic, P. (1972), 'Psychological study of human judgment: implications for investment decision making', *Journal of Finance*, **27**, 779-99.

Smiles, S. ([1859] 1969), *SELF-HELP with Illustrations of Conduct & Perseverance*, London: John Murray.

Smiles, S. (1875), *Thrift*, London: John Murray.

Smith, A. ([1759] 1982), *The Theory of Moral Sentiments*, ed. by D.D. Raphael and A.L. Macfie, Indianapolis, IN: Liberty Classics. (First published in 1759).

Smith, A. ([1776] 1981), *An Inquiry into the Nature and Causes of the Wealth of Nations*, Vols. I and II, ed. by R.H. Campbell and A.S. Skinner, Indianapolis, IN: Liberty Classics. (First published in 1776).

Smith, V.L. (1991), 'Rational choice: The contrast between economics and psychology', *Journal of Political Economy*, **99**(4), 877-97.

Sonuga-Barke, E.J.S. and P. Webley (1993), *Children's Saving: A Study in the Development of Economic Behaviour*, Hove, UK: Lawrence Erlbaum Associates.

Srinivasan, T.N. (1992), 'Comment on Ando et al., Saving among young households. Evidence from Japan and Italy', *Scandinavian Journal of Economics*, **94**, 251-52.

Stacey, B.G. (1982), 'Economic socialization in the pre-adult years', *British Journal of Social Psychology*, **21**, 159-73.

Strotz, R.H. (1956), 'Myopia and inconsistency in dynamic utility maximization', *Review of Economic Studies*, **23**(3), 165-80.

Strumpel, B. (ed.) (1974), *Subjective Elements of Well-Being*, Paris: OECD.

Strumpel, B. (ed.) (1976), *Economic Means for Human Needs: Social Indicators of Well-Being and Discontent*, Ann Arbor, MI: Survey Research Center, University of Michigan.

Sutherland, S. (1995), *The MacMillan Dictionary of Psychology*, 2nd ed., Hants, UK: The MacMillan Press Ltd.

Swedberg, R. (ed.) (1993), *Explorations in Economic Sociology*, New York: Sage.

Swieringa, R.J. and K.E Weick (1982), 'An assessment of laboratory experimentation in accounting', *Journal of Accounting Research*, **20**, 56-101.

Tarde, G. (1902), *La psychologie économique*, Alcan: Paris. (2 volumes).

Tesser, A. and D. Shaffer (1990), 'Attitudes and attitude change', *Annual Review of Psychology*, **41**, 479-523.

Thaler, R. H. (1980), 'Toward a positive theory of consumer choice', *Journal of Economic Behavior and Organization*, **1**, 39-60.

Thaler, R.H. (1981), 'Some empirical evidence on dynamic inconsistency', *Economic Letters*, **8**, 201-7.

Thaler, R.H. (1985), 'Mental accounting and consumer choice', *Marketing Science*, **4**(3), 199-214.

Thaler, R.H. (1990), 'Anomalies: saving, fungibility, and mental accounts', *Journal of Economic Perspectives*, **4**, 193-205.

Thaler, R.H. (1992), *The Winner's Curse. Paradoxes and Anomalies of Economic Life*, New York: The Free Press.

Thaler, R.H. (1994), 'Psychology and savings policies', *American Economic Review*, **84**, Papers and Proceedings, 186-192.

Thaler, R.H. and E.J. Johnson (1990), 'Gambling with the house money and trying to break even: the effects of prior outcomes on risky choice', *Management Science*, **36**(6), 643-60.

Thaler, R.H. and H.M. Shefrin, (1981), 'An economic theory of self-control', *Journal of Political Economy*, **89**, 392-406.

Tobin, J.J. and F.T. Dolbear (1963), 'Comments on the relevance of psychology to economic theory and research', in S.Koch (ed.), *Psychology: A Study of a Science*, Vol. VI, New York: McGraw-Hill, 677-83.

Tuchman, B.W. (1979), '*A Distant Mirror. The Calamitous 14th Century.* Harmondsworth, UK: Penguin Books Ltd.

Tversky, A. and C.R. Fox (1995), 'Weighing risk and uncertainty', *Psychological Review*, **102**(2), 269-83.

Tversky, A. and D. Griffin (1991), 'Endowment and contrast in judgments of well-being', in R.J. Zeckhauser (ed.), *Strategy and Choice*, Cambridge, MA: The MIT Press, 297-317.

Tversky, A. and D. Kahneman (1982), 'Availability: a heuristic for judging frequency and probability', in D. Kahneman, P. Slovic, and A. Tversky (eds), *Judgment Under Uncertainty: Heuristics and Biases*, Cambridge: Cambridge University Press, 163-78.

Tversky, A. and D. Kahneman (1986), 'Rational choice and the framing of decisions', *Journal of Business*, **59**(4, Pt. 2), S251-S278.

Tversky, A. and D. Kahneman (1992), 'Advances in prospect theory: cumulative representation of uncertainty', *Journal of Risk and Uncertainty*, **5**, 297-323.

Tversky, A., P. Slovic, and D. Kahneman (1990), 'The causes of preference reversal', *American Economic Review*, **80**, 204-17.

Vanden Abeele, P. (1988), 'Economic agents' expectations in a psychological perspective', in W.F. van Raaij, G. van Veldhoven, and K.-E. Wärneryd (eds), *Handbook of Economic Psychology*, Dordrecht: Kluwer Academic Publishers, 478-515.

van Raaij, W.F. (1984), 'Micro and macro economic psychology', *Journal of Economic Psychology*, **5**, 385-401.

van Raaij, W.F. (1989), 'Economic news, expectations and macro-economic behavior', *Journal of Economic Psychology*, **10**(4), 473-93.

van Raaij, W.F. and H.J. Gianotten (1990), 'Consumer confidence, expenditure, saving, and credit', *Journal of Economic Psychology*, **11**, 269-90.

van Raaij, W.F., G. van Veldhoven, and K.-E. Wärneryd (eds), *Handbook of Economic Psychology*, Dordrecht: Kluwer Academic Publishers.

van Tilburg, M.A.L. and J.C. Vruggink (1994), 'Saving in an experimental set-up. Development of an experimental set-up and a test of the Behavioral Life-Cycle Hypothesis on the basis of two pilot experiments', Department of Economic Psychology, Tilburg University, Master's Thesis.

van Veldhoven, G.M. and C. Keder (1988), 'Economic news and consumers' sentiment', in Proceedings from the 13th Annual Conference of the International Association for Research in Economic Psychology, Leuven, Belgium.

Veblen, T. ([1899] 1953), *The Theory of the Leisure Class. An Economic Study of Institutions*, New York: The New American Library.

Viard, A.D. (1993), 'The productivity slowdown and the savings shortfall: a challenge to the Permanent Income Hypothesis', *Economic Inquiry*, **40**, 549-63.

Wahlund, R. (1989), 'Perception and judgement of marginal tax rates after a tax reduction', in K.G. Grunert and F. Ölander (eds), *Understanding Economic Behaviour*, Dordrecht: Kluwer Academic Publishers, 135-79.

Wahlund, R. (1991), *Skatter och ekonomiska beteenden. En studie i ekonomisk psykologi om främst skattefusk och sparande utifrån 1982 års skatteomläggning*, [Taxes and economic behaviors. An economic-psychological study on tax evasion and saving with particular emphasis on the Swedish tax system change in 1982], With an English summary, Doctoral dissertation. Stockholm: The Economic Research Institute at the Stockholm School of Economics.

Wahlund, R. and J. Gunnarsson (1996), 'Mental discounting and financial strategies', *Journal of Economic Psychology*, **17**, 709-30.

Wahlund, R. and K.-E. Wärneryd (1987), 'Aggregate saving and the saving behavior of saver groups, *Skandinaviska Enskilda Banken Quarterly Review*, **3**, 52-64.

Walker, C.M. (1996), 'Financial management, coping and debt in households under financial strain', *Journal of Economic Psychology*, **17**, 789-807.

Walras, L. ([1926] 1954), *Elements of Pure Economics or the Theory of Social Wealth*, London: George Allen and Unwin Ltd. (First published in French, 1874).

Ward, S. and D.B. Wackman (1973), *Effects of Television Advertising on Consumer Socialization*, Cambridge, MA: Marketing Science Institute.

Wärneryd, K.-E. (1986a), 'Introduction: the psychology of inflation', *Journal of Economic Psychology*, **7**, 259-68.

Wärneryd, K.-E. (1986b), 'Economic and psychological approaches to the study of economic behavior: similarities and differences', in B. Brehmer, H. Jungermann, P. Lourens, and G. Sevón (eds), *New Directions in Research on Decision Making*, Amsterdam: North-Holland, 29-58.

Wärneryd, K.-E. (1988), 'Economic psychology as a field of study', in W.F. van Raaij, G. van Veldhoven, and K.-E. Wärneryd (eds), *Handbook of Economic Psychology*, Dordrecht: Kluwer Academic Publishers, 3-41.

Wärneryd, K.-E. (1989), 'On the psychology of saving: an essay on economic psychology', *Journal of Economic Psychology*, **10**, 515-41.

Wärneryd, K.-E. (1991), 'The psychology of saving: from micro- to macroeconomic psychology, in G. Antonides, W. Arts, and W.F. van Raaij (eds), *The Consumption of Time and the Timing of Consumption: Toward a New Behavioral and Socio-Economics*, Amsterdam: North-Holland, 176-94.

Wärneryd, K.-E. (1993), *The Will to Save Money. An Essay on Economic Psychology*, CentER for Economic Research, Tilburg University: Discussion Paper No. 9322.

Wärneryd, K.-E. (1994), 'Psychology + economics = economic psychology?', in H. Brandstätter and W. Güth (eds), *Essays on Economic Psychology*, Berlin: Springer-Verlag, 31-52.

Wärneryd, K.-E. (1996a), *Personality and Saving,* CentER for Economic Research, Tilburg University, VSB-CentER Savings. Project, Progress Report 39.

Wärneryd, K.-E. (1996b), 'Saving attitudes and saving behavior', in C. Roland-Lévy (ed.), *Social and Economic Representations*, Paris: Université René Descartes, Institut de Psychologie, IAREP 21st Colloquium, 798-811.

Wärneryd, K.-E. (1996c), 'Risk attitudes and risky behavior', *Journal of Economic Psychology*, **17**, 749-70.

Wärneryd, K.-E. (1997), 'Demystifying rational expectations theory through an economic-psychological model', in G. Antonides, W.F. van Raaij, and S. Maital (eds), *Advances in Economic Psychology*, Chichester: Wiley & Sons, 211-36.

Wärneryd, K.-E., P. Davidsson, and R. Wahlund (1987), *Some Characteristics of Swedish Self-Employed*, Stockholm School of Economics, Economic Research Institute, Research Paper 6328.

Wärneryd, K.-E. and B. Walerud (1982), 'Taxes and economic behavior: some interview data on tax evasion in Sweden', *Journal of Economic Psychology*, **2**, 187-211.

Wärneryd, K.-E. and R. Wahlund (1985), 'Inflationary Expectations', in H. Brandstätter and E. Kirchler (eds), *Economic Psychology*, Linz: Rudolf Trauner Verlag, 327-35.

Weber, M. ([1930] 1952), *The Protestant Ethic and the Spirit of Capitalism*, London: George Allen & Unwin Ltd.

Weber, M. (1968), *Economy and Society. An Outline of Interpretive Sociology*, ed. by G. Roth and Claus Wittich, Berkeley, CA: University of California Press.

Webley, P. and S.E.G. Lea (1993), 'Towards a more realistic psychology of economic socialization', *Journal of Economic Psychology*, **14**, 461-72.

Webley, P., M. Levine, and A. Lewis (1991), 'A study in economic psychology: Children's saving in a play economy', *Human Relations*, **44**, 127-46.

Weil, D.N. (1991), 'What determines savings? A review essay', *Journal of Monetary Economics*, **28**, 161-70.

Weiner, B. (1985), 'An attributional theory of achievement motivation and emotion', *Psychological Review*, **92**, 548-73.

Williams, R.A. and L.V. Defris (1981), 'The roles of inflation and consumer sentiment in explaining Australian consumption and saving patterns', *Journal of Economic Psychology*, **1**(2), 105-20.

Winnett, A. and A. Lewis (1995), 'Household accounts, mental accounts, and savings behaviour: some old economics rediscovered?', *Journal of Economic Psychology*, **16**, 431-48.

Winslow, E.G. (1986), 'Keynes and Freud: psychoanalysis and Keynes's account of the "Animal Spirits" of capitalism', *Social Research*, **53**, 549-78.

Yoshikawa, H. (1995), *Macroeconomics and the Japanese Economy*, Oxford: Oxford University Press.

Zeckhauser, R. (1986), 'Comments: Behavioral versus Rational Economics: What you see is what you conquer', *Journal of Business*, **59**(4, Part 2), S435-S449.

Zelitzer, V.A. (1993), 'Making multiple monies', in R. Swedberg (ed.), *Explorations in Economic Sociology*, New York: Sage, 193-212.

Zullow, H.M. (1991), 'Pessimistic rumination in popular songs and news-magazines predict economic recession via decreased consumer optimism and spending', *Journal of Economic Psychology*, **12**(3), 501-26.

Index